...ISH EMPIRE & COMMONWEALTH	AMERICA, ASIA & AFRICA	
		1880
	1881 1st. South African War	
	1882 Battle of Tel-el-Kebir	
	1884-5 Berlin Colonial Conference	
Canadian Pacific Railway		
Indian National Congress	1886 Gold discovered on Rand	
		1890
1895 { Jameson Raid / Venezuela Crisis		
Battle of Omdurman	1898 Philippines annexed by U.S.A.	
1899 2nd. South African War		
Commonwealth of Australia		1900
	1902 Anglo-Japanese Treaty	
	1904 T. E. Roosevelt President	
	1904-5 Russo-Japanese War	
Morley-Minto Reforms		
Union of South Africa		1910
	1911 Agadir Crisis	
	1912 Woodrow Wilson President	
R L D	W A R	
	1917 U.S.A. at War	
Montagu-Chelmsford Reforms		
Amritsar Massacre		1920
Irish Free State		
Imperial Conference		
Statute of Westminster		
		1930
Ottawa Agreements	1931 Japanese Invasion of Manchuria	
	1932 F. D. Roosevelt President	
India Act	1935 Abyssinian War	
Irish Free State re-named Eire	1936 Anglo-Egyptian Treaty	
		1940
Fall of Singapore	1941 Pearl Harbour	
R L D	1942 Battle of El Alamein A R	
	1945 { Truman President / Atom Bomb	
End of Indian Empire		
Burma independent		
	1950 Korean War	1950
	1952 Eisenhower President	
	1953 Hydrogen Bomb	
		1955

MODERN TIMES

A Brief History from 1880 to 1955

Modern Times

A BRIEF HISTORY FROM 1880 TO 1955

I. M. M. MACPHAIL, M.A., Ph.Dr.

Principal Teacher of History, Clydebank High School

LONDON

EDWARD ARNOLD (PUBLISHERS) LTD

First published, 1961
Reprinted, 1961

MADE AND PRINTED IN GREAT BRITAIN BY
WILLIAM CLOWES AND SONS, LIMITED, LONDON AND BECCLES

PREFACE

One of the chief aims of history teaching in schools, according to many educationalists, is to help young people to be better citizens by learning about the background of the times they live in. But too often the school history book stops short at a date long before the children were born, and the last chapter, as like as not, is only a vague summary of the events of the previous decade. There has recently, however, been a tendency to place more emphasis on the study of modern times, e.g. in the syllabus for the new Ordinary Level examination for the Scottish Certificate of Education. This book starts with the days when our oldest living Prime Minister, Sir Winston Churchill, was a mere child and ends with the year of his resignation from office; and an attempt has been made to accord to the study of the later part of the period as detailed and objective a treatment as that generally given to the earlier. Although the focus is mainly on Britain and the Commonwealth, there is a full account of the development of the major European states and of the U.S.A. in the twentieth century. In addition, there are chapters on Parliament and on central and local government which should help to elucidate the modern political scene.

This is an age when the politician's vocabulary is full of terms such as dollar gap, invisible exports, credit squeeze, automation, and a history of modern times cannot ignore the economic problems of the day. The diagrams included will, it is hoped, lighten the task of learning about the "dismal science". Social history has also been treated at some length but it is regretted that for considerations of space it was found necessary to omit sections on the literature, art and music of the period. These subjects, however, should normally be adequately dealt with outside the history classroom.

Exercises at the end of each chapter are intended to promote individual study and a fuller knowledge of the period. Numerous source extracts provide glimpses of history being made and should stimulate the young historian to further reading and research.

It is a pleasure for me to acknowledge the assistance I have received from many friends, and, in particular, from my colleague, Mr. J. E. V. Ralston, who read the whole book in proof and gave helpful advice and criticism.

I. M. M. MACPHAIL

CONTENTS

PLATES

MAPS

DIAGRAMS

ACKNOWLEDGMENTS

We should like to thank the following authors, executors and publishers for permission to reprint copyright extracts:

From *The Life of Andrew Carnegie*. Copyright 1923 by Burton Hendrick, reprinted by permission of Doubleday & Company, Inc. and William Heinemann Limited; from *A History of Technology* by Singer, Holmyard, Hall and Williams and *Life of William Temple, Archbishop of Canterbury* by F. A. Iremonger, by permission of The Clarendon Press; from *The World Crisis* by Sir Winston Churchill and *Hitler—A Study in Tyranny* by Alan Bullock, by permission of Odhams Press, Ltd; from *The Black and Tans* by Richard Bennett, by permission of Vista Books; from *King George V* by Sir Harold Nicolson, by permission of the author; from *My Life of Revolt* by David Kirkwood and *Atomic Energy* by Egon Larsen, by permission of Messrs. George G. Harrap & Co., Ltd; from *Life of Earl Oxford and Asquith* by J. A. Spender and C. Asquith and *The History of the Czechs and Slovaks* by R. W. Seton Watson, by permission of The Hutchinson Publishing Group; from Lenin's *The State and Revolution* by permission of Messrs. Lawrence & Wishart, Ltd; from Margot Asquith's *Autobiography*, by permission of Messrs. Eyre & Spottiswoode (Publishers) Ltd; from Viscount Alanbrooke's War Diary in *The Turn of the Tide* by Sir Arthur Bryant, by permission of Messrs. Collins; from *Mahatma Gandhi—His Own Story* by C. F. Andrews, by permission of Messrs. George Allen & Unwin, Ltd; from *After Ten Years* by Ritchie Calder, with the author's permission; from *Rowing* by R. C. Lehmann, by permission of John Lehmann, Esq; from *Our Everest Adventure* by Sir John Hunt by permission of Messrs. Hodder & Stoughton, Ltd; the *Daily Telegraph* for an extract "Wembley Stormed" and an account of the Lindbergh flight; *The Times* for an extract from Lloyd George's speech at Limehouse in 1909; H.M. Stationery

Office for "Question Time in the House of Commons", April, 1946 (Hansard). Every effort to trace the copyright owner of W. T. Stead's *Last Will and Testament of Rhodes* has failed.

PHOTOGRAPH ACKNOWLEDGMENTS

We would like to thank the following for their kind permission to reproduce the photographs used in this book:

The Mansell Collection for those of Queen Victoria, Gladstone, the Boer War, Mafeking Night in London, Blériot and Marconi; Radio Times Hulton Picture Library for those of C. S. Rolls, Women Bus Conductresses, 1917, Suffragettes, Ramsay MacDonald, Keir Hardie, the Assassination of Francis Ferdinand, Rail Strike, 1919, French Troops in the Ruhr, Waterloo Station during General Strike, 1926, Digging Air-raid Trenches in Hyde Park, 1938 and Sleeping in the Tube, 1940; The Cambridge University Press for that of Lord Rutherford; The *Belfast Telegraph* for that of Sir Edward Carson and the Ulster Volunteers; The Imperial War Museum for "Your country needs you" and for the photographs of Chamberlain and Hitler, the Surrender of Singapore, General MacArthur, Churchill crossing the Rhine, Lloyd George at the Front, 1916 and the Sinking of the "Ark Royal"; The *Daily Mail* for examples of the campaign to "make Germany pay"; Fox Photos, Ltd, for that of the Battle of Britain Pilots; The Keystone Press for that of Gandhi; The Punjab Photo Service for that of Lord Mountbatten and Mr. Rajagopalachari; The Travellers Club for that of Lord Salisbury.

CHAPTER I

GLADSTONE AND THE
IRISH QUESTION

Beginning of Modern Times. There are many reasons for starting the story of modern times in 1880. In that year, when Gladstone became Prime Minister of a Liberal Government, the Irish question came to the forefront of British politics, which were destined to be bedevilled by it for the next fifty years. It was only six years before that the first working-men were elected to Parliament, and the 1880's saw the emergence of a working-class movement, still small but significant for the future. At this time also a national system of education was being organized following the Acts of Parliament of 1870 and 1872, while the education and emancipation of women were being advanced as a result of the founding of Girton College (1869), Newnham (1871) and numerous girls' high schools in the 1870's. The British people during this period became conscious and proud of the British Empire, and as other countries also cherished imperialist ambitions there ensued "the scramble for Africa". It was at this time, too, that the British began to be dependent on cheap food from overseas—grain from the prairies of the American Mid-West, and, a little later, chilled mutton from Australia and New Zealand and chilled beef from America. At sea, the sailing-ship was giving way to the steamer, although the best-known of the clippers, the *Cutty Sark*, which had been launched as late as 1869, the year of the opening of the Suez Canal, was still able to outpace most steamers. Steel was taking the place of iron in industry, and Britain's long-held industrial supremacy began to face challenges from the United States and Germany. New developments became possible through the applications of electricity; the Atlantic cable had been laid in 1866, the telephone invented by Graham

Bell in 1876, and the incandescent filament lamp by Swan and Edison just before 1880. The first four-stroke internal combustion engine was constructed in Germany in 1876 also and the first motor-cars of Benz and Daimler soon appeared on the roads. In medicine, a new era began with the experiments in immunization by inoculation of Louis Pasteur in 1881. Even in the realms of sport and popular entertainment, a change was evident. The last public hanging took place at Oxford in 1868; by 1880 spectators thronged to football and cricket matches, and golf, bowls, tennis and rowing all attracted enthusiasts. The institution of Bank Holidays in 1871 and of Saturday half-holidays a little later gave the ordinary man-in-the street the opportunity of sharing in the fruits of leisure enjoyed hitherto only by the middle and upper classes. In many different spheres, then, Britain was at the beginning of modern times in 1880.

Queen Victoria and her Prime Ministers. In 1880 Queen Victoria had already reigned for over forty years. For some time after the death of her husband, Albert, the Prince Consort, in 1861, she had lived in strict retirement, usually at Osborne House, Isle of Wight, or at Balmoral Castle on Dee-side. But, thanks mainly to the persuasion of Disraeli, when Prime Minister from 1874 to 1880, she had begun to appear more often in public. In 1887, at her Golden Jubilee, she participated fully in the ceremonies and sedately enjoyed the glories of the occasion. By 1897, the year of her Diamond Jubilee, she was revered by her subjects and accepted as the personification of all the great achievements of nineteenth-century Britain. Queen Victoria was a constitutional monarch, supposed to accept the advice of her ministers; but she liked to express her views on political and other matters and was annoyed when her opinion was ignored. When a Prime Minister was to be chosen and there was a choice between peer and commoner, she preferred the peer. In 1880 she would have had Lord Hartington, the Liberal leader in the Commons, or Earl Granville, the Liberal leader in the Lords, before Gladstone but they declined in his favour; in 1885 she chose Lord Salisbury instead of Sir Stafford Northcote, the Conservative leader in the Commons, and, similarly, in 1894,

Lord Rosebery in preference to Sir William Harcourt, the Liberal leader in the Commons. She detested Gladstone, of whom she once complained that he addressed her as if she were a public meeting; and in 1886 she went so far as to describe him as "this half-crazy and really in many ways ridiculous old man". She was of course more naturally in accord with Conservative beliefs in the monarchy, the aristocracy, the Church of England and the Empire, while she was appalled by the Liberal leader's policies in foreign affairs and in Ireland and by the republican ideas of some of his Radical colleagues. The Queen's antipathy to Gladstone increased by reason of her friendship with the Conservative leader, Disraeli. When he became Prime Minister in 1874, he won for himself an exceptional position as the Queen's adviser and friend through his discretion, tact and flattery (which last, he once confessed, should be "laid on with a trowel so far as royalty is concerned"). Disraeli, who had been created Earl of Beaconsfield in 1876, did not long survive his defeat in the election of 1880, dying the following year. He and Gladstone, rivals for so long, were unable to regard one another in a normal manner and often resorted to extremely abusive language in their arguments. Disraeli's acquisition in 1878 of Cyprus, of which he was so proud, Gladstone denounced as "insane—an act of duplicity not surpassed and rarely equalled in the history of nations". Disraeli on the other hand referred to Gladstone (in a private letter) as "an unprincipled maniac—extraordinary mixture of envy, hypocrisy and superstition" and (at a public banquet) as "a sophistical rhetorician inebriated with the exuberance of his own verbosity". It is possible to see from these quotations the bitterness that existed between the two statesmen and also the difference between the political vocabulary of their period and today. It is hardly necessary to add that neither statesman was as bad as he was painted by the other.

Midlothian Campaign, 1879–80. In the last two years of Beaconsfield's Ministry events at home and abroad had begun to affect the Conservative chances of victory at the next election. The "Great Depression" in agriculture and industry caused widespread unemployment and distress, agitation and outrages increased daily in Ireland, obstruction by Irish M.P.s held up business in the House of Commons, and military reverses in South Africa and Afghanistan made the splendours of the new imperialism seem rather tarnished. But without doubt it was Gladstone's election campaign in Midlothian which focused attention on the Government's difficulties and shortcomings and was mainly responsible for its downfall. Gladstone, who had emerged from retirement because of his indignation over the Bulgarian atrocities, was now, at the age of seventy-one, standing as Liberal candidate for Midlothian, the county with which his forebears were associated. He made his headquarters at Dalmeny House, the seat of his young friend and colleague, the Earl of Rosebery, later to be Prime Minister also. From Dalmeny he toured the constituency and other parts of south Scotland in November 1879 and again in March 1880, making speeches in public halls, in the open air and on railway platforms. The main burden of his attack on "Beaconsfieldism" was the need to place morality before material interests in foreign and imperial affairs. "Remember," he enjoined upon his hearers, "that the sanctity of life in the hill villages of Afghanistan among the winter snows is as inviolable in the eyes of Almighty God as can be your own." His tone of righteous indignation infuriated the Conservatives, and it was at this time that Beaconsfield in a letter characterized Gladstone as "an unprincipled maniac". In the late Victorian age, religion and morality exercised great influence in Britain, especially in Scotland, and Gladstone's appeals met with an enthusiastic response. The Liberals won a resounding victory (gaining 52 of the 60 seats in Scotland) and the Queen had reluctantly to accept Gladstone as her Prime Minister. The Midlothian campaign was the first occasion when a party leader went "on the stump" at an election, but Gladstone's success led to the practice becoming general. It also revealed the marked cleavage that still exists in Britain in the sphere of foreign affairs. Liberals and Socialists, following Gladstone, emphasize respect for the interests of other nations and sympathy with the oppressed, while Conservatives, following Beaconsfield, give priority to British interests and security.

Political Parties in 1880. It has often been remarked that in the politics of Victoria's reign one can see "the swing of the pendulum", which brought each party alternately into power—Liberals in 1868, Conservatives in 1874, Liberals in 1880 and 1885, Conservatives in 1886, Liberals in 1892, Conservatives in

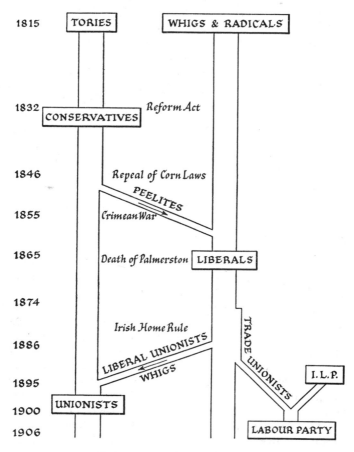

British Political Parties

1895. The two great parties of the latter half of the nineteenth century, the Liberals and the Conservatives, dominated the political scene. As Gilbert put it—

> "Every boy and every gal
> That's born into the world alive
> Is either a little Liberal
> Or else a little Conservative."

But that is an over-simplification. In 1880 the Liberals included at least two main groups—the right-wing Whigs and the left-wing Radicals. Gladstone, who had become Prime Minister for the second time, himself occupied a position between the two groups: his opinions were nearer to those of the Radicals but his friendships were mainly with the Whigs, of whom there were eight in his Cabinet of eleven. The WHIGS, like the Marquis of Harting-ton and Earl Granville, represented the old landowning aristocracy, differing little from the Conservatives, with whom they later joined forces over the question of Irish Home Rule. The RADICALS were not numerous in Parliament but had strong support among the working-classes. Socialism was just beginning to be discussed, mainly among middle-class people, but the Radical slogan at the 1880 election was not very revolutionary— "A Free Church, Free Schools and Free Land". Prominent among the Radicals in the Liberal party was Joseph Chamberlain, a wealthy screw-manufacturer and former Mayor of Birmingham, which, he claimed, had been "parked, paved, assized, marketed, gas-and-watered, and improved—all as the result of three years' active work" (1873–76). The Conservatives (often still called by their old name, "Tories") had also a left wing, the TORY DEMO-CRATS, who favoured a policy of social reform along the lines of Beaconsfield's policy. When Beaconsfield died a year after the election of 1880, the leadership of the Conservative party went to the Marquis of Salisbury in the House of Lords. In the 1880 Parliament, a small Conservative ginger-group was led by one of the Tory Democrats, Lord Randolph Churchill (father of Sir Winston Churchill), and was nicknamed the "FOURTH PARTY". The "third party" was that of the IRISH NATIONALISTS, a strong compact body under the leadership of Parnell. They were now advocating "Home Rule" or repeal of the Union of 1800 and saw to it that Irish grievances were fully ventilated, obstructing the business of the House of Commons whenever possible.

"A Most Distressful Country." There was little doubt that the Irish question was the most important problem confronting the new Government. It was indeed not to be solved until the twentieth century; and, even yet, there are many who think the present set-up in Ireland not a permanent settlement. Despite Gladstone's efforts in his first ministry (1868–74) to "pacify Ireland", the situation in 1880 was worse than ever. The depression in agriculture had hit Ireland badly. The harvests of 1877 and 1878 were the worst since the "Potato Famine", and with the influx of cheap wheat from the American prairies, Irish grain could no longer be sold at a profit in Britain. Rents still remained high, and evictions became increasingly common, 10,457 in 1880 as against 2,177 in 1877. In reprisal the Irish started "moonlighting". Outrages were committed at night (and sometimes by day)—burning of cornstacks, mutilating of cattle and even murder. Out of this agrarian unrest the IRISH NATIONAL LAND LEAGUE was formed by Michael Davitt, a former Fenian, and Parnell, with the latter as president. Its purpose was to press for land reforms by peaceful and constitutional methods, although many of the members were not so moderate as their leaders. CHARLES STEWART PARNELL was an Anglo-Irish Protestant landlord, son of an American mother who had brought him up to hate the English; and hate them he did, with icy bitterness. In the previous Parliament, Parnell had led the Irish Nationalist M.P.s in a campaign of obstruction which produced frequent all-night sittings and made ordinary business in the House almost impossible. Not long after the new Parliament met, Parnell made his famous speech at Ennis in County Clare, urging that anyone who took a farm from which a tenant had been evicted should be "isolated from his kind as if he were a leper of old". The first person to suffer this treatment was not an Irish tenant but an English land agent in County Mayo called Captain Boycott; and "boycotting" soon became an effective weapon in the hands of the Irish. Truly the condition of the country was such as to justify the line in *The Wearing of the Green*—"She's the most distressful country that's ever yet been seen."

Repression and Reform. Gladstone had often supported the cause of oppressed minorities abroad but, although he sympathized with the Irish, he had now reluctantly to agree with his colleagues that law and order must first be enforced in Ireland. A Coercion Act was passed despite determined Irish Nationalist opposition in the House of Commons, one sitting lasting for forty-one hours. (It was on this occasion that there was introduced the device of the closure, by which a debate can be brought to an end by a straightforward motion to that effect.) The Coercion Act (1881) suspended the Habeas Corpus Act so that the authorities could imprison any suspected persons without trial. Along with this repressive measure, the Government brought in a Bill for land reform, embodying the proposals of a Royal Commission set up in 1879. This new Land Act (1881) gave Irish tenants the rights known as the "3 F's"— (1) Fair Rents, to be fixed by a Land Court; (2) Fixed Tenure, so long as this rent was paid; (3) Free Sale of the tenant's interest in the holding, which meant that the tenant would be compensated for any improvement he had carried out. It also made provision for advancing 75 per cent of the purchase price to a tenant who wanted to buy his holding. This Act was effective in ending the abuses of "landlordism" but for a time its usefulness was negatived by Parnell's opposition and his advice to Irish tenants not to use the Land Courts. Parnell felt bound to oppose the new Act as much of the financial support for the Irish Nationalist movement came from the Irish-American organization, Clan-na-Gael. This was composed of extremists who were determined to achieve Home Rule and who had no wish to see the Irish peasant content under the British flag. The Government became more and more incensed by Parnell's tactics and the continued outrages. Finally, declaring that "the resources of civilization are not yet exhausted", Gladstone allowed Forster, the Chief Secretary for Ireland, to imprison Parnell and some of his colleagues in Kilmainham Jail in Dublin. To Gladstone, who

had so recently been expatiating on the rights of Afghans and
Boers, this policy of coercion was distasteful. Nor did it lead to
any improvement in Ireland: as Parnell prophesied, "Captain
Moonlight" took his place. The outrages continued unabated and
men who had served on a jury that convicted a terrorist were
even shot down in the street. In the spring of 1882, therefore,
Gladstone arranged for the release of Parnell, who promised to do
his best to restore order. This KILMAINHAM TREATY, as it was
called, led to the resignation of Forster, who felt that he had been
slighted in the matter. His place was taken by Lord Frederick
Cavendish, son of the Duke of Devonshire and a relative by
marriage of Gladstone. He was highly regarded on all sides and
the whole country was shocked when on the afternoon of his
arrival in Dublin he was murdered along with the Under-
Secretary, Thomas Burke, when taking a walk through the
Phoenix Park. They were hacked to death with surgical knives by
terrorists called "The Invincibles". The PHOENIX PARK MURDERS
(1882) ruined any chance of a peaceful settlement. Parnell actually
thought of resigning his seat in disgust and expressed in scathing
terms his denunciation of what had happened. A new COERCION
ACT (1882) was passed, suspending trial by jury (as Irish juries
had been refusing to convict), only to be followed by more
outrages, including twenty-six murders in Ireland and the
dynamiting of buildings in England. Slowly, however, tenants
began to take advantage of the Land Act and a slight improvement took place under the firm but sympathetic rule of the
Viceroy, Earl Spencer.

"Crofters' War." While these troubles were going on in
Ireland, there prevailed in the Scottish Highlands and Islands
similar agrarian discontent, but fortunately there was comparatively little violence or terrorism. Although the worst of
the Clearances were over, the crofters still suffered from rack-
renting and evictions; and inspired by the Irish example, some
of them formed a Land League to fight the landlords by all
means available short of violence. Crofters in Lewis, Skye and
Wester Ross refused to accept eviction notices from the sheriff
officers; and, in answer to appeals from the local authorities,

soldiers and sailors were sent north to maintain law and order. In 1882, the gunboat *Jackal* steamed north to Glendale in Skye to intimidate crofters who refused to answer a summons to appear in court. Near Portree, there occurred the "BATTLE OF THE BRAES", when the sheriff, accompanied by a troop of Glasgow policemen, was met with stones from an angry crowd. Prompted by the Scottish Liberal M.P.s, the Government were forced to investigate and remedy the crofters' grievances. A Royal Commission under Lord Napier was set up in 1883 and the Commissioners toured the crofting counties, collecting evidence from crofters, factors, landlords, doctors and ministers. It was not until 1886 that at last the CROFTERS ACT was passed, guaranteeing to the crofters security of tenure and giving powers to a Crofters Commission to cancel rent arrears, reduce rents and assess improvements made by the crofters. Unfortunately, by giving the crofters security in their holdings, it tended to perpetuate the very small and uneconomic crofts which had been produced by repeated sub-division. Although the crofters felt that they had won a victory over the landlords, the agitation did not die down for some years. Land-hungry cottars (men without crofts) made raids to seize land, especially in the Western Isles. In 1887 there occurred the LEWIS DEER DRIVE: several hundred cottars, whose families were starving after a poor harvest and an unsuccessful fishing season, raided a deer-forest in the company of Lowland newspaper-reporters and slaughtered the stags and hinds. They returned home just before troops arrived from the south; the ringleaders surrendered themselves and stood their trial in Edinburgh, their acquittal leading to enthusiastic scenes in the High Street of the capital. The Liberals' action in passing the Crofters Act enhanced their reputation in the crofting counties, which for long remained loyal to their Liberal tradition.

Colonial Difficulties. During the troubles in Ireland and Scotland the Government also had to deal with difficulties that arose from the colonial annexations made by their predecessors in office. Gladstone had already criticized "Beaconsfieldism" in Afghanistan, the Transvaal and elsewhere; but he was so involved in home affairs at first that he could not carry out his proposal for "disannexation" until after the Boers of the Transvaal proclaimed their independence and wiped out at MAJUBA HILL on the borders of the Transvaal a British force sent against them (1881). What was Gladstone to do? In the Cabinet there was a split, the right-wing Whigs pressing for the restoration of British military supremacy before independence would be granted and the left-wing Radicals advocating immediate "disannexation". Gladstone, after all his public criticism of the Conservative annexations, could hardly do otherwise than grant the Boers their independence. Unfortunately, as this concession followed so soon after the Majuba Hill reverse, it gave the Boers the impression that the British had yielded to force; their contempt for British military power was to last for a long time and to lead to trouble in the future. In AFGHANISTAN, where the British had pushed forward to prevent Russian penetration, Beaconsfield's policy had already met with a reverse: the British envoy and his mission were murdered (1879) and a British army routed at Maiwand near Kandahar (1880). Gladstone's Government had just come into office before this defeat, which was followed by a memorable march of 313 miles over almost road-less country in twenty-three days by a relieving force under Sir Frederick Roberts to save the small force besieged in Kandahar. As a result of this march from KABUL TO KANDAHAR and a victory over the Afghans, British prestige was restored. British forces were withdrawn, however, and an understanding arrived at with the new Amir so that Afghanistan became a friendly buffer-state effectively blocking a Russian advance.

Egypt. When Disraeli purchased the Suez Canal shares from the bankrupt Khedive Ismail, Gladstone foretold that Britain would inevitably become involved in Egyptian politics. Events were soon to prove him right. The Khedive's debts had amounted in 1874 to over £100,000,000 (part of it incurred by lavish expenditure on the opera *Aida*, which he had commissioned from the composer Verdi for the opening of the Suez Canal) and, despite the £4,000,000 he obtained from Britain in 1875, he was soon in difficulties again. As a result, there was set up in 1876 an

Anglo-French Commission in the interests of the Khedive's foreign creditors. At their instigation, the Khedive was deposed in 1879 by his nominal sovereign, the Sultan of Turkey, and replaced by his son, Tewfik, who proceeded to rule through the British and French officials of the Dual Control. This provoked a nationalist movement, which led to a mutiny in the army in 1881. Egyptian officers complained that Turks were preferred to them in promotions and that payments of interest to foreign investors came before arrears of pay. The slogans of "Egypt for the Egyptians!" and "Out with the foreigners!" received popular support and the Khedive was compelled to yield to nationalist demands that his foreign officials should be dismissed. ARABI PASHA, an Egyptian colonel and leader of the army rebels, was made Minister of War. The French were anxious for an Anglo-French occupation of Egypt but Gladstone was at first reluctant to adopt such a policy. A combined Anglo-French naval squadron was sent to Alexandria to intimidate the Egyptians; but instead rioting started in Alexandria and fifty Europeans were killed. In the end, the French, who were busy with their newly-annexed colony of Tunisia, withdrew from Alexandria and the British were left to carry on alone. The Alexandria shore batteries, recently strengthened by Arabi's men, were bombarded by the British Navy, an event which brought about the resignation of one member of Gladstone's ministry, John Bright, the veteran Radical, who had strong pacifist sympathies. Gladstone tried unsuccessfully to persuade France, Italy and Turkey to combine in a joint intervention in Egypt; but it was a British force under Sir Garnet Wolseley that destroyed Arabi's army at TEL-EL-KEBIR (1882), following a night march across the desert. Gladstone was still against the annexation of Egypt, but he felt it would be impossible to withdraw the troops stationed there without causing chaos in the Middle East. In 1883 he sent out to Egypt as British Agent and Consul General, Sir Evelyn Baring (later Lord Cromer), who was to be an effective ruler of Egypt for the next twenty-three years; and so began the long British occupation of Egypt that was to last, in one form or another, for almost three-quarters of a century.

Sudan. More trouble in the same region followed almost immediately for Gladstone's Government. A religious movement had begun among the Muslims in the Sudan, who had resented Egyptian rule and, in particular, recent attempts to suppress the slave trade by European officials, one of whom was General Gordon. Under the leadership of the MAHDI (a word similar to "Messiah"), the Sudanese defeated Egyptian troops in several small skirmishes and finally annihilated an Egyptian army led by a British general, Hicks, in 1883. It was with an order to evacuate the military garrisons still left in the Sudan that GENERAL GORDON was sent by the Government early in 1884. Gladstone had viewed with alarm the ever-increasing responsibilities incurred by the British since Disraeli's purchase of the Suez Canal shares; but he made a mistake in his choice of Gordon for the task of evacuation. Gordon had earned a national reputation for himself as a Christian gentleman and dauntless fighter in China, and had already been employed in the Sudan as Governor-General under the Khedive of Egypt. He reached Khartoum but, instead of evacuating the garrisons, he settled down to making plans to "smash the Mahdi" and recover the Sudan. The Government were unwilling to lose any more British lives but, as the Mahdi's followers conquered more and more of the Sudan, Gladstone was pressed to send reinforcements. Gordon could have escaped down the Nile but preferred to wait on at Khartoum until it was too late. When at last, in January 1885, a relief force under Wolseley reached the beleaguered garrison at Khartoum, it was only to find that Gordon had been killed two days earlier by the Mahdi's followers. Wolseley withdrew his troops and no attempt was to be made to re-conquer the Sudan for almost twelve years. The news of Gordon's death provoked a storm of anger in Britain. Gladstone received a severe rebuke from Queen Victoria in a telegram, which became publicly known; the title Gladstone had been given by his admirers, G.O.M. ("Grand Old Man") was inverted by his critics into M.O.G. ("Murderer of Gordon"). Never in his whole career was Gladstone so unpopular as he was in 1885.

Political and Social Reforms. During most of the time when

Gordon was at Khartoum, Gladstone had been busy in the House of Commons over the Franchise Bill which, by giving the right to vote to male householders in country districts and small towns, was a big advance towards complete manhood suffrage. Chamberlain and the Radicals had been disappointed because Irish affairs had interfered with their programme of reforms. Certainly some useful measures had been passed—the CORRUPT PRACTICES ACT, restricting the amount of money that could be spent at elections; the first EMPLOYERS' LIABILITY ACT, granting compensation for accidents to workmen; the MARRIED WOMEN'S PROPERTY ACT, giving married women rights of ownership. But electoral reform had still to be tackled and at last the Whigs in the Cabinet had to agree. The THIRD REFORM ACT (1884), which was accompanied by a Redistribution Act, had important political consequences. Among other results, it led to the gradual disappearance of the Whigs; and as the Irish electorate was trebled, Parnell and his followers were assured of a victory in almost every Irish constituency except in the north-east. Just before the end of Gladstone's ministry, a separate Scottish Office was created, mainly at the instigation of Lord Rosebery. It was during this Parliament of 1880–85 that CHARLES BRADLAUGH, the famous freethinker who had been elected M.P. for Northampton, was denied the right to take his seat in the House of Commons for first refusing to take the oath and later for offering to do so "as a matter of form". Gladstone, although a very religious man himself, supported Bradlaugh's claim on the Liberal grounds of liberty of conscience while the Conservatives, especially Lord Randolph Churchill, made the most of the "Radical Atheist". Bradlaugh was on one occasion expelled from the House only after ten policemen had been summoned to deal with him; after being re-elected four times, he was finally allowed to take his seat in 1886.

Salisbury's First Ministry, 1885. When the Liberals were defeated in the House of Commons by a combined Irish and Conservative majority, there was no immediate election as the new electoral rolls were not yet ready. Gladstone handed over the reins of office to the Conservative Lord Salisbury, who formed "a ministry of caretakers", as Chamberlain called them. During this "stop-gap" government, one important act dealing with Ireland was passed. This was a LAND PURCHASE ACT, introduced by Lord Ashbourne and usually called after him; it extended the provisions of the Land Act of 1881 by allowing the Irish peasant a 100 per cent loan instead of a 75 per cent loan to buy his holding. By this time, Gladstone had come to the conclusion that there was no real alternative to Home Rule for Ireland. He was aware that this would not be acceptable to all his colleagues, particularly the Whigs, and when he heard that some Conservatives were thinking along the same lines, he felt relieved. He knew that such a measure would go through the House of Lords only with difficulty and that the best chance for it would be with Conservative rather than Liberal backing. Parnell, who has been called "the uncrowned King of Ireland" and for the next year or so was to earn the title of "the arbiter of British politics", saw like Gladstone that the best chance for an Irish Home Rule Bill would be under a Conservative Government. After private discussions with the Conservative leaders, Parnell instructed all Irishmen in British constituencies to "vote Tory" in the election at the end of 1885, an action which, it was estimated, lost the Liberals about 30 seats. These losses were, however, offset to some extent by Liberal gains due mainly to the success of Chamberlain and his Radical speeches. Although his UN-AUTHORIZED PROGRAMME was strongly criticized by his Whig colleagues, and not even approved by Gladstone, it exerted a strong appeal to the newly-enfranchised masses. Among other proposals he advocated "Free Schools, Disestablishment of the Welsh Episcopal Church and the Presbyterian Church of Scotland, Crofters' Rights, Small-holdings ('Three acres and a cow'), Payment of M.P.s." Like Gladstone in 1879–80, he toured the country, holding large audiences spell-bound by his eloquence. It was confidently forecast that "Radical Joe" (the be-monocled business-man with an orchid perpetually in his buttonhole) would succeed Gladstone as Prime Minister. But the election brought about a deadlock: the Liberals had a majority of 86 over the Conservatives, while Parnell and his followers numbered exactly 86 ("the 86 of '86"). Parnell was master of the House of Commons but Home Rule was not to be easily achieved.

Home Rule Bill, 1886. There had been no definite agreement in the Conservative Cabinet about Home Rule, and when Gladstone's son, Herbert, disclosed to the press that his father had decided on Home Rule as the only solution, the Conservative leader, Salisbury, who had never been keen on the proposal, was quick to repudiate it. He had no desire to split his own party over such a distasteful measure and preferred Gladstone to have the trouble of handling it. Unfortunately for Gladstone, his decision displeased many of his colleagues; most of the Whigs opposed it and also Chamberlain, who saw that his Radical programme was likely to be jeopardized for the sake of Home Rule and who bore Parnell a grudge for persuading Irishmen in Britain to vote Conservative at the election. Gladstone, now in his seventy-seventh year, went on doggedly to propose an independent Parliament for Ireland and, along with it, a scheme of land purchase that would cost £50,000,000 and would make the Irish peasants proprietors of their soil. He introduced the Home Rule Bill with an eloquent speech of three and a half hours, and the debates on the Bill throughout were of a very high standard. Lord Salisbury showed how wrong Parnell was in hoping for Home Rule from the Conservatives by a speech in which he deeply offended the Irish:—"All men are not capable of self-government as the English race is. There are the Hottentots, for instance, and the Indians. The alternative is to enable the Government of England to govern Ireland." Lord Randolph Churchill seized on the resentment felt by the Protestants of Northern Ireland at being placed under a Catholic majority and coined the oft-used phrase: "Ulster will fight and Ulster will be right". Despite Gladstone's final moving appeal in the House of Commons—"Ireland stands at your bar, expectant, hopeful, almost suppliant"—the Bill was defeated, 93 Liberals voting against it. The Liberal party received a blow in 1886 from which it did not recover for twenty years and Irish Home Rule seemed as far off as ever. The name UNIONIST, adopted by the Liberals who voted with Chamberlain to preserve the union with Ireland, was later applied also to the Conservatives and is still popularly used for "Conservative" in some places. It was in this year, which has been called "the most dramatic in modern English party history", that a SCOTTISH HOME RULE ASSOCIATION was formed, partly as a protest against the appointment of an Englishman, Sir George Trevelyan, to the new post of Secretary for Scotland. One beneficial measure that was well received in north and west Scotland was the Crofters Act, already mentioned.

Conservatives and Ireland. The election of 1886 brought the Conservatives under Lord Salisbury into power with the prospect of support from the Liberal Unionists, who included not only the Radical Chamberlain but also many of his former Whig colleagues. Chamberlain's Radical programme was still advocated by some Liberals but during the later 1880's, when unemployment was rife, there was a ferment of agitation which produced a new militant trade unionism and led to the formation of the Independent Labour Party in 1893. Before Salisbury's Ministry was more than a few months old, the brilliant but brief career of Lord Randolph Churchill, the Chancellor of the Exchequer and probable successor to Salisbury as Premier, came to an end with his resignation over a minor dispute. His place was taken by a former Liberal, George J. Goschen, while some years later (1895) Chamberlain also entered a Conservative Cabinet. Salisbury, Prime Minister from 1886 to 1892, and again from 1895 to 1902, concerned himself mainly with imperial and foreign affairs (which are considered in later chapters). The Conservative solution for Irish problems was based on the maintenance of law and order or, as Salisbury expressed it, "twenty years of resolute government". But they also had something positive to offer, which it was hoped would "kill Home Rule by kindness". First, as the Liberals had already proposed in their Land Acts, financial assistance was to be given to the Irish peasants for land purchase to end their grievances about rent and compensation; secondly, the Irish were given an opportunity of governing themselves in a limited sphere, when county councils were set up. The new Chief Secretary for Ireland was Salisbury's nephew, ARTHUR J. BALFOUR, previously regarded as a dilettante and ridiculed as "the darling of perfumed drawing-rooms". He revealed himself a firm and determined Chief Secretary, whom the Irish soon christened "Bloody Balfour". Another CRIMES ACT was passed, a new procedure, the guillotine, being invented to overcome obstruction in the House of Commons; by this Act Resident Magistrates could try offenders without a jury. Within a year, six Irish M.P.s were in prison undergoing hard labour and over twenty M.P.s were imprisoned in all. To help the Government pass their coercive measure, *The Times* published a series of articles, PARNELLISM AND CRIME, which insinuated that Parnell had condoned the Phoenix Park Murders. At a judicial committee of inquiry, it was later revealed that one of the most incriminating documents, a facsimile of which *The Times* reproduced, had been forged. The forger, a disreputable Irish journalist, Richard Pigott, was forced under a grilling cross-examination to admit his guilt. He fled the country that same night and finished up by blowing his brains out in a Madrid hotel. The British sense of fair play brought a large measure of sympathy for Parnell and his cause, and the Government's harsh treatment of the Irish was widely criticized. British support for Home Rule, however, was shaken when Parnell was cited as co-respondent in a divorce case brought by a Captain O'Shea against his wife. The divorce case meant that Parnell lost the support of the Roman Catholics in Ireland, and the Irish Nationalist party split up into Parnellites and Anti-Parnellites. He himself died in 1891 within a year of the divorce case but the split lasted for a long time after. Balfour improved on Lord Ashbourne's Act (1885) by another LAND PURCHASE ACT (1891) in which the Government undertook to lend up to a total of £20,000,000 to enable tenants to buy their holdings. (Another Act passed in 1903, when Balfour himself was Prime Minister, helped to complete the process, the land being bought by the Government and handed over to the peasants, who paid back the loan in annual sums, "annuities", up to 1932, when the Irish Free State Government stopped them.) COUNTY COUNCILS, which had been set up in England and Scotland in 1888 and 1889, were introduced to Ireland in 1898. This innovation was hailed as "one of the most beneficial pieces of legislation ever passed for Ireland". Men who had hitherto had no outlet for their political energy except in agitation could now busy themselves over local problems.

"An Old Man in a Hurry." Gladstone, who felt dedicated to the cause of Irish Home Rule, was in his eighties when his last chance came in 1892, the election of that year giving the Liberals and Irish Nationalists a majority over the Conservatives and Liberal Unionists. Gladstone's chief preoccupation in his short fourth Ministry (1892–94) was with the SECOND HOME RULE BILL. Lord Randolph Churchill's description of the previous Bill of 1886 being introduced "to gratify the ambitions of an old man in a hurry" was even more appropriate in 1893, the aged Prime Minister displaying amazing energy. The Bill was passed by the Commons but, as everyone expected, thrown out by the Lords by an overwhelming majority. The only other important measure was a LOCAL GOVERNMENT ACT (1894), setting up Parish Councils. Gladstone retired a few months later after a parliamentary career of over sixty years. When he died in 1898, he was described by the Conservative A. J. Balfour as "the greatest member of the greatest deliberative assembly the world has ever known".

Rosebery's Ministry. Gladstone was succeeded in 1894 not by the Liberal leader in the House of Commons, Sir William Harcourt, but by Lord Rosebery, Queen Victoria again showing her preference for a peer over a commoner, as she had done in 1885 when Lord Salisbury was chosen instead of the Conservative leader in the House of Commons. Rosebery had had a brilliant political career up to the time of his becoming Prime Minister, but his Ministry was not a success except in an unusual respect, his horses winning the Derby in the two years he was in office. (He was said to have announced when at Eton that he had three ambitions—to become Prime Minister, to win the Derby and to marry an heiress; he did achieve all three, his wife being one of the Rothschilds.) It was during Rosebery's Ministry that Sir William Harcourt, Chancellor of the Exchequer, greatly increased the Death Duties because of heavy naval expenditure.

They were to be increased still further by successive Chancellors until they have become responsible for the break-up of many of the old landed estates in Britain. It was with a sigh of relief that Rosebery resigned in 1895 after an adverse vote in the House of Commons. At the ensuing election the Conservatives and Liberal Unionists combined and the Liberals were decisively defeated. The Irish question was to be dormant until just before the First World War when the Liberals at last were able to surmount the obstacle of the House of Lords. It had been the main issue in British politics for a generation and more, and the bitterness engendered then was sufficient to keep the Home Rule movement alive despite the improvements effected by Liberals and Conservatives. Unfortunately, by fomenting the strife between the Protestant north and the Catholic south, the Conservatives kept open a festering sore in Ireland which has not been healed even at the present day.

SOURCE EXTRACTS

A   *Start of Boycotting*

"What are you to do to a tenant who bids for a farm from which his neighbour has been evicted?" (*Cries of "Kill him!" "Shoot him!"*) "You must shun him on the roadside when you meet him, you must shun him in the streets of the town, you must shun him at the shop counter, you must shun him at the fair and at the market-place, and even in the house of worship—by isolating him from his kind as if he were a leper of old, you must show him your detestation of the crime he has committed, and you may depend upon it, that there will be no man so full of avarice, so lost to shame, as to dare the public opinion of all right-thinking men, and to transgress your unwritten code of laws."

Parnell at Ennis, September 16th, 1879.

B   *Irish Home Rule*

... "Ireland stands at your bar, expectant, hopeful and almost suppliant. ... She asks a blessed oblivion of the past, and in that oblivion our interest is even deeper than hers. You have been asked tonight to abide by the traditions of which we are heirs. What traditions? By the Irish traditions? Go into the length and breadth of the world, ransack the literature of all countries, find if you can a single voice, a single book, in which the conduct of England towards Ireland is anywhere treated except with profound and bitter condemnation. Are these the traditions by which we are exhorted to stand? No, they are a sad exception to the glory of our country. They are a broad and black blot upon the pages of its history, and what we want to do is to stand by the traditions of which we are heirs in all matters except in our relations with Ireland. . . . She asks also a boon for the future; and that boon for the future, unless we are much mistaken, will be a boon to us in respect of honour, no less than a boon to her in respect of happiness, prosperity and peace. Such, sir, is her prayer. Think, I beseech you: think well, think wisely, think, not for the moment, but for the years that are to come, before you reject this Bill."

Gladstone in House of Commons, June 9th, 1886.

EXERCISES

1. (*Extract "A".*) What events led Parnell to propose such a policy?
2. (*Extract "B".*) On what occasion was Gladstone speaking?
3. Identify the authors of the following and explain where necessary:

   (*a*) "Flattery should be laid on with a trowel so far as royalty is concerned."

   (*b*) "This half-crazy and really in many ways ridiculous old man."

   (*c*) "A sophistical rhetorician inebriated with the exuberance of his own verbosity."

   (*d*) "Remember that the sanctity of life in the hill villages of Afghanistan among the winter snows is as inviolable in the eyes of Almighty God as can be your own."

   (*e*) "The resources of civilization are not yet exhausted."

   (*f*) "Ulster will fight and Ulster will be right."

   (*g*) "The darling of perfumed drawing-rooms."

   (*h*) "Introduced to gratify the ambitions of an old man in a hurry."

   (*i*) "Three acres and a cow."

   (*j*) "All races are not capable of self-government as the English race is. There are the Hottentots, for instance, and the Indians."

4. Explain: Fourth Party, "swing of the pendulum", boycotting, moonlighting, 3 F's, Ministry of Caretakers, "the arbiter of British politics", Radical Joe, "the 86 of '86", Unionists, "Battle of the Braes".

5. Write short notes on: Kilmainham Treaty; Phoenix Park Murders; Majuba Hill; "Parnellism and Crime"; Charles Bradlaugh; "Unauthorized Programme"; Lewis Deer Drive.

6. Write notes on: Midlothian Campaign; Irish Land Acts; Charles Parnell; Irish Home Rule Bill (1886); "Crofters' War"; Lord Rosebery; Lord Randolph Churchill.

7. Explain and criticize Gladstone's Irish policy.

8. What was the Conservative policy for Ireland at the end of the nineteenth century?

9. Write a speech for or against Gladstone's colonial policy.

10. Describe the problems encountered by Gladstone at home and abroad in his second Ministry, 1880–85.

CHAPTER II

IMPERIALISM IN AFRICA

The Age of Imperialism. Although the British Empire had been expanding for centuries, it was only in the last quarter of the nineteenth century that the British people began to feel conscious and proud of their "Empire on which the sun never sets". By giving Queen Victoria a new title, Empress of India, by the purchase of the Suez Canal shares, and by the "forward" policy in South Africa, Afghanistan and the Middle East, Disraeli's Ministry (1874–80) had contributed largely to this changed attitude. At the same time other European nations were looking enviously at Britain; her wealth and trade supremacy were generally regarded as resulting from her possession of an overseas empire. France, keen to wipe out the memory of her humiliating defeat in the Franco-Prussian War (1870–71), sought colonial gains in Africa and in the Far East. Germany and Italy, having so recently achieved national unity and independence, began to think that their prestige required colonies; in other words, nationalism gave birth to imperialism. Many European statesmen agreed with Joseph Chamberlain's remark—"The day of small nations has passed away: the day of empires has come." Even the United States, whose anti-colonial feeling had been so strong, began to build up an overseas empire by the annexation of the former Spanish colonies of Cuba and the Philippines. Among the European powers, this new interest in colonies in the last quarter of the nineteenth century led to a contest for possessions overseas and, in particular, a "scramble for Africa", still a comparatively undeveloped and unexploited continent. From this "scramble" Britain, already long established there, was to emerge with the lion's share.

Britain and Imperialism. Inevitably, the problems of the Empire came to occupy much of the Government's attention in the last two decades of the century. The most important imperial questions confronting the politicians at Westminster were:

(a) Defence of the Empire, involving strategic considerations such as the security of trade routes (e.g. Suez Canal) or frontier disputes (e.g. Venezuela or the Transvaal) or the control of buffer-states (e.g. Afghanistan).

(b) Imperial co-operation between the self-governing parts of the Empire and the Mother Country.

(c) Annexation of new territories for reasons of security or trade or prestige.

(d) Grants of self-government.

(e) Treatment of "backward" races.

(f) Development of natural resources of the colonies.

There were divided views in Britain about these problems of empire. All parties were more or less in agreement about the first two although there still lingered a few "Little Englanders" in the Liberal party. So far as imperial co-operation was concerned, Liberals (Forster, Chamberlain and Rosebery) were foremost in setting up the Imperial Federation League in 1884; and it was Rosebery who coined the phrase "THE BRITISH COMMONWEALTH OF NATIONS" in a speech in Australia in the same year. About annexation and self-government there were strongly-held opposite views. When Gladstone denounced

"Beaconsfieldism", he was thinking mainly of Beaconsfield's annexations, and most Liberals (except for a few Whigs) tended to follow Gladstone's lead in this respect. Grants of self-government the Conservatives resisted, in Africa as in Ireland, as harmful to British interests and also as premature, because of the presumed unfitness of the peoples concerned. To withdraw British rule, it was argued, would mean giving the colonies over to chaos and civil war. So far as the majority of the British people were concerned, imperial expansion was regarded with pride. Some of the pioneers of the Labour movement, e.g. Keir Hardie, were indeed critical but they were only a small minority group. These lines from *Land of Hope and Glory,* written by A. C. Benson, a master at Eton, expressed what many felt:

> "Land of Hope and Glory, Mother of the Free,
> How shall we extol thee, who are born of thee?
> Wider still and wider shall thy bounds be set;
> God who made thee mighty, make thee mightier yet."

This was the period when Kipling's poems and stories about the British soldier had an enormous vogue. His *Departmental Ditties* (1886), *Plain Tales from the Hills* (1886), *Soldiers Three* (1889), *Barrack Room Ballads* (1892) and others did not merely entertain a vast public: they helped to foster the belief that the British, instead of the "lesser breeds without the law", had been divinely chosen to take the major share of the "WHITE MAN'S BURDEN". When he wrote the poem *The White Man's Burden* for the American people at the time of the annexation of the Philippines, Kipling stressed the fact that empire-building involved obligations to the inhabitants of the territories annexed. Many of the British people were already not only aware of this "White Man's Burden" but proud to share in the "civilizing mission" involved—suppressing the slave trade, starting medical services, education, etc. Unfortunately, not all the empire-builders shared these views and their arrogance to native races sowed the seed of much racial bitterness at a later period.

Opening up Africa. The new interest in Africa had begun long before Chamberlain became Colonial Secretary. The journeys of explorers like Speke, Livingstone and Stanley had opened up the interior of the "Dark Continent". H. M. STANLEY (1841–1904), after his meeting with Livingstone at Ujiji (where he gave his greeting "Dr. Livingstone, I presume?"), explored the country round Lake Tanganyika with him. Later, in three years of exploration (1873–77), during which he lost most of his companions and his hair went white, he mapped Lake Victoria Nyanza, confirming Speke's claim that it was the source of the Nile, and then crossed over to the Congo river, following it to the sea. His book *Through the Dark Continent* (1878) was widely read; his account of the wonderful resources and commercial possibilities of the Congo roused the interests of Leopold II, King of the Belgians, who was later to allow the development of the Congo Free State to degenerate under Belgian officials into the worst kind of exploitation of the natives. Tales of the ivory, rubber and palm oil in the region led to claims by the Portuguese and French; and the latter sent an expedition under Count de Brazza to claim the north bank of the Congo in 1880, the year before they occupied Tunis. It was in the next year, 1882, that the British sent their expedition to Egypt and reluctantly became involved in the occupation of that country; but other countries were keen to acquire colonies and the scramble for Africa was about to begin.

The Scramble for Africa. A lecture-tour by H. M. Stanley in Germany was responsible for the founding in 1884 of a SOCIETY FOR GERMAN COLONIZATION by Karl Peters, who at the end of the same year landed with two other Germans on the East African coast near Zanzibar and cajoled the native chiefs in the interior to sign treaties recognizing German sovereignty. The British had been active in this area for some time. It was through Sir John Kirk, Consul-General at Zanzibar from 1866 to 1887 that the slave trade was finally suppressed; and it was another Scotsman, Sir William Mackinnon, chairman of the British India Steam Navigation Company, who was offered by the Sultan of Zanzibar control of his mainland possessions in 1876, only to find that Disraeli's Government would not agree to support him. On the other side of Africa, German traders were also busy making agreements with tribal chiefs in Togoland, Kameruns South-west Africa, and in so doing had just forestalled British attempts to do the same; but the British had already long before occupied other parts of West Africa—the Gold Coast, Gambia and Sierra Leone, while a trading company was operating in Nigeria. Even before Peters had started on his "empire-building", the European powers had met in a Colonial Conference at Berlin to discuss the partition of Africa (1884–85). At this BERLIN COLONIAL CONFERENCE, which was attended by fourteen Powers including the U.S.A., it was recognized that possession of part of the coastline by a Power gave it the right to regard the hinterland as its sphere of influence. The Powers also bound themselves to suppress slavery and look after the welfare of the native races. The Congo Free State was set up as an independent state and King Leopold of Belgium chosen to administer it. Italy, forestalled by the French in Tunisia, managed to annex part of the Red Sea coast in 1884 and founded her first colony, Eritrea.

British Expansion. Britain was at first not unduly alarmed by the interest displayed by other Powers in Africa. Gladstone regarded sympathetically Germany's colonial aspirations. In 1885 he remarked: "If Germany is to become a colonizing Power, all I can say is, God speed her! She becomes our ally and partner in the execution of the great purposes of Providence for the advantage of mankind." Salisbury, his successor as Prime Minister, was more interested in securing and safeguarding the new territories but managed to avoid conflict with the other Powers over the colonies. Britain's method of expansion at this time was by chartered companies, that is, trading companies of private individuals who had been granted royal charters. This was a cheap and effective method of colonial expansion, similar to that followed in the seventeenth century. The ROYAL NIGER COMPANY (1886) and the BRITISH EAST AFRICA COMPANY (1888) were taken over by the Crown in the 1890's and became the protectorates of Nigeria and British East Africa (later Kenya), as also did Nyasaland and Uganda. The burden of the work involved in establishing British Control in these parts was undertaken by two men, Sir Harry Johnston in Nyasaland, Tanganyika and Uganda and Frederick Lugard (later Lord Lugard) in Nigeria and Uganda. To the south of these areas the BRITISH SOUTH AFRICA COMPANY (1889) was busy under the direction of Cecil Rhodes in annexing territories. By the end of the century almost all Africa had been partitioned among European Powers; the parts still under native rulers were Morocco and Ethiopia or Abyssinia, where an Italian expedition had met with a disastrous defeat in 1896, while Liberia in West Africa was a state for freed American negro slaves. Despite the international rivalries and jealousies, the partition of Africa did not lead to armed hostilities between the Powers. Their differences were settled peacefully after negotiation; for example, when Salisbury was Prime Minister in 1890 the British and Germans put an end to their disputes in East Africa by exchanging the islands of Zanzibar and Heligoland, the island off the German coast that had been in British hands since 1807.

Chamberlain the Imperialist. The Liberal split over Home Rule in 1886 left Chamberlain high and dry for a time. The Radical ideas of the "Unauthorized Programme" of 1885 could not very well be put into effect by Salisbury and the Conservatives, with whom he joined forces against the Liberals. The Tory Democrats were no longer prominent in the Conservative party since the departure of Lord Randolph Churchill from the Cabinet. But some of the legislation at the end of the century could be ascribed to Chamberlain's influence—the Local Government Act of 1888 setting up county councils, the granting of free elementary education in 1891, and the Workmen's Compensation Act of 1897, which created an improved scheme for workmen. In contrast to the "Little Englanders" in the Liberal party, Chamberlain had always been interested in the Empire and was one of the founders of the Imperial Federation League in 1884. It was nevertheless a surprise to most when in 1895 he chose the office of Colonial Secretary, hitherto regarded as of minor importance. His first year in office was his most difficult as it saw the quarrel with the U.S.A. over Venezuela and British Guiana and the disastrous blunder of the Jameson Raid. But having

survived the storm that burst about his head, he went on to
carry out many of the plans he had conceived for colonial
development. Chamberlain regarded the colonies as "undeveloped estates" awaiting development "for the benefit of
their population and for the benefit of the greater population
which is outside". It was during his administration of the colonies
that the LONDON SCHOOL OF TROPICAL MEDICINE was established
under Sir Patrick Manson ("Mosquito Manson"), scientific
methods in agriculture encouraged, slavery suppressed in the
few areas where it still survived, Nigeria opened up by railways,
and regular shipping services begun for the West Indies fruit
trade. On the occasion of Queen Victoria's Diamond Jubilee,
representative units from the various armies in the Empire
appeared in military parades in London and a conference of
colonial premiers was organized by Chamberlain, although
no positive or agreed action was taken. Similarly, another
COLONIAL CONFERENCE was held at the time of King Edward
VII's coronation in 1902 just after the Boer War. Chamberlain
proposed the setting up of a permanent Imperial Council but
again without result. Imperial co-operation was a plant of slow
growth. Actually, in 1885 Australian troops were sent to help the
British in the Sudan and during the Boer War (1899-1902)
over 30,000 Canadian, Australian and New Zealand troops
arrived in South Africa. But the self-governing colonies were
sensitive about anything that looked like surrendering their
independence. One of the major difficulties that Chamberlain
saw in the development of imperial federation was that Britain
still held to her ideas about free trade while her colonies were
gradually building up tariff walls. It was this that turned his
mind from 1903 onwards to advocacy of tariff reform and the
abandonment of Free Trade.

Rhodes the Empire-Builder. The most important figure in
the expansion of Britain's empire in South Africa was undoubtedly Cecil Rhodes. Compelled to leave England for
South Africa as a boy of seventeen for health reasons, he made
a fortune in the diamond-diggings at Kimberley, returning at
intervals to England where he managed to take a degree at

Oxford by the time he was twenty-eight. He was a mixture of idealist and hard-headed business-man. At the age of nineteen, on a long journey over the African veld he had experienced something like a vision of the world peaceful and content under the leadership of the English-speaking peoples and he dedicated himself with a solemn vow towards achieving that aim. His ideal was not so much one of British domination as one of a partnership of free nations; he once sent £10,000 to Parnell as he felt that a grant of Irish Home Rule would strengthen rather than weaken the Empire. His immense fortune he intended to use for these aims and he left the bulk of it to Oxford University to found scholarships for the best men from the Dominions, the United States and Germany. He was only thirty-four when by writing out a cheque for £5,338,650 he made a successful take-over bid in 1887 for the interests of his main rival at Kimberley, the Jew "Barney" Barnato, and brought into existence the De Beers Consolidated Mines Co., the largest diamond concern in the world. He had also considerable invest-ments in the gold mines of the Rand and in the 1890's his income was estimated at over £1,000,000 a year. He had by this time launched out into a new career, that of empire-builder. He had already helped in the annexation of Bechuanaland in 1884, but his plans went far beyond Bechuanaland and the Transvaal. In the BRITISH SOUTH AFRICA COMPANY, which was formed by royal charter in 1889 to open up the territory to the north of the Transvaal, he was managing director, and in the following year he became Prime Minister of Cape Colony. To secure a route for a railway that would in time, he hoped, run all the way "from Cape to Cairo" through British territory, the agents of the chartered company, prominent among them DR. L. S. JAMESON, pushed forward into what is now Southern Rhodesia. They set up Fort Salisbury in 1890 and warded off a threatened Boer invasion across the Limpopo river in 1891. LOBENGULA, the chief of the warlike Matabele tribe, had signed treaties with the British who for some time regarded him as an independent ruler. But when the settlers began to move into the best grazing lands of the Matabeles, hostilities broke out in 1893. Rhodes's lieutenant,

Dr. Jameson, made short work of the fighting, as he was able to use machine-guns, then a novelty, against the natives' spears and rifles. Lobengula died in hiding, and his land, thus forcibly acquired, became known as RHODESIA. In Cape Colony itself, Rhodes proved an able Prime Minister, working in co-operation with the leader of the Afrikaners in the colony, Hofmeyr. The one main obstacle to the development of Rhodes's plans was the Transvaal republic, the President of which was Paul Kruger, an inveterate hater of the British since the time when as a boy he had taken part in the Great Trek. It was the Jameson Raid in 1895, an attempt to solve the problem of the Transvaal by force, that was finally to bring disaster to Rhodes's scheme, as we shall see below. He was compelled to resign the premiership of Cape Colony and died in 1902 just before the end of the Boer War, his last words being, "So little done, so much to do". He was buried, according to his wish, in the Matopo Hills in Southern Rhodesia.

Transvaal. Since the Transvaal had received back its independence from Gladstone in 1881, it had found itself gradually hemmed in on all sides by British colonies or protectorates except on the north-east where lay the Portuguese colony of Mozambique. A railway was built from the Transvaal through this colony with a terminus at Delagoa Bay and it was used by the Boers in preference to the southern routes through the British colonies. If Kruger and the Boers had difficulties with Rhodes and the British over his encirclement, these were small compared with the problems that arose over the British population that had crowded into the Transvaal after the discovery of gold on the Rand in 1886. The Afrikaners of the Transvaal were mainly farmers of Dutch origin (hence the name "Boer", which means farmer). The gold-mining industry that suddenly grew up attracted a cosmopolitan, but mainly British, crowd of gold-diggers, business-men and pure adventurers; and soon Johannesburg changed from a mining-camp to a "boom" town, while still retaining the unsavoury features of a mining-camp that repelled and disgusted the strictly religious Boers. "Oom Paul" (Uncle Paul, as Kruger was called by his fellow-Boers) was determined that these UITLANDERS (or foreigners) should pay heavily for the privilege of gold-mining in the Transvaal. Before long there were as many Uitlanders as male adult Boers and it was estimated that they provided nineteen-twentieths of the Government's revenue, which rose from £178,000 in 1885 to over £4,000,000 in 1899. Appeals for the right to vote and even for some form of local government in Johannesburg were brusquely turned down, "Oom Paul" letting the Uitlanders know that if they did not like conditions in the Transvaal they could leave at any time. In 1894 the period of residence necessary for naturalization was raised from five to fourteen years, as many of the Uitlanders were almost ready to qualify. The Uitlanders' grievances received sympathetic support from the British in Cape Colony and especially from Rhodes, who saw Kruger and the Transvaal as obstacles to his plans for united South Africa. In 1895 there was talk of a revolt by the Uitlanders on the Rand, and Rhodes, realizing that such a revolt would make intervention possible, began to smuggle arms into Johannesburg and make preparations to back up with armed force the rising when it came. This was the background to the disastrous Jameson Raid.

Jameson Raid. Dr. Jameson, the agent of the chartered company (as the British South Africa Company was known), had collected a small force of about 500 armed "police" on the border of the Transvaal in readiness for a raid to help the Uitlanders as soon as a revolt would begin. He even had an undated letter ready, purporting to be a call for assistance from the Uitlanders, whose women and children were said to be "at the mercy of well-armed Boers". But as 1895 wore on, the Uitlanders, angry though they were about their grievances, showed little enthusiasm for a revolt. Jameson, whose success in the Matabele War had made him think of himself as another Clive, at last lost patience and set off with his small force for Johannesburg at the very end of December, 1895, thinking the Uitlanders would rise to greet their liberators. News of the raid caused a sensation in South Africa and in Britain. Rhodes at once resigned his post as Prime Minister of Cape Colony and later his position in the British South Africa Company. In London, Chamberlain, the Colonial

Secretary, and the Government disclaimed all responsibility, while the British public, impressed by the fake letter, regarded Jameson as a hero. But the raid turned out a fiasco; Jameson and his men were rounded up within four days and the few Uitlanders who had risen were easily suppressed. Kruger, magnanimously and astutely, handed over Jameson to the British authorities for trial. He was imprisoned, released after a short period because of ill-health, but lived to become Prime Minister of Cape Colony in 1904. The Jameson Raid caused a great deal of criticism throughout the world; and it was obvious that the British had no friends in Europe. It was at this time that the phrase "splendid isolation" was first used. The German Kaiser, William II, infuriated the British public by sending to Kruger a telegram of congratulations. There was even talk of war with Germany. The parliamentary inquiry set up afterwards was considered almost everywhere in Europe as a travesty; a Moscow newspaper wrote of "the scandalous and disgraceful sham of investigation". Chamberlain had been accused of complicity but the report of the committee of inquiry exonerated him. Since then, documents not available at the enquiry have revealed that he was aware of the plans of Rhodes, although neither he nor Rhodes would have sanctioned Jameson's Raid until after a rising in Johannesburg. As a consequence of the Raid and the inquiry, not only was British prestige abroad lowered but a disastrous blow was dealt to the chances of friendly co-operation in South Africa. Rhodes's Afrikaner friends in Cape Colony felt that they had been duped, the Boers of the Orange Free State drew closer to those in the Transvaal, and Kruger was encouraged to be even more intransigent in his attitude.

Boer War, 1899–1902. The British and the Boers slowly drifted into war after the Jameson Raid. With the money contributed by the Uitlanders in taxation, arms were imported into the Transvaal from Germany and German officers arrived to train the Boers in the use of artillery. War was finally declared by Kruger in October, 1899, before British reinforcements were due to arrive from overseas and just when the fresh green grass on the veld provided feeding for the horses of the Boer "commandos".

With memories of Majuba Hill, the Boers hoped for a speedy victory. The Boers in the Orange Free State came in at once on the side of the Transvaal and over 13,000 Afrikaners from Cape Colony and Natal ultimately joined them. The Boers had the advantage of fighting in their own country, and most of them

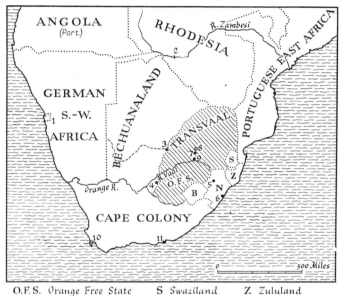

O.F.S. *Orange Free State*	S *Swaziland*	Z *Zululand*
B *Basutoland*	N *Natal*	

1 *Walfish Bay (Brit.)*	5 *Ladysmith*	9 *Vereeniging*
2 *Victoria Falls*	6 *Durban*	10 *Cape Town*
3 *Mafeking*	7 *Johannesburg*	11 *Port Elizabeth*
4 *Kimberley*	8 *Pretoria*	

South Africa, 1899

had been accustomed from youth to handling a rifle and living the rough life of the veld. The war had three phases:—(1) the early period (October–December 1899) of Boer successes over the small, unprepared British forces; (2) the middle period (January–August 1900) when a greatly enlarged British army defeated the Boers in open battles; (3) the long-protracted "mopping-up" operations (1900–02) against the guerrilla tactics of the remaining commandos. The British army has often started off badly in a war but it was a shock nevertheless for the British people, at the time intensely jingoistic, to learn that the Boers were besieging three British forces at Kimberley, Ladysmith and Mafeking, and that when the main British army arrived and split into three columns, two were heavily defeated and the other held up. The British newspapers in mid-December 1899 spoke of "BLACK WEEK", although Queen Victoria said to the pessimistic Balfour, the deputy Prime Minister, "We are not interested in the possibilities of defeat: they do not exist." In the second phase of the war GENERAL REDVERS BULLER, the army commander, was made the scapegoat and was superseded by Lord Roberts of Kandahar (see page 23) and Lord Kitchener of Khartoum, fresh from his victory in the Sudan (see page 51); more troops were sent out from Britain and contingents arrived from the colonies. The three besieged towns were relieved in the first half of 1900. The news of the RELIEF OF MAFEKING, where Colonel Baden-Powell had held out for 217 days, was received in London with scenes of unparalleled enthusiasm, so that Mafeking Night was remembered for years afterwards. The Boers, hopelessly outnumbered (in all 87,000 Boers served in the war as against 449,000 on the British side), gradually broke up into smaller commandos and turned to guerrilla tactics. The third phase, the "mopping-up", took a long time as the commandos proved difficult to pin down; one of the commando leaders, CHRISTIAN DE WET, led the British troops such a dance that he came to be much admired by the British public. Kitchener then resorted to a policy of clearing out the civilian population so that the commandos could no longer be supplied. By a system of 8,000 blockhouses, joined by miles of barbed wire, Kitchener's army cleared the Transvaal, evacuating the women and children and burning the farmsteads. The women and children were taken away to concentration camps, where unfortunately, because of the lack of organization, over 26,000 of them perished from disease and malnutrition (that is, more than the total British losses in the war).

South African Settlement. The South African War had deeply shaken the complacency of the British people. Victory had not come so easily as they had confidently expected when the khaki-clad soldiers had embarked for Africa, with the bands playing *Goodbye, Dolly Gray* and *Soldiers of the Queen*. The nation was shocked also when it learned of the high rate of rejection (40 per cent in the whole country and 60 per cent in some industrial areas) of recruits for the army because of low physical standards; the report of an investigating commission set up after the war led to the passing of an Act in 1906 to provide free meals for poor children. Opposition to the war came from some of the Liberals and the newly-formed Labour party; and these were labelled "pro-Boers" and "traitors" by the jingoistic section of the population. The young Welsh lawyer and "pro-Boer" Liberal M.P., David Lloyd George, later to be a wartime Prime Minister himself, escaped from an incensed crowd at Birmingham only by being smuggled out of the Town Hall disguised as a policeman. It was an English lady, Emily Hobhouse, whose revelations about the concentration camps compelled the Government to take action. The Boers were ever grateful to her and to the Liberal leader, Campbell-Bannerman, who condemned "the methods of barbarism" used by the British in South Africa. An election in 1900, the so-called "Khaki Election", had returned Salisbury's Government to office; but despite the Government's slogan, "A vote against the Government is a vote for the Boers" over two million votes were cast for the Liberals and the newly-born Labour party as against almost two and a half millions for the Government. The existence of this large element of sympathy for the Boers made easier the way to a final settlement. Peace was signed at Vereeniging in 1902, the veteran Salisbury retiring from the post of Prime Minister in favour of his nephew, A. J. Balfour, almost immediately afterwards. By the TREATY OF VEREENIGING, the Boers of the Transvaal and the Orange Free State acknowledged British sovereignty and were promised self-government as soon as possible; the British Government wisely made a grant of £3,000,000 to enable the Boers to re-establish themselves on their farms. This was a generous provision and helped to conciliate the Boers. In the immediate post-war years, reconstruction went on apace under Lord Milner, Governor of the two Boer states, with the aid of a loan of £35,000,000 from Britain. Milner and Chamberlain wisely started a plan for promoting self-government gradually; but in 1906 a Liberal Government came into power under Sir Henry Campbell-Bannerman and one of the new Prime Minister's actions was to establish full independence in the Transvaal right away, the Orange Free State gaining its independence the following year (1907). Balfour, the ex-Premier and leader of the Unionist opposition, criticized the Liberal decision in the superlatives beloved of politicians—"the most reckless experiment ever tried in the development of a great colonial policy". The experiment was daring but it was successful. The South African leader, Smuts, paid the Liberals a striking tribute: "They gave us back our country in everything but name. After four years! Has such a miracle of trust and magnanimity ever happened before?" The next step was to unite the two predominantly British colonies, Cape Colony and Natal, with the two Boer colonies, the Transvaal and the Orange Free State. The co-operation of the recent enemies was easier because of the Boers' memory of the Liberals' support during the war. "Three words" said Botha, the Transvaal prime minister "made peace and union in South Africa: 'methods of barbarism'." The new constitution, creating the UNION OF SOUTH AFRICA, came into effect in 1910. The value of this generous treatment of a defeated foe was to be seen in 1914 when the South Africans, led by Smuts and Botha, former enemies of Britain, came into the war against Germany on the British side.

Cromer in Egypt. Britain's position in Egypt and the Sudan was very different from what it was in South Africa or indeed anywhere else in the whole continent. That was because Gladstone, after the suppression of Arabi Pasha's nationalist revolt in 1882, was unwilling to annex Egypt outright or to abandon it, the Suez Canal being of so great importance to Britain. In theory, Egypt remained part of the Ottoman Empire, in theory also the Khedive was still head of the Egyptian Government,

BRITAIN IN THE LATE VICTORIAN AGE. *Left*: Gladstone addressing a crowd from the balcony of Lord Rosebery's house in Edinburgh at the conclusion of his Midlothian campaign, 1880 (see p. 15). *Centre*: Queen Victoria. *Right*: Lord Salisbury speaking in the House of Lords.

THE SOUTH AFRICAN WAR (see p. 46). *Left:* A British propaganda drawing showing Boers displaying the white flag as a ruse. In war each side attempts to portray the enemy as "beyond the Pale". *Right:* Hysterical scenes in London on Mafeking night, May 18th, 1900.

and there was an international commission representing the bond-holders or creditors of the Government. But the British army was in constant occupation and the British agent or consul-general, Sir Evelyn Baring (later LORD CROMER) became in effect the ruler of Egypt. Appointed in 1883, he was to remain there until 1907 and, although on his last drive through the streets they were lined by British troops, he completed in a quarter of a century a programme of work that brought real benefit to Egypt. His first task was to establish Egyptian finances on a sound footing. Strict economy was observed and corruption suppressed so that by 1888 the budget had been made to balance. From then on, a great scheme of reconstruction was undertaken. The old irrigation works at Cairo were improved and a huge dam was built at Aswan further up the Nile, making it possible to provide more irrigation and to double the area of land under cultivation. Railways were constructed and trade increased. The fellaheen or peasants, who had been oppressed and exploited for centuries, were now treated as free men; forced labour and flogging were abolished and the law was justly and fairly administered. The Egyptian army was re-organized and trained; and, under the Sirdar or Commander-in-Chief, Sir Herbert Kitchener, was made fit to undertake the conquest of the Sudan. Nationalist feelings had persisted since 1882 and they were roused, just before Cromer's departure in 1907, by the DENSHAWAI AFFAIR. A party of British officers shooting pigeons in the Nile delta near the village of Denshawai was attacked and one of them was killed. The public hangings and floggings that followed were widely criticized at home and abroad and inflamed Egyptian nationalist feeling. A pro-British Prime Minister was assassinated in 1910 and anti-British agitation increased when Egypt became a British protectorate at the beginning of the First World War, as the Turkish Sultan, the nominal sovereign, entered the war as an ally of Germany. It was not until after the Second World War that British forces were finally withdrawn.

Conquest of Sudan. The Sudan had been for long under the despotic rule of the Khalifa, who succeeded the Mahdi when he died in 1885. In three successive campaigns (1896–97–98)

4

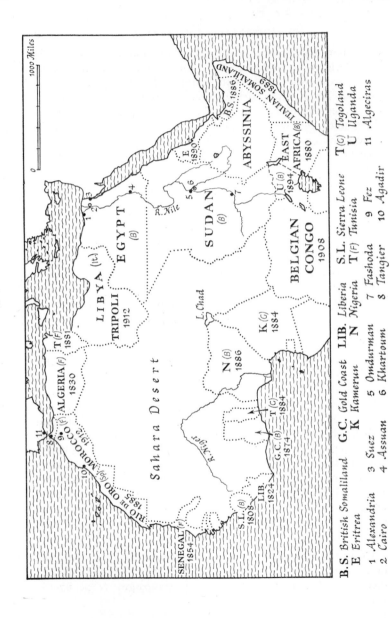

Northern Africa, 1914

B.S. *British Somaliland* G.C. *Gold Coast* LIB. *Liberia* S.L. *Sierra Leone* T(G) *Togoland*
E *Eritrea*   K *Kamerun*   N *Nigeria* T(F) *Tunisia*   U *Uganda*

1 *Alexandria*   3 *Suez*   5 *Omdurman*   7 *Fashoda*   9 *Fez*   11 *Algeciras*
2 *Cairo*   4 *Assuan* 6 *Khartoum*   8 *Tangier*   10 *Agadir*

KITCHENER undertook the conquest of the Sudan, building a railway to secure his line of communication and advancing gradually southwards until in 1898 he reached Omdurman, the new capital founded by the Mahdi on the Nile opposite Khartoum. There he met and defeated the Khalifa's forces, who were mown down by British machine-guns. The BATTLE OF OMDURMAN was notable for a full-scale cavalry charge (one of the last to be made), the 21st Lancers, among them a young subaltern called Winston Spencer-Churchill (later to be known as Sir Winston Churchill), sweeping down on the Sudanese. Soon after the battle of Omdurman there happened the FASHODA INCIDENT, which nearly led to war between the British and the French. A French force under a Captain Marchand had reached the Nile at Fashoda, nearly 500 miles south of Khartoum, after a remarkable journey from the Congo and had hoisted the French tricolour. Kitchener pushed south with gunboats and a few hundred men and, hoisting the British and Egyptian flags, requested Marchand to withdraw. Neither would withdraw and neither wished to start hostilities so that the matter was referred to the home governments. British public opinion was solid behind the Government's demand that the French should withdraw as the control of the headwaters of the Nile was considered essential to the welfare of Egypt. The French climbed down as they could not count on the support of their only ally, Russia, in such a cause and could not face a war on their own. When the Anglo-French Entente was signed in 1904, the French recognized Egypt and the Sudan as a British sphere of influence. The Sudan in 1898 came under joint British and Egyptian rule, and in less than ten years order was restored, the slave trade suppressed, agriculture and trade improved, schools and law-courts set up. The ANGLO-EGYPTIAN CONDOMINIUM was to last till 1956, when the Sudanese were granted self-government, despite the Egyptian claim to retain sovereignty over the Sudan.

Problems of Imperialism. The story of British imperialism in Egypt, the Sudan and South Africa is not quite the same as that of imperialism in other parts of Africa, where the British were dealing with backward, primitive races. But together they show the variety of problems facing the empire-builders and cast a light on the motives that encouraged them to continue. In 1882 Chamberlain, then a Radical, had said about Egypt: "We voluntarily undertook our responsibility in Egypt and duty, interest and humanity require us to stick to it. Cairo too is on the way to the Cape. Along it we will find sales for our goods, fields for our enterprise, scope for our philanthropy. There are roads to make, markets to open, lands to till, and slaves to emancipate." These three motives, commercial profit, adventure, humanitarianism, appealed to different people in varying degrees. Cecil Rhodes summed up imperialism similarly but briefly— "philanthropy and five per cent". There was also the conviction, shared by high and low, rich and poor, that the British people were undeniably the best to be entrusted with the "civilizing mission" of suppressing slavery, providing medical services and schools, starting schemes of irrigation, building roads and railways. The awareness of the "white man's burden", the obligations to the colonial races involved in empire-building, was not always shared however by the empire-builders themselves. Some of these contemptuously spoke of the coloured people as "niggers", regarding them as fit only to be "hewers of wood and drawers of water". Today "imperialism" is often criticized or referred to in a derogatory sense but there has usually been a humanitarian side to it. LORD LUGARD, one of the greatest colonial administrators of the twentieth century, expressed a modern attitude to imperialism when he defined it as a "DUAL MANDATE". Britain was to act as a trustee with a double duty, first, to develop the natural resources of a colony so that the native population benefited most and, secondly, to allow the world at large to share in the resulting benefits. Another important aspect of imperialism, the granting of self-government, was already being hotly discussed in India by the beginning of the twentieth century but in tropical Africa little was heard of it at that time. Lord Lugard evolved in Nigeria and Uganda the method of "INDIRECT RULE" through native chiefs, village headmen and elders, the British officials interfering as little as possible and acting rather as advisers and supervisors. In this way the natives were encouraged to take their share of government and were not faced with a sudden uprooting of old ways and customs. Lugard's principles of the "Dual Mandate" and "Indirect Rule" were applied to other colonies also. But complications arose in colonies like Southern Rhodesia, where there is a large body of British settlers, or Kenya, where there are also many British settlers and immigrants of another race (Indians, mainly engaged in trade) or Northern Rhodesia, where there is a large element of the native population employed in industry. As a result, progress towards self-government has gone at different speeds in the different colonies, as we shall see later.

SOURCE EXTRACTS

A   *Rhodes on the English Empire-builders*

I contend that we are the first race in the world and that the more of the world we inhabit, the better it is for the human race. I contend that every acre added to our territory provides for the birth of more of the English race, who would otherwise not be brought into existence. Added to which, the absorption of the greater portion of the world under our rule simply means the end of all wars. Here and now I decide that I shall work for the furtherance of the British Empire, for the bringing of the whole world under British rule, for the recovery of the United States, for the making of the Anglo-Saxon race into one Empire. What a dream! But yet it is probable! It is possible!

Letter to W. T. Stead, 1878.

B   *Chamberlain on the New Imperialism*

The same change has come over the Imperial idea. Here also the sense of possession has given place to a different sentiment—the sense of obligation. We feel now that our rule in these territories (in tropical climes where the native population must always outnumber the white inhabitants) can only be justified if we can show that it adds to the happiness and prosperity of the people; and I maintain that our rule does, and has brought security and peace and comparative prosperity to countries that never knew these blessings before.

In carrying out this work of civilization we are fulfilling what I believe to be our national mission, and we are finding scope for the exercise of those faculties which have made of us a governing race. I

do not say that our success has been perfect in every case, I do not
say that all our methods have been beyond reproach; but I do say that
in almost every instance in which the rule of the Queen has been enforced, there has come with it greater security to life and property, and
a material improvement in the condition of the bulk of the population.

Joseph Chamberlain at the Royal Colonial Institute, 1897.

EXERCISES

1. (*Extract* "*A*".) Suggest the likely comments made by a German,
   an Irishman and an educated African on Rhodes's claim for the
   English race.
2. (*Extract* "*B*".) In this extract, Chamberlain admits that not "all
   our methods have been beyond reproach". Which annexations do
   you think he has in mind?
3. Explain: Little Englander, British Commonwealth of Nations,
   "White Man's Burden", "Black Week", blockhouse system,
   pro-Boers, fellaheen, dual mandate, indirect rule.
4. Give the authors of the following and explain where necessary:
   (*a*) "Wider still and wider shall thy bounds be set;
         God who made thee mighty, make thee mightier yet."
   (*b*) "The day of small nations has passed away: the day of empires
         has come."
   (*c*) "Philanthropy and five per cent."
   (*d*) "So little done, so much to do."
   (*e*) "We are not interested in the possibilities of defeat: they do
         not exist."
   (*f*) "Methods of barbarism."
5. Write short notes on: H. M. Stanley, "Oom Paul", Kruger Telegram, Siege of Mafeking, Denshawai Affair, Battle of Omdurman, Fashoda Incident, Treaty of Vereeniging, Lord Lugard.
6. Write notes on: Scramble for Africa, Cecil Rhodes, Jameson Raid,
   South African War (1899–1902), Cromer in Egypt.
7. Give an account of the career of Joseph Chamberlain. (Refer to
   other chapters in this book.)
8. Outline the part played by Great Britain in Egypt and the Sudan
   from 1881 to the outbreak of the First World War.
9. What were the main colonial issues during Salisbury's ministries
   and how were they dealt with?
10. What were the causes of the South African War (1899–1902)?
    Give a brief account of the war and the post-war settlement.

CHAPTER III

ECONOMIC CHANGES, 1880–1914

"Top Nation." Since the middle of the nineteenth century Britain had enjoyed a period of prosperity unparalleled in her history. Her wealth and her supremacy in world trade gave her people a pride in themselves and their country that was at its height in the 1860's; this "mid-Victorian complacency" may be compared to the somewhat similar mood in the United States in the middle of the twentieth century. What were the reasons for Britain's outstanding position in the world a hundred years ago? Without going into a detailed explanation, it can be said briefly that no country was so highly industrialized as Britain, and that no country could compare with her in the vastness of her colonial empire. By the middle of the century, she could be called the workshop or factory of the world, the forge and foundry of the world and the carrier of the world's goods. Britain was responsible for the bulk of the world's production of machinery, cotton, linen, woollen, iron and leather goods. Her bankers financed merchants and governments in other countries and her ships carried more than half the cargoes of the world. Her railway system, the most highly developed of any country, helped her industries and her trade. London, her capital, was easily the largest and wealthiest city in the world, and the English "milord" was renowned throughout Europe for his affluence, his elegance and his love of sport. The successful merchant or factory-owner bought himself a country estate and his sons or daughters married into the older aristocracy. British farming had been highly profitable for over a century, and the landed aristocracy, not then burdened with the crushing taxation of modern Britain, lived well on their rents. Some of the oldest families had also profited greatly from the industrial revolution, e.g. the Duke of Hamilton and the Duke of Northumberland from their mining royalties and the Marquis of Bute from his properties in Cardiff. The Duke of Bedford, according to Disraeli, was in 1875 the wealthiest of Queen Victoria's subjects, with an income of over £300,000 a year; but a man with £50,000 a year, in those days when income tax was less than 1s. in the £, was better off than someone today with an income of a million a year. It is little wonder that there was complacency in the mid-Victorian age, in "the heyday of British Capitalism" as it has been called.

Overseas Trade. The key to all this prosperity seemed to many, both British and foreigners, to be Britain's vast overseas trade. Based originally on her colonies, it was by 1880 world-wide and was constantly expanding. The most recently acquired market had been in the Far East, where China had been compelled in two short wars to open certain ports to British trade. The policy of colonial annexation that led to the scramble for Africa was often, though not always, caused by a desire to gain new markets or at least to prevent other European powers from doing so. To protect her empire and trade, Britain maintained the largest navy in the world and proudly called herself "Mistress of the Seas". Since the early nineteenth century, Huskisson, Peel and Gladstone had successively abolished export and import duties with a view to stimulating trade. The unprecedented prosperity the country enjoyed in mid-century many ascribed to FREE TRADE, as trade seemed to have boomed ever since the last duties had been swept away. It was hoped that in time other countries would follow Britain's lead but in the meantime it seemed vital for Britain to keep to Free Trade. Britain, it was argued, was a manufacturing country which needed to import her raw materials —cotton from America, wool from Australia, flax from the Baltic, jute from India, timber from Canada and the West Indies, and iron ore from Sweden and Spain. Cheap raw materials meant cheap manufactured products, which could be exported all over the world. Free trade also meant cheap food—grain from Eastern Europe, tea from India and China, sugar from the West Indies, coffee from Brazil, and, later, chilled beef and mutton from Australia, New Zealand and America. Cheap food helped to keep wages at a low level and thus reduced the cost of the manufactured article. When Joseph Chamberlain's proposals for tariff reform were adopted by the Unionist party, they were heavily defeated at the ensuing election in 1906, the Liberals raising the cry of "dear bread". Linked with Britain's overseas trade was the investment of money in other countries like Egypt, India, Canada, South America, South Africa, where the railways, docks, plantations and mines might be owned, wholly or partly, by British investors, who often reaped handsome

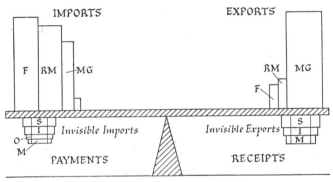

F	Food, tobacco, wines, etc.	I	Interest on overseas investments
RM	Raw materials	O	Overseas expenditure by Government
MG	Manufactured goods	M	Miscellaneous (tourist trade,
S	Shipping		banking, insurance, etc.)

Balance of Trade

dividends. By the 1880's it was estimated that the total British investments overseas amounted to nearly £1,500,000,000, bringing an annual return of at least £75,000,000; in 1913, the comparable figures were £4,000,000,000 and £200,000,000. In addition, British insurance companies and British bankers did business all over the world. The services of banking, insurance and shipping, together with overseas investments, brought in vast sums of money to Britain, just as exported goods and raw materials did, and were called "INVISIBLE EXPORTS". They helped to build up the great wealth of which British people were so proud.

"The Great Depression." All was not well, however, with British trade, industry or agriculture in the late Victorian age. Indeed the twenty years or so from 1873 onwards contrasted so markedly with the prosperous 1850's and 1860's that it is common to speak of the "Great Depression" of the last quarter of the

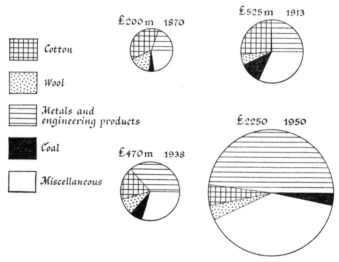

British Exports (Values), 1870-1950

nineteenth century. It was not confined to Britain only: many other countries suffered severe setbacks but Britain experienced special difficulties. (1) First of all, agriculture, the oldest industry of all, was facing competition from cheap food imported from overseas, which meant that the "Golden Age" of British farming was at an end. (2) Although Britain's production of coal, iron, steel, textile goods, etc., was increasing all or most of the time, her industrial supremacy was being challenged by the United

States and Germany. By the end of the century, both of these countries surpassed Britain in steel production. The Germans also began to forge ahead in the new electrical and chemical industries, an advance that according to some observers was due to their more highly developed system of technical education. (3) Further, although Britain still led the world in shipping and shipbuilding, the fierce competition between steamer and sailing-ship, coupled with improvements in marine engines, led to a severe reduction in freight rates, which hit worst of all "the carrier of the world's goods". The building of railways in other countries made them less dependent on British ships than formerly; and at the very end of the century Britain's long-standing supremacy on the Atlantic crossing was broken by German liners. (4) A series of financial crises at home, like the failure of the City of Glasgow Bank in 1879, helped to bring about worse depressions in industry by undermining public confidence. Unemployment among trade unionists, for whom alone there are figures, rose to over 10 per cent at different times and naturally the working-classes suffered distress. The words "unemployed" and "unemployment" date from the 1880's. It is no surprise, therefore, that this period saw a great amount of political agitation, strikes, demonstrations, the formation of new trade unions, the beginnings of socialism and of an organized labour movement in this country.

Decline of Agriculture. Disraeli had prophesied at the time of the repeal of the Corn Laws in 1846 that British agriculture would be ruined as a result of free trade. Instead, there followed almost thirty years of farming prosperity, the "Golden Age" of British farming. This did not happen because of free trade but because of many other factors—new methods and machines, improved drainage, artificial fertilizers, an assured market for the produce of the farm. Farming profits were good and rents and wages increased; most of the farm buildings and many of the farmworkers' houses of today date from this period. Disraeli's prophecy was to come true just when he himself became Prime Minister. Cheap corn came flooding into Britain from the prairies of the Middle West, opened up in the great period of railway construction following the American Civil War. There was also a series of bad harvests in the 1870's. That of 1879 was said to be the worst of the century; the wet weather not only ruined the crops but also caused outbreaks of pneumonia in the cattle and liver-rot in the sheep. In years of bad harvests there is normally one compensation: prices are high. But this did not happen in 1879 as prices were kept low by imported American grain, grown in the fertile virgin soil of the prairies, where the new McCormick reaper-and-binder could do the work of many men. Some Conservatives thought that Disraeli might have restored the Corn Laws to protect the home farmer, but in his opinion protection was "not only dead but damned". Too many people in the towns depended in 1879 on cheap bread for Disraeli to risk again all the agitation of the "hungry forties". The price of wheat fell from 71s. a quarter in 1839 to 23s. in 1894, and the price of a loaf from 10d. to 5d. Other branches of farming also suffered at this time. Already, Australian wool, imported first in the fast clippers like the *Cutty Sark* and then by steamers after the opening of the Suez Canal in 1869, was arriving in such large quantities as to make sheep-farming in Scotland and Wales less profitable. Another and more serious blow to sheep-farming was forecast in 1878, when a French ship landed 5,500 carcasses of mutton from Argentina at Le Havre. Soon afterwards in 1880, a Clyde-built ship, the *Strathleven,* with refrigerating plant designed by Clydeside engineers, arrived in London from Melbourne with 40 tons of frozen beef and mutton. New Zealand soon followed suit and by 1886 was responsible for most of the 30,000 tons of frozen mutton shipped to Britain. Another method of food preservation was by canning. In Britain, tinned meats were at first produced mainly for sailors, but by the 1880's the products of Chicago's meat-packing industry were being bought by the British housewives. Cattle-boats continued long after this time also to bring live cattle from Canada, Argentina and elsewhere. Later, tinned salmon from British Columbia and tinned fruits from California began to reach the British shops and added variety to the diet of the town-dwellers.

Farming Changes. How did British farmers react to the

depression in agriculture? Some gave up the struggle and, selling out to neighbours, emigrated. There was a constant stream of emigration of country-dwellers, farm-workers as well as farmers, in the late Victorian age. Those who stayed at home adapted themselves in different ways to the changed conditions. Imported meat, especially chilled or frozen, could not fetch such high prices as the best home produced like the "prime Scotch beef" obtained from Aberdeen-Angus cattle. The British arable farmer, ruined by cheap grain, tended to turn his arable land into grazing and began to raise stock rather than crops. The improvement of pasture by LEY-FARMING in Scotland and Wales was one of the bright features of this period; it was in the 1880's that R. H. Elliott of Roxburghshire evolved the Clifton Park system —an eight-year rotation of roots, corn, roots, corn and four years of grass, which enabled him to maintain the ground in a condition of high fertility. STOCK BREEDING became a profitable business. Agricultural shows encouraged the production of the best cattle, sheep, pigs and horses. Breeders from all over the world came to Britain (and still come) to buy British livestock. Farmers near the large towns, in order to cater for the large urban population, turned to potato-growing and DAIRY-FARMING, and the early morning railway trains carried the milk-cans up to town. In addition, farmers began to take an interest in poultry-keeping to supply eggs and fowls for the town-dwellers, fruit-farming (raspberries and strawberries for jam-making) and market-gardening (fruit and vegetables). By the beginning of the twentieth century British farming had undergone many changes but it was not until the First World War (1914–18) that it enjoyed prosperity again.

Industry. The late nineteenth century also saw many changes in the chief British industries. In the TEXTILE INDUSTRY, cotton still led the field although it had suffered a set-back during the American Civil War (1861–65), when cotton supplies from the southern states were stopped by the northern blockade and many mills closed down never to reopen. From this time the cotton industry began to look elsewhere for other sources of supply in addition to the American plantations; Indian and Egyptian cotton was imported in increasingly large quantities, and later on other new sources were found in the West Indies. Lancashire cotton garments were worn all over the world, by miners and ranchers in the United States, by negroes in Africa and Indians in the Far East. English woollen cloth, especially when made into bespoke suits by Savile Row tailors, was considered the finest in the world; and the Harris tweed from the Western Isles, worn at first by a few sportsmen, began about 1900 to enjoy a wider reputation. Jute, a new textile fabric made in Dundee ("Jute-opolis"), was used for sacking and also for a floor-covering, linoleum, the manufacture of which was centred in Kirkcaldy, Fife. COAL-MINING was still considered one of the basic industries of the country. Apart from its domestic uses for fuel and gas-lighting, it was essential for the iron industry, for the railways and steamships, for steam engines generally and even for electricity as the generating stations depended entirely at first on steam-power operating the turbines. Coal exports also steadily increased—from 11 million tons in 1850 to 29 million tons in 1880, 44 million tons in 1900 and 73 million tons in 1913. In the latter half of the century the by-products of coal were being utilized; coal tar was used to produce aniline dyes and also to provide the smooth tarmacadam road surface which the faster-moving bicycles and motor-cars demanded.

Coming of Steel. The iron industry had been revolutionized by the BESSEMER PROCESS (patented in 1856), which made possible the production of cheap steel. By Sir Henry Bessemer's method, 5 tons of cast steel could be produced in 30 minutes whereas formerly it took 15 days and nights to produce 50 lbs. The Bessemer process was not at first successful in Britain because of the difficulty of dealing with the phosphorus present in most British iron ores; as a result Britain began to import non-phosphoric ores from Sweden and Spain. (Bessemer had not realized this difficulty during his experiments as he had used haematite, a non-phosphoric iron ore found in Wales and Cumberland.) The discovery about 1866 on the shores of Lake Superior of an extensive orefield containing rich deposits of non-phosphoric ore had made possible the rapid growth of the

Carnegie Steel Company at Pittsburgh, under the direction of Andrew Carnegie, son of a Dunfermline handloom weaver. Carnegie (who was later to give away over £70,000,000 in benefactions) helped to give the United States the first place in the world in steel production. By 1878 two cousins, SIDNEY GILCHRIST THOMAS, a police-court clerk and amateur chemist, and Percy Gilchrist, a metallurgist, made it possible to use phosphoric ores by lining the Bessemer converter with materials which would absorb the phosphorus. Basic slag, a by-product of this Gilchrist–Thomas process, proved an excellent fertilizer for grass and clover and is widely used today in Britain. The other method of making cheap steel, invented in 1858 by two German brothers naturalized in England, Frederick and William Siemens, and improved about 1864 by a Frenchman, Pierre Martin, was known as the SIEMENS-MARTIN OPEN-HEARTH PROCESS and was also made suitable for phosphoric ores, by the Gilchrist–Thomas improvement. Still another process was invented by William Siemens, the ELECTRIC FURNACE, which could develop very high temperatures (as high as 3,500°C.) but was not so widely used because of being more expensive. It was due to the Gilchrist–Thomas improvement that Germany came to the fore as a producer of steel; the phosphoric minette ores of Lorraine, annexed from France in 1871, could now be used. By the end of the century steel had replaced iron in most of its uses—armaments, railways, ships, buildings. Immense structures like the American skyscrapers were now possible. The Eiffel Tower, 984 feet high, was built in 1887–89 and the Forth Bridge, with its two main spans of 1,710 feet each, between 1882 and 1890. But Britain, which had led the world for so long and which was the country where the new inventions were first tried out, had despite her wonderful achievements fallen into third place in steel production behind the United States and Germany.

Electricity. It was in the 1870's that electricity began to be applied to various processes in industry and transport and to improve the amenities of ordinary life. The telegraph had been in use for a long time and in 1866 the Atlantic cable had at last been laid. Then in 1876, the telephone was invented by GRAHAM BELL, a Scotsman living in Boston, Massachusetts. By 1912, when the Post Office took charge of the telephone system in the country, there were only 400,000 telephones in operation. By 1912, also, wireless communication had already been established. GUGLIELMO MARCONI, born of Italian and Irish parents, sent signals from Poldhu in Cornwall to St. John's, Newfoundland in 1901. The arrest of the murderer Dr. Crippen following a wireless message from a transatlantic liner in 1910 and the sinking of the *Titanic* after collision with an iceberg in 1912, when wireless distress signals were picked up by many ships but not by the ship which lay only a few miles off, focused the attention of the world on the possibilities of wireless communication. ELECTRIC LIGHTING by arc lamps was installed in lighthouses before 1860 and the Gaiety Theatre façade was illuminated from 1875 by six arc lamps. Domestic lighting with illumination of low intensity came only after the invention of the filament lamp by two men, the American, EDISON and the Englishman, SWAN about the same time (1878–79). The steam turbine, which was invented in 1884 by CHARLES PARSONS, son of the Earl of Rosse, was soon utilized to drive dynamos and generate electricity. The early power stations were small and varied greatly in voltage, frequency and the rate charged to consumers. The first really large power station in Britain was planned for Deptford by S. Z. DE FERRANTI, who was unique at the time in advocating transmission at a high voltage, 10,000 volts instead of the usual 2,500 volts. The Deptford station started in 1889; but there were many difficulties and large power stations did not become common till much later. HYDRO-ELECTRIC POWER has been used in Britain mainly on a small scale until recent times. A Frenchman, Berges, was the first to transform into electricity the power in a waterfall, which he called "white coal" (1878). The first hydro-electric British power station was erected at Foyers near Loch Ness in 1895–96 by the British Aluminium Company, which later (1909) built a larger one at Kinlochleven on the west coast of Scotland. Factories, which had been erected first for water-power and had changed to steam-power, now began to install electrical power machines. Electricity was also used in various forms of transport

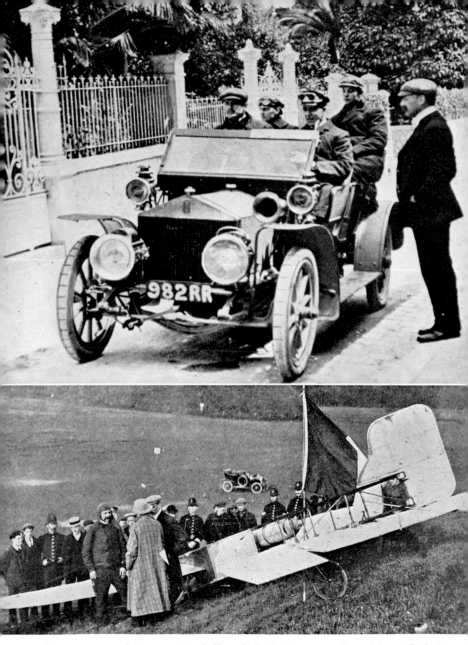

THE COMING OF THE MODERN AGE I. *Top:* C. S. Rolls sets out from Monte Carlo in 1906 on his record-breaking run to London in a T.T. type 4 cyl. Rolls-Royce car (see p. 69). *Bottom:* Blériot lands at Dover, July 25th, 1909 (see p. 70). One of the most significant moments in British history.

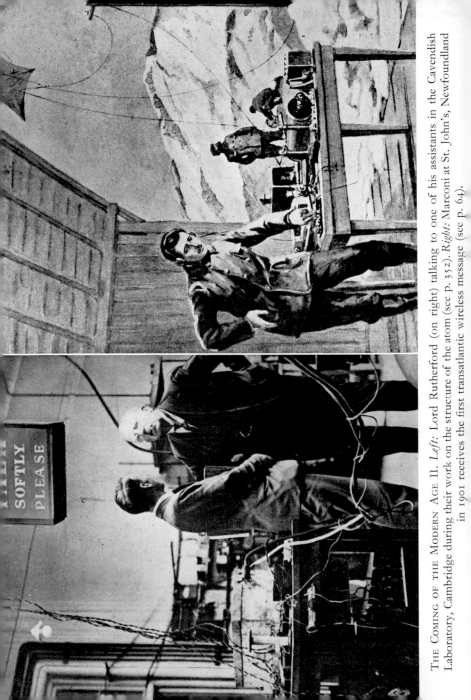

THE COMING OF THE MODERN AGE II. *Left:* Lord Rutherford (on right) talking to one of his assistants in the Cavendish Laboratory, Cambridge during their work on the structure of the atom (see p. 352). *Right:* Marconi at St. John's, Newfoundland in 1901 receives the first transatlantic wireless message (see p. 64).

which date from the 1880's—tramways, railways, motor-cars. The invention by AMBROSE FLEMING of the thermionic valve in 1904 was to increase still further the applications of electricity in wireless, television and electronics generally.

Ships. Although steamships had been in common use for many years, the heyday of the CLIPPER, the fast and beautiful merchant sailing ship, was as late at the 1860's. It was in 1870 that one of the most memorable ocean races of all time took place between the Aberdeen-built *Thermopylae* and the Dumbarton-built *Cutty Sark*. They raced from Shanghai to London, the *Thermopylae* winning by 4 days in 115 days; but the gallant fight put up by the loser's captain and crew after the rudder had been broken in a storm won the admiration of the British public. The saving of fuel and time effected by the opening of the SUEZ CANAL in 1869 and by the TRIPLE-EXPANSION ENGINE (invented by A. C. Kirk in 1876) helped to deal a death-blow to the clipper. (The *Cutty Sark*, the last of the great clippers, is preserved today as an example of the beautiful sailing-ships of long ago.) Few sailing-ships were being built by the end of the century and, at last, steamers could be seen that were not fitted for sails. It was in the 1870's also that an attempt was made to improve the conditions of life at sea and end the scandal of overloaded ships by the passing of the Merchant Shipping Act, which made loading lines (the PLIMSOLL LINES) compulsory. As sail gave way to steam, so iron hulls gave way to steel. Some STEEL-HULLED STEAMERS had been built during the American Civil War (1861–65) to run the northern blockade, as they were considered lighter and faster. But early steel was not considered reliable; it was not until the Siemens-Martin process produced sound, trustworthy steel that the Admiralty at last decided to change over. H.M.S. *Iris,* the first steel warship, was launched at Pembroke Dockyard in 1877; and, by the end of the century, steel had taken the place of iron in most shipyards. The superiority of the TURBINE ENGINE in ships was brought forcibly to the notice of the public in 1897 by the sensational appearance at the Jubilee naval review at Spithead of a small, 100-foot ship, Charles Parsons's *Turbinia,* which with its speed of 34·5 knots was able to outdistance the fastest destroyers. The Admiralty, reluctant to introduce changes, was compelled to build two turbine-driven destroyers and by 1905 was completely converted to the turbine engine in place of the old reciprocating engine. The *King Edward,* the first civilian steamer with turbine engines, was launched at Dumbarton on the Clyde in 1901; and the Cunard sister-ships, the Tyne-built *Mauretania* and the Clyde-built *Lusitania,* were both given turbine engines in 1907. For some years German ships had held the "BLUE RIBAND" OF THE ATLANTIC and the British Government decided, for the sake of British prestige, to aid the Cunard Company in the building of these ocean liners, as the company was threatened by a "take-over bid" from the American, J. Pierpont Morgan. In 1909 the *Mauretania* crossed from Queenstown to New York in 4 days, 11 hours, a time that was not to be beaten for twenty-two years. The maiden voyage in 1912 of the rival White Star liner, the *Titanic,* built at Belfast, was the occasion of one of the greatest disasters at sea: the liner struck an iceberg and went down almost three hours later with a loss of 1,490 persons. The disaster led to the introduction of certain improvements: life-saving equipment and life-boats, adequate for a full complement, life-boat drill and wireless installation were made compulsory on ocean liners. By that time, several changes had been carried through in the British Navy as a result of the efforts of Admiral Fisher ("Jacky" Fisher). The importance of submarines and torpedoes was at last recognized, and, in order to achieve higher speeds and greater cruising distances, OIL FUEL was substituted for coal. It was to ensure an oil supply that the British Government made arrangements with the Persian Government for a long-term concession of Persian oil-fields and so acquired a new interest in the Middle East. It was in 1912 that the first big ship, the Danish *Selandia,* was driven by a diesel engine. RUDOLF DIESEL, a German professor, had invented this engine in 1897; its successful use in the *Selandia* was unfortunately followed by the mysterious drowning of the inventor on the crossing from Antwerp to Harwich in 1913. It was not until the 1920's that the diesel engine became common.

Railways. The British railway system was more or less established by the middle of the nineteenth century. Although "the battle of the gauges" had gone in favour of the 4 ft. 8½ in. gauge, it was as late as 1892 that the Great Western Railway completed the changeover from the 7-ft. gauge to the standard gauge. Railways had long since displaced canals for inland transport; but it was at the end of the century that the largest canal of all, the Manchester Ship Canal, was opened. The change from iron to steel rails was only one of the many improvements that belong to the latter part of the nineteenth century. Locomotives were made more powerful; and after the 1860's long-distance trains no longer needed to stop frequently at stations to replenish the boilers but were able while in motion to take up water with scoops from troughs placed between the rails. This innovation, together with more efficient braking and signalling systems, made possible much higher speeds, culminating in the famous "RACE TO THE NORTH" in August 1895 when long-distance records were established that have not been surpassed. The North British express from King's Cross to Aberdeen by the east coast route covered 523½ miles in 8 hours, 40 minutes, and the Caledonian night express from Euston to Aberdeen did the 541 miles in 8 hours, 32 minutes with four stops included. Comfort for passengers on long-distance journeys was vastly increased: sleeping-cars, heated carriages and restaurant cars were introduced in the 1870's and corridor-trains in 1890. It was in the 1870's also that, with the coming of luxury Pullman cars, second-class coaches began to disappear from British railways, leaving on most lines, to puzzle foreign visitors, only two classes, first and third. Of many unfortunate railway accidents, that which most shocked the public was the TAY BRIDGE DISASTER on the 28th December 1879, when the bridge, completed only a year before, collapsed at the height of a terrible storm, the Edinburgh–Dundee express with 79 people aboard being thrown into the Tay. The present Tay Bridge was completed in 1887 and, three years later, the Forth Bridge, a wonder of modern engineering. An engineering feat of a different kind was the construction in 1863 of the first UNDERGROUND RAILWAY, which was to form part of London's "Inner Circle", completed in 1884. When the first London "Tube" was constructed in 1890 at a much lower level from the City to the Elephant and Castle, it was decided to use ELECTRIC TRACTION. By the 1900's the greater part of London's underground system was electrified but for the rest of Britain the steam locomotive was still standard.

Road Transport. Travelling on the roads a century ago was a leisurely affair. The stage-coach had disappeared except in remote country districts such as the Trossachs and the Lake District where it served the tourist trade till the twentieth century. The fastest horse carriage to be seen was likely to be a four-in-hand, popular with the landed gentry; it was the favourite method of travel with the American "steel king", Andrew Carnegie, on his annual visits to the British Isles. Tollgates every few miles held up the traveller until 1859 in England and 1883 in Scotland. Steam-carriages, which had been popular in the 1830's were no longer seen because of ruinous tolls, competition from the railways, and the famous "RED FLAG" ACT (1865). This Act forced on power-driven vehicles a speed-limit of 4 m.p.h.; a man was to walk in front with a red flag by day or a red lamp at night. The fastest vehicle on the road in 1870 was the new type of bicycle known as "penny-farthing", with pedals on the large front wheel. This was considered a racing machine, and tricycles were used by ladies and older men. The first SAFETY BICYCLE, with rear-wheel drive and wheels of different sizes, came about 1874; but it was the Rover safety bicycle, designed by J. K. Starley of Coventry in 1885 and incorporating most of the features of the modern bicycle, that started the craze for cycling at the end of the century. PNEUMATIC TYRES (an invention patented as far back as 1845 by J. W. Thomson) were made in 1889 by J. B. Dunlop, a Scottish veterinary surgeon in Ireland, for his son's tricycle; and the Dunlop Company, formed in the same year, was soon making large profits. Many other improvements quickly followed— ladies' bicycles, free-wheels, three-speed gears. To many a young man in the 1890's, freewheeling on his pneumatic-tyred bicycle downhill on the new tarmacadam road surface seemed the nearest possible approach to flying. By the end of the century, the motor-car had, rather tardily, made its appearance on British roads, some years after it had been developed abroad. The first MOTOR VEHICLES were produced in Germany in the 1880's by Gottlieb Daimler and Karl Benz. By 1890, cars with Benz engines were being built in France and Belgium; and in 1895 a race from Paris to Bordeaux (735 miles) was won by a 4-h.p. Panhard with an average speed of 15 m.p.h. Similar progress in Britain was held up by the "Red Flag" Act, which was at last repealed in 1896. The first cars in Britain were of foreign makes, but in 1896 the English DAIMLER COMPANY was formed in Coventry. Among early British pioneers of the motor industry were Lord Austin, who designed his first motor vehicle, a three-wheeler, in 1895 when working for the Wolseley Sheep Shearing Machine Company, and F. W. Lanchester, who in 1896 produced the first properly designed motor-car, anticipating modern designs in many respects. By 1914 the motor-car had displaced the horse-drawn coach as the vehicle for wealthy people; and (an omen for the future) the Rover Company was selling for less than £150 a light car, a two-seater with a 6-h.p. engine. In the towns there were other forms of transport. The horse-drawn omnibus had been popular in London since Shillibeer started his bus-service between the City and the Edgware Road in 1829. Without fixed stopping places, rival bus-drivers would race one another through the busy streets. HORSE-DRAWN TRAMS, popular for long in the United States, were introduced in 1860 at Birkenhead and soon afterwards in London. Steam locomotives were used on tram-ways in towns in the west of England and the Midlands, and cable haulage was to be found in a few towns like Edinburgh, which retained the cable trams until well on in the twentieth century. ELECTRIC TRAMS and electric trains had a common parent, an electric tramway opened at Berlin in 1881. The first electric line in the British Isles was opened in 1883 on the beach at Brighton, followed soon afterwards by the Giant's Causeway line in Northern Ireland, the current being taken at first from a third line and later from an overhead wire. Manchester had electric trams in 1890, Leeds in 1891, Glasgow trams changed over to electricity by 1902 and London by 1905. In the capital, the hansom-cab had been for years the gentleman's way of getting quickly to his destination and just before the 1914–18 war it was yielding place to the motor-taxi.

Flying. Since the first balloon flights in 1783, the main technical achievements were for long confined to improving the shape of the balloon and using a power-driven propeller on the undercarriage. There was thus gradually evolved a dirigible balloon or AIRSHIP. In 1852 such an airship with a steam engine driving the propeller achieved a speed of 5 m.p.h. in a flight in France; but steering was possible only if there was little wind. The electric motor and, later, the petrol engine took the place of the steam engine, and by the end of the century many flights had been made. The French led the way in their encouragement of flying; in 1901 Santos Dumont, a Brazilian aeronaut, won fame (and a prize of 100,000 francs) for a flight round the Eiffel Tower in an airship. In Germany FERDINAND ZEPPELIN had been working for some time on a rigid airship, the balloons or bags containing the hydrogen being enclosed in a cigar-like framework of light metal. He had his first successful flight in 1900 and from then to 1914 he built several airships, called zeppelins after him. An air-service was started between Berlin and Lake Constance in 1910, the first in the world. The earliest British attempts were not successful, the first rigid airship, the *Mayfly* breaking in two while being manœuvred from her shed in 1911. In the First World War the Germans used zeppelins as well as aeroplanes to bomb Britain but they were slow and vulnerable, many being brought down. Experiments with GLIDERS gave men the experience and the ideas to design heavier-than-air machines, capable of sustained flight. The German OTTO LILIENTHAL was one of many who tried to imitate the flight of a bird with his gliders, and he made over 2,000 successful flights before his death in a gliding accident. The historic flight by the brothers ORVILLE and WILBUR WRIGHT at Kitty Hawk, North Carolina, in December 1903 did not greatly impress people in Britain and Europe at the time. When the two brothers came to France in 1908, however, interest grew and in the following year many important flights were made. LOUIS BLÉRIOT crossed the Channel in July 1909, and Henry Farman, an Anglo-French aviator, flew over 140 miles in France. Britain woke up to the possibilities of the new machine. Nation-wide publicity was given to the air-races staged by the *Daily Mail*; although the large money-prizes generally went to Frenchmen, aviators like GRAHAM WHITE and S. F. Cody became national heroes. Britain, after a late start, was making up the leeway when war broke out in 1914. During the First World War, the number of British aeroplanes rose from 600 to over 22,000; and it was a British plane that was first to cross the Atlantic in 1919. It may be asked why the British should have shown themselves so far behind other nations in the early development of the motor-car and aeroplane. It has been suggested that their lead in the industrial revolution had given the British people a feeling of over-confidence and superiority so far as the steam-engine and the steam-ship were concerned and that they were at first blind to the advantages and potentialities of the petrol engine and the aeroplane. In time, they were to equal and surpass the achievements of other nations both in motor engineering and in aviation.

New Developments in Industry. We have already seen how the application of electricity brought changes to industry and transport. Work was performed in cleaner, brighter surroundings as a result and a whole series of factory acts helped to bring other benefits to the workers. By the end of the period there were not nearly so many works where the owner and the employer were the same person, and the old personal relationship between master and men was tending to die out. The formation of LIMITED LIABILITY COMPANIES after the Companies Act of 1862 meant in time that the ownership of the factory or shipyard passed into the hands of shareholders who might know nothing and care little about the work, while the management was the concern of a board of directors who might hold only a small proportion of the shares. Large COMBINES were sometimes formed to gain control of an industry; this tendency to monopoly capitalism showed itself earlier in the gigantic trusts of the United States (where anti-trust laws were passed) and in the cartels in Germany. Although there were certain advantages, the consumer and employee felt themselves at the mercy of the combines, which might fix prices at a higher rate or reduce wages. The earliest large British combine, the Salt Union, managed to raise the prices of salt from 2*s*. 6*d*. to 10*s*. 6*d*. a ton soon after it was formed in 1888. Another development that is associated at this period mainly with the United States was MASS-PRODUCTION. This involved the division of the manufacturing process into simple operations which could be performed easily by workmen. The conveyor-belt assembly line of Henry Ford's automobile works at Detroit had nothing to equal it in Britain or elsewhere before 1914. American firms with factories in Britain, like the Singer Sewing Machine Company, introduced the new methods, and British firms began to copy them. The United States also led the world in the use of petrol, the preservation of food, and plastics (although the first synthetic plastic, celluloid, was made by Alexander Parkes at Birmingham in 1865). American production of coal, iron and steel, grain crops and food in general, outstripped Britain's by the beginning of the twentieth century; and Americans were able to take a pride in their economic position similar to that felt in our country in the middle years of the nineteenth century. Britain's other great rival, Germany, also led her in certain respects—in steel production, in the application of electricity to industry, in motor engineering, in chemical manufactures, in the speed of her transatlantic liners, in her export of cheap metal manufactures, and was challenging Britain in other spheres. But, despite this greatly increased competition from the United States and Germany, which persuaded many to support Chamberlain's proposals for tariff reform to protect British industries and agriculture, the bulk of the British people still held to the belief in Britain's supremacy as an industrial and commercial nation. The Edwardian era (1901-10), which is remembered with nostalgic pride by those old enough to have lived in it and enjoyed its comforts, seems now to have been a transitional period in our economic history when the British people were living on the fat accumulated in the Victorian age. The First World War was to accentuate and expose difficulties which had already begun to reveal themselves long before.

SOURCE EXTRACTS

A   *Birth of American Steel Industry*

It was not until the advent of Bessemer that the Americans found how lavishly nature had endowed them. . . . That solid mountain of iron, the greatest ore-bed known to man, the richest in metallic content, the most easily mined, the most readily transported—and at the same time practically free from phosphorus—that, in fine, is the story of the Lake Superior fields. Such a miraculous conjunction of forces a nation has seldom had laid at its feet. Not until recent years has the economic historian fully grasped the significance of these two concurrent facts— the evolution of a method for making unlimited quantities of cheap steel, and the discovery of immense beds of iron ore that were perfectly adapted to this method. The result has been to give industrial leadership to the United States. *Burton Hendrick: Life of Andrew Carnegie.*

B   *Steam-Turbines*

Parsons planned from the start that his turbine should drive a direct-coupled electrical generator, but as the maximum speed of dynamos at that time was only about 1,200 r.p.m. he had to design a new high-speed direct current generator and this was as revolutionary as the turbine. His two patents granted in 1884—No. 6735 for "improvements in rotary motors actuated by fluid pressure and applicable also to pumps" and No. 6734 for high-speed generators—were of supreme importance. In the same year he built his first direct-current turbo-generator; it was non-condensing, generated 7·5 kilowatts at 100 volts and ran at the astonishing speed of 18,000 r.p.m. Steam was admitted at the centre and flowed axially in equal proportions to eliminate unbalanced axial thrust on the rotor. . . . In 1887 he made a compound reaction turbine with high- and low-pressure stages, and in 1888 the first turbine-driven generating set was installed in a public power station; this was the first of four 75 kilowatt turbo-alternators running at 4,800 r.p.m. for the Forth Banks Power Station of the Newcastle and District Electric Lighting Company.

Singer, Holmyard, Hall and Williams: A History of Technology.

EXERCISES

1. (*Extract "A".*) Explain why the author considers that industrial supremacy passed to the United States because of the two facts he

mentions. What is the connection of Andrew Carnegie with this great change?

2. (*Extract "B".*) What important developments followed from Parsons's inventions?

3. Explain: invisible exports, Jute-opolis, haematite, "Race to the North", Red Flag Act, penny-farthing, cartel, anti-trust laws, conveyor-belt, assembly line.

4. Write notes on:
The Great Depression, *Cutty Sark, Strathleven, Turbinia, Mauretania, Titanic,* Bessemer system, Gilchrist–Thomas process, Rudolf Diesel, Otto Lilienthal.

5. Account for the decline of British agriculture after 1873. To what extent had it recovered before 1914?

6. What were the main developments in transport and communications between 1880 and 1914?

7. Give an account of the chief applications of electricity to industry and transport before 1914.

CHAPTER IV

THE LABOUR MOVEMENT

"The Leap in the Dark." The passing of the Second Reform Act (1867), and the meeting of the first Trades Union Congress (1868)—these events which happened before the beginning of our period were of great significance for the British Labour movement. In 1867, also, there was published the first volume of Karl Marx's *Das Kapital,* based mainly on his studies in the British Museum, but it had scarcely any effect in this country for a long time. The Second Reform Act was the first step in the enfranchisement of the working-classes. The Conservative Prime Minister, the Earl of Derby, whom Disraeli had persuaded into adopting the measure, was expressing the doubts of many of his colleagues when he called it "a leap in the dark". Carlyle, historian and philosopher, went further and described it as "shooting Niagara". Disraeli hoped that the newly-enfranchised artisans would show their gratitude by returning the Conservatives to office, but the elections of 1868 produced a Liberal government and Disraeli's turn did not come till 1874. For a while, it seemed that the artisans were content to support either Liberal or Conservative politicians. The first working-men to gain seats in Parliament were two miners, Thomas Burt and Alexander MacDonald, who were returned in 1874 as Liberals; and it was with Liberal party labels that a few trade unionists made their appearance in later parliaments. Industrial problems naturally came more and more into the public eye. The first meeting of the TRADES UNION CONGRESS in 1868 followed the appointment of a Royal Commission on trade unions. Gladstone's ministry (1868–74), adopting the recommendations of the Royal Commission, gave the trade unions legal recognition, so that they were at last able to sue in the law courts against dishonest officials. But, by another Act of the same parliament, the unions' powers of picketing during strikes were restricted. The grievances of the trade unionists were redressed during Disraeli's ministry (1874–80), when an Act allowing "peaceful picketing" was passed. Some increase in trade union activity began to be evident from this time onward. Those were the days of "craft unionism" when only a small percentage of workers (less than 10 per cent) were members of trade unions, which were confined to the "aristocracy of labour", the skilled craftsmen such as engineers, joiners, shipwrights, etc. The unions acted more like friendly societies, dealing with sickness and accident payments, and strikes were avoided as likely to reduce their funds. An attempt to start a union among farm-labourers was made in 1872 by JOSEPH ARCH of Warwickshire; his union attracted members in the Midlands and East Anglia, where some of them were bold enough to demand a guaranteed wage of 15s. for a 60-hour week. But farming was just then beginning to feel the effects of overseas competition. Farmers were not unwilling to dismiss employees and the union collapsed. The "Great Depression", which started in the 1870's, was to last on and off for a long time.

The accompanying unemployment, distress and poverty formed the background to a ferment of agitation and unrest out of which came many more trade unions and an organized labour movement. Although the leaders of the main parties tended to ignore this new force, the Radicals in the Liberal party and the Tory Democrats in the Conservative party were alive to it. "The leap in the dark", about which Derby and others had misgivings, had introduced a new element into British politics; and by the end of the century there had arisen a new political party that less than twenty-five years later was to be called upon to form a government.

Marxism. Karl Marx's *Das Kapital*, or *Capital*, which has been called "the Bible of Communism", produced scarcely any effect in Britain when it was published in 1867, and his ideas made slow progress in this country in comparison with other countries of Europe. The Social Democratic Federation, one of the bodies that combined to form the British Labour Party, was based on Marx's teachings. Marx's daughter was one of its keenest members and its founder, Hyndman, produced in 1881 a pamphlet explaining Marxism called *England for All*. But the S.D.F. did not receive much support at any time. In many countries of the world today, however, Communist governments are in power, and the influence of Marxist doctrines is so widespread that they must be studied if the history of modern times is to be appreciated. Marxism is sometimes called Communism, sometimes Bolshevism, and sometimes revolutionary Socialism. It is more than a political creed for it expresses also a philosophy of history. Marx's views are contained not only in *Capital*, which is concerned mainly with economics, but also in certain other documents and books, such as the COMMUNIST MANIFESTO of 1848, his *Critique of Political Economy* (1859) and in a lengthy correspondence with his great friend and collaborator, FRIEDRICH ENGELS. In *Capital*, Marx made much of his theory of "surplus value", according to which the working-man, whose labour is the source of value, is exploited by the capitalist, who appropriates the "surplus value" after paying the worker a subsistence wage. Marx writes of the "Iron Law of Wages", by which wages are driven down to the subsistence level, and the "Law of Increasing Misery", according to which the poverty of the working-classes becomes worse with the growth of capitalism. To prevent this "exploitation" by the capitalists, the working-classes or proletariat must combine to establish collective ownership of all means of production, distribution and exchange. Capitalism in one sense paved the way for this collectivism or public ownership; by the "Law of the Concentration of Capital", larger and larger units such as trusts, combines and monopolies are created in a capitalist society, thus crushing the small business-men, shopkeepers, etc., and forcing them into the ranks of the wage-earners or proletariat. Marx maintained that capitalism contained within itself the seeds of its own downfall—financial crises, depressions, destructive imperialist wars between capitalist states, until the working-classes are driven to revolt. This picture does not seem like that of a modern capitalist society, where trade unions, friendly societies, co-operative societies, building societies and the welfare state have combined to elevate the workers' conditions. At the time of his Manifesto (1848) and later, however, it seemed true enough to say: "The proletariat have nothing to lose but their chains. They have a world to win. Workers of all countries, unite!" A successful revolution, well prepared and organized by a class-conscious working-class or their leaders, would be followed by a temporary "DICTATORSHIP OF THE PROLETARIAT", which would in turn lead to a classless, communist society or state.

Materialist Conception of History. Marx's political philosophy is based on "the materialist conception of history". It involves an interpretation of history according to which the economic factor is fundamental to all others. The economic structure of a society, be it feudal or capitalist or communist, is, he maintained, the basis on which the laws, the constitution, the moral code and social life are built. Feudalism and all that went with it—military organization, the Great Council of the tenants-in-chief, oaths of fealty, homage, chivalry—were based on the economic structure of society, the manorial system. According to Marxists, the growth of Christianity can be ascribed to the economic conditions of the Roman Empire, which produced misery among the lower classes, making them accept willingly the gospel or message of Christ's redemption and the eternal bliss vouchsafed to those who believe. Another important element in the Marxist philosophy of history is the theory of the CLASS WAR. This is to be seen in the struggle of the bourgeoisie or middle class against the feudal barons at the end of the Middle Ages and of the proletariat against the capitalists in modern industrial times. To a Marxist historian, the Civil War in England was due primarily not to religious nor political causes; it is represented by them as a class struggle in which the bourgeoisie overcame the feudal and royal powers that had survived from the Middle Ages. The transition from a feudal to a bourgeois society, from a bourgeois or capitalist society to a communist society, Marx described as an inevitable process. History was thus mainly a record of the class war according to him, and the creation of a class-conscious proletariat was a necessary preliminary to the revolution that would establish Communism. Britain, Marx thought, was most likely to have the first Communist revolution as it possessed the most class-conscious working-class or proletariat at his time. Some of Marx's theories, such as those of surplus value and the increasing misery of the working-classes, are no longer held seriously, and later thinkers, such as the Russian revolutionary leader, Lenin, have adapted and added to Marxism. Today, however, both as a political programme and as a philosophy of history, it is accepted as the official creed of the many Communist states that have come into existence in the twentieth century, while it also underlies the political thought and writing of Socialists in Western Europe.

Depression and Unemployment. As we have seen in the chapter, "Economic Changes, 1880–1914", the words "unemployment" and "unemployed" date from the 1880's. It is difficult to estimate the numbers of unemployed in a period when there were no labour exchanges at which unemployed workers could register. Among trade unionists, themselves a small fraction of all the workers, unemployment was over 10 per cent in 1879–80 and again in 1886; but it was more usually the unskilled or the semi-skilled outside the unions who found it hardest to obtain regular work or even any work at all during a depression. In those days, when there was no unemployment benefit, hardship and distress were common. The description of London's poor in the twelve volumes of *Life and Labour of the People in London,* written by Charles Booth, a wealthy shipowner who started his investigations in the East End of London in 1888, revealed the depths of misery in which a large section of the unskilled, casual and "sweated" workers eked out an existence. Over 30 per cent, Booth estimated, were living in poverty, below the subsistence level, and in East London the proportion of such people was over 60 per cent. A book by another Booth, GENERAL WILLIAM BOOTH, who had founded the Salvation Army in 1879, was also published about the same time. It appeared in 1890, the year when H. M. Stanley's *In Darkest Africa* was published, and Booth called it *In Darkest England— The Way Out.* Booth's picture of the "submerged tenth" of the population shocked the consciences of the whole religious world and almost a quarter of a million copies of his book were bought. The Salvation Army, which tried to reach the outcasts of society, was not the only religious body engaged in work in the slums: many church missions for the relief of distress were set up and run by Christian men and women who devoted their lives to this charitable work. In 1884 TOYNBEE HALL was founded in Whitechapel as a University Settlement, the headquarters of young men from Oxford and Cambridge who were willing to engage in social service. (C. R. Attlee, Labour Prime Minister from 1945 to 1951, was at one time Secretary of Toynbee Hall.) It must not be thought that the twenty years after 1873 were years of unrelieved depression for British workers. There were periods of trade recovery, e.g. 1880–82 and 1886–90, when only 2 per cent of trade unionists were unemployed. Over the whole period, too, the standard of living improved, at any rate for those who were in regular employment. Between 1873 and 1896 wages actually rose by about 5 per cent, and, as the prices of food fell with the import of cheap grain and frozen meat, it has been estimated that "real wages", as distinct from "money wages", rose by almost

37 per cent. The average consumption of tea, sugar, meat and other foods also increased. But such averages meant little to an unemployed man with an empty stomach: six months or less without a wage could suffice to bring a man and his family to destitution and make them easy victims to illness and disease.

Socialists and Fabians. Although Ireland was the main topic of discussion in Parliament in the 1880's, there was a great deal of political agitation outside Parliament throughout the period, in which middle-class speakers and workers played a large part. Much of it was attributed to the influence of Henry George's *Progress and Poverty,* a book published in America in 1879. The author himself came to Britain on a lecture-tour in 1881 and thereby helped greatly to popularize his views. Henry George, like Robert Owen long before him, considered that poverty was due not to weakness of character or original sin but to the defective organization of society. Henry George was not a socialist and his main proposal was for a "single tax" on land, to end the landlord's exploitation of the community. But he started men thinking of a reorganization of society along socialist lines. It was in the early 1880's that Karl Marx's views began to influence people in Britain. The first Marxist group in this country was formed by H. M. HYNDMAN, who had been converted to Socialism by reading *Das Kapital* in a French translation. He set forth the Marxist doctrines in a pamphlet *England for All,* and, although Marx quarrelled with Hyndman over the pamphlet, it won many converts. The SOCIAL DEMOCRATIC FEDERATION (S.D.F.) which Hyndman eventually formed in 1884, was intended to pave the way for a workers' revolution. They adopted the red flag as the revolutionary symbol, and their favourite slogan was based on that of Marx's Manifesto: "Workers of all nations, unite; you have nothing to lose but your chains". Hyndman, who had been educated at Eton and Cambridge and had played cricket for Sussex, became known as "the Socialist in a top hat", as he was invariably dressed in top-hat and frock-coat. Although some workers joined the S.D.F. and although in their speeches the "bourgeoisie" was constantly under attack, most of the leaders were themselves of the middle-class, and included at one time or another William Morris, the poet and artist, Joynes and Salt, two former schoolmasters at Eton, and Champion, an ex-army officer who spent much of his time drilling the unemployed for the revolution that never came. The FABIAN SOCIETY, founded also in 1884, was another middle-class group, who studied problems connected with socialism and hoped to influence people by their writings. (The name of the society recalls the Roman General, Fabius, whose delaying tactics helped to defeat Hannibal.) The Fabians, who included some brilliant writers such as George Bernard Shaw, Beatrice and Sidney Webb, H. G. Wells and Graham Wallas, believed in the "inevitability of gradualness", advocating evolutionary Socialism instead of the revolutionary Socialism of Marx; they formed and still form an influential group in the labour movement.

Liberal Radicals. The newly-enfranchised working-classes, unimpressed by the Fabians or the S.D.F., gave an enthusiastic reception to Joseph Chamberlain's Radical UNAUTHORIZED PROGRAMME at the 1885 election. It was not Socialist but contained proposals for free schools, payment of M.P.s, "three acres and a cow" for country dwellers, and disestablishment of the churches of Scotland and Wales. Chamberlain's popularity was such that many regarded him as a future Radical Prime Minister; but his break with the Liberals over Home Rule for Ireland ruined such hopes. Eleven trade unionists were elected in 1885 as Liberal Radicals and there were also a few middle-class Radicals in Parliament. The prospects of a strong Radical party faded how-ever with Chamberlain's departure and the forced retirement of Sir Charles Dilke, another brilliant Radical, who was involved in a divorce suit. At the election of 1892, however, Gladstone himself, in order to win a majority for his last attempt at Irish Home Rule, produced in a speech at Newcastle a Radical manifesto, similar to Chamberlain's "Unauthorized Programme" of 1885. Gladstone's NEWCASTLE PROGRAMME, which was considered very advanced and shocked many of his party, was far removed from Socialism. It promised the disestablishment of the Welsh and Scottish churches, local veto on the sale of alcoholic liquors, land reform and provision of allotments,

6

employers' liability for accidents, payment of M.P.s, triennial
parliaments, parish and district councils. Only the last two of
these proposals were carried out in Gladstone's short-lived
parliament. When the Liberals came into power in 1906, Radicals
in the party like Lloyd George pressed for the granting of
various social reforms like old age pensions, unemployment and
health insurance, control of sweated industries, etc., and greatly
increased taxation of the rich to enable these reforms to be carried
out. These may be said to mark the beginning of the "Welfare
State" and enabled the Liberals to retain the support of the working-class voters despite the appeal of the new Labour party.
With the decline of the Liberals after the First World War and
the growth of a strong Labour party, Radicalism no longer
counted as a force in politics, and the name is now associated
mainly with the nineteenth century.

Working-class Agitation. The working-class movement
grew apace in the late 1880's. Salisbury's ministry of 1886–92
had to deal with a constant succession of demonstrations,
strikes and disturbances, which seemed to presage a revolution.
In 1887, when over twenty Irish M.P.s were in jail and gunboats were sent north to the Isle of Lewis to deal with irate
crofters, and while weekly demonstrations occurred in London,
Lord Salisbury must have thought ruefully of the consequences
of "the leap in the dark" taken by his colleagues in 1867. The
climax of the London agitation occurred on the famous "BLOODY
SUNDAY", November 13th, 1887, when thousands of marchers,
converging on Trafalgar Square, were dispersed by police and
soldiers, the Foot Guards and Life Guards being called out.
Two of the ringleaders, John Burns, an engineer and member of
the S.D.F., and R. B. Cunninghame Graham, a Scottish laird and
Liberal M.P., were badly injured and were later sent to prison.
It was again in London that the working-class movement next
showed its strength in a series of STRIKES in 1888–89. The first
strike was on a small scale but it aroused great public interest.
A few hundred girls, unorganized in any union, and working in
deplorable conditions in Bryant and May's match factory in the
East End of London, came out on strike in July 1888. Many of

them suffered from "phossy jaw", a painful disease caused by working with phosphorus and known to doctors as necrosis, by which the teeth and jawbone often rotted away. They were helped by MRS. ANNIE BESANT, a prominent freethinker and Fabian Socialist, who appealed for funds and soon had over £400 collected. Public opinion favoured the match-girls, and in a fortnight they had won. The unskilled workers, hitherto outside trade unions, were now trying to organize themselves. A union was formed by London gas-workers and when they presented a demand for an eight-hour day, the employers agreed without a strike. The example of the gas-workers encouraged the unskilled thousands who laboured in dockland. At that time, when ships docked in, hundreds of dock-labourers fought with one another like wild beasts in order to receive from a clerk, who was protected in an iron cage, a ticket that entitled the labourer to a day's work. The organizing of the dockers into a union was an extremely difficult task but it was carried through successfully by a young docker, BEN TILLETT, in 1889. Along with two young Socialist engineers, John Burns and Tom Mann, he managed to call out all the dockers from the Port of London with a demand for a guaranteed 6d. an hour for all. Burns and Tillett were first-rate open-air orators and each day organized meetings and demonstrations which attracted public attention. The dockers had no funds but this strike for "the Dockers' tanner" evoked much public sympathy. Subscriptions poured in, over £30,000 coming from overseas, most of it from Australia, where there was already a strong labour movement. The organizing of strike pay and relief tickets was carried out by Tillett with great efficiency. After four weeks the employers yielded to the strikers' demands, Cardinal Manning, the veteran leader of English Catholics, acting as mediator in the negotiations. The GREAT DOCK STRIKE of 1889 had important results. The public was impressed by the efficiency of the strike-leaders and was inclined to regard them with greater sympathy. New unions sprang up, differing from the older ones in certain respects: they usually included all or most of those engaged in an industry (e.g. the General Railway Workers' Union) instead of being confined to those in certain crafts. These GENERAL UNIONS were less concerned with friendly society activities and they were more inclined to adopt an aggressive policy to raise wages and improve conditions. The number of trade unionists rose between 1889 and 1892 from three-quarters of a million to over one and a half millions. The old unions also tended to become more militant, and, although the union leaders still mainly followed the Liberals, the working-classes began to regard in a new light Socialists like Burns and Mann, who had played such notable parts in the Great Dock Strike.

Keir Hardie's Early Career. London had been the focus for most of the industrial and political agitation of the 1880's. It was, however, from Scotland that the impetus came for the formation of a new political party to represent the working-classes. Keir Hardie, the founder of the Independent Labour Party, was born in 1856 in a Lanarkshire mining village in a single-roomed thatched cottage with an earthen floor. His family lived on the verge of poverty and starvation, as his father, a carpenter, was often out of work. When he was only eight, he was for a time the only wage-earner in the house, earning 3s. a week for a 12½-hour day. He went down the mines at ten and spent all day alone as a trapper, opening and shutting a door for ventilation purposes. His mother taught him to read but he was seventeen before he could write his name. He studied hard in the evenings and by the time he was twenty he had gained some fame locally as a lay preacher and a temperance orator. It was because of his ability as a speaker that he was chosen to lead a deputation of miners to protest about a reduction in wages. As a result, not only he but his brothers also were dismissed from their jobs, and the Hardie family was "black-listed" by all the Lanarkshire mine-owners. He then became a journalist and was appointed Secretary of the Scottish Miners, organizing the Ayrshire miners into a union that managed to extract a wage-increase from the mine-owners. Disillusioned with the Liberals, whom he had at first supported, he was strongly impressed by Henry George, the American author of *Progress and Poverty,* on a tour he made in Scotland. Hardie turned to Socialism as the solution to the

problems of the workers. He was defeated in his first attempt to
enter Parliament in 1888 at a by-election in Mid-Lanarkshire,
refusing to stand down in favour of the Liberals on the condition
of financial assistance in a future election. A few weeks later, at
a meeting in Glasgow he was elected secretary of a newly-
formed SCOTTISH LABOUR PARTY, under Cunninghame Graham
as president. This was the first Labour party in Britain but its
programme was more Radical than Socialist—adult suffrage,
payment of M.P.s, abolition of the House of Lords, Scottish
Home Rule, state insurance against sickness, accidents, old age
and death, nationalization of banks, mining royalties and
transport, local veto of alcoholic liquors, free education, taxation
of land values and incomes. Keir Hardie was returned in 1892 as
Labour M.P. for West Ham, one of three independent Labour
M.P.s elected along with eleven trade unionists who were Liberal
M.P.s. It was at this election that Gladstone made his appeal to
the working-classes in his radical "Newcastle programme", but
once elected he became engrossed in Irish Home Rule. From the
start of his parliamentary career, Keir Hardie made it clear that
he was there to represent the working-classes. Wearing a rough
tweed suit and cloth cap, he was driven to the House by his
supporters in a two-horse brake, with a cornet player on the box.
Two years later, he was almost ostracized for his outspoken
criticism of the Government's failure to move a vote of sympathy to the relatives of over 200 miners killed in a terrible
mining disaster, although the House had approved an address of
congratulation to Queen Victoria on the birth of a grandson
(the future Edward VIII) on the same day.

Keir Hardie and the Labour Party. In 1892–93 there was
another periodic slump and the employers took the opportunity
to hit back at the unions. Wage-cuts were imposed, workers were
locked out, and some of the new unions almost collapsed. At
Featherstone, Yorkshire, two men were killed and many
wounded when troops opened fire at a miners' demonstration.
It was in this atmosphere that there met in Bradford in 1893
under the chairmanship of Keir Hardie a conference representing
various sides of the labour movement—some of the new trade

unions, the Social Democratic Federation, the Fabian Society (one of the representatives being George Bernard Shaw), the Scottish Labour Party, and, among others, Robert Blatchford, editor of the popular *Clarion* newspaper and author of the best-seller of the 'nineties, *Merrie England* (over a million copies of which were sold, most of them at 1*d.* each). The result of this conference was the INDEPENDENT LABOUR PARTY, whose aim was stated as "the collective ownership and control of the means of production, distribution and exchange", in other words, Socialism, with immediate objectives of the 8-hour day and unemployment and sickness benefits. The Social Democratic Federation refused to co-operate, and also, for some time, the older trade unions. When at the ensuing election in 1895, all the 28 I.L.P. candidates, including Keir Hardie, were defeated, the older trade unionists were even more critical. During the South African War (1899–1902) Hardie, like most of the Labour movement and many of the Liberals, was pro-Boer, a fact which did not prevent his being returned to Parliament at the "Khaki Election" in 1900. A few months before the election, delegates from the Trades Union Congress at last met with some of the Independent Labour Party, the Co-operative Societies, the Social Democratic Federation and the Fabian Society to form the LABOUR REPRESENTATION COMMITTEE, with James Ramsay MacDonald, an I.L.P. member, as its secretary. This Labour Representation Committee bound its members to work together in Parliament "in the direct interest of labour" but it was not a purely Socialist or working-class body. In 1906, it became the parliamentary Labour party. The I.L.P. continued alongside the Labour party for years and always to the left of it. (Further to the left was the S.D.F. which left the L.R.C. in 1901, most of the members joining the Communist party when it was formed in Britain in 1920.) Keir Hardie was to become a strong anti-imperialist and pacifist, opposing British participation in the First World War. He died in 1917, and, although no longer so influential as he had been, he was considered by all the great pioneer of the labour movement.

The Law and the Trade Unions. Once the South African

War was over, the Labour Representation Committee began to gather strength. The Liberals were disunited, their great leader, Gladstone, leaving by his death in 1898 a gap which there was no one obvious to fill. For the period of the Unionist ministries of Salisbury (1900–02) and Balfour (1902–5), the labour movement was under pressure from different sides. The trade unions were shocked when, following a strike on the Taff Vale Railway in 1900, the railwaymen's union was found liable for damages and loss of profits during the strike. Despite an appeal to the House of Lords, the Amalgamated Society of Railway Servants had to pay £23,000 damages. This TAFF VALE DECISION roused the ire of the trade unions and the new Labour Representation Committee. After the 1906 election, when the L.R.C. became the Labour Party and the Unionists were heavily defeated, there were 29 Labour M.P.s and 24 "Lib.–Lab." M.P.s. The Liberal ministry at once had the Taff Vale Decision overturned by the TRADES DISPUTES ACT (1906), which declared that trade unions were not liable for civil wrongs. In 1908 the trade unions were again in hot water. A railway clerk, Osborne, decided to go to law to prevent his union spending its funds for political purposes, mainly to pay Labour M.P.s a salary of £200 a year. Osborne won his case and many other trade unionists took advantage of this OSBORNE JUDGEMENT. This obviously affected the working-class members of Parliament, who were dependent on trade union funds for their incomes. In 1911, however, payment to M.P.s of a salary of £400 a year became the law; and in 1913 the right to impose political levies was restored to the trade unions, provided that any objector could "contract out". The Liberals, persuaded by Lloyd George, the Welsh Radical Chancellor of the Exchequer, enacted various other measures, the Health Insurance and Unemployment Insurance Acts of 1911, in order to keep their working-class support from fading away to the Labour party. This period, immediately prior to the First World War, although to many today it seems like one of halcyon days, was disturbed by industrial unrest, strikes and lock-outs, not to mention the threat of civil war over Ireland. During strikes, the Liberal Government was compelled to send troops to work in the docks and to guard the Welsh mines; and Tom Mann, the veteran dockers' leader, was sent to jail for appealing to the soldiers to remember that they were working-men's sons. These actions of the Government naturally did not help them to retain working-class support, and after the First World War the Labour party rapidly grew in strength.

General Strike. The boldest attempt made by the trade union movement this century to influence politics was the General Strike of 1926. One of the first actions taken by Baldwin's Government (1924–29) had been to restore the Gold Standard. This was not a complete return to the gold standard of pre-war days when a gold sovereign or half-sovereign was still preferred to banknotes by many people. What was introduced in 1925 was the Gold Bullion Standard, by which Britain engaged to buy gold from or sell gold to foreign merchants and bankers at a fixed rate and of a stated minimum quantity. The Bank of England impressed upon the new Chancellor of the Exchequer, Winston Churchill (who had re-joined the Conservative party after years in the Liberal party) that this measure would restore Britain's position as the financial centre of the world. Unfortunately it had the effect of making it more difficult for British exporters to sell their goods, and British trade received a set-back. The British producers were compelled either to raise their prices (which curtailed their markets) or reduce wages. The effect of the restoration of the GOLD STANDARD was soon seen in the coal industry. The miners, still bitter from their experience of the immediate post-war years, refused to accept a wage-cut in 1925, but a "show-down" in the industry was postponed by a subsidy from Baldwin's Government after the railwaymen and transport workers had threatened to ban the transport of coal. A ROYAL COMMISSION was again appointed, as had already been done in 1919. This commission was not in favour of nationalization but proposed that the Government should buy out the royalty-owners (the owners of the land where the coal was mined) and that the industry should be re-organized. Most important, it came out against subsidies and proposed a reduction of wages coupled with a longer working day. The reaction of the miners was immediate. With the slogan "Not a minute on the day, not a penny off the pay", they rallied the whole trade union movement behind them. Remembering how their threats had influenced the Government already into paying a subsidy, the trade union leaders threatened a GENERAL STRIKE, i.e., a strike of all the major industries and transport services. When Baldwin and the Government refused to give way and promise subsidies, the strike began on May 4th, 1926. It lasted only nine days, but for at least half of that time it paralysed the life of the community. Young men of Conservative sympathies or of no political allegiance at all acted as amateur bus-drivers and tram-drivers and helped at the docks. The Government controlled broadcasting, still in its infancy, and Winston Churchill after a few days produced the *British Gazette* so that in the absence of other newspapers the Government were able to influence public opinion more than the strikers. A speech in Parliament by Sir John Simon, an eminent Liberal lawyer, had a profound impression on the more moderate trade unionists. He argued that general or sympathetic strikes to coerce the Government into some action were illegal and suggested that workers who had broken their contracts to their employers by taking part in strikes could be sued for damages. On May 12th, the general strike was called off by the trade union leaders in the expectation that the question of wages and hours would be re-opened. The miners felt that once more they had been let down by the other unions and struggled on with their strike for several months. One result of the General Strike was the passing of the TRADES DISPUTES ACT (1927), which declared illegal general or sympathetic strikes or any strikes aimed at coercing the Government or the nation. It also reversed the provision of the Trade Union Act of 1913 about political funds, for which in future a trade unionist would have to "contract in" instead of "contracting out" and which were thereby considerably reduced. When the Labour party achieved power after the Second World War, one of their first actions was to restore the provision about "contracting out" of the political levy by the Trades Disputes Act of 1946, which also declared that a strike to be officially recognized must be preceded by negotiation.

Labour's Rise to Power. At the 1906 election the new Labour party had won 29 seats, in addition to 24 held by Liberal trade unionists, but in the 1910 elections their numbers declined. The country at that time was torn and divided over the dispute about the House of Lords, and the Liberal party still received the bulk of working-class support in the fight between "the Peers and the People". JOHN BURNS, a former Socialist leader who also had been prominent in the Great Dock Strike, was actually made a member of the Liberal Cabinet in 1905, the first working-man to reach that position. When war broke out in 1914, Burns resigned from the Cabinet on pacifist grounds; but, although the Labour party leader, James Ramsay MacDonald, was also a pacifist, the party and the trade unions generally supported the war. ARTHUR HENDERSON, the new leader after MacDonald, joined Asquith's government in 1915 as a junior minister, an appointment that the Liberals hoped would make it easier to deal with the Labour movement. Henderson was also a member of the small War Cabinet formed by Lloyd George, while other minor posts were held by Labour M.P.s. At the election in 1918 at the end of the war, the Labour party, calling itself "the Party of Workers by Hand and Brain", put forward, for the first time, a Socialist programme, involving nationalization or public ownership and control of industries, transport, etc. They won only 63 seats in this "Khaki Election", but with the growth of unemployment and wage-reductions in the post-war years they obtained 144 seats in the 1922 election, becoming the official Opposition for the first time. In the 1923 election the Conservatives lost a hundred seats but were still the largest party, with 256 members as against 191 Labour members and 158 Liberal members. Baldwin, the Conservative Prime Minister, resigned and RAMSAY MACDONALD became the first Labour Prime Minister. His was a minority government, dependent on Liberal support, and it lasted less than a year after which Baldwin was Prime Minister for four years. Labour was again to form a minority government in 1929; although this time it was the largest party, it was easily outnumbered by the combined Conservative and Liberal vote. It was not until 1945, after the Second World War, that the

Labour party was able to form a government under CLEMENT
ATTLEE with a clear majority.

SOURCE EXTRACTS

A *William Temple and Sweated Industries*

Nearly twenty years later a Sweated Industries Exhibition was held
at Oxford. Here Temple saw the results of a *laissez-faire* industrial
system: match-boxes made at the rate of 2*d.* a gross, the worker having
to find paste, hemp (for tying up) and firing to dry wet boxes, spending
two hours a day in fetching and returning her work, and receiving 8*s.*
a week for ten hours' toil a day; trousers which were basted, machined,
finished and pressed at a net wage of 6*s.* a week for twelve hours' hard
daily work; artificial flowers for the making of which the worker
provided her own paste, and earned an average of 10*s.* a week for a
fourteen hours' day; stall after stall decked with the produce of free
enterprise including one devoted to the wages and hours that prevailed
in the industry of "Bible-folding". Temple, in co-operation with the
Christian Social Union, was responsible for collecting the committee
which organized the Exhibition, and in the handbook he wrote—"While
we glory in an Empire whose flag is said to stand for Justice, we are
convicted by the facts at our own doors, of stupid coarseness, of
ignorant sensibility and of wanton oppression. We form Army Corps,
we build Dreadnoughts, we discuss endlessly what metaphysics are to
be taught to children in our schools. But if we listen, there is still the
desolate cry of the Son of Man: 'I am hungry and ye give me no meat'."

F. A. Iremonger: Life of William Temple, Archbishop of Canterbury.

B *Churchill on the General Strike, 1926*

Among other things, the General Strike provided a perfect example of
the style of speech of Mr. Winston Churchill, the Chancellor of the
Exchequer. Most of the very great speeches I have heard were spoken
in very simple words. That is where Mr. Winston Churchill differs
from the others. His speeches are full of surprising phrases. I think he
has the largest vocabulary of any man in the House and he is by far the
most dramatic speaker.

He was never more dramatic than at the close of the General Strike of
1926. During the Strike he had been responsible for the publication of
The British Gazette, a miserable little sheet of news that was the object

of much ridicule. After the collapse of the General Strike a debate took place in the House. The Labour party lashed Mr. Churchill. It seemed a deliberate attempt to taunt him into fury. He did not disappoint his baiters. He took up their challenge in a heroic style of speech. In flashing phrases he denounced the wickedness and folly of the General Strike. Then he began to warn the Trade Union elements of what would happen if they did it again. The whole House waited for the momentous words. Would he threaten to declare a state of Civil War? Would he call out the Army in a civil dispute? Would he arrest the leaders? Very solemnly he proceeded with his warning: "If ever this and if ever that . . ." Then working to his climax with the most awesome solemnity, he paused and said "Then I will publish another *British Gazette!*" For a moment the House could not collect its wits. Then there came such a crash of laughter as I have never heard in the House. The Conservatives were in a frenzy of delight. Our boys could not resist the ridicule and joined in the laughter. That astonishing performance made another General Strike impossible.   *Kirkwood: My Life of Revolt.*

EXERCISES

1. (*Extract "A".*) What were the main features of "sweated industries"? What was being done to remedy the abuses of the system?
2. Explain: peaceful picketing, the aristocracy of labour, Iron Law of Wages, Law of Concentration of Capital, submerged tenth, collectivism, "inevitability of gradualness", real wages, "Bloody Sunday", Newcastle Programme, "phossy jaw," contracting-in, *laissez-faire.*
3. Identify the authors of the following and explain where necessary:
   (*a*) "A leap in the dark."
   (*b*) "The proletariat have nothing to lose but their chains."
   (*c*) "Not a minute on the day, not a penny off the pay."
   (*d*) "The Party of Workers by Hand and Brain."
4. Write short notes on: Charles Booth, General William Booth, Henry George, Social Democratic Federation, Fabian Society, Ben Tillett, John Burns.
5. Write notes on: Great Dock Strike, Keir Hardie, Liberal Radicals, General Strike of 1926.
6. Give an account of the development of trade unions from 1880 to 1914.
7. Trace the growth of the Labour party up to 1914.

8. What was done between 1880 and 1914 to secure better conditions for British workers? (The answer should be based on this chapter and on the relevant material from the chapters on the political history of this period.)

CHAPTER V

THE LATE VICTORIAN AGE

The Age of Progress. The mid-Victorian period of the 1860's has been described as an age of complacency and as the heyday of British capitalism. Naturally, the British people were satisfied, even smug, about their economic and political supremacy in the world; and in the 1870's Disraeli gave them an added pride in the Empire. The inventions of science, the speeding-up of transport, the advance of medical knowledge, the improvements in public health, the extension of the franchise, the expansion of the educational system—all seemed to spell one word: "Progress". The belief in progress as inevitable remained strong throughout the whole Victorian period. This belief accorded well, too, with the new theory of evolution, the progress of nature that had culminated in Man. But the 1870's also brought the Great Depression, so that in the 1880's, a decade of unemployment, strikes and new political movements, many people began to question the smug acceptance of the idea that Britain was the best place in the world and the nineteenth century the best period in the world's history. Among the foremost critics of Victorian complacency was MATTHEW ARNOLD (1822–88), son of Dr. Thomas Arnold, the famous headmaster of Rugby, and himself an Inspector of Schools as well as poet and literary critic. Arnold attacked the middle-class of his time as "Philistine" and the aristocratic class as "Barbarian" so far as the arts and culture were concerned. "One has often wondered," he wrote, "whether there is anything so unintelligent, so unapt to, perceive how the world is really going as an ordinary young Englishman of our upper class." Britain, he argued, might lead the world in political and economic power, but she was far behind the other countries of Western Europe in her appreciation of culture. When the London newspapers were full of praise for a new and rapid train service between north and south London, Arnold criticized the Londoner who considered it was "the highest pitch of development and civilization when his letters are carried twelve times a day from Islington to Camberwell and from Camberwell to Islington and if railway trains run to and fro every quarter of an hour. He thinks it is nothing that the trains only carry him from an illiberal, dismal life at Islington to an illiberal, dismal life at Camberwell, and that the letters only tell him that such is the life there." THOMAS CARLYLE (1795-1881), the Scottish philosopher and historian who became "the Sage of Chelsea", was contemptuous of the Victorian pride in material progress. "To whom is this wealth of England wealth?" he asked. "Who is it that it blesses, makes happier, wiser, beautifuller, in any way better?" JOHN RUSKIN (1819-1900), another critic of literature and art, tended finally to social reform as a protest against the sordid conditions of industrial Britain; and WILLIAM MORRIS (1834-96), one of the founders of the Socialist League, was a distinguished artist who tried to improve popular taste in interior decoration, never ceasing to advise people: "Have nothing in your home except what you know to be useful and believe to be beautiful". The AESTHETIC MOVEMENT of the 1880's and 1890's was a protest against the lack of culture or Philistinism in Britain. It believed in "art for art's sake", going to extravagant lengths in detaching itself from the world. The aesthetic type was ridiculed by W. S. Gilbert in the opera *Patience* (1881). The poet Bunthorne, who walked down Piccadilly with a lily in his hand, was—

"A most intense young man,
A soulful-eyed young man,
An ultra-poetical, super-aesthetical
Out-of-the-way young man."

The movement in the 1890's even went so far in its reaction against the Philistines' pride in progress as to pride itself on being decadent. But the aesthetic movement itself led to a reaction, particularly after the appearance of OSCAR WILDE (1856–1900), the brilliant literary leader of the decadent 1890's, in a notorious law-suit. The Edwardian era found poets and artists in a search for new ideas and new ideals.

Religion and Science. Doubts about the Bible story of the Creation had been expressed ever since Sir Charles Lyell's *Principles of Geology,* published in 1821–33, argued that certain fossils could be proved to be millions of years old. Most nine-teenth-century Christians who believed in the literal truth of every word and sentence of the Bible also tended to accept the date of the Creation as about 4004 B.C., the year calculated by Archbishop Ussher in the seventeenth century. (The exact time of the Creation of Man, according to Ussher, was 9 a.m. on Saturday, October 23rd, 4004 B.C.) To these Christians the assertions of Lyell and other geologists about the age of the earth seemed almost blasphemy. Darwin's *Origin of Species* (1859) and, still more, *The Descent of Man* (1871) accepted the geologists' theories about the age of the earth, as millions of years were considered necessary to allow for the development of the various species. Darwin's suggestion in *The Descent of Man* that men and apes were probably descended from a common stock was generally misunderstood and was also taken by Christians as denying the truth of the story of man's creation in *Genesis.* "Is man an ape or an angel? I am on the side of the angels," remarked Disraeli. The conflict between religion and science seemed irreconcilable: either the Bible or the theory of evolution was true, but not both. The great protagonist of the theory of evolution in the never-ending controversy between scientists and the churches was T. H. HUXLEY (1825–95), a noted zoologist. Huxley could detect no purpose in evolution. He maintained: "The purpose manifested in evolution, whether for adaptation, specialization or biological progress, is only an apparent purpose. It is just as much a product of blind forces as is the falling of a stone to earth or the ebb and flow of tides." To others, however, evolution showed a purposeful development that accorded with the commonly accepted ideas about the progress of mankind towards what Tennyson called "the one far-off divine event to which the whole creation moves". Gradually many Christians found that they need not accept the literal truth of the story of Creation in *Genesis* in order to be Christians. But there were still many others who, believing in the Divine inspiration of the Bible, refused to allow one word or sentence to be called untrue. The researches of the nineteenth-century scholars who revealed discrepancies in the Bible or upset long-accepted theories or traditions about the Bible were considered in some quarters to be born of the Devil and were labelled scornfully "the HIGHER CRITICISM". Bishop Colenso of Natal, who published a book in 1862, criticizing the traditional view that Moses was the author of the Pentateuch (the first five books of the Bible) was unanimously condemned by his fellow-bishops. Robertson Smith, Professor of Hebrew in the Free Church College of Aberdeen, who followed Colenso in his article on the Bible in the *Encyclopaedia Britannica* in 1875 was charged in the church courts with heresy as a result. In the United States, Fundamentalists (those who believe in the literal truth of the Bible) were still so strong in 1925 that a young schoolteacher in Dayton, Tennessee, was accused of breaking the state laws by teaching his pupils the theory of evolution. His trial (called "the monkey trial" by the American papers) revealed that many people still believed in the Divine inspiration of every word of the Bible. But in the mid-twentieth century most church members in Britain have ceased to regard such a tenet as important.

Church of England. The Victorian Age differed radically from earlier and later periods so far as religion was concerned. Apart from some of the aristocracy and some of the lower classes, strict religious observance was considered proper. For the middle-class family (and the Victorian Age has been called the age of the middle class), it was common for all, young and old, to go to church twice on Sunday, for the children to have Sunday School also, and for family prayers to be said twice a day. (The hours recommended by Mrs. Beeton in her famous book, *Household Management,* were 8.45 a.m. and 10 p.m.) The puritanical Sabbath observance of the Scottish Presbyterians and the English Nonconformists, which they had retained since the seventeenth century, had spread in the nineteenth century to Church of England circles also. Lord Shaftesbury, a leading Anglican, strongly opposed the suggestion that bands should be allowed to play in the London parks on Sundays. Shaftesbury called himself "an Evangelical of the Evangelicals", those who believe in the necessity of conversion for a Christian and also in the literal interpretation of the Bible. Some of the more extreme EVANGELICALS were called "Low Church" as distinct from the "High Church" party, whom they opposed mainly because of the introduction of more ritual into the Anglican service. The HIGH CHURCH or Anglo-Catholic clergy in the Church of England owed their inspiration to the Oxford Movement of the first half of the nineteenth century and were often very devout, energetic and sincere men who felt that the basic doctrines and the church services could be greatly improved. According to Gladstone, himself a devout Anglican, the normal Church of England service had formerly been "dishonouring to Christianity and disgraceful to the nation; the church was bare, the service plain, the music terrible, the indifferent congregation lounging or asleep". A more ornate ceremonial, the placing of the cross, candles or flowers on the altar, the wearing of vestments, the use of incense and other ritual were introduced by Anglo-Catholic "High Church" clergy to enable their congregations "to worship the Lord in the beauty of holiness". People were encouraged to take Holy Communion every Sunday instead of only twice a year as Queen Victoria and most other Anglicans did. But "High Church" ritual was regarded by many as "halfway to Rome"; and in 1874, at Queen Victoria's own request, Parliament passed the PUBLIC WORSHIP REGULATION ACT in order to stop what the Prime Minister, Disraeli, called "ritualistic high jinks". Although some clergy were sent to prison, Anglo-Catholic ritualist practices continued, and on the whole the effect of the High Church movement was to revitalize the Church of England.

English Catholics and Nonconformists. From the time of

7

the Oxford Movement, there had been a drift of Anglo-Catholics to the Roman Catholic Church, two of the converts, Newman and Manning, becoming Cardinals. MANNING was one of the outstanding diplomats of the Catholic Church. He played a leading part in the Vatican Council at Rome in 1870, when the dogma of papal infallibility was promulgated. He later became very interested in social reform, encouraged General Booth in his Salvation Army work, helped to bring the London Dock Strike of 1889 to an end, and started the League of the Cross, a Catholic association to encourage teetotalism. The Roman Catholic Church in England changed its character in the latter half of the nineteenth century: from being a small, rather select church it was greatly enlarged through the influx of Irish Catholics to industrial cities like London, Liverpool and Birmingham. The rapid growth of the Catholic Church and its recruitment of distinguished Anglo-Catholics continued into the twentieth century and gave further cause to the keen Protestants of the Church of England for criticism of High Church practices. But the strongest opposition to the Roman Catholic Church and the Anglo-Catholics came from outside the Church of England, from the NONCONFORMISTS. The Methodist Church which Wesley had founded was still imbued with the Evangelical spirit he displayed. Lay preachers were permitted in the Methodist, Baptist and other Nonconformist denominations and they were often as eloquent as any clergyman. Lloyd George and Keir Hardie were only two of the many Labour and Liberal politicians who first earned fame as lay preachers. In the late nineteenth century indeed the difference between Anglican "Church" and Nonconformist "Chapel" was not only one of religion but also of politics. Those who attended the Church of England were generally Conservative but might be Liberal (as Gladstone was) while those who attended the Nonconformist chapels were almost invariably Liberal or, later, Labour. Some prominent Radicals were also known as "freethinkers", however; the most notable was CHARLES BRADLAUGH, who refused to take the oath as M.P., and there were many grades of free-thinkers—sceptics, agnostics, atheists. The most religious century in England since the Reformation produced at its close more critics of religion than any previous period. But if there were sceptics on the one side, there were enthusiasts on the other. It is difficult to realize today how completely absorbed in religion Victorian people became at certain times called "revivals". Some American revivalists of the twentieth century have attracted great audiences but none of them could compare with the famous pair, Dwight L. Moody and Ira D. Sankey, who held gospel meetings all over the country in 1873, 1881 and 1892. Many of the MOODY AND SANKEY hymns became popular, and it is estimated that over fifty million copies of their *Sacred Songs and Solos* have been sold. One of the last great revivals started in 1904 in Wales, the leader being a young miner, Evan Roberts. There were certain Nonconformist preachers whose ordinary services were like revival meetings. Pre-eminent among these was CHARLES H. SPURGEON (1834–92), who once preached to a congregation of 24,000 in the Crystal Palace. Books of his sermons, which he delivered extempore and which were later taken down in shorthand, were eagerly read by thousands who had never seen Spurgeon. Queen Victoria herself was a regular reader of his sermons. Her preference (oddly enough for the Supreme Governor of the Church of England) was for the Presbyterian service of the Church of Scotland and her favourite preacher was Dr. Norman MacLeod, a prominent Highlander and minister of the Barony Church, Glasgow, from 1851 to 1872.

Scottish Churches. In the second half of the nineteenth century there were two principal churches in Scotland, the CHURCH OF SCOTLAND, corresponding to the Church of England in its official connection with the state, and the FREE CHURCH OF SCOTLAND, which came into existence at the Disruption in 1843. The Free Church was not the only church that stood outside the Established Church. The UNITED PRESBYTERIAN CHURCH (the U.P. Church), formed out of earlier secessions from the Church of Scotland, differed from the Free Church in certain respects. The Free Church stood for a state-established church, although they denied the right of the state to interfere in the internal affairs of the Church, while the U.P. Church was "Voluntary",

i.e. opposed to state establishment. In the church services, the
U.P. Church went much further than the Free Church in the
singing of hymns (particularly after the revival meetings of
Moody and Sankey) and in 1872 the use of instrumental music in
the church was sanctioned. Many in the Free Church still
maintained that only the psalms should be sung, while organs
were considered as Anglican innovations and contemptuously
referred to as "kists o' whistles". Some U.P. ministers, also, were
prepared to accept the Westminster Confession of Faith only
with certain qualifications, while it remained a fundamental
standard of the Free Church. By the end of the century, however,
a large majority of the Free Church were prepared to unite with
the U.P. Church. By this time, the foreign missions of the Scottish
churches were to be found in many parts of Africa and India, and
the claims of missionaries that separate missions caused confusion
were among the arguments presented in favour of a union
between two similar churches. In 1900 the Union was carried
through and a UNITED FREE (U.F.) CHURCH was formed,
leaving outside a small but determined minority in the Free
Church, whose members became known as the "WEE FREES".
The dispute over church property (buildings and funds) between
the "Wee Frees" and the new United Free Church led to a legal
case of great constitutional importance and provoked violent
scenes in Scotland, a gunboat being sent to the Isle of Lewis
where feelings ran high. The FREE CHURCH CASE, which went
through the Scottish courts and was finally settled in favour of the
"Wee Frees" in the House of Lords in 1904, was memorable both
for the dialectical skill with which R. B. Haldane, counsel for
the U.F. Church and later Secretary for War, dealt with theologi-
cal questions such as predestination. and also for the overturning
of the decision by an Act of Parliament immediately thereafter,
a demonstration that Parliament is the supreme authority in the
land. In 1874 the PATRONAGE ACT had been repealed and it was
inevitable that there should be another union, this time with the
established Church of Scotland. Some of the U.F. Church did
not like the idea of the church being controlled by the state in
any degree whatsoever or of being supported by public taxes

(the teinds). It was not until the twentieth century that union took place. When Acts were passed in Parliament in 1921 and 1925, declaring the Church's independence of the state and putting an end to the system of teinds, the way was clear and in 1929 1,457 parish churches and 1,441 U.F. churches combined to form the new Church of Scotland. The state connection is still maintained, however, by the Queen sending to the General Assembly each May the LORD HIGH COMMISSIONER, who takes up his residence as her representative in the Palace of Holyroodhouse. The first oath taken by the Queen on her accession was one to maintain "the government, worship, discipline, rights and privileges of the Church of Scotland"; and it is the royal custom, when in Scotland, to attend Presbyterian services even although the sovereign is head of the Church of England. The Roman Catholic Church expanded very rapidly in Scotland as in England, through Irish immigrants flooding into the industrial areas, particularly Clydeside. But there were Protestant as well as Catholic immigrants from Ireland and unfortunately the Irish brought over with them their bitter hatred of one another. The Orangemen in Scotland started their Irish custom of celebrating the 12th of July, the anniversary of King William's victory at Boyne Water (actually fought on 1st of July, 1690). Every "TWELFTH OF JULY", the Protestant v. Catholic feud would boil up because of the Orange Walks (or processions), often deliberately causing trouble by marching through Catholic districts. In 1875, street fighting went on for days in Partick, Glasgow, after the centenary celebrations of Daniel O'Connell's birth. The rivalry extended to the sphere of sport, and hooligans, calling themselves Catholic or Protestant, fought one another on the terracing at football matches between Hibernians and Heart of Midlothian in Edinburgh and between Celtic and Rangers in Glasgow.

Scientific Advances. Many of the important advances in science have already been described in Chapter III. Generally scientific discoveries and inventions were regarded as beneficial to mankind. But many of them were used to make warfare more efficient and more ruthless. The high-explosive shells and bombs of the First World War were made possible by the Swedish inventor and manufacturer, ALFRED NOBEL (1833–96), who first produced nitro-glycerine and gun-cotton on a large scale. Nobel was also responsible for the production of dynamite and blasting-gelatine, widely used for industrial purposes. As he did not wish to be remembered only for his manufacture for warlike ends, he left a sum of money equal to almost £2,000,000 to provide the Nobel science, medicine, literature and peace prizes. The application of electricity, as we have seen, brought tremendous changes to industry, transport and communications. Electricity also opened up other avenues of research that were to lead to developments of great significance for mankind. SIR WILLIAM CROOKES (1832–1919) first earned fame by applying the use of the spectroscope to chemistry, discovering the rare thallium in that way. He helped to identify the very light gas, helium, which had been discovered by Lockyer in 1868 spectroscopically in the sun before it was discovered on the earth. Crookes experimented with electrical discharges through gases at low pressures and he invented the Crookes's tube, now called the cathode-ray tube. When he was president of the British Association in 1898, he prophesied that, unless nitrogenous fertilizers could be obtained synthetically, the world would be faced with a disastrous food shortage, a warning that was fortunately heeded and led to the successful industrial production of such fertilizers. Crookes was also a benefactor of mankind by his invention of a type of lens (the Crookes lens) that protected the eyes of glass-workers and others exposed to the harmful light-rays of certain industrial processes. It was while experimenting with Crookes's tube that a German professor of physics, WILHELM RÖNTGEN, discovered in 1895 that, when the cathode rays struck a metal plate in the tube, they turned into rays which could penetrate flesh but not bones and wood but not metal. These rays he modestly named X-rays but on the continent they are more commonly called Röntgen-rays and are used for a variety of purposes. In the following year, 1896, a French professor, Becquerel, discovered by accident that some uranium in his possession was giving off radiation. In the course of investigating the nature of these "Becquerel rays" (as they were called), Becquerel's assistant, MARIE SKLODOWSKA CURIE, made her discovery of radium. She was the daughter of a Polish professor and it was at the Sorbonne, in Paris, where she was studying chemistry, that she met her husband, PIERRE CURIE, professor of physics, with whom she carried out a brilliant piece of research. They managed to extract 1/10th of a gramme of the new element, radium, from 10,000 kilogrammes of uranium pitchblende they had received from a Bohemian silver-mine. Radium has proved particularly valuable in the treatment of certain diseases such as cancer; and radio-therapy, although it has to be used with care, has been hailed as a blessing by many sufferers. The Curies, however, had not only discovered a new element but had also revolutionized men's thinking about the structure of matter. The matter in radium, they found, was turning into radiation so that, according to their calculations, in 1,600 years half of any given quantity of radium would disappear. Scientists began to evolve a new theory of atomic structure and to reconsider the relations between matter and energy. It was in the Cavendish laboratory at Cambridge that in 1897 Professor J. J. THOMSON (later Sir John J. Thomson) proved the cathode-rays to be composed of fast-moving particles of negative electricity which he named electrons. Thomson and a young New Zealander, Ernest (later Lord) Rutherford, began their collaboration in researches that led to the utilization of atomic energy, as we shall see in a later chapter.

Medical Improvements. The most outstanding contribution made to medical science in the second half of the nineteenth century was undoubtedly that of the Frenchman LOUIS PASTEUR (1822–95), who was not himself a medical man but a chemist. He was engaged in investigating why wine and beer went sour when he realized the importance of microscopic organisms, usually known as germs, which are invisible to the naked eye. In 1867, he became Professor of Chemistry at the Sorbonne in Paris just after he had saved the French silk industry from disaster by showing that the disease attacking the silkworms was caused by two kinds of bacteria, which he was able to isolate. He then began to experiment on animals and, basing his theory on Jenner's practice of vaccinating to confer immunity from smallpox, he reduced the death-rate from cholera among poultry from 10 per cent to 1 per cent. Then, in a famous experiment in 1881 with sheep and goats, he inoculated one group with weakened germs of anthrax so that, after a slight attack of the disease, they became immune. Later, when both groups were exposed to anthrax, those inoculated survived, while the others succumbed to the disease. This experiment was the first stage of a development in the war against disease that has gone on ever since: doctors have worked hard first to discover and isolate the germs of a disease and later to find a way of inoculating as Pasteur did, thereby creating immunity. Pasteur's most striking triumph was the production of a vaccine for protection against hydrophobia or rabies, caused by bites from mad dogs. When in 1885 he inoculated a boy who had been bitten by a mad dog and the boy survived, the whole of Europe was full of praise for Pasteur. Three years later there was built by public subscription the Pasteur Institute in Paris; and today there are over sixty similar Pasteur Institutes for research in different parts of the world. It was a German scientist, ROBERT KOCH (1843–1910), professor at Berlin University, who first proved (what Pasteur himself had suspected) that infectious diseases were caused by bacteria. Koch's discovery of the bacillus of tuberculosis in 1882 was followed by his discovery of the bacillus of cholera, an achievement for which he was given £5,000 by his Government. The consequences of these discoveries were tremendous. From the middle of the century, men had regarded a pure water supply as important; now it was realized that a contaminated water supply could be a breeding-ground for the microbes of diseases. Public authorities were encouraged in their efforts to provide proper sanitation and an abundant, pure supply of water for all. Immunization against the water-borne disease of typhoid (from which the Prince Consort died and his son, the future Edward VII, nearly died) was started in 1896 by SIR ALMROTH WRIGHT, who used dead microbes. This typhoid vaccine was used only at the end of the South African War (1899–1902), during which more soldiers died of typhoid (or enteritis) than from enemy action; but it was of great service in the First World War and typhoid is now a comparatively rare disease. The principle of destroying the breeding-grounds of the microbes was put into effect in the tropics when it had been shown by SIR RONALD ROSS (1857–1932), after years of painstaking research in India, that malaria was caused by a parasite carried by the mosquito. It was not until an American army surgeon, Major-General Gorgas, showed that yellow fever was caused by another type of mosquito that it was possible, by clearing the mosquito-infested swamps of the Panama Isthmus, to finish the construction of the Panama Canal, which was started in 1881 and was at last opened in 1914. Another medical development of this period was the first successful brain operation by William (later Sir William) MacEwan in 1876. It is not surprising that the death rate in England and Wales fell from 22·3 per thousand in 1871 to 13·8 per thousand in 1911 and from 22·3 to 15·1 per thousand in Scotland over the same period.

Exploration. It was just after the middle of the nineteenth century that Africa, the "Dark Continent", was opened up by the journeys of explorers like Speke, Livingstone and Stanley. The interior of another continent, Australia, was similarly explored about the same time; the epic character of the crossings from south to north by the Irishmen, Burke and Wills, in 1860 and the Scotsman, MacDowall Stuart, in 1862 was equalled by that from west to east of John Forrest (later Lord Forrest and first Prime Minister of Western Australia) in 1875. Explorers in the latter part of the century were at pains to find some fresh regions for their efforts. SIR FRANCIS YOUNGHUSBAND (1863–1942), soldier and colonial administrator, was one of the first two Englishmen to reach India overland from China in 1887 and he led a mission to Tibet in 1903–4, when the "forbidden city" of Lhasa first became revealed to the world. This was also the period when the more difficult peaks of the Alps were conquered; and British climbers who had formed the Alpine Club in 1858–59 took a large part in popularizing the sport of mountaineering. The Matterhorn, the last of the great Alpine peaks to be conquered, was scaled in 1865 by EDWARD WHYMPER and his party, four of whom were killed on the descent. Whymper later succeeded in climbing many other mountains, including Chimborazo in Ecuador. Mountaineers went all over the world in search of "first ascents"; and so, by the end of the century, giants like Aconcagua in Chile, Kilimanjaro in Africa, Mount St. Elias in Alaska were conquered. Expeditions were made to the Himalayas and the Karakorams but Everest and the higher mountains were still deemed impossible. New routes were pioneered up difficult rock faces and gullies in the Alps and also in the Scottish Highlands, Wales and the Lake District. Polar exploration also offered scope to the adventurous. FRIDTJOF NANSEN (1862–1930), Norwegian champion athlete, swimmer and ski-runner, daringly undertook in 1893 to let his ship, the *Fram,* specially built for him in a Scottish shipyard, drift across the frozen Arctic Ocean. Leaving the *Fram* with one companion, he travelled across terrible ice and snow in a dash for the North Pole. But they were compelled to give up within 200 miles of the Pole and after more than a year of hardships and hair-breadth escapes from death, they were fortunate in reaching a camp of British explorers. It was in the early twentieth century that the Poles were reached at last.

Victorian Football. In the late Victorian age, Britain led the world in sport as she did in so many other spheres. Her pre-eminence was not seriously challenged before the twentieth century, except in countries like Australia and the United States where the people could claim kinship with the British. British sports have since then become familiar all over the world; and English words connected with sports have been adopted into other languages—football, golf, hockey, goal, kick, match, fair play, and of course sport itself. Why did Britain occupy such a dominating position in the world of sport? The existence of a wealthy aristocracy with plenty of leisure encouraged sports and recreations like hunting, horse-racing, polo, golf, cricket. Organized games and competitions like football, hockey, rowing, athletics, grew out of the English public school system, whereby boys living together and playing together gradually evolved rules for their games. When the Saturday half holiday became general in the 1880's, it was natural that, with the great increase in players and spectators, games should become more organized. The FOOTBALL ASSOCIATION was formed in 1863 by "Old Boys" of public schools who had met in London the previous year to draw up rules. The dribbling game preferred by the Football Association thus became known as Association Football or "soccer", while the carrying code of the RUGBY UNION, formed (principally by the Blackheath and Richmond clubs) in 1871, became known as "rugger". The F.A. Cup was first played for in 1871, the Cup-winners being the Wanderers, a team of public school old boys, who won it so often that in 1878 the Cup became their absolute property. They handed it back to the Association, however, to be a perpetual trophy; but it had to be replaced in 1895 when it was stolen from a shop-window in Birmingham after Aston Villa had won it. The first international between Scotland and England was played in 1872 at Kennington Oval, the result being a goalless draw. In 1873, when the Scottish Rugby Union and the Scottish Football Association were founded, the competition for the Scottish Cup was won by the Glasgow club, QUEEN'S PARK, which had provided the entire Scottish team in the international of the previous year. Queen's Park developed out of the Y.M.C.A. and is now the only amateur side left in senior football in Britain, their ground, Hampden Park, being one of the largest in the world. The most famous amateur football club in England in the nineteenth century was the CORINTHIANS, formed in 1882 by leading university and public school players. By 1890 professionalism was rampant, and the amateur clubs gradually dropped out of senior competition, forming themselves into a separate association in 1906. The team formation in the early days of Association Football was different from that of today—a goalkeeper, two backs, two half-backs and six forwards instead of the present line-up. In 1888, the winners of the Scottish and English Cups, Renton and the West Bromwich Albion, played for "the championship of the world"; Renton, the winners, have long since disappeared from the game, but West Bromwich Albion are still to the fore. The numbers and positions of players in RUGBY FOOTBALL also varied considerably in the early days: the team of fifteen became common but it was arranged as three backs, two half-backs and ten forwards, then as one full back, three three-quarter backs, two half-backs and nine forwards, and so to the present formation. In 1895, when the Rugby Union was trying to stamp out professionalism, the Northern Union was formed to promote professional rugby; it is now known as the RUGBY LEAGUE, it is strong in the north of England and its rules differ in some respects from those of the Rugby Union (e.g., there are thirteen players in a team instead of fifteen).

Other Sports. Cricket, which had been a popular sport in England since the eighteenth century, entered a new phase in 1873, when the county championship was instituted, Nottinghamshire and Gloucestershire sharing the title. In 1876 the first properly organized Australian TEST MATCHES were played at Melbourne. The name "The Ashes" goes back to 1882 when Australia beat England at the Oval and a sporting paper published the notice "In Memoriam"—"In loving memory of English cricket, which died at the Oval on August 29, 1882. The remains will be cremated and the ashes taken to Australia". The great hero of nineteenth-century cricket was DR. W. G. GRACE (1848–1915). "W. G." was a very tall, bearded doctor who had a practice in Bristol and played for Gloucestershire. He was only sixteen when he was chosen to play for South Wales and in 1871 he made his highest aggregate of 2,739 runs in one season. He was an all-round cricketer and in one season took 192 wickets, while his highest score in first-class cricket was 344. For over fifty years he played in village, county, test matches and he helped to increase the popularity of cricket, the crowds thronging the grounds where he played. On one occasion, when he was quite clearly stumped early in the innings, the umpire refused to give him "out", in order not to disappoint the crowd. Other sports were also organized on a popular basis in the second half of the nineteenth century. The first OPEN GOLF CHAMPIONSHIP was held at Prestwick in 1866, when the prize was a champion belt, while LAWN TENNIS dates from 1874, when rules were drawn up for the game, the first championships being held at Wimbledon in the following year. ROWING had become established first at Eton, then at Oxford and Cambridge, as the manly sport *par excellence*. The University Boat Race was first held as far back as 1829 and the Regatta at Henley in 1839; the oarsmen from the two older universities normally provided the winners at Henley and the only serious challenges came from American and Australian crews. The rules of rowing then (and for long after) debarred from competition not only professionals who had won money prizes but also those engaged in manual work, as it was felt that these had an unfair advantage over gentlemen who did no work. It was also the universities that organized ATHLETICS. The first amateur athletic meeting was staged at Oxford by Exeter College in 1850 and included races over two miles cross-country, 140 yards, 100 yards, and one mile with ten flights of hurdles. The first inter-university meeting was held in 1864 and an Amateur Athletic Club to promote amateur athletics was founded in 1866. It was in 1886 that W. G. George, a professional runner, put up a record for the mile, 4 minutes, 12¾ seconds, that was to last for almost forty years. The Amateur Athletic Association dates from 1880 and the modern Olympic Games from 1896, when they were staged at Athens and the marathon race (from Marathon to Athens) was won, appropriately enough, by a Greek shepherd. By the end of Victoria's reign, Britain was still pre-eminent in most sports except cricket, in which occasionally Australia proved superior, and yachting, in which the Americans invariably beat their British challengers for the America's Cup, prominent among them Sir Thomas Lipton, with his five yachts, all named *Shamrock*.

Class Distinctions. When we look back on Victorian times we are struck by the many differences from our own day. What is difficult to realize is the extent to which class distinctions prevailed last century. There were many reasons for this—the lack of education among the lower classes, the vast range of incomes (in those days of low taxation) from the wealthy landowner to the slum-dweller, the acceptance by nearly all, including the poor, of wealth and comfort as the birth-right of some and of grinding poverty as the lot of others. As they sang in church or chapel on Sundays—

"The rich man in his castle,
The poor man at his gate,
God made them high or lowly,
And order'd their estate."

In the days before death duties and supertax had been devised to "soak the rich", it was possible for an upper-class family to maintain, in good condition, a country estate and a town house. There were few outlets in Victorian days for women in industry and business, so that domestic servants were available in plenty and at low wages—perhaps £2 a month (all found) for a house-maid; and even houses of the small villa type had at least one "maid's room". The calendar of events for those in "high society" was one that presupposed a comfortable income and ample leisure—the London season that made necessary for women who could afford it a visit to a Paris dressmaker and provided for the young débutantes who were presented at Court a round of wonderful private parties and balls and visits to Ascot, Henley or Cowes; the mass exodus from London in the month of August when the Highlands were full of Englishmen and Americans for the grouse-shooting and angling; and the return to England for the pheasant-shooting and the fox-hunting. For the middle classes the late Victorian age was also one of comfort, if not of the extravagance and gaiety of high society. The middle-class paterfamilias preferred a solid, respectable house—it may be in a terrace, with three or four storeys ranging from the subterranean scullery, where the servant toiled, to the attic, where she slept, or in a detached house well-enclosed and screened from vulgar gaze by rhododendron, laurel or privet hedge. Middle-class holidays in those days often meant taking a house for a couple of months at the coast or in the country and removing there the whole family—servants, pets and all. But most middle-class people at one time or another took a trip abroad. The Englishman in his Norfolk jacket and knickerbockers was a conspicuous figure on the Continent; and it was certainly Englishmen who opened up the Alps for mountaineering and ski-ing. Holidays for the working-man and his wife and family, who lived in a room-and-kitchen house with few amenities, might mean only a day or two at Margate, Blackpool, Dunoon or Portobello. There were also, for the children, the annual excursion to the country for the Sunday School treat or picnic and the week of the Fair, when the travelling shows visited the Common. But for many older people, particularly during periods of unemployment, there could be no holidays at all. Many an old man or woman, in those days of no old age pensions, had no chance of going away from their homes except to the workhouse or poorhouse. There were shadows as well as splendours about the late Victorian age.

SOURCE EXTRACTS

Oxford Crew's Training and Diet, c. 1895

7 a.m. Out of bed, and without bathing or washing dress immediately in flannels. A cup of milk and a biscuit.

7.15 Out of the house. A brisk walk with one sharp run of 150 yards.

7.50 Back to the house. Bath, etc.

8.30 Breakfast.—Fish, plainly cooked, without sauce. Soles, whitings and smelts are best. Salmon is not allowed. Cutlets or beefsteaks, or grilled chicken. Eggs, boiled or poached or fried, sometimes scrambled. Mustard and cress or water-cress. Toast. Limited amount of butter. Marmalade is allowed only during the last fortnight of training. Not more than a cup and a half of tea.

11. At Putney, when the state of the tide permits it, exercise in the boat . . .

1 p.m. Lunch.—Cold meat. Tomatoes plainly made into a salad with oil and vinegar. Toast. Small quantity of butter. Oatmeal biscuits. One glass of draught beer or claret and water.

3 or 4 (according to tide). Work in the boat.

6.30 Dinner.—Fish, as at breakfast. An *entrée* of pigeons or sweetbread or spinach and poached eggs. Roast joint (not pork or veal), or else chicken with potatoes, mashed or boiled, and boiled vegetables. Stewed fruit with rice pudding, Sometimes jelly. Two glasses of draught beer or claret and water. For dessert, figs, prunes, oranges, dry biscuits and one glass of port wine.

9.50   A glass of lemon and water or a cup of water-gruel.

10.   Bed.

(Note.—Once or twice during training there is a "champagne night" when champagne is substituted for beer or claret and water; but this only occurs when the crew have been doing very hard work, or when they show evident signs of being over-fatigued and require a fillip.)

R. C. Lehmann: Rowing.

EXERCISES

1. Explain: Sage of Chelsea, "Philistine", Higher Criticism, funda-mentalism, High Church, freethinkers, "Wee Frees", "kists o' whistles", Twelfth of July.
2. Identify the authors of the following and explain where necessary:
    (*a*) "The trains only carry him from an illiberal, dismal life at Islington to an illiberal, dismal life at Camberwell."
    (*b*) "Have nothing in your home except what you know to be useful and believe to be beautiful."
    (*c*) "Is man an ape or an angel? I am on the side of the angels."
    (*d*) "Ritualistic high jinks."
    (*e*) "The remains will be cremated and taken to Australia."
3. Write short notes on: Matthew Arnold, *Descent of Man,* T. H. Huxley, Cardinal Manning. Moody and Sankey, Alfred Nobel, Sir William Crookes, Marie Curie, Sir Ronald Ross, Edward Whymper, Sir Francis Younghusband, W. G. Grace.
4. Give an account of the career of Louis Pasteur and estimate its importance in the history of medicine.
5. Write a short history of golf or rowing or athletics or football (association or rugby) in the nineteenth century.

CHAPTER VI

EDWARDIAN LIBERALISM

Edward VII. When Queen Victoria died in January 1901, her eldest son, the Prince of Wales, was already sixty years of age. A bearded, portly, dignified man of the world, he had long since outlived the youthful indiscretions which led Bradlaugh, one of the republicans of the 1870's, to express the hope that "the present Prince of Wales would never dishonour this country by becoming its King". He was fond of social life and engaged in all the pursuits and sports of the gentlemen of his day. By the time he came to the throne he confined himself mainly to the sports of yachting and horse-racing. His interest in yachting, which had taken him annually to Cowes, had diminished somewhat since his nephew, the German Kaiser, William II, became a member of the Royal Yacht Squadron, trying to outdo his uncle in everything and earning the nickname of "Boss of Cowes". A royal victory in the Derby is always popular with the British people; Edward VII achieved this supreme triumph of the turf in 1909, while another possible victory in 1913 was prevented by a fanatical suffragette who committed suicide by throwing herself in front of the King's horse. Every year Edward VII spent about three months abroad, visiting Biarritz in the spring and Marienbad (in Austria) in the autumn. He was in Biarritz when Campbell-Bannerman resigned in April 1908 and the new Prime Minister, Asquith, kissed hands in a foreign hotel, the only British Prime Minister to do so. Edward introduced to Britain the Homburg hat and the fashion (enforced upon him by his stoutness) of leaving undone the bottom button of the waistcoat. Although he was a stickler for etiquette, he broke with royal tradition by forming a friendship with the wealthy Jew, Sir Ernest Cassel, at a time when there was a strong anti-Semitic feeling. His outings in the yacht of Sir Thomas Lipton, who owned a vast network of grocery stores and who competed several times for the America's Cup before he was admitted to the exclusive Royal Yacht Squadron, caused the Kaiser to sneer at his uncle "going boating with his grocer". Edward's coronation in 1902 was an affair of wonderful splendour, the first for sixty-four years, and a memorable occasion for all concerned. It had to be postponed for a few months because of an operation upon the King for appendicitis (which then became the fashionable operation). There were strong objections in Scotland to his taking the title Edward VII on the grounds that, in an early

8

similar case, James VI of Scotland had been called James I of the United Kingdom. The sympathy evoked by his illness helped to have the objections passed over, but similar objections were raised again in 1953 at the time of the coronation of Queen Elizabeth. Edward VII had less interest in politics than Queen Victoria partly because she had not allowed him to read government papers till he was fifty-five. His visit in 1903 to Paris, where he aroused popular enthusiasm, is said to have helped in bringing about the *Entente Cordiale* with France in the following year. During his brief reign and that of his son and successor George V, the powers of the monarchy declined while the respect of the British public for it increased.

note ✳   **Balfour's Ministry (1902–5).** A. J. Balfour, who succeeded his uncle, the Marquess of Salisbury, in 1902 was a Scottish laird with an English background (Eton and Cambridge). An intellectual rather than a man of action, author of a treatise on philosophic doubt and an essay on Handel, a first-class player of tennis and golf, he maintained an aloofness in politics and never managed to inspire much enthusiasm among his followers. His politics resembled those of his uncle and have been defined as "conservatism unadulterated"; he believed that the first duty of a government is to govern, not to introduce legislation, and that the less interference there is with the mechanism of administration the better. He started off his ministry, however, by undertaking personal responsibility for an EDUCATION BILL that excited a very acrimonious controversy. This Bill had been planned by an able civil servant, Robert (later Sir Robert) Morant, and its main purpose was to establish a secondary school system in England and Wales. Some people who had become alarmed at the rapid, industrial progress of Germany attributed it in part to their much more highly developed educational system; it was also pointed out that Switzerland was then spending 1*s.* per head of population on secondary education in comparison with less than a penny in England and Wales. The English and Welsh school boards were abolished and education, both elementary and secondary, was now put under the control of county councils— "board schools" thus became "council schools". (In Scotland, elementary and secondary schools remained under the control of parish school boards until 1918.) The controversial part of the Bill was a proposal to save the church schools by subsidizing them from the rates. Some Nonconformists opposed this with such bitterness that, after the Bill became law, they actually went to prison rather than pay rates for an Anglican school. Education and religion had led men into a defiance of the law, and this was also a principal feature of the policy followed by the suffragettes, who started violent agitation after the formation of the Women's Social and Political Union under Mrs. Emmeline Pankhurst in 1903. A lawsuit which went to the House of Lords and which had serious consequences for Balfour's Government was the TAFF VALE CASE, decided in 1901 when Salisbury was Prime Minister (see page 87). Balfour's attempt to damp down the agitation by referring the matter to a Royal Commission was regarded by the workers as a mere shelving of the problem. There was still another grievance of organized labour and also of the Liberals—the employment of CHINESE COOLIES as "indentured labourers" in the mines of the Transvaal. Some objected to the exploitation of the Chinese, whose condition they described as "slavery" (Winston Churchill later described this as a "terminological inexactitude") and also to the danger of undercutting white men's wages, although in fact white men seldom performed such work in the mines. The Education Act, the Taff Vale Case and Chinese Labour question all tended to weaken the Government's position in the country as by-election after by-election showed, nor was the *Entente Cordiale* with France at first very popular. But it was almost certainly Chamberlain's proposals for tariff reform that brought upon the Government the greatest public disfavour.

Tariff Reform Campaign. Britain's trade prosperity, which was at its height in the 1850's and 1860's, had followed the coming of free trade in the 1840's, and to many it seemed that the prosperity was due to the free trade. But with the onset of the "Great Depression" in the 1870's, the decline of agriculture and the increased industrial competition from other countries like the U.S.A. and Germany, there was a growing demand for tariffs or import duties to protect the British farmer and industrialist. At first it had been hoped that Britain's example in establishing free trade would be followed by the rest of the world, but instead tariff walls seemed to be raised rather than lowered. As Chamberlain's own connection was with the iron and steel industry, he was not blind to the serious threat of German competition. Articles of all sizes and purposes, stamped "Made in Germany", were flooding British markets. But when Chamberlain brought the question of protection or free trade to the forefront of politics in 1903, it was primarily because of his disappointment with the Colonial Conference of 1902. The Dominion premiers had declined his suggestion of an Imperial Council and had proposed a system of mutual imperial preference in trade. This meant lowering tariffs on each other's goods, but while the Dominions all had tariffs, Britain had none to lower. There was still another reason for Chamberlain's adoption of tariff reform. Before the South African War he had been advocating one of the reform proposals of his old Radical days—old age pensions; but the expenditure entailed by the war had been considerable and the pensions for old folks had to be postponed. Now it seemed to him that tariffs would help to provide the revenue that could be devoted to pensions. Chamberlain found that his Cabinet colleagues were not all happy about his proposals, and he resigned his post as Colonial Secretary to promote his tariff reform campaign. This he conducted in his old rampaging, electioneering style; FREE TRADE VERSUS PROTECTION became the political question of the day. There was one obvious disadvantage, however, from an electioneering point of view: as the colonies exported mainly food to Britain, foreign food would have to be taxed at the ports to enable the Dominions to have preference. The cry of "the poor man's bread" was raised by the Liberal Free Traders and in the end proved decisive. The chief effect of Chamberlain's tariff reform campaign was thus to harm the Unionist party and unite the Liberals. Not only did the Unionists lose the next election in 1906 and two succeeding elections but they were labelled thereafter as the party that wanted to deprive the working man of his cheap food. Chamberlain's own active career came to an end in 1906 when he had a stroke. One of his sons, Sir Austen Chamberlain, was a Conservative Foreign Secretary from 1924 to 1929 and another, Neville Chamberlain, was Prime Minister from 1937 to 1940, although neither possessed the political stature of his father. It is doubtful now whether the introduction of tariffs would have been either as beneficial as the Protectionists made out or as ruinous as the Free Traders forecast. During the First World War, the Liberal Chancellor of the Exchequer, Reginald McKenna, mainly in order to raise more revenue, introduced 33⅓ per cent duties on imported motor-cars, clocks, watches, musical instruments, cinema films. These became known as "safeguarding duties" as they gave protection to British industries, specially vulnerable to foreign competition. McKenna's Duties were continued (with a short break) until 1932 when a flat-rate tariff of 10 per cent on all imports was imposed.

Liberals in Power. Balfour resigned office at the end of 1905 in the middle of an international crisis over Morocco. Sir Henry Campbell-Bannerman, the Liberal leader, took over from Balfour, and the ensuing election in January 1906 was marked by a Liberal landslide, the new Government having a record majority of 356. CAMPBELL-BANNERMAN, or C.-B. as he was called, was another Scotsman, son of a Lord Provost of Glasgow, and an astute politician. He was not destined to hold office for long, as he resigned through ill-health in 1908, dying of cancer a few weeks later. When he became Prime Minister, he immediately put a stop to the immigration of Chinese labourers to South Africa and granted self-government to the Transvaal, where his criticism of the "methods of barbarism" in the Boer concentration camps was gratefully remembered. His action was in the true Gladstonian spirit but it angered the Unionists, who denounced it as "criminal levity" and accused the Liberals of "throwing away the fruits of victory". Balfour himself described it as "the most reckless experiment ever tried in the development of a great colonial policy"; but it proved a successful experiment and the Liberal action was justified in 1914 when the former enemies of Britain, Generals Botha and Smuts, rallied to their side and in a brief campaign overran German colonies in Africa. Campbell-Bannerman was followed in 1908 by H. H. ASQUITH, a brilliant lawyer and debater, who had done much to demolish Chamberlain's arguments for tariff reform, following Chamberlain in a campaign round the country. As Asquith was cautious and deliberate in his approach to a problem, he was in time ridiculed for the answer he gave to many questions in Parliament —"Wait and see". There were many able men in this Liberal cabinet: two of them, Lloyd George and Winston Churchill, later became Prime Ministers, while Sir Edward Grey is reckoned one of Britain's greatest foreign secretaries and R. B. Haldane won great praise for his reforms at the War Office. John Burns, the engineer and trade unionist who had helped to organize the Great Dock Strike, was appointed President of the Board of Trade, the first working-man to attain cabinet rank, although he lost popularity with his former Labour colleagues by accepting the post. In many respects—social reforms, political reforms, army and navy reforms, foreign affairs—this Liberal period must be considered one of the most important in the history of modern Britain. It lasted from the end of 1905 to the middle of the First World War, although there were two elections in 1910, which diminished the Liberal majority.

Lloyd George, the Welsh Radical. During this period, the dominant personality in the Liberal cabinet was David Lloyd George. He was to achieve even greater fame as a wartime Prime Minister but it was in the heated controversies of the Edwardian era that he won renown as the ablest debater and politician on the Liberal side. He was born in 1863 in Manchester, the son of a Welsh schoolmaster, a brilliant man who died at an early age; and he was brought up in a Welsh village, Llanystumdwy, by his uncle, Richard Lloyd, the local shoemaker. Richard Lloyd, a man of intelligence and strong convictions, was a lay preacher in the local Baptist chapel and the young Lloyd George grew up in a typical Welsh Nonconformist household, in which religion and politics were constantly discussed. One of Lloyd George's early memories was of the evictions of those tenants in the parish who had voted Liberal in the 1868 election, the last to be contested at the hustings. Gladstone attracted his early admiration; when only seventeen years of age, he and his brother walked fourteen miles in an evening merely to obtain a copy of a newspaper with a full report of one of Gladstone's Midlothian campaign speeches. Lloyd George trained for the law but before he became a fully-qualified solicitor, he acquired valuable experience as a journalist by writing on political topics for a local newspaper and also as a speaker (in Welsh and English) on temperance questions and on religion. He was returned at a by-election in 1890 as Liberal M.P. for Caernarvon Burghs, a seat he was to hold for fifty-five years. He soon became prominent in the House of Commons as a vigorous critic of the Conservative Government and of his own party; for a time he and a few other Welsh M.P.s acted almost as an independent party. Lloyd George was for many years the main advocate of Welsh Church Disestablishment, a burning question in Wales, where the Nonconformists of all sects united in criticizing the exaction of tithes from them to support what they regarded as an alien church. Home Rule for Wales and Scotland was considered by most Welsh and Scottish Liberals to be the inevitable consequence of a grant of self-government to Ireland; but it was not until 1914 that an Irish Home Rule Bill finally became law and Welsh and Scottish hopes perished in the wreck of the First World War. Lloyd George won national prominence as a critic of the Government, particularly of Chamberlain, during the South African War (1899–1902) and was labelled "pro-Boer". Some of his speeches provoked violent demonstrations and riots; at Birmingham, the home town of Chamberlain, he only escaped from an irate crowd by adopting the disguise of a policeman. In the Liberal Government of Campbell-Bannerman, he was President of the Board of Trade and when Asquith became Prime Minister, he became Chancellor of the Exchequer. In the long-protracted quarrel over the "People's Budget" of 1909 and the Parliament Bill, he was the leading Government speaker both in the parliamentary debates and in mass meetings, at which his eloquence could rouse his audience to a pitch of enthusiasm, seldom equalled in this country. He was genuinely keen on social reform and warned his fellow-Liberals in 1906: "If at the end of an average term of office it were found that a Liberal Parliament had done nothing to cope seriously with the social conditions of the people, to remove the national degradation of the slums and widespread poverty and destitution in a land glittering with wealth, that they had not provided an honourable sustenance for deserving old age, . . . then would a real cry arise in this land for a new party and many of us here in this room would join in that cry". Lloyd George was a man of great personal charm and, although possessed of a biting tongue, he was on friendly terms with many of his political rivals. His persuasive powers and dynamic energy helped him greatly in the office of Prime Minister which he held from 1916 to 1922, and he is regarded as one of the greatest war ministers Britain has had.

Social Reforms—(a) Children and Criminals. The social reforms of the three Liberal ministries of the period 1906–14 fall into five main groups, affecting (1) children, (2) criminals, (3) relief of poverty and sickness, (4) trade unions, (5) the redistribution of wealth effected by the Budget of 1909 and later Budgets. Among the first reforms carried through by the Liberals were those dealing with children. The nation had been shocked by the revelation that in the South African War 40 per cent of the recruits were rejected as unfit (the figures in some areas like Glasgow and Liverpool were as high as 60 per cent). As the low standard of nutrition was blamed, a PROVISION OF MEALS ACT (1906) was passed to provide school-meals for necessitous children. Little advantage was taken of the Act in some areas, however, only 200,000 children benefiting by it in 1911. In 1907 MEDICAL INSPECTION IN SCHOOLS became compulsory, thus making it possible to start treatment earlier for many ailments; and in the same year the first infant welfare centre was established at St. Pancras, London. Other Acts of 1907–8 dealt with juvenile delinquents. The PROBATION SYSTEM was introduced and provision was made for reclaiming young offenders by detaining them for two or three years in institutions, called Borstals after the prison at Borstal, Kent, where the system was first tried out. Another Act, the "CHILDREN'S CHARTER", laid down that children should not be sent to prison, that their identity should not be made public in the press, and that probation should be tried first if possible. Formerly, imprisonment was regarded as punishment for wrongdoing, and prison life was made as degrading and as unpleasant as possible. An attempt at improvement of prison life was made by Winston Churchill, the young Home Secretary, who, mindful of his own prison experiences during the South African War, tried to organize libraries and entertainments for prisoners. Following the famous case of Adolf Beck, who was twice wrongly convicted through mistaken identification, the CRIMINAL APPEAL ACT was passed, allowing appeals to bring up not only points of law but also points of fact.

Social Reforms—(b) Poor, Sick and Unemployed. The

shadow of the workhouse that darkened the retirement of old people in England was removed by the OLD AGE PENSIONS ACT (1908), by which those over seventy were to receive 5s. a week (a married couple 7s. 6d.). In Scotland, where outdoor relief had always been the rule, the pension was equally welcome. The sums were deliberately left small, so that (it was argued) the virtues of thrift and self-help would be encouraged. Two other Acts went some way to lessening the sting of unemployment, poverty and disease among the working-classes. The NATIONAL HEALTH INSURANCE ACT (1911) made possible medical attention for all manual workers and for non-manual workers earning less than £160 a year. They were compelled to pay 4d. a week out of their wages, the employer paying another 3d. and the state 2d. —thus providing Lloyd George with his slogan, "9d. for 4d.". There was an outcry at first from employers and doctors; meetings were held in the Albert Hall and elsewhere by indignant individuals who declared that they would not "lick Lloyd George's stamps". But the scheme took on and many a doctor was in time pleased to have a "panel" of National Health patients as the core of his practice. An UNEMPLOYMENT INSURANCE ACT followed, providing unemployment benefit for the workless in certain industries such as the building trades and shipbuilding where unemployment risks were highest; the provision was extended to other trades in 1920. Labour exchanges had been set up before then to render easy the finding of jobs for un-employed. Similar insurance schemes had been in existence in other countries, in Germany, New Zealand and Australia but in the United States they were not introduced until many years later. Workers outside the scope of the Factory Acts were protected by the SWEATED INDUSTRIES ACT (1909), which laid down minimum wage-rates in industries where the work was done on contract, generally in the workers' homes, and the SHOPS ACT (1911), which among other benefits introduced the weekly half-holiday for shop-assistants. All these reforms of the Lib-erals helped to ameliorate social conditions to a certain extent but they did not succeed in removing working-class discontent. Despite these reforms and the Trade Union Acts of 1906 and 1913, passed to reverse the Taff Vale Decision and the Osborne Judgement, industrial agitation became more intense before 1914, when strikes (especially unofficial or "wildcat" strikes, as they are dubbed) became more numerous and violent.

People's Budget. In the first two years of the Liberal ministry (1906–8), the House of Lords rejected three Education Bills and a Licensing Bill. That the Liberal Government, with the largest majority in the House of Commons of the period, should have its Bills turned down was, according to the Liberals, due to party prejudice. Balfour, the former Unionist Prime Minister, had tactlessly remarked after the 1906 election that his party, although defeated, "would continue to control the destinies of the Empire". When a Unionist M.P. referred to the House of Lords as "the watchdog of the constitution", Lloyd George was quick to point out that it was rather "Mr. Balfour's poodle". For centuries, no budget had been rejected by the House of Lords until 1909, but the budget which Lloyd George opened in that year contained such drastic increases in taxation that the House of Lords took the unprecedented step of rejecting it. What were the reasons for the new taxation? It was, said Lloyd George, "a war budget for raising money to wage implacable war against poverty and squalidness". But it was also a war budget in a different sense, as greatly increased expenditure was required to build eight new Dreadnought battleships in order to keep Britain ahead of her rival, Germany. (The number of Dreadnoughts required had originally been four, then raised to six, and finally pushed up by Unionist agitation to eight—"We want eight, and we won't wait.") Among the novel features of this budget which aroused the ire of the Unionist opposition were:—(1) a graduated income-tax, rising as high as 1s. 9d. on the largest incomes, with allowances for children and a distinction between earned and unearned incomes; (2) an extra tax aimed at the rich, a supertax on all incomes over £5,000 per annum; (3) a heavy tax on licensed premises and increased duties on tobacco and alcohol, raising the price of a bottle of whisky from 3s. 6d. to 3s. 9d.; (4) taxes on motor-cars (in the form of licences) and on petrol, to be paid into a Road Fund for repair and improvement of the roads; (5) a tax on mining royalties, to be paid into a separate Miners' Welfare Fund; (6) land taxes (which were found difficult to impose), one on "unearned increment" in land values, another on the value of undeveloped land and minerals, and a third on the expiry of leases. That Lloyd George was using the budget as a means of redistributing wealth for social rather than for fiscal reasons or by "soaking the rich", as it was more bluntly put, was clear to all; hence the name—the "People's Budget", and hence the howl of execration with which it was greeted by the Unionists. The Liberals must have realized that the Lords were almost bound to reject the budget; when that happened they welcomed the "show-down" with the Lords as the issue was one over which the Liberals could count on the support of the bulk of the people. The upshot was a struggle in which each side used the bitterest invective in attacking the other. It was after seventy parliamentary days of hard debating and many all-night sittings that the budget, introduced in April, was passed by the Commons in November, only to be thrown out as anticipated, by the Lords. Lloyd George defended the budget by attacking the peers in speeches at Limehouse and Newcastle that earned him the name of "robber gull" from Lord Lansdowne, the Unionist leader in the House of Lords, and caused the Duke of Beaufort, in hunting parlance, to express the wish to see "Lloyd George and

Winston Churchill in the middle of twenty couple of dog hounds". The budget was not to be passed till the Liberals decided to challenge the powers of the Lords. The passing of a Parliament Bill to curtail the veto of the House of Lords was to take another year and involve the country in two elections. After the first election in January 1910, when the Liberals were returned to power with a reduced majority, the Lords passed the budget without a division on the eve of the introduction of the 1910 budget. Since then, by one of the clauses in the Parliament Act of 1911, no budget is ever debated in the House of Lords. One result of the Parliament Bill controversy, which proved long and acrimonious, was that some disgruntled Unionists started a movement with the slogan, B. M. G. ("Balfour Must Go") to oust Balfour from the leadership of the party. His successor, a Glasgow business-man named Bonar Law, was more forthright than Balfour; and in his first speech as leader castigated the Liberals as "artful dodgers, dealers in trickery and cant, and Gadarene swine rushing down a steep place".

Irish Home Rule. The passage of the Irish Home Rule Bill just before the outbreak of war showed at least one of the main disadvantages of a delay of two years in settling the fate of a Bill as a result of the new Parliament Act of 1911. The more protracted the passage of the Bill, the deeper the passions aroused. The bitterness of the Parliament Bill struggle had been due in some measure to the Unionists' knowledge that an Irish Home Rule Bill would be an inevitable consequence. The Home Rule Bill, introduced in 1912, was resisted tooth and nail by the Unionists in the House of Commons and was only passed in 1914 by reason of the Parliament Act. It provided for an Irish Parliament but reserved certain matters (defence, foreign affairs, finance and trade) for the Imperial Parliament. According to Asquith, it was to be followed by similar Bills for Scotland and Wales. The Unionist tactics were not merely to delay the Bill, but to arouse such opposition in Ulster that the Government would be forced to drop it. Lord Randolph Churchill's slogan—"Ulster will fight and Ulster will be right"—was revived. In a speech before 10,000 people at a fête held in July 1912 at Blenheim

Palace, Bonar Law gave a pledge ("the Blenheim pledge")—
"I can imagine no length of resistance to which Ulster will go
which I shall not be ready to support". SIR EDWARD CARSON,
a Protestant barrister from Dublin who became leader of the
Protestant Orangemen in Ulster, declared he was "ready to
break any and every law in the cause". Their encouragement was
hardly needed in Ulster where the Orangemen feared that "Home
Rule means Rome Rule". Belfast and the north generally were
also more industrialized than the south, and it was felt that it was
unfair to place the go-ahead, economically advanced minority
in the north at the mercy of the backward south. Whether the
Unionists were more actuated by sympathy for Ulster or by a
desire to bring down the Liberal Government is open to question.
In 1922, Carson, the Orangemen's leader of 1911–14, declared
in his maiden speech in the House of Lords that he and all
Irishmen had been "mere puppets in the political game that was to
get the Conservative party into power". That Unionists, who
would normally deplore any suggestion of resisting authority,
should take up such an intransigent attitude is evidence of the
rancour of party politics at the time. In 1911, the Orangemen
formed for themselves a force, over 80,000 strong, known as the
ULSTER VOLUNTEERS, the first private army in the British Isles
for over a century. A "Solemn League and Covenant", on the
model of the Scottish covenant of the seventeenth century, was
drawn up in 1912 and signed by over 200,000 Ulstermen, who
pledged themselves to "use all means which may be found
necessary to defeat the present conspiracy to set up a Home Rule
Parliament in Ireland". Asquith's tendency to "wait and see"
did not help matters: he should have had "Carson's Army"
declared illegal and suppressed it or he should have introduced
at an early stage some measure of separate rule for Ulster or done
both. But he was against both ideas and, as a result of his policy
of drift, the situation became worse. Another volunteer army
was formed in 1913, this time in the south of Ireland, where there
was growing support for the movement of SINN FEIN ("We
Ourselves"), which advocated that the question of their Government should be solved by the Irish people themselves. The

Ireland

problem of how to deal with any armed resistance in Ulster, when the Home Rule Bill would become law, was troubling Asquith, who hoped if possible to avoid the use of force. Things were not made easier by the Unionist leader Bonar Law, who made an appeal to Army officers, then generally considered to be Unionist, to disobey orders when the time came. It was in the spring of 1914, when troops were about to be moved north to Ulster to protect Army depots from possible raids, that there occurred the CURRAGH INCIDENT. The officers at the Curragh camp near Dublin were given to understand by the War Office that, in the event of trouble in the north, those who had homes in Ulster would be allowed to "disappear" for the time being and that any others who had conscientious objections to serving in Ulster should resign from the Army. It was learned that one brigadier-general and 57 (out of 70) officers in a cavalry brigade would accept dismissal if ordered to Ulster. The Secretary for War was blamed for allowing this to happen and resigned, while there was a public outcry against what was called an "officers' mutiny". A month later, 30,000 rifles and three million rounds of ammunition, purchased in Germany, were landed at Larne in Ulster. Another gun-running attempt at Howth near Dublin was successful despite the intervention of police and soldiers, but three men were killed. A proposal to allow the northern counties to vote for their exclusion from the terms of the Home Rule Act was turned down by the Irish Nationalists, who were against the partition of their country. Just then, the attention of the whole population of the British Isles was diverted to the trouble in Europe that led the nations into the First World War. Irish Home Rule was postponed with tragic consequences for Ireland. It is difficult today to realize the extent to which Ireland and Britain were roused in 1914 when civil war seemed imminent. Neither Asquith's Government nor the Unionist opposition can be considered as free from blame for the parts they played; and almost certainly the Germans were persuaded by the trouble over Ireland that Britain would not fight in 1914 and therefore took the decisive step of invading Belgium.

End of an Era. There are other important aspects of Edwardian politics which are dealt with elsewhere in other parts of this book—the creation of the Triple Entente by the signing of treaties with France and Russia, the far-reaching changes in the Army and Navy, the parliamentary struggle over the House of Lords, the violent agitation of the suffragette movement, and the growth in power of the trade unions and the new labour movement. It would seem to us nowadays to have been a most troubled period; yet to the post-war generation, faced with different but to them even greater problems, the period "before the war" appeared as halcyon days that would never return. The reign of Edward's successor, George V, before the war broke out is usually considered as part of the Edwardian era; and certainly the years 1901–14 had more in common with Victorian times than with the period immediately succeeding the war. The great increase in prices resulting from the war of 1914–18 made pre-war prices seem fantastically cheap; and to the troubled generation of the 1920's life in Edwardian times in general seemed much easier and more leisurely. But it is always easy to exalt the glories of the past and forget the darker side of things. Among new developments of the period which were to be of importance in the post-war era were the Boy Scout and Girl Guide movements, the advent of the electric trains and trams, the motor-car (for the well-to-do) and the char-à-banc (for others), the aeroplane races staged by the *Daily Mail,* the use of wireless on ships (although it did not prevent the *Titanic* disaster of 1912). The war of 1914–18 was to bring even more changes and to mark a cleavage from the days of the Edwardian era.

SOURCE EXTRACT

Lloyd George at Limehouse, July 30, 1909

They are now protesting against paying their fair share of the taxation of the land and they are doing so by saying:— "You are burdening the community; you are putting burdens upon the people which they cannot bear". Ah, they are not thinking of themselves. (*Laughter.*) Noble souls! (*Laughter.*) It is not the great dukes that they are feeling for, it is the market gardener (*laughter*), it is the builder, and it was, until recently, the smallholder. (*Hear, hear.*) In every debate in the House of Commons they said: "We are not worrying for ourselves. We can afford it with our broad acres: but just think of the little man who has only got a few acres;" and we were so very impressed with this tearful appeal that at last we said, "We will leave him out." (*Cheers.*) And I almost expected to see Mr. Pretyman jump over the table and say— "Fall on my neck and embrace me". (*Loud laughter.*) Instead of that he stiffened up, his face wreathed with anger, and he said, "The Budget is more unjust than ever". (*Laughter and cheers.*) Oh! No! We are placing the burdens on the broad shoulders. (*Cheers.*) Why should I put burdens on the people? I am one of the children of the people. (*Loud and prolonged cheering and a voice, "Bravo David, stand by the people and they will stand by you".*) I was brought up amongst them. I know their trials; and God forbid that I should add one grain of trouble to the anxiety which they bear with such patience and fortitude. (*Cheers.*) When the Prime Minister did me the honour of inviting me to take charge of the National Exchequer (*A voice, "He knew what he was about", and laughter*) at a time of great difficulty, I made up my mind in framing the Budget which was in front of me that at any rate no cupboard should be bared (*Loud cheers*), no lot would be harder to bear. (*Cheers.*) By that test I challenge them to judge the Budget. (*Loud long-continued cheers, during which the right hon. gentleman resumed his seat.*) Afterwards the audience rose and sang. *For he's a jolly good fellow.*   The Times.

EXERCISES

1. What differences are there between the modern style of reporting political speeches and the Edwardian style as illustrated in the above extract?
2. Explain: "Boss of Cowes", Lloyd George's stamps, National Health panel, "Mr. Balfour's poodle", Dreadnought, Blenheim Pledge, Ulster Volunteers, Sinn Fein, B.M.G.
3. Identify the authors of the following and explain where necessary:
   (*a*) "Going boating with his grocer."
   (*b*) "A terminological inexactitude."
   (*c*) "The most reckless experiment ever tried in the development of a great colonial policy."
   (*d*) "We want eight and we won't wait."
   (*e*) "I would like to see Lloyd George and Winston Churchill in the middle of twenty couple of dog hounds."

(f) "Artful dodgers, dealers in trickery and cant, and Gadarene swine rushing down a steep place."

(g) "I can imagine no length of resistance to which Ulster will go which I shall not be ready to support."

4. Write brief notes on: Education Act of 1902; Chinese Labour in Transvaal; Old Age Pensions Act; National Health Insurance Act; Sir Edward Carson.

5. Write notes on: A. J. Balfour; Sir Henry Campbell-Bannerman; Tariff Reform; People's Budget; Third Irish Home Rule Bill.

6. Give an account of the career of Joseph Chamberlain and estimate his importance in the history of his period. (See other chapters also.)

7. What was done in the period 1906–14 to improve the conditions of the British working-classes?

8. What claims has the Liberal ministry of 1906–14 to be considered one of the most important in the history of modern Britain? (Refer to other chapters for foreign affairs and constitutional reforms.)

CHAPTER VII

THE END OF ISOLATION

Salisbury. The Marquess of Salisbury, whose name is usually associated with the foreign policy of isolation, never became popular like "Dizzy" or "the People's William" or "Radical Joe", but he is regarded as one of Britain's greatest prime ministers. One of the famous family of Cecil, Salisbury was an aristocrat who viewed with disdain the extension of the franchise to the working-classes and criticized Disraeli's Reform Act of 1867 as a "political betrayal". He conducted the diplomatic negotiations before the Congress of Berlin in 1878 and accompanied Beaconsfield to Berlin as Foreign Secretary, becoming leader of the Conservative party after Beaconsfield's death in 1881. Salisbury was appointed Prime Minister for three terms—in 1885, from

1886 to 1892, and from 1895 to 1902. For most of his time as Prime Minister he also held the office of Foreign Secretary and his main interest was in foreign and imperial affairs. He had no desire to emulate Disraeli's "spirited foreign policy" and his period in office has been called one of "intelligent inaction". Although Britain's situation during his terms of office has often been described as "splendid isolation", he criticized those who claimed that Britain could remain aloof from the Continent. "We are a part of the community of Europe and we must do our duty as such," he said in 1888. When he became Prime Minister for the third time in 1895, Europe was already divided into two camps—the TRIPLE ALLIANCE, which comprised Germany, Austria-Hungary and Italy and the FRANCO–RUSSIAN ALLIANCE formed in 1894. Britain had an agreement with Italy since 1888; but it was restricted to the sphere of the Mediterranean and was designed to protect British and Italian interests there against Russia and France. Apart from that agreement, Britain stood in isolation from the European alliances in 1895 and remained so until after Salisbury retired in 1902. There were some disadvantages in this policy of isolation. In 1895, a dispute arose with the U.S.A. over the frontier between British Guiana and Venezuela. When Salisbury refused the American demand to submit the matter to arbitration, the President of the U.S.A., Cleveland, adopted a belligerent attitude and insisted on the dispute going to arbitration. Neither side really wanted war but the reaction in Europe to the Jameson Raid on the Transvaal revealed Britain as a country without a friend so that Salisbury eventually decided to accept arbitration over the Venezuela dispute. It was early in 1896, during the period of the Jameson Raid and the Venezuela crisis, that a Canadian M.P. referred admiringly to the "great Mother Empire" standing "splendidly isolated" in Europe. Many people in Britain were proud of this "splendid isolation"; and the phrase has commonly been regarded as applicable to Salisbury's policy from 1895 to 1902. It must be remembered, of course, that Salisbury regarded Britain as "part of the community of Europe" and was willing to act in co-operation with the other Powers, as he did over the question of Crete in 1897–8

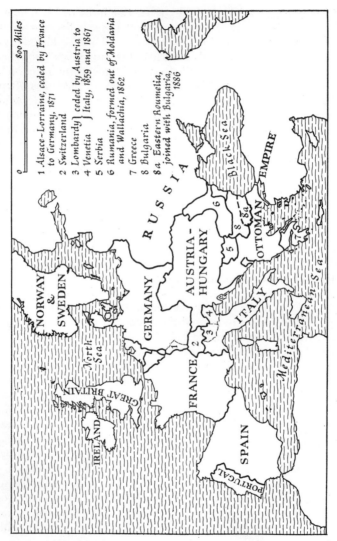

1 Alsace-Lorraine, ceded by France to Germany, 1871
2 Switzerland
3 Lombardy } ceded by Austria to Italy, 1859 and 1867
4 Venetia
5 Serbia
6 Rumania, formed out of Moldavia and Wallachia, 1862
7 Greece
8 Bulgaria
8a. Eastern Roumelia, joined with Bulgaria, 1886

Europe, 1886

and in connection with the Boxer Rebellion in China in 1900. He was, however, unwilling to enter into any definite alliance that would commit Britain to a war. He felt that the entry of Britain into a war should depend on the attitude of the British public. When asked by the Belgians what action Britain would take if Belgium were invaded by the French or Germans, Salisbury would not give a definite commitment despite the Treaty of London (1839), by which Britain and other Powers had guaranteed Belgian independence and neutrality. As time went on, Salisbury tended to become more aloof from his colleagues, spending much of his time at the Cecil family seat, Hatfield, where he relaxed by riding in dignified fashion round the park on a tricycle or engaging in experiments in his private laboratory. He resigned office in 1902, a year after Queen Victoria's death, and died a year later. The resignation of Salisbury, the last peer to be Prime Minister, marked the end of the Victorian age, the end of the epoch of active empire-building and the end of isolation in foreign affairs.

End of Isolation. What were the reasons for Britain's isolation at the end of the nineteenth century? In the first place, Salisbury and his colleagues felt that British imperial interests in Africa, Asia and America were more important than entanglements in European affairs. Secondly, the British were proud of their great empire and strong navy, which made them the leading world power, while their island position gave them added security. Thirdly, Britain had quarrels of one kind or another with the other European Powers—Russia (over the Far East), France (over the Sudan), Germany (over South Africa)—and also with the U.S.A (over Venezuela). These disputes and the world-wide criticism levelled at Britain over the South African question made some of the leading statesmen in Britain, like Chamberlain, realize the disadvantages of the policy of isolation. Salisbury himself saw that if Britain was to remain without an ally, it would be wise to cut down the risks of war by settling any disputes with other Powers. The trouble that flared up between Britain and France over the Sudan and led to the Fashoda Incident in 1898 prevented an approach to the French. In the same year, an offer to settle differences was made to Russia but her advances in China (where Britain controlled 80 per cent of the trade) prevented a settlement. Britain next turned to Germany, to which Chamberlain made approaches in 1898, 1899 and again in 1901 without any success; but neither Salisbury nor the rest of the Cabinet were keen on any alliance with Germany that would involve them in a European war, while Germany was not prepared to quarrel with her neighbour, Russia, for the sake of Britain. The friendship shown by the Germans to the Boers of the Transvaal, the start of a German naval programme that challenged Britain's supremacy at sea, and the Kaiser's visits to Turkey and other parts of the Near East, all tended to make the British regard Germany with suspicion. At the time, Germany did not consider it at all likely that Britain could possibly end her isolation by joining France or Russia because of their disputes overseas. It was the fear of Russia's expansionist policy in the Far East (she had seized Port Arthur in 1898 and occupied Manchuria in 1900) that decided Britain to abandon her diplomatic isolation by the ANGLO-JAPANESE ALLIANCE of 1902, but it was limited to preventing further Russian expansion and only bound Britain to remain neutral in the event of a Russo-Japanese War. This was followed soon afterwards by an Anglo-French rapprochement. Delcassé, French Foreign Minister from 1898 to 1905, was promoting a policy of isolating Germany, and ever since the Fashoda Incident of 1898 he had hoped for an agreement which would allow France a free hand in Morocco. He had already persuaded Italy to sign a secret agreement recognizing French rights in Morocco in return for French recognition of Italian rights in Tripoli. Visits by Edward VII to Paris and by the French President to London helped the atmosphere of the Anglo-French negotiations, which were concluded by the signing of the ANGLO-FRENCH TREATY of 1904. By this treaty, Britain and France recognized each other's rights in Egypt and Morocco respectively, and settled long-standing disputes over Siam, the New Hebrides, while France renounced the fishing rights on the "French Shore" of Newfoundland in return for some territories in West Africa. The British Foreign Secretary, Lord Lansdowne, insisted that it was only a settlement of colonial differences, but the French hoped that it would lead to a closer understanding in European affairs. The friendly relationship that developed from 1904 on was called the *Entente Cordiale*. The RUSSO-JAPANESE WAR of 1904–5, in which Russia was decisively defeated by the Japanese, might have been expected to disrupt

F	Formosa	K	Korea	M	Manchuria

1	Harbin	4	Port Arthur	7	Nanking
2	Vladivostok	5	Peking	8	Shanghai
3	Tokyo	6	Lhasa	9	Hong Kong

Expansion of Japan before 1941

the *Entente*, as the British were allies of the Japanese and the French were allies of the Russians. When on Trafalgar Day (of all days) in 1904 the Russian fleet, passing through the North Sea on its way out to the Far East, fired on an English fishing-vessel on the Dogger Bank, in mistake for a Japanese torpedo-boat, many thought war was imminent. But, partly through the good offices of Delcassé, the Russians offered a full apology and compensation. At the same time, the rapid expansion of the German navy alarmed the British, who started upon a vast programme of naval construction (involving a new type of battleship, the *Dreadnought*) and began to look upon Germany as the French had done for years—a probable enemy in a future war. It was, however, the Moroccan crisis of 1905–6 that did most to strengthen the ties between Britain and France.

First Moroccan Crisis, 1905–6. The Germans, who had for long eyed with jealousy the British and French advances in Africa and elsewhere overseas, were determined to secure "a place in the sun". Their chief interest in Morocco, where they feared that the French would soon attempt to gain control, was to obtain an Atlantic base for the new German navy at Casablanca. France's ally, Russia, was powerless following her humiliating defeat at the hands of the Japanese, and it seemed to Germany a good time to intervene. The German Kaiser, WILLIAM II, landed from his yacht at Tangier and in a speech there assured the Sultan of Morocco that he recognized the independence of Morocco. At the same time a demand was made for an international conference to settle the question of Morocco. Delcassé wanted to refuse this request but he received little support from his own colleagues or from the British Government and was compelled to resign. His resignation, following on the Kaiser's provocative speech, made Britain and other nations realize the dangers of allowing Germany to win a diplomatic triumph. An international conference of twelve Powers (including the U.S.A.) was summoned to meet at ALGEÇIRAS, a Spanish town near Gibraltar, and sat for several months in 1906. France received staunch support from Britain, Russia, Italy and Spain. Although Germany's demand for an "open door" in Morocco for all nations was conceded, the control of the police and the traffic in arms was put in the hands of the French and Spanish, which was equivalent to a diplomatic victory for France. On the suggestion of the new British Foreign Secretary, Sir Edward Grey, the military and naval experts of Britain and France actually met during the conference to discuss combined action. France was thus more assured of British support against Germany on a future occasion as a result of the Moroccan crisis. In the following year, the British and the Russians patched up their quarrels in Asia: Russia recognized Afghanistan, Tibet and Southern Persia as British spheres of influence, while Britain recognized Turkestan and Northern Persia as Russian spheres of influence. Although the ANGLO-RUSSIAN TREATY of 1907 was also, like the Anglo-French Treaty of 1904, restricted to colonial questions, it helped to create a TRIPLE ENTENTE in Europe that was bound to be considered as a counterpoise to the Triple Alliance. Britain's isolation had ended despite herself.

Pre-War Crises. The Moroccan crisis of 1905–6 was the first of a series of crises, at three-year intervals, in 1908, 1911 and 1914, that led to the outbreak of the First World War. In 1908, when the "Young Turks'" rebellion forced the old, despotic Sultan, Abdul Hamid, to grant a constitution, AUSTRIA-HUNGARY seized the opportunity to annex Bosnia and Herzegovina, the territories which had been under military occupation by them since the Treaty of Berlin (1878). Strong protests were made against this annexation by the Turks, the Serbs and the Russians. The Turks were in the midst of a constitutional crisis and were powerless to act. The Serbs already hated Austria-Hungary because many of their fellow-Slavs, the Croats and Slovenes, were subjects of the Austrian Empire, in addition to the newly-annexed Bosnians, and the Serbs also felt that this annexation thwarted their hopes of an outlet to the sea. (The present Yugoslavia, which means "Land of the Southern Slavs", is made up of Serbs, Croats, Slovenes, Bosnians and others.) Russia, the "Big Brother" of the Slav states in the Balkans, was only too willing to accede to the Serbian request for help and was angered by this Austrian advance into the Balkans, which they regarded as their sphere of interest. Austria-Hungary refused the demands of Russia, Britain and France for another conference (similar to that of Algeçiras) and was supported by Germany. The Kaiser, William II, had himself been very annoyed by the Austrian action, as he regarded the Turks as under his special protection because of his interest in the Berlin–Baghdad railway project.

Later, however, he boasted of standing by his ally like "a knight in shining armour". For a time war seemed likely but the Russians, not yet recovered from their defeat of 1904–5, had to climb down. Both the Russians and the Serbs were furious at this rebuff and

The dotted lines show the old boundaries before the Balkan Wars, 1912–'13

A-H *Austria-Hungary*	M *Montenegro*
S *Serbia*	Al *Albania*
R *Rumania*	G *Greece*
B *Bulgaria*	TA *Turkey in Asia*
Bo *Bosnia*	TE *Turkey in Europe*

1 *Sarajevo*   2 *Belgrade*   3 *Sofia*   4 *Constantinople*

Balkan Boundaries, 1913

vowed not to let it happen again. The next crisis occurred again in Morocco. When the French in 1911 sent troops to occupy Fez, the capital of Morocco, which had been the scene of a rising, the Germans sent to the port of Agadir, on the Moroccan coast, the gunboat *Panther*, followed by the cruiser *Berlin*. This "Panther-spring" seemed to bring Europe once more to the brink of war. But the French premier was willing to appease Germany, which was prepared to allow the French a free hand in Morocco in return for certain French territories in West Africa. Britain's attitude in this AGADIR CRISIS was announced in a speech at a Mansion House banquet by the Chancellor of the Exchequer, Lloyd George, who warned Germany that in the event of war Britain would take the side of France. The Germans were all the more impressed by this warning as up to this time Lloyd George had been regarded as one of the pacifist section of the Liberal Cabinet. Following the Agadir crisis, the British War Office and Admiralty began to prepare plans for landing an expeditionary force in France, in the event of a Franco-German war. Further conversations took place between the defence ministries of the two countries, the French undertaking to take over the naval defence of the Mediterranean in time of war and thereby free the British Navy for other duties. War was drawing nearer with each crisis, and the *Entente Cordiale* was being transformed into an alliance. The years 1912 and 1913 saw further trouble in the Balkans. Taking advantage of the weakened condition of the Ottoman Empire, the states of Serbia, Bulgaria, Greece and Montenegro, encouraged by Russia, formed themselves into a Balkan League to drive the Turks out of Europe. The FIRST BALKAN WAR (1912) was over in six weeks, but quarrels arose over the division of the spoils. Serbia was keen to acquire Albania for an outlet to the sea but Austria-Hungary stepped in to prevent this. In the SECOND BALKAN WAR (1913) Bulgaria was defeated by her former allies, the Serbs and Greeks, assisted by the Rumanians; but although the Serbs acquired more territory they still nursed their grievances against Austria-Hungary. It was out of this Austro-Serbian distrust and hatred that there developed the crisis that brought about the First World War of 1914–18.

Outbreak of War. The heir to the Austrian Empire, the ARCHDUKE FRANZ FERDINAND, and his wife were visiting Sarajevo, a town in Bosnia on June 28, 1914 (a day which

happened to be the National Day of all the Serbian peoples)
when they were assassinated. The assassin was a nineteen-year-
old student, Gavrilo Prinzip, one of three "Young Bosnians" who
had received arms for the purpose from a secret society, the
"Black Hand", organized by Serbian army officers. Europe was
aghast at the shocking crime but few realized that it would lead
to war in little over a month. Trouble in the Balkans seemed to be
almost an annual fever, so that people became used to it. Austria-
Hungary, thirsting for revenge and feeling that the time had
come to settle once and for all with her troublesome neighbour,
delivered an ultimatum to Serbia which no self-respecting
government could accept. In other words, the Austrians hoped
for a short, sharp war that would finish off Serbia as an independent state. The German Kaiser, who had gone off on his summer
cruise of the Norwegian fjords, had previously assured the
Austrians of German support in any action they would take.
Serbia actually accepted eight of the ten demands in the Austrian
ultimatum, offering to submit the remaining two points to
international arbitration. The Austrians refused to accept
Serbia's reply and declared war. By now the whole of Europe
was alarmed. Russia was determined to protect Serbia and
obviously the war might spread further. The Russian and the
Austrian War Offices were afraid of being caught napping and
ordered mobilization while their foreign ministers were still
arguing. William II, the German Kaiser, and Nicholas II, the
Russian Tsar, were cousins and they interchanged telegrams
(written in English, signed "Willy" and "Nicky", and later
called the "Willy-Nicky" correspondence), in which they expressed their hopes that peace could be preserved. Both Germany
and France however declared their intentions of supporting their
allies, Austria-Hungary and Russia, in the event of war. The
British, apart from sending their fleets to their war-stations,
hoped to the end for a peaceful settlement, so that it was not
clear to the Germans whether Britain would remain neutral or
not. To the Germans and other continental nations it seemed also
that Britain was too engrossed in its own internal quarrel over
Ireland to be able to intervene in Europe. Some members of the

British Cabinet were against entering the war and, when war was declared, actually resigned. Neither they nor the majority of the Cabinet knew to what extent Britain had been committed to helping France by the military and naval conversations of 1912. What decided the British Cabinet finally was the German decision to invade France through Belgium. As recently as 1908, the official British Foreign Office view had been doubtful about intervening to protect Belgium from a German invasion. But since then the bonds between Britain and France had been strengthened by successive crises; and the wave of public sympathy for "gallant little Belgium" left the Government with little room for doubt. An ultimatum was sent to Germany, asking her to withdraw her troops from Belgian soil in accordance with the TREATY OF LONDON (1839), which guaranteed Belgian independence and neutrality. It was this treaty which the German Chancellor is said to have referred to as "a scrap of paper", words which only went further to arouse anger against the "Huns", as some British newspapers were quick to label the Germans. The British ultimatum was ignored and Britain was at war by August 4th, 1914. On the previous evening, Sir Edward Grey, the Foreign Secretary, looking out over London and seeing the lights go up in the city streets, had said: "The lamps are going out all over Europe: we shall not see them lit again in our lifetime." The first great European war for a century was about to begin.

Causes of War. We have traced the events leading up to the outbreak of war, seeing how one crisis led to another. What were the causes of the war? Which power was chiefly responsible? Many books have been written, discussing questions of "war guilt", and almost half a century later it is still not possible to answer them satisfactorily. Underlying other causes of war were the various rivalries in Europe. The oldest of all was that between France and Germany: when Alsace and Lorraine had been taken from France by Germany in 1871, Gladstone forecast that it would in time lead to a European war, and the idea of a war of revenge had never been far from the minds of the French military leaders. The other main rivalry was that between Britain and Germany over various issues—colonies, trade and the building of the German fleet. Colonies and trade alone would not have provoked a war, but the competitive building of warships made each country sensitive about its prestige and suspicious of the other's intentions. Why, the Germans asked, should they not have a navy as big as Britain's? The question seems reasonable enough, but to the British at that time the only purpose behind the German naval programme was to challenge and defeat Britain. The rivalry in the Balkans between Austria-

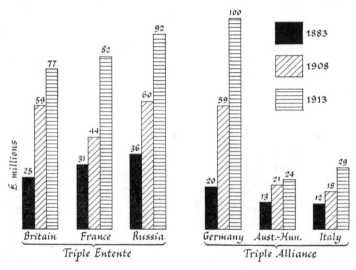

Armaments Expenditure, 1883–1913

Hungary and Serbia over Bosnia-Herzegovina actually provoked the assassination that led to war. But a large-scale war would not have ensued were it not for the added rivalry between Austria-Hungary and Russia, which since its withdrawal from the Far East after 1905 had turned with renewed interest to the Near East and was only too ready to support the Serbs against the Austrians. Another main cause of the war was without doubt the division of Europe into two armed camps—the

Triple Alliance of Germany, Austria-Hungary and Italy (which had however safeguarded itself against a war with Britain and France) and the Triple Entente of France, Russia and Britain, which gradually evolved as crisis succeeded crisis into what was tantamount to an alliance. These alliances had been formed to preserve peace but by 1914 their existence was more likely to transform a local conflict into a large-scale war. The armaments race between the Powers was another important cause of the war. *Si vis pacem para bellum* (If you wish peace, prepare for war) was an old Latin tag. But when both sides prepared for war feverishly, piled up weapons, built larger and larger warships, extended the periods of compulsory military service, there was a tendency for the men in charge of the defences of a country to become "trigger-happy" when international tension developed. In the earlier crises, one or other side was not prepared for war and gave way—Germany in 1905–6, Russia in 1908, Germany in 1911 —but the countries which had suffered rebuffs were left smarting and all the more determined not to be so treated again. National pride, coupled with suspicions of other Powers, led to declarations of "honour" and "vital interests" (such as in Lloyd George's speech in 1911 during the Agadir Crisis) that made it difficult to climb down; considerations of national pride and prestige thus played their part in driving the peoples of Europe along the road to war. In 1914 the various Powers reckoned that they were ready to fight; and, having built up large land and sea forces for war, they accepted the drift towards war as inevitable. Which of the countries concerned was chiefly responsible for the outbreak of war has been argued over and over again— Serbia, Austria-Hungary, Russia, Germany, France. Even Britain has been blamed—for not making her intentions clear early enough. It was in order to avoid a similar accusation that in 1939, when war threatened between Germany and Poland, the British Government issued a guarantee to Poland to protect her in case of invasion; but it still did not prevent the outbreak of war.

British Army and Navy Reforms. It was in the decade before the First World War that Britain carried through sweeping changes in the Army and Navy that helped her to weather the storms of 1914–18. The Liberals, who were in power, had in Gladstone's first ministry (1868–74) made many reforms in the Army; but weaknesses had been revealed in the South African War (1899–1902) and no one could claim that the British Army was at all comparable with the continental armies. The Secretary for War from 1905 to 1914 was R. B. HALDANE, an outstanding lawyer and an able administrator. His knowledge of Germany, where he had studied philosophy, had made him aware of Britain's military weakness; and although he remained an opponent of the compulsory military service on which Germany based her strength, he introduced other changes that derived from Germany. He copied their idea of a permanent GENERAL STAFF, which would plan operations; hitherto planning had been left until a war started. The old Volunteers and yeomanry regiments were replaced by a well-organized TERRITORIAL ARMY ("the Terriers"), intended primarily for home defence but destined to play its part in France soon after the outbreak of war. For such an eventuality, plans were made for an EXPEDITIONARY FORCE, to be ready to leave the country at short notice. In schools and universities, OFFICERS' TRAINING CORPS were started to provide a "pool" of officers for war time. Haldane received little credit for his work when war started as his well-known sympathy for Germany led to a public outcry which forced him to resign; but one of the first actions of Sir Douglas Haig, the British Commander-in-Chief when the war ended in 1918, was to send to Haldane a letter of thanks for his work that had made victory possible. The changes in the Navy were begun in Balfour's Ministry by ADMIRAL SIR JOHN FISHER, First Sea Lord of the Admiralty from 1904 to 1910, and were continued by WINSTON CHURCHILL, First Lord of the Admiralty from 1911 to 1914. A great expansion in the Navy was considered necesssary by the rapidly-growing sea-power of the Germans, which the British strongly resented as they felt it could be aimed only at the British Empire. The *Entente Cordiale* made it possible from 1904 for the Mediterranean fleet to be reduced in strength and a larger Atlantic fleet to be based on Gibraltar, while new naval bases,

THE FATEFUL YEAR, 1914. *Top:* Carson (centre) reviews the Ulster Volunteers (see p. 125). *Bottom:* The arrest of Prinzip, the assassin of the Archduke Ferdinand at Sarajevo (see p. 140). One of the most dramatic photos ever taken.

THE FIRST WORLD WAR, 1914–18. Lloyd George (with hat raised) visits British trenches in France. (*Inset*) The famous Kitchener recruiting poster of 1914 (see p. 160).

more useful for dealing with Germany, were constructed at Rosyth on the Firth of Forth, Invergordon on the Cromarty Firth and even in the distant Orkneys at Scapa Flow. To meet the threat created by Germany's new warships, larger and faster capital ships were built, the prototype battleship, the *Dreadnought*, launched in 1906 and ready for service the same year, displacing 18,000 tons instead of the 16,000 tons of existing battleships, attaining with the new turbine engines 21 instead of 18 knots, and carrying ten instead of four 12-inch guns. The *Dreadnought* made all existing battleships obsolete; the Germans found themselves compelled not only to build equally large ships but also to widen the Kiel Canal from the North Sea to the Baltic, a task not completed till 1914. As Britain desired her navy to be twice the size of any other navy, there was a keen competition in naval construction as a result. "Jacky" Fisher was a firm believer in efficiency and was ruthless in carrying out changes, many of which ran counter to the traditional conservatism of the Navy. He was all for scrapping obsolete ships and replacing them with new ships; he was aware of the importance of torpedoes, submarines, electrical and hydraulic equipment; and he broke with tradition by placing engineer officers on the same rank as the rest and making all undergo some engineering and scientific training. It was in Churchill's first few years at the Admiralty that the revolutionary change from coal to oil fuel was made; this enabled ships to achieve higher speeds and longer cruising ranges and it also increased Britain's interests in the Middle East, where the ANGLO-PERSIAN OIL COMPANY started to work the Persian oilfields under a concession from the Persian Government. Bigger ships with bigger guns were designed and built, the calibres being increased from 12-inch to $13\frac{1}{2}$-inch, then to 15-inch and even 16-inch. As a result of all this planning, Britain was able to face her commitments in 1914 and survive the dangers of the next four years.

Hague Peace Conferences. It must not be thought that all Europe was engaged in an armaments race before 1914. Two disarmament conferences were held at the Hague, and every year from 1901 until 1914 a Peace Prize was awarded out of funds

10

left by the Swedish engineer and inventor, Alfred Nobel (see page 102). The FIRST HAGUE CONFERENCE was summoned in 1899 at the request of the Russian Tsar, Nicholas II, to consider "a possible reduction of the excessive armaments which weigh upon all nations". Twenty-seven nations sent delegates but the Tsar's proposals for limiting armaments were coolly received. Some cynics suggested that his motives were not entirely humanitarian, as he was also interested in reducing the burden of taxation in Russia. There was some support for the suggestion that arbitration between states should take the place of war, but Germany and Britain, among others, were strongly against it. Salisbury bluntly declared that no Power would allow questions of honour and vital interest to be decided by a third party. The Tsar had to be content with a vague and general statement that armaments should be reduced to "a level that would permit the increased well-being of humanity". Certain conventions were however signed about—(1) the laws and customs of war on land; (2) the extension of the GENEVA CONVENTION of 1864 for the protection of wounded and sick to cover war at sea; (3) the prohibition for five years of aerial bombing, the use of poison-gas and "dum-dum" (soft-nosed, expanding) bullets. Britain, which along with Portugal voted against the ban on "dum-dum" bullets, was criticized for using this type of bullet, considered inhumane, in the fighting on the north-west Indian frontier. A COURT OF ARBITRATION, with permanent judges and officials, was set up but arbitration was not made compulsory. Although it was used for settling the Anglo-Russion dispute over the Dogger Bank episode of 1904, it did not prevent the many crises before 1914. A SECOND HAGUE CONFERENCE was called in 1904 at the instance of Theodore Roosevelt, the President of the United States, but because of the Russo-Japanese War it did not meet till 1907. It tried to extend the principle of arbitration by making it compulsory except in questions of honour and vital interest, the very questions that lead to war. The British proposals for restricting armaments to their existing levels did not appeal to other nations, particularly the Germans, who suspected that the British, having just greatly strengthened their fleet, desired to keep other fleets permanently at a lower level. The Hague Conference also adopted the new rules of war laid down by the Second Geneva Convention of 1906, relating to the treatment of wounded, prisoners of war, etc. The international RED CROSS organization, founded by the Swiss banker, Jean Henri Dunant in 1864 at Geneva, did much in the two world wars towards ensuring that the Geneva and Hague Conventions were observed. There was thus a strong feeling against war despite the extensive preparations being made by the various governments. One of the most widely-read books of the pre-war period was *The Great Illusion* (1910), written by an English pacifist, NORMAN ANGELL, who set out to show the economic futility of war, as neither side could ever recoup the vast expenditure before and during the war. Still, although *The Great Illusion* was translated into many languages and received much acclaim in the last twelve months before war broke out, it did not prevent the nations arming themselves. Germany increased its peace-time military strength by 170,000 men, Russia increased the period of compulsory military service by six months, while France extended her period of service from two to three years. The governments of Europe went on drifting into war, much to the alarm of Colonel House, who toured Europe on a peace mission for the American President Woodrow Wilson in May 1914 and who reported: "The situation is extraordinary; it is militarism run stark mad. . . . It only needs a spark to set the whole thing off." The assassination of the Austrian Archduke in June 1914 provided the spark.

SOURCE EXTRACT

The Tragedy of Sarajevo

On the afternoon of June 28 the Archduke and his wife entered Sarajevo. The murder had been carefully planned. At least seven assassins had taken their stations at various points upon the probable royal route. Every one of the three bridges had its two or three murderers in waiting. The first attempt was made on the way to the Town Hall; but the bomb slid off the back of the motor-car and its explosion only wounded two officers of the suite. After the miscreant had been caught, the Archduke proceeded to the Town Hall and received in a mood of natural indignation the addresses of welcome. The police precautions had seemed to be lax, and the owner of the motor-car, Count Harrach, who sat beside the driver, accosted the Governor, Potiorek: "Has not Your Excellency arranged for a military guard to protect his Imperial Highness?" to which the Governor replied impatiently, "Do you think Sarajevo is full of assassins, Count Harrach?" The Archduke proposed to alter the return route and to visit the Hospital to which the wounded officers had been taken. . . . Count Harrach wished to stand on the left footboard to protect the Archduke. "Don't make a fool of yourself," said Franz Ferdinand.

The four cars moved out into the dense crowds in the original order, but at a faster pace. At the entrance to Franz Joseph Street the crowd, uncontrolled by the police, made a lane and by a fatal error the cars turned back to the original route. Governor Potiorek, who sat facing the Royal Visitors, told the chauffeur that he had taken the wrong turning. The car slowed down and came close to the right-hand pavement. A young man fired two shots at three yards' range. The archduke continued to sit upright; his wife sank upon his breast. A few murmured words passed between them. For a few moments no one realized that they had been shot. But the Archduke had been pierced through the artery of his neck and the Duchess through the abdomen. The assassin, a Serbian student named Prinzip, was seized by the crowd. He died in prison, and a monument erected in recent years by his fellow-countrymen records his infamy, and their own. Such was the tragedy of Sarajevo.

Winston S. Churchill: World Crisis.

EXERCISES

1. What were the reasons for the plot to assassinate the Archduke of Austria in June 1914?
2. Explain: French Shore, "a place in the sun", "Panther-spring", *Entente Cordiale,* Willy-Nicky correspondence, Black Hand, the Terriers, dum-dum bullets.
3. Identify the authors of the following and explain where necessary:
   (a) "A knight in shining armour."
   (b) "A scrap of paper."
   (c) "The lamps are going out all over Europe; we shall not see them lit again in our lifetime."

(d) "The situation is extraordinary: it is militarism run stark mad."

4. Write short notes on: Venezuela dispute; Dogger Bank Incident; Balkan Wars of 1912–13; Haldane's army reforms; Fisher's navy reforms.

5. Write notes on: Anglo-Japanese Treaty, 1902; Anglo-French Treaty, 1904; Agadir Crisis; Hague Peace Conferences.

6. Why is British foreign policy at the end of the nineteenth century described as one of "splendid isolation"?

7. Describe and account for the change in British foreign policy at the beginning of the twentieth century.

8. What were the reasons for the outbreak of war in 1914?

9. Why did Britain go to war in 1914?

10. Which of the powers do you consider chiefly responsible for the outbreak of war in 1914?

CHAPTER VIII

THE FIRST WORLD WAR

Opening Campaign. As far back as 1905, the chief of the German General Staff, Count von Schlieffen, had worked out a plan of campaign for the war on two fronts which Germany would have to fight one day against France and Russia. Schlieffen died in 1913 but it was his plan that the German War Office put into operation in 1914. This SCHLIEFFEN PLAN was to mass the German strength on the Western Front against the French and to depend mainly on their Austrian allies on the Eastern Front against the Russians, who were expected to be slow in mobilizing. On the Western Front, most of the German forces were to be concentrated in the north so that the armies on the right wing would carry a heavier punch. As a result, the German overall superiority on the Western Front was to be 3 to 2 and in the north 3 to 1. (The Germans were also superior in fire-power, particularly in heavy artillery and in machine-guns, sixteen of the latter to an infantry battalion in comparison with only two in a British or French battalion.) By invading neutral Belgium, it was hoped to drive through to Paris in a few weeks and near there to inflict on the enveloped French forces an overwhelming defeat or "Cannae" (as the German military experts called it, after the famous victory of Hannibal over the Romans). The Schlieffen Plan was watered down by his successors, although his dying words had been: "See you make the right wing strong!" In addition, the Germans met with greater opposition than they had anticipated. Belgium did not provide the walk-over the Germans had expected when they crossed the Belgian frontier on August 4th. The Belgian fortified town, Liége, put up a gallant defence, delaying the Germans for a few days, and it was August 19th before the Belgian army retreated from Brussels. The British Expeditionary Force under Sir John French also went into action against the Germans in Belgium at Mons, where they were compelled, like the French army at Namur, to retreat. The B.E.F. (as it was soon to be familarly known) numbered only 80,000; the Kaiser was supposed to have called it "a contemptible little army" and the name "Old Contemptibles" was proudly adopted by the survivors later. The French War Office had known of the Schlieffen Plan for years but had worked out no real counter-plan, preferring instead to pursue an aggressive policy by advancing into Lorraine, the territory they had lost in 1870. In Lorraine, however, only a few miles were gained at the expense of over 300,000 casualties. By the end of August the Germans had driven through Belgium and Northern France and the armies of the right wing were swinging round to the south to within twenty miles of Paris. Fortunately for the French, the German advance had not been so effective as had been anticipated; originally they had hoped to envelop Paris and instead they were still well to the east. The French attack on Lorraine, unsuccessful as it was, and the quicker mobilization of the Russians had caused the German High Command to send troops to both these fronts so that the punch of the right-wing armies was weakened. Their timetable had been upset also by the unexpected resistance of the Belgians and the B.E.F.

Battle of the Marne. The French Government in alarm left
Paris for Bordeaux at the beginning of September and the defence
of the city was undertaken by General Galliéni. It was then that
the French commander, Joffre, decided on a counter-attack from
the line of the river Marne. This BATTLE OF THE MARNE
(September 6th–9th) is considered one of the decisive battles

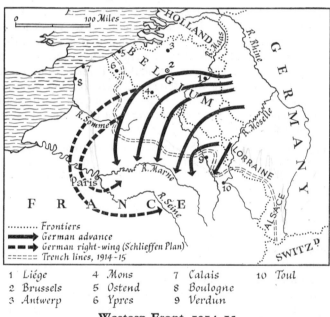

1 Liége	4 Mons	7 Calais	10 Toul
2 Brussels	5 Ostend	8 Boulogne	
3 Antwerp	6 Ypres	9 Verdun	

Western Front, 1914–15

of the world. The B.E.F. played an important part by driving
through the gap between two German armies; and the French
general, Foch, later to be Commander-in-Chief of the allied
armies, managed to hold off all German assaults on his thinly
held part of the line. The defenders of Paris were able to launch
a powerful attack on the German flank, General Galliéni
rushing reinforcements to the battle front from the railway

stations in taxis ("the taxis of the Marne"). The Germans began to withdraw and in their retreat tried to seize the Channel ports to make communications more difficult for the British. This "RACE TO THE SEA" involved attempts by both armies to outflank one another. The B.E.F. managed to hold on to the coastline, the toughest fighting taking place in October and November just inside the Belgian frontier at YPRES ("Wypers" to the British soldier). After the battle of Yypres half of the B.E.F. were casualties. The British were to hold on to Ypres for the rest of the war and it has been estimated that more British blood has been shed there than anywhere else in the world. By the end of 1914, the German, French and British armies on the Western Front had dug themselves in, their trenches protected by sandbags and barbed wire, stretching from the North Sea to the Alps. The lines of the trenches were not to be altered greatly in the next four years.

Trench Warfare. In the South African War, trenches had been dug occasionally to protect soldiers from rifle or gun fire; but these had been shallow and were occupied only for brief periods. In the First World War, there were often two or three or more lines of trenches, some with dug-outs, the living and sleeping quarters of soldiers for weeks on end. In front of the trenches were sandbags and barbed-wire entanglements; and across the "No-man's-land" was a similar system of German trenches. Why did warfare become static in 1914? The answer is to be found in the much greater fire-power made possible by improved rifles, machine-guns and high-explosive shells. The increased fire-power and the elaborate trench systems meant that to be on the defensive was easier than to be on the offensive. It was later reckoned that a break-through required a numerical superiority of 3 to 1. Naturally, the generals on both sides at first pinned their hopes on achieving such a superiority; and as the British had the smallest army of all, the attention of the War Office was concentrated mainly on recruiting more soldiers. Civilians like Lloyd George, the Chancellor of the Exchequer, emphasized the importance of matching the German fire-power. The War Office, proud of the British regular soldier's skill with his Lee-Enfield rifle, was reluctantly compelled to increase the number of machine-guns from two to sixteen by the end of 1915 and eventually to eighty for a battalion. There were, in all, three proposed methods for breaking the deadlock in the west:— (1) the massing of men and artillery at a decisive point; (2) the use of a new weapon to effect surprise and achieve local superiority, as the Germans tried with poison-gas and the British with tanks; (3) the opening of a new front that would enable the western allies to link up with Russia and by supplying her with armaments utilize her vast man-power—the theory of the "Easteners", prominent among them Winston Churchill, as against that of the "Westerners", mainly the generals at the War Office.

The Eastern Front. The Germans had expected that the Russian "steam-roller", although powerful when in motion, would take some time to get going. Partly because of mobilizing before the other countries and partly because of a desire to ease the German pressure on the Western Front, the Russian armies made an advance into East Prussia. As a result of this Russian advance, the Germans, who were thinking of the battle in the west as already won, transferred two army corps from Belgium to East Prussia at the end of August. The quick advance of the Russian "steam-roller" may thus have saved France, for the Schlieffen Plan was never fully executed as a result. Under the veteran general, Hindenburg, and his able assistant, Ludendorff, the two main Russian armies were tackled separately and defeated at the battles of TANNENBERG and the Masurian Lakes in August and September 1914. Tannenberg was a name well known in German history because of a resounding defeat suffered by the Teutonic Knights in 1410 at the hands of the Poles and Lithuanians. The overwhelming victory there in 1914 (90,000 Russian prisoners were taken) gained for HINDENBURG a reputation as the best German general of the war, and it helped him to become President of Germany in 1925. His partner, Ludendorff, was later to win fame on the Western Front; but little credit was given to the man who may be said to have won the battle for the generals, Colonel Hoffman, the Chief of Staff. The Russians had more success against the Austrians, who actually suffered reverses

1 Danzig   3 Masurian Lakes   5 Vienna   7 Belgrade
2 Tannenberg   4 Warsaw   6 Budapest

Eastern Front, 1914–15

both on their Russian and Serbian fronts. The "ram-shackle Empire" of Austria-Hungary (as Lloyd George called it) included many subjects of Slavonic race, such as Czechs, Slovaks, Croats, Bosnians, Poles, whose sympathy was with the Serbs and Russians. Some of them tried to get out of the army by cutting off their trigger-fingers or by laming themselves until self-mutilation was made a capital offence. Others deserted at the first opportunity so that a large Czechoslovak Legion had been formed in Russia by 1917. As in the west, so in the east a stalemate ensued after the first campaigns and the armies settled down to trench warfare, which lasted more or less till the collapse of the Russians in 1917. On the first Christmas Day of the war, there was much fraternization on the Eastern Front: soldiers visited the enemy trenches with presents of food and drink and sang carols together. There was less of this fraternization on the Western Front, although at one place in the frontline some British soldiers produced a football for a friendly match with their German enemies. Once the generals and War Offices got to hear of this fraternization, strict orders were sent to officers to ensure that their men would not engage in such irregular conduct again. The fraternization was all the more remarkable as in every country newspaper propaganda made the enemy out to be a barbarian and a savage. By 1915, the Germans were faced with the two-front war Bismarck had always tried to avoid; but the prospect of victory still attracted the German generals.

Dardanelles Campaign. Before the end of 1914, Winston Churchill's active and fertile mind was turning to other schemes for using Britain's command of the seas in outflanking the enemy instead of "chewing barbed wire" in Flanders. When Turkey came into the war on Germany's side at the end of October 1914, the problem of maintaining contact with Russia became acute. Churchill's proposal that Britain should force a passage through the Straits of the Dardanelles and the Sea of Marmora and take Constantinople had much to recommend it. It would provide a route for the supply of arms to Russia, permit military aid to be given to the Serbs, rally other Balkan states to the allied cause, and safeguard the vital waterway of the Suez Canal. Brilliantly conceived, the plan was badly executed. A combined naval and military operation late in 1914 or early in 1915 would in all probability have been successful. But neither the War Office nor the Admiralty was keen to risk losing their treasured resources: soldiers were needed on the Western Front and a lost battleship took years to replace. The element of surprise, so important in an operation of this kind, was lost by a preliminary bombardment of the Turkish forts at the mouth of the Dardanelles in November 1914. The Turks started to improve their defences with German help. As the War Office was adamant in refusing to provide troops, an attempt to force the Straits by shelling the forts on either side into silence was begun in February 1915 by the Navy. Bad weather and minefields in the Straits made operations slow and difficult; and when three warships were sunk by mines on March 18th, the naval attack was called off. The Turkish land forces had thus been given plenty of warning. They dug themselves in and increased their forces from two to six divisions. When at last Kitchener and the War Office decided that they could afford to send a military force, the time for an easy passage to Constantinople had gone. Landings were made on the GALLIPOLI peninsula near Cape Helles on April 25th by troops sent from Egypt, mainly soldiers of the Australian and New Zealand Army Corps (A.N.Z.A.C.). Deeds of dauntless courage and incredible endurance were performed, and April 25th is still observed as ANZAC DAY. But most of the effort and sacrifice of the "Anzacs" was rendered valueless by bungling. The landings were made or attempted on the tip of the peninsula instead of at the narrow waist; almost every beach was an inferno for the disembarking troops except one, where no attempt was made to push on and capture the peninsula. There was an absence of leadership and a lack of co-ordination on the British side that allowed the German general, LIMAN VON SANDERS, in control of the Turkish defences to hold the peninsula, except for the small "bridgeheads" on the beaches. In August another landing was made further up the peninsula at Suvla Bay, but again there was only a half-hearted attempt to push across the peninsula. The hero of the Turkish defence was a young officer, KEMAL, who later became dictator of Turkey. The British forces retained their meagre footholds till the end of 1915 when they were at last evacuated to Egypt. The Dardanelles disaster left the Russians still without an easy line of supply. The Balkan states, Greece and Rumania, still delayed coming into the war on the allied side, while Bulgaria chose to join Germany and Serbia's resistance collapsed. The Turks were able, after the Dardanelles failure, to deal more easily with the British troops in MESO-POTAMIA, where General Townshend with nearly 10,000 British and Indian troops was compelled to surrender at Kut-el-Amara in 1916. At home, the press had been howling for a scapegoat for a long time. Lord Fisher, the First Sea Lord, who had been

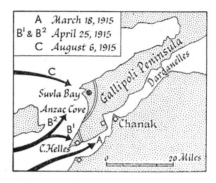

Dardanelles Campaign, 1915

against the scheme from the start, resigned and Churchill, the First Lord of the Admiralty, was forced to do so also. His brilliant project had miscarried because of a lack of co-opera-tion in the War Office and Admiralty and blunders on the spot; but his impetuosity had led to the naval attacks, which did little more than provide a warning to the Turks. By the beginning of 1916, Churchill had left the House of Commons and was in the trenches in Flanders as lieutenant-colonel of the Royal Scots Fusiliers.

Big Offensives. The alternative strategy of massing troops and guns and hurling them against the enemy trenches was tried throughout the war by both sides. Many generals seemed unable to think of any strategy other than that whereby they could achieve sufficient superiority on what they considered the

decisive Western Front. What happened instead was a WAR OF
ATTRITION, the wearing down of each other's strength. Various
offensives in 1915 did little more than push in a "salient" (a
bulge in the line) or create another. The German offensive
in the spring of 1916 on the Western Front was actually planned
as a campaign of attrition. By forcing the French to defend
VERDUN, one of the frontier forts which had played an important
part in French history and which they were unwilling to abandon
without a terrific struggle, the Germans hoped "to hammer the
French on the anvil of Verdun". The French held on for months
and, under the command of General Pétain, they checked the
German advance. The French fought grimly as men do in defence
of their native soil: "Ils ne passeront pas" ("They shall not
pass") became the cry. In the end, Verdun remained in French
hands; both German and French armies had been bled white
(almost 600,000 casualties between the two armies) but still the
war went on. In July 1916, a combined British and French
offensive was launched on the Somme in the north of France.
After a heavy artillery barrage lasting seven days to pound the
enemy out of existence, the British troops poured across in waves
towards the German trenches only to be mown down by machine-
gun fire. At the end of the first day, there were 60,000 casualties
(the heaviest loss suffered by the British Army in one day in
all its history) for a gain of only a mile or so of shell-shattered
German territory. The BATTLE OF THE SOMME went on until
November 1916, by which time over 600,000 casualties (killed,
wounded and prisoners) had been sustained on each side.
The flower of Kitchener's volunteer army was destroyed in these
months, and Britain henceforth had to rely on the soldiers
raised by conscription, which started early in 1916. (In all,
six million served in the British forces and over half of these
were volunteers.) The Germans had borne heavy losses since
1914 and at the end of 1916, according to Ludendorff, by this
time their leading general, they "had been fought to a standstill
and were utterly worn out". Their Austrian allies had suffered
heavy losses at the hands of the Russians in 1916; and the
Russian success had brought Rumania into the war at last.

Germany managed, despite the Battle of the Somme, to send troops to the Eastern Front to hold up the Russians and administer a knock-out blow to Rumania. But although Rumania's wheat and oil supplies were welcome, the fighting of 1916 had left Germany exhausted. The Germans were thus forced to remain on the defensive in 1917, but both British and French generals were able to conceive plans for breaking the enemy line, although they met with no more success than in 1916. The French offensive under NIVELLE was rendered ineffective by the Germans, who had learned of the French plans and withdrew from their trenches to the well-fortified Hindenburg line. The force of the initial barrage and the first attacks of the infantry were thus wasted but Nivelle continued for three more weeks, the French troops suffering such heavy casualties that many of the survivors refused to fight. Pétain, the hero of Verdun, was appointed to take over the command and restore its morale. During the period when the French were getting over their mutinies, the British Commander-in-Chief, Sir Douglas Haig, undertook an offensive to break through Flanders to the Belgian coast. Little heed was paid to warnings about the boggy ground to be covered in the initial stage, as the High Command was confident of a rapid advance which would take the troops clear of the swamp in forty-eight hours. Their hopes were not justified. The preliminary barrage destroyed the elaborate system of drainage in the reclaimed swamp of PASSCHENDAELE (north-west of Ypres), the rain came down day after day, and forty-eight days later British forces were still in the mud of Passchendaele. It was on drier ground at Cambrai that in November, towards the end of the battle at Passchendaele, tanks made their first really successful break-through. After four ghastly months, four miles of ground had been gained at a cost of over 400,000 casualties. Sir Douglas Haig was strongly criticized at the time and later. In his defence, it has been said that the offensive helped to relieve the pressure on the French after the period of the mutinies; but the French never asked for an offensive of such a kind or in such a place. Haig's Chief of Staff, who visited the battlefield for the first time when it was all over, wept when he saw the mud. "Good

God! Did we really send men to fight in that?" he said. It was because of the fearful carnage at Verdun, the Somme and Passchendaele that, in the Second World War, the leading figure on the British side, Winston Churchill, was always careful to avoid such costly offensives.

Home Front. The first year of the war produced a burst of patriotic enthusiasm that sent men and youths flocking to the recruiting offices to volunteer in answer to the call of LORD KITCHENER, the victor of Omdurman, now Secretary for War. Probably one of the most effective posters of all time was that showing Kitchener with pointing finger and, underneath, "Your Country Needs YOU". The suffragettes dropped their agitation for the franchise; and women began to take men's places in offices, in factories, on the farms. By reason of their large contribution to the war effort, there was little difficulty at the end of the war in having a Bill passed, enfranchizing women over thirty years, those under that age being still considered unfit to vote. Ireland and Irish Home Rule were dead issues in Britain; and it was a song about Ireland, the popular hit of 1914, that was sung everywhere for the first few years of the war and particularly by the soldiers marching, at home or in Flanders:

"It's a long way to Tipperary, it's a long way to go;
　It's a long way to Tipperary, to the sweetest girl I know.
Goodbye, Piccadilly! Farewell, Leicester Square!
　It's a long, long way to Tipperary, but my heart's right there!"

The Sinn Feiners were, however, still anti-British; and at Easter 1916 some of the more extreme Volunteers, who had possessed arms since 1913, staged a rebellion that fizzled out after a weekend, the ringleaders being executed with one or two exceptions. Among those executed after this EASTER RISING was Sir Roger Casement, who had been in Germany since 1914, and had landed near Tralee on the Kerry coast from a U-boat, and one of the few spared was a young mathematics lecturer, Eamon De Valera, who was lucky enough to have been born in New York and who became, long after the war, Prime Minister of

Ireland. As 1915 wore on, the nation's mood became more tense. People began to realize that Kitchener's prophecy that the war would last at least three years was nearer the truth than anyone had thought in 1914. Big offensives in the west brought news of a little ground gained and long casualty lists, published regularly in the newspapers. There were charges of grave shortages of shells and the Chancellor of the Exchequer, Lloyd George, took over the newly created Ministry of Munitions. His dynamic energy and his ability to cut "red tape" soon brought results. Trade unions did not like his introduction of "diluted" labour on jobs hitherto regarded as reserved for skilled tradesmen; but high wages helped to keep things quiet and when strikes broke out, as they did in Glasgow, the ringleaders were imprisoned or deported to Ireland. (Some of these, like David (later Lord) Kirkwood, became prominent figures in the Labour party after the war.) The Dardanelles failure brought about a change in the Government in May 1915, when the Unionists joined the Liberals in a COALITION GOVERNMENT with Asquith still as Prime Minister. In December 1916 Asquith was replaced by LLOYD GEORGE after a series of intrigues and a press campaign which boosted the "Welsh Wizard" as a man to "do it now" and derided Asquith for his tendency to "wait and see". One of Lloyd George's first steps was to set up a small WAR CABINET of ministers relieved of the burden of looking after departments and devoting themselves to the conduct of the war. Among those who joined this War Cabinet was General Smuts, the former Boer general who along with General Botha had conducted a successful campaign against the Germans in their colonies of South-west Africa and East Africa. Lloyd George's leadership saw Britain through the dark days of 1917, the year of heavy U-boat sinkings, food shortages and rationing, air raids, and ever-mounting casualties in Flanders. Air raids had become more frequent as the war went on. At first the Germans used zeppelins, fourteen of them reaching London in September 1916; but later they turned to aeroplanes, the worst raid occurring on July 6th, 1917, when several German planes appeared over London at 10 a.m. and bombed the city for an hour, hundreds of people being

11

killed. Lloyd George had many difficulties to contend with as Prime Minister—quarrels with the War Office and the generals over the strategy on the Western Front and with the Admiralty over the introduction of the convoy system as a protection against U-boats. Although head of the Coalition, many of his own party, including the leader, Asquith, were his bitter enemies. But he throve on opposition and emerged triumphant in 1918 as "the man who won the war".

Naval Warfare. Despite Germany's efforts to build a large navy, she was still well behind Britain in 1914, mainly because of the work of Admiral Fisher. The main German High Seas Fleet remained in its harbours for most of the first two years of the war; but the possibility that it might emerge kept the British fleets waiting in their new Scottish harbours—at Scapa Flow in the Orkneys, in the Cromarty Firth and in the Firth of Forth. Each side was afraid of what the other could do, the Germans

War at Sea, 1914

of the British Grand Fleet, which was stronger than their own High Seas Fleet, and the British of the German torpedo-boat and U-boat (short for *Unterseeboot* or submarine). Three British cruisers were sunk by one U-boat off the east coast of England in one day in September 1914 and another cruiser a few days later. When the alarm was raised at Scapa Flow that a U-boat periscope had been sighted, Admiral Jellicoe took the Grand

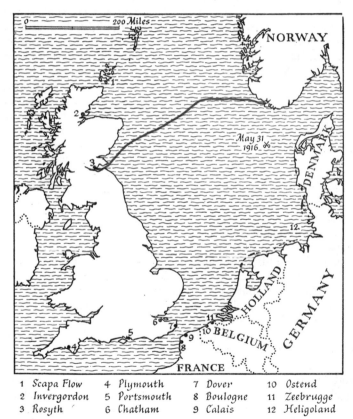

1	Scapa Flow	4	Plymouth	7	Dover	10	Ostend
2	Invergordon	5	Portsmouth	8	Boulogne	11	Zeebrugge
3	Rosyth	6	Chatham	9	Calais	12	Heligoland

North Sea, 1914–18

Fleet for safety to the west of Scotland till he was ordered back to the east coast. During the first year of the war, the British gradually disposed of various units of the German navy that were scattered about the oceans of the world. One German squadron, commanded by Admiral Graf von Spee, did much damage off the South American coast and sank all but one of a British squadron off Cape Coronel on the Pacific coast of South America in November 1914. A month later, however, the tables were turned and all but one of Graf von Spee's squadron were sunk at the FALKLAND ISLANDS. It was in February 1915 that the Germans announced a blockade of Great Britain, which was carried out by U-boats, among their first victims being an American ship. Soon after, the giant Cunarder, *Lusitania*, was torpedoed off the Irish coast not far from Cork; nearly 1,200 lives were lost, including many Americans. This U-boat blockade was to lead in time to the intervention of the United States in the war. The only large-scale naval battle of the war was fought on May 31st, 1916 and is called by the British the BATTLE OF JUTLAND and by the Germans the Battle of the Skagerrak. The actual fighting was chiefly between the battle-cruisers, faster but less heavily armoured than the battleships. The Germans under Admiral Hipper, fired with great accuracy and sank two of the four cruisers in Admiral Beatty's squadron. The battleships of the fleets hardly made contact and through the night the German ships managed to steam back home. At first the news of Jutland was received with gloom in Britain because of the British losses. Admiral Jellicoe, in charge of the British fleet, was criticized for his cautiousness; but as Winston Churchill wrote later in his history of the war, Jellicoe was "the only man who could have lost the war in one afternoon". A successful torpedo attack on the British battleships might have disastrously altered the balance of naval power and brought Britain to defeat within a year. The German fleet only engaged in very minor raids after Jutland and the fighting was left to the U-boats, which in February 1917 started UNRESTRICTED WARFARE, firing on all ships, allied and neutral, sailing to the British Isles. In April of that year, 423 ships, totalling 875,000 tons, were sunk and by the end of May there were less than 5 million tons of merchant shipping available, so that the Government saw defeat as a distinct probability before the end of the year. The United States were also very much alarmed and angry at the sinking of American ships, despite their strong protests. When the British Secret Service discovered a telegram from Zimmerman, the German Foreign Minister, to Mexico inviting them to enter the war in return for the American states of Texas, Arizona and New Mexico, the American Government was at once informed. The United States delayed no longer and declared war on Germany in April 1917. At the instance of Lloyd George, the Admiralty introduced the convoy system in May and it was at once successful in reducing sinkings. Other methods of overcoming the new menace of the sea were also employed: destroyers, submarines and Q-ships (warships camouflaged as merchant ships) were also sent to hunt down the U-boats. By the end of 1917 the German threat to Britain's supplies had been defeated and the first United States soldiers were arriving in Europe.

The Year of Victory. During 1917 the Germans, exhausted after the blood-baths of the first two years of war, were able to hold on in the hope that the U-boat campaign would be successful. Gradually things improved for them. The French and British offensives had been much more costly to the Allies than to the Germans. The Russian front collapsed even before the revolution of November 7th placed the Bolsheviks in power. In March 1918 the Russian leaders, Lenin and Trotsky, were compelled to accept the humiliating terms of the Treaty of Brest–Litovsk, by which the Baltic lands and Poland went to Germany and Austria, the Ukraine and Finland became independent and large reparation payments were to be made—a much more severe treaty than the Treaty of Versailles, of which the Germans complained so bitterly after 1919. The Austrians, strengthened by German troops, inflicted a shattering defeat on the Italians at CAPORETTO; over 300,000 Italians were captured and even more deserted. The Italians were kept in the war, however, by British and French reinforcements being rushed to Italy and in October 1918 defeated the Austrians at Vittorio

Veneto. Only in the Middle East did the British have any military success in 1917: the Turks were at last after centuries driven out of PALESTINE by Allenby, who was joined there by Lawrence, the hero of the Arabian desert, where he had organized a revolt of the Arabs against the Turks. When 1918 opened with American soldiers already in France, President Wilson in a

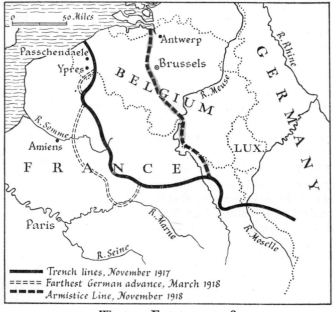

Western Front, 1917–18

speech to Congress outlined the basis of peace discussions in his famous FOURTEEN POINTS. These included "open covenants openly arrived at", the restoration of territories conquered by Germany, "autonomous development" for the peoples of the Austro-Hungarian and Turkish Empires, and "a general association of nations" to preserve peace. A big German offensive under LUDENDORFF, to defeat the Allies before substantial help arrived from America, started in March 1918 and, after a terrific artillery barrage and poison-gas attack, broke the British line to a depth of about forty miles in a few days. The French General Foch was appointed Commander-in-Chief of the allied armies in France in order to secure better co-ordination. Once more Paris was threatened and by July the Germans had again reached the Marne. One unexpected consequence of the German advance was a lowering of the soldiers' morale when they found that, contrary to the propaganda about the starving British, the captured trenches had plenty of food. In a second battle of the Marne, the Germans were slowly driven back. It was near AMIENS, against the German right flank, that the decisive battle of the year began on August 8th. By clever planning and well-concealed preparations, the British General Rawlinson and his Australian Chief of Staff, General Monash, were able to concentrate great masses of troops, guns and tanks. Using the tanks as a spearhead, the British infantry advanced eight miles in the first day. August 8th was for General Ludendorff "the black day of the German Army in the history of the war". He knew that the Germans no longer had a chance of victory and although he kept his armies intact as the Allies (Americans as well as British and French) dealt blow after blow, he advised the German Government to seek peace. The British blockade was telling on the civilian population and also the army; and new troops arriving in the front line were jeered at by those leaving it: "Blacklegs! you are prolonging the war!" Already Bulgaria had surrendered in September and the Austro-Hungarian Empire was in the midst of breaking up when proposals for an armistice were made by Germany and Austria-Hungary on the basis of President Wilson's Fourteen Points. Mutinies broke out among the German sailors, revolution seemed just around the corner, the German and Austrian Emperors abdicated and peace came at last on November 11th, 1918—Armistice Day.

End of the War. What had been called "Armageddon" and "the war to end wars" was over. Although the fighting had been confined mainly to Europe and the Middle East, almost the whole world had been brought into the war. The casualties had been tremendous—in all, over 8 million dead and many more millions wounded. Britain's losses had been 812,000 dead (in comparison with 298,000 in the Second World War) but, with overseas troops included, over a million, France's 1,393,000 and Germany's 2,050,000 dead. In Britain the first reaction to the news of victory was one of elation. The bitter feeling against the Kaiser (it was often called "the Kaiser's War") showed itself in a slogan at the election in December 1918—"Hang the Kaiser". But William II

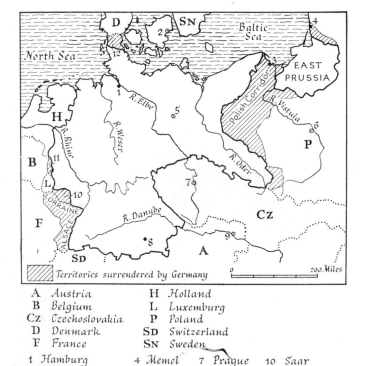

A	Austria	H	Holland
B	Belgium	L	Luxemburg
Cz	Czechoslovakia	P	Poland
D	Denmark	SD	Switzerland
F	France	SN	Sweden

1	Hamburg	4	Memel	7	Prague	10	Saar
2	Copenhagen	5	Berlin	8	Munich	11	Malmédy
3	Danzig (Free City)	6	Warsaw	9	Vienna	12	Slesvig

Germany after 1919

was safely at Doorn in Holland, where he remained till his death in 1941. What had been responsible for the final success of the Allies? (1) First must be reckoned their numerical superiority. The war had really been one of Britain, France, Italy, Russia (and, in its place after 1917, the U.S.A.) against Germany, whose ally Austria-Hungary had proved a broken reed. (2) In the war of attrition on the Western Front, the German losses had drained the nation of its strength. (3) British sea-power had once more proved a vital factor in enabling Britain to conduct war in many different theatres and also to impose a blockade on Germany that made its resistance crumble in 1918. (4) The skilful use of the new weapon, the tank, had given the Allies tactical superiority in the decisive campaign of 1918. (5) Finally, the Germans had no war leader to compare with Lloyd George, who had been able to keep the British fighting spirit high to the end, or Clemenceau ("Tiger"), who had rallied the French from their despair in 1917.

The Peace Treaties. The Peace Conference which met for six months at Versailles in 1919 was dominated by the "BIG FOUR"—President Wilson, Lloyd George and the French and Italian premiers, Clemenceau and Orlando. WOODROW WILSON, who had been Democratic President of the United States since 1912, was faced with a difficult situation at home as the Republican party had gained a majority in Congress in 1918 and were highly critical of his intervention in European affairs. Wilson's Fourteen Points provided a basis for the peace discussions, and the Covenant (or Constitution) of a LEAGUE OF NATIONS was drawn up in April 1919. The TREATY OF VERSAILLES, which the Germans accepted only with great reluctance, was signed in the Hall of Mirrors in the Palace of Versailles, where in 1871 the German Empire had been proclaimed. It provided for a League of Nations and dealt with the defeated Germany as follows:—

(1) *European Territories.*—Alsace-Lorraine was restored to France, a small area, Eupen and Malmédy, to Belgium, a large area of Eastern Germany to a new Poland (which also included Russian and Austrian territory), and provision was made for holding plebiscites to ascertain the wishes of the people in certain disputed districts.

(2) *Colonies.*—The German colonies were handed over to the League of Nations, which afterwards entrusted the government of them to various powers; of these "mandated" territories Britain was given control of East Africa (or Tanganyika), the Union of South Africa control of South-West Africa, France control of the Cameroons. Japan, which had been at war with

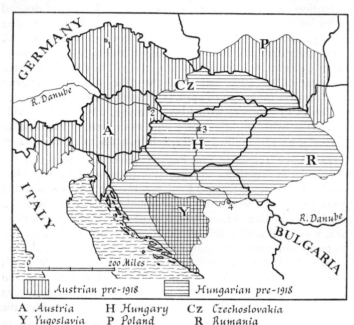

A *Austria*	H *Hungary*	Cz *Czechoslovakia*
Y *Yugoslavia*	P *Poland*	R *Rumania*
1 *Prague*	2 *Vienna*	3 *Budapest*　4 *Belgrade*

Territories lost by Austria-Hungary, 1919

Germany since 1914, assumed control of most of the German Pacific Islands.

(3) *Security.*—Germany's army was to be limited to 100,000 men, the navy's battleships to six, and submarines and military aircraft were prohibited; the Allies were to occupy the Rhineland

for at least fifteen years, and the east bank of the Rhine was to be demilitarized to a depth of thirty miles.

(4) *Reparations*.—The Saar coalfield was to be worked for the good of the French for fifteen years (after which a plebiscite would be held), all Germany's large merchant ships and a quarter of her fishing fleet were to be handed over, reparations for civilian damages were to be paid and a Reparations Commission was to be set up to assess total damages and methods of payment.

(5) *War Guilt*.—Kaiser William II was denounced for his crimes against international morality (but he was never tried as the Dutch refused to hand him over).

In this treaty the victors had tried to give expression to the principle of "SELF-DETERMINATION", to punish Germany by depriving her of her colonies and making her pay reparations, and to secure her neighbours from future aggression. They managed, however, to create problems as well as solving them; and Hitler was able later to gain sympathy in his protest against what he called the Versailles *Diktat* (or "dictated peace"). The most unfortunate aspect of the Peace Settlement was that the U.S.A. never ratified it. President Wilson's party was defeated in the elections of 1920 and his Republican successors went back to the traditional American policy of isolation.

The Austro-Hungarian Empire was carved up by the Treaties of ST. GERMAIN (signed by Austria in 1919) and TRIANON (signed by Hungary in 1920). Three new states were created:—
(1) Czechoslovakia, composed of the Czechs of Bohemia and Moravia, formerly subjects of Austria, and the Slovaks, formerly subjects of Hungary; (2) Yugoslavia ("the land of the Southern Slavs"), which included the Serbia of 1914 and Croatia, Bosnia, Herzegovina and Slovenia; (3) Poland, which after over a hundred years was restored to approximately the same size as the state partitioned among Austria, Prussia and Russia in the eighteenth century. Unfortunately, drawing frontier-lines proved a difficult task and many racial minorities were included in the new national states. Over three million Austrian Germans were included inside the Czechoslovak frontiers, which followed the mountain ranges of Bohemia. To provide Poland with an

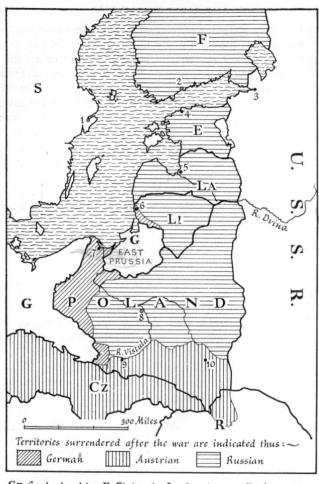

Territories surrendered after the war are indicated thus:∼

Ⓗ *German*	Ⓗ *Austrian*	Ⓗ *Russian*

Cz *Czechoslovakia* **F** *Finland* **LA** *Latvia* **R** *Rumania*
E *Estonia* **G** *Germany* **Li** *Lithuania* **S** *Sweden*
U.S.S.R. *Union of Soviet Socialist Republics*

1 *Stockholm*	5 *Riga*	9 *Cracow*
2 *Helsinki*	6 *Memel*	10 *Lwow*
3 *Petrograd (Leningrad)*	7 *Danzig (Free City)*	
4 *Tallinn*	8 *Warsaw*	

Poland and Baltic States after 1919

access to the sea, many Germans were left in the "Polish Corridor". In addition, Austrians in the South Tirol became Italian subjects, while Italians on the Adriatic coast were included in Yugoslavia. (After the war, however, Italy managed to have Fiume, on the Italo-Yugoslav frontier, handed over to her.) Thus, applying the principle of self-determination meant creating new problems for the future. It was some years before the fate of the Turkish Empire was finally decided. Several independent states were set up in the Middle East and, in fulfilment of a promise in the Balfour Declaration of 1917 to set up a "national home for the Jews", Palestine came into existence as a separate state under a British mandate. Like many other peace settlements, there were enough seeds of trouble sown in 1919–20 to produce more wars a generation later. But the hopes of the world's peace were with the new League of Nations, which seemed to herald a new era.

SOURCE EXTRACTS

A   *The Battle of the Somme* (*A German account*)

The men in the dug-outs waited ready, a belt full of hand-grenades around them, gripping their rifles and waiting for the bombardment to lift from the front defence zone on to the rear defences. It was of vital importance to lose not a second in taking up position in the open to meet the British infantry who would be advancing immediately behind the artillery barrage. Looking towards the British trenches through the long trench periscopes held up out of the dug-out entrances, there could be seen a mass of steel helmets above their parapet showing that their storm-troops were ready for the assault. At 7.30 a.m. the hurricane of shells ceased as suddenly as it had begun. Our men at once clambered up the steep shafts leading from the dug-outs to daylight and ran singly or in groups to the nearest shell craters. The machine-guns were pulled out of the dug-outs and hurriedly placed into position, their crews dragging the heavy ammunition boxes up the steps and out to the guns. As soon as in position, extended lines of British infantry were seen moving forward from their trenches. . . . They came on at a steady pace as if expecting to find nothing alive in our front trenches. . . . A few minutes later, when the leading British line was within 100 yards, the rattle of machine-gun and rifle

fire broke out from along the whole line of craters. . . . Red rockets
sped up into the blue sky as a signal to the artillery, and immediately
afterwards a mass of shells from the German batteries in the rear
tore through the air and burst among the advancing lines. Whole
sections seemed to fall, and the rear formations, moving in closer
order, quickly scattered. The advance rapidly crumpled under this
hail of shells and bullets. All along the line men could be seen throwing
their arms into the air and collapsing never to move again. Badly
wounded rolled about in their agony, and others less severely injured
crawled to the nearest shell-hole for shelter. . . .

Gerster: Die Schwaben an der Ancre.

B   *Admiral Beatty at the Battle of Jutland*

This is a moment on which British naval historians will be glad to
dwell; and the actual facts deserve to be recorded. The *Indefatigable*
had disappeared beneath the waves. The *Queen Mary* had towered up to
heaven in a pillar of fire. The *Lion* was in flames. A tremendous
salvo struck upon or about her following ship, the *Princess Royal*,
which vanished in a cloud of spray and smoke. A signalman sprang
on to the *Lion*'s bridge with the words: "*Princess Royal* blown up, sir."
On this the Vice-Admiral said to his Flag Captain, "Chatfield, there
seems to be something wrong with our ——— ships today. Turn two
points to port", i.e. two points nearer the enemy.

W. S. Churchill: The World Crisis.

EXERCISES

1. (*Extract "A".*) Why did the British make such slow progress
   on the Somme in 1916 and such rapid progress at Amiens in 1918?
2. (*Extract "B".*) Why does this incident at the battle of Jutland
   appeal to Churchill as "a moment on which British naval historians
   will be glad to dwell"?
3. Explain: "Old Contemptibles", the taxis of the Marne, the race to
   the sea, 1914, No-man's-land, Anzac, Q-ships, Kitchener's army,
   Welsh Wizard, Fourteen Points.
4. Identify the authors of the following and explain where necessary:
   (*a*) "See you make the right wing strong!"
   (*b*) "Hammer the French on the anvil of Verdun."
   (*c*) "Ils ne passeront pas!"
   (*d*) "Good God! Did we really send men to fight in that?"

(e) "Your Country Needs YOU."

(f) "The only man who could have lost the war in one afternoon."

(g) "The black day of the German army in the history of the war."

(h) "There seems to be something wrong with our ——— ships today. Turn two points to port."

5. Write short notes on the following: Schlieffen Plan, Battle of the Marne, trench warfare, Battle of Tannenberg, Siege of Verdun, Battle of the Somme, Battle of Passchendaele, Battle of Jutland, Battle of Caporetto, Fourteen Points.

6. Write notes on the following: Dardanelles campaign, Submarine warfare 1914–18, Home front, 1914–18, Treaty of Versailles. ✔

7. Describe the part played by the British in the defeat of Germany in the First World War. ✔

8. Account for the final success of the Allies against Germany in the First World War. ✔

9. Give an account of the Peace Treaties, 1919–20. ✔

CHAPTER IX

BRITAIN BETWEEN THE WARS

Post-war Problems. The signing of the Armistice on November 11th, 1918, was followed a few weeks later by a parliamentary election in Britain. It was called the "Khaki Election", because so many men were still in uniform, and the "Coupon Election", as the candidates willing to support the Coalition Government received letters of recommendation or "coupons" from the Coalition leaders. Some of the slogans reflected the mood of Britain at the end of the war—"Hang The Kaiser!", "No More War!", and "Make Germany Pay!" The result of the election, which was the first in which women voted, was a triumph for Lloyd George and the Coalition. People expected Lloyd George, "the man who won the war", to use his great ability to make Britain "a fit country for heroes to live in"—

a phrase which was often to be thrown in his face in later years. But Lloyd George himself was busy for a time at Versailles in peace-making and it was not long before problems began to multiply themselves at home. In Britain, after a short-lived boom when industry was making up for the shortages caused by the war, a slump ensued. Many of the old pre-war markets had been lost to Britain as a result of the war when other countries had to be self-sufficient. The cotton industry found itself faced with competition from Japan and India where labour was much cheaper. After a long spell of full employment with good wages, unemployed workers took badly to the change, even although the hardship was relieved by the weekly unemployment benefit. Unemployment mounted slowly from 3 per cent of the insured workers in midsummer 1920 to over 20 per cent a year later. Attempts were made by employers to regain their lost markets by cutting wages, sometimes by as much as one-third; but many workers refused to accept them and for six months the Lancashire cotton-mills were closed. The coal-miners faced a similar threat but a stoppage in a key industry such as coal-mining was bound to be more serious as it involved other industries. In 1919, just after the war, the miners had threatened to go on strike for a shorter working day of seven hours, higher wages, and nationalization of the mines. The strike had been averted by the Government setting up a Royal Commmission on the industry under Sir John Sankey. This SANKEY COMMISSION recommended in favour of accepting the miners' demands. Although the recommendation of nationalization had been by the narrow majority of only one vote and although a Government is not compelled to accept the findings of a Royal Commission, the miners were left with a permanent grouse at the Government's unwillingness to adopt the proposal for nationalization. The threat of a breakdown had been got over temporarily by granting a government subsidy to the mine-owners to prevent reducing pay. But more troubles developed in the mines. The price of coal dropped catastrophically from 85s. a ton in 1920 to 24s. in 1921; and the mine-owners felt compelled to resort to a reduction in wages. The miners finally had to face a "lock-out", after they refused to accept

THE AFTERMATH OF THE FIRST WORLD WAR. *Top:* Army lorries being used as London buses during the 1921 Rail Strike. *Bottom:* Examples of the *Daily Mail* campaign to "make Germany pay" (see p. 175).

THE RISE OF LABOUR. *Top:* Pioneering Days. Keir Hardie (with beard) waiting to address a May Day rally in 1912 (pp. 84–6). *Bottom:* Victory demonstration in the Royal Albert Hall, 1924—Ramsay MacDonald, Prime Minister with members of the first Labour Cabinet, on his left Margaret Bondfield and J. H. Thomas (with bow tie) (see p. 182).

the owners' terms. Again the Government helped with a subsidy, but the miners were still bitter over the non-fulfilment of the Sankey Commission recommendations. In Ireland, something like civil war raged until the end of 1921, when the Irish Treaty brought a solution of a kind to the question that had vexed British politics for so long. But the Government's position was weakening as the Coalition, formed for wartime purposes, began to break up. A scandal blew up in the summer of 1922 over the Birthday

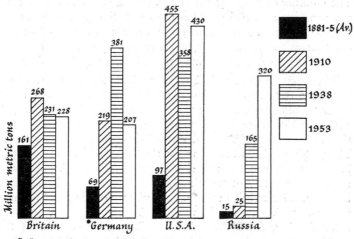

* German figures include lignite.
1953 figures for West Germany only.

Coal Production, 1881–1953

Honours List. Not only was there strong criticism directed against one of the new peers but allegations were freely made that peerages had been granted to those prepared to pay money into Lloyd George's political fund. The wonderful reputation Lloyd George had built up during the war had become tarnished. The Versailles settlement of 1919 had led to troubles in Europe that were also blamed on Lloyd George. He had been unsuccessful in his attempts to get the French to co-operate over the

12

problem of Germany's payment of reparations. The fall of the
Coalition Government came in October 1922 over the handling
of a crisis in the Middle East where the Turks led by Mustapha
Kemal, the hero of the Dardanelles defence, drove the Greeks
out of the part of Asia Minor they had acquired in the peace
settlement. The prospects of another war, which seemed probable
through Lloyd George's support of the Greeks, was too much
for the British people who had just fought "the war to end wars".
The Unionists broke away from the Coalition and in the ensuing
election were returned with a majority of almost a hundred over
the other parties. Lloyd George was never to regain office and
the Liberal party, which he had wrecked by the split between
himself and Asquith, was fated to dwindle away from then on.

The Irish "Troubles". The Home Rule Act of 1914, which
had taken over two years to pass, had been suspended and was
never to be enforced. After the collapse of the Easter Rising of
1916, the Volunteers and Sinn Fein combined under the leadership of EAMON DE VALERA, one of the rebels of Easter 1916.
The 73 Sinn Fein M.P.s elected at the "Khaki Election" of 1918
justified their name by ignoring the Parliament in London and
meeting separately in Dublin. Lloyd George, who had been a
keen Home Ruler before the war and was to spend several months
in 1919 at Versailles helping to make a peace based on self-
determination, found himself in a dilemma. The crux of the
problem was whether, by this same principle of self-determination, the Protestants in the six northern counties should be allowed
to separate from the rest of Ireland. The solution of the problem
by the partition of Ireland, already proposed in 1914, was revived
in a Government of Ireland Act (1920), providing for separate
parliaments for northern and southern Ireland. But the Sinn
Feiners were adamant against the partition of Ireland, particularly
their leader, De Valera, who had been elected "President of the
Irish Republic" in 1917 but spent most of the next four years in
prison in England or in exile in the United States. At the beginning
of 1919, the Sinn Feiners set up an alternative government in
Dublin, levied taxes and organized an IRISH REPUBLICAN ARMY.
It was not long before the "troubles" began. Policemen and

soldiers were ambushed and shot down by the I.R.A.; and any Irishman friendly with the British was likely to find himself a corpse with a notice pinned on his clothing—"Executed by Order of the I.R.A.—Spies and Informers Beware". In the municipal and district council elections in 1920 the Sinn Feiners had an overwhelming majority; even Londonderry (of which Orangemen are so proud) had a Catholic mayor. In the same year the Lord Mayor of Cork, Terence MacSwiney, who had been imprisoned for possessing "treasonable documents", died after a hunger-strike that lasted seventy-four days and evoked the attention of the whole world, especially of the many Irish sympathizers in the United States. The leader of the Sinn Fein resistance movement was MICHAEL COLLINS ("the big fellow" as he was called), who boldly and coolly organized sabotage, ambushes and murder and went about Dublin with a price of £10,000 on his head and without any attempt at disguise. To reinforce the R.I.C. (the Royal Irish Constabulary) several thousand British ex-servicemen, selected for their toughness, were recruited. They were fitted out with black caps and belts and khaki (sometimes black) tunics and trousers and were promptly nicknamed the BLACK-AND-TANS. But they failed to restore order and before long over 300 police-stations in Southern Ireland were abandoned. The Ulster Volunteers of the pre-1914 period were at the same time embodied in the Army and the restoration of law and order became more like civil war. Another force, the Auxiliary Division of the R.I.C., composed of British ex-officers, earned a reputation as bad as that of the Black-and-Tans. The Auxiliaries and Black-and-Tans tried to outdo the I.R.A. in violence, and their actions aroused resentment in Britain as well as in Ireland. Asquith, the former Liberal Prime Minister, commented: "Things are being done in Ireland which would disgrace the blackest annals of the lowest despotism in Europe." Asquith was naturally keen to blame his old rival, Lloyd George, for the Irish "troubles". But General Sir Hubert Gough (who had been leader of the officers in the Curragh Incident of 1914) also condemned the conduct of affairs in Ireland: "The British Government committed worse crimes in

Ireland than Germany had ever committed in France." On one occasion, following the shooting in their beds of fourteen British Army officers (who had been sent over to Ireland as secret agents to beat Collins at his own game), the Black-and-Tans opened fire on the spectators at a football match in Dublin. A week later, they cleared the people off the streets of Cork and set the Town Hall and other buildings on fire, causing over £3,000,000 worth of damage. At last, in the summer of 1921, Lloyd George took the bold step of opening negotiations with the Sinn Fein leaders, despite protests by members of the Cabinet that law and order must be restored first. The Irish leaders themselves were not keen to accept the proposed solution, which involved the partition of Ireland, and De Valera repudiated the final settlement, which was arrived at in December 1921. The Irish Treaty made the twenty-six counties of Southern and Western Ireland into a FREE STATE with the same rights as those possessed by Canada, in other words, dominion status. The six counties of Northern Ireland were to have their own government and parliament and were also to be represented at Westminster. The Sinn Feiners were persuaded to sign the treaty by promises made by Lloyd George that changes in the boundaries between Northern and Southern Ireland would be carried out under the terms of the treaty; and they later bitterly denounced the British Cabinet for having deceived them. The solution pleased hardly anyone. Michael Collins, who had started negotiations with reluctance, was murdered by his fellow-Irishmen for having betrayed Ireland by agreeing to the partition. But the Irish Free State was born and the Irish at last had their chance to govern themselves.

Free Trade v. Protection. The break-up of the Coalition brought the Unionists into power but not for long. As the Irish question was now settled, they now reverted to their old name of "Conservatives", although the name "Unionist" was still preferred in Northern Ireland and also, to a lesser extent, in Scotland. BONAR LAW (1858-1923), the new Prime Minister, was a son of the manse, born in New Brunswick, Canada, where his father was a Presbyterian minister. He was brought up in

Scotland, however, and was a dominant figure in the iron trade in Glasgow. He succeeded Balfour as Unionist leader in 1912 and was vitriolic in his attacks on the Liberals over Irish Home Rule. But he joined the Coalition Government of Asquith in 1915 and stood by Lloyd George in the "split" of 1916, becoming a member of the War Cabinet. He was noted for his ability to make lengthy speeches on complicated financial matters with hardly a note. Bonar Law was fated to hold office only for a short time: he resigned for health reasons after a few months and died soon afterwards. The appointment of STANLEY BALDWIN (1867–1937) as his successor came as a surprise to many. The Conservative leader in the House of Lords, the Marquess of Curzon, had confidently expected to succeed Bonar Law. But the day for a Prime Minister in the House of Lords had gone and George V sent for Baldwin, Chancellor of the Exchequer of less than a year's standing and hardly known to the public. Like Bonar Law, he had been engaged in the iron industry and entered Parliament fairly late in life. Earlier in 1923, as Chancellor of the Exchequer, he had effected a settlement of British debts with the United States that was very much criticized at the time and later, especially as Britain's own debtors, including France, made little attempt to do the same. He was to be Prime Minister three times, but his first ministry was short-lived. His solution for relieving unemployment was the protection of home industries from foreign competition by tariffs on imported goods. Remembering how Joseph Chamberlain's Tariff Reform campaign of 1903–6 had been wrecked by Liberal cries of "Dear Bread", he proposed to omit food from his list of tariffs. Even that gesture would not convince the British people, brought up to believe that their standard of living depended on free trade. Baldwin went to the country in December 1923 to ask for a mandate for protection but the popular vote went against him. When Parliament met in January 1924 the Conservatives were still the largest party with 256 members, the Labour party had jumped up to second place with 191 members, and the Liberals (with Asquith and Lloyd George reunited at last in the "old cause" of free trade) numbered 158. An interesting constitutional situation had arisen. Baldwin resigned as he felt that the country had rejected him and his policy. Asquith, the Liberal leader, decided that the Labour party had the right to form a Government, even though it was only second largest, and he felt that he and the Liberals could check any tendency to go to extremes. Ramsay MacDonald then formed the first Labour Government in the history of Britain.

MacDonald's Labour Government. James Ramsay Mac-Donald (1866–1937) was born and brought up at Lossie-mouth on the Moray Firth. His early life was a hard struggle. He became a clerk in a London office and spent much of his spare time "improving" himself at evening classes. He joined the I.L.P. soon after it was formed in 1893 and began to earn his living as a writer on politics and economics. He was appointed Secretary of the Labour Representation Committee in 1900 and Chairman of the Labour party in 1911, although he was compelled to resign that office at the beginning of the 1914–18 war because of his pacifist views, becoming leader of the party again in 1922. His handsome appearance, his eloquence, his moderation combined to make him a Prime Minister who would attract rather than frighten the British public. It was not an easy task for him to form a Cabinet, as apart from Arthur Henderson, who had served in Lloyd George's War Cabinet, none of the Labour party had Cabinet experience. MacDonald himself became Foreign Secretary as well as Prime Minister; and two former Liberal peers, Lord Haldane and Lord Chelmsford, were persuaded to join the Cabinet. The rest of the Cabinet were mainly trade unionists with a sprinkling of intellectuals like Sidney Webb, one of the founders of the Fabian Society. The left-wingers of the Labour party, prominent among them a group of I.L.P. members from Clydeside, felt disgruntled at the absence of Socialism from the Government's policy. "Jimmy" Maxton, former Glasgow school-teacher, said bluntly: "Socialism is a very definite class war which cannot be fought with kid gloves." But the Labour Government was a minority government and depended for its existence on the Liberals. Only one important measure of social reform was carried through, the HOUSING ACT, for which the Minister of Health, John

Wheatley, one of the Glasgow I.L.P. group, was responsible. This made possible generous grants for the building of cheaper houses; and town councils began to carry out slum clearances on a larger scale. Ramsay MacDonald's own achievements as Foreign Secretary made a favourable impression on the country. After a long period of difficulties with the French over German reparations, he helped to persuade the French to accept a scheme, the Dawes Plan, which allowed Germany to pay reduced reparations. Another effort he made at international co-operation was not so favourably received. He recognized the Bolshevik Government as the legal Government of Russia. When he went on, however, to try and arrange a trade treaty with Russia, he met with such opposition from Conservatives and Liberals that he resigned. The chances of a Labour victory in the ensuing election were not improved by the publication a week before the polling-day of a letter purporting to be from a Russian, Zinoviev, head of the Comintern or Third Socialist International, which engaged in Communist propaganda. This letter, which urged British Communists to undermine the loyalty of the British Army, created a furore in the country. Although the RED LETTER was denounced by the Soviet Government as a crude forgery, it added strength to the conviction of many people that a Labour Government would tend to lead to Communism (then more often called "Bolshevism"). The Conservatives under Baldwin came back with a large majority, and although the total Labour poll had risen by about a million the Labour party had lost almost forty seats in the House of Commons. The Liberals had been the victims of the short-lived Labour régime; their numbers dropped to forty and their leader, Asquith, was defeated, retiring soon afterwards to the House of Lords with an earldom, the usual honour for retired Prime Ministers. The Liberals were thus left without much influence in Parliament. The Asquith–Lloyd George split, their support of MacDonald's short ministry, and the workings of the electoral system had combined to defeat them.

Baldwin's Second Ministry. The most important event during the five years (1924–29) of Baldwin's second ministry was the General Strike of 1926 which has been described in Chapter

IV. Much useful legislation was passed under this Conservative Government. Three Acts which are dealt with elsewhere were the Equal Franchise Act of 1928 and the Local Government Acts of 1928 and 1929. The ELECTRICITY SUPPLY ACT of 1926 set up a Central Electricity Board, and the consumption of electricity was soon doubled as pylons with electricity cables spread over the country. A tax on betting, which brought about the introduction of the "tote" or totalisator on race-courses, was attacked by those who felt that gambling was immoral—a sign that the Nonconformist conscience of the nineteenth century was still alive. Further evidence of the Nonconformist conscience came when the Commons twice rejected a revised PRAYER BOOK, agreed to by the Church of England and the House of Lords but regarded as Anglo-Catholic by the Presbyterians, Methodists and Baptists of the House of Commons. An important act of social reform in the tradition of his father, "Radical Joe" Chamberlain, was Neville Chamberlain's WIDOWS', ORPHANS' AND OLD AGE PENSIONS ACT, which provided ten-shillings a week for widows of working-men with allowances for children under fourteen. It was also during this ministry, in 1926, that a conference of United Kingdom and Dominion ministers agreed upon the famous formula which was later to be incorporated in the Statute of Westminster (1931) and which recognized the Dominions as "autonomous communities" equal in status with the United Kingdom as members of "THE BRITISH COMMONWEALTH OF NATIONS". What with all these measures and the more peaceful atmosphere in Europe that had prevailed since the Locarno Agreements of 1925 (see page 196), the Conservative Government felt that they had good reason to be satisfied with their term of office. When they went to the country at the election of 1929 they were hopeful of victory; a poster, showing a placid, contented Stanley Baldwin with a pipe in his mouth and the words "SAFETY FIRST" below, was their chief weapon in the electoral campaign. But the newly-enfranchised electors (the electorate had increased by over five millions as a result of the Equal Franchise Act of 1928) contained many working-class voters who were more impressed by the constant shadow of unemployment that darkened the country; and they went to the polls in the hope that the Labour party might produce some remedy, still untried, which might be successful. Ramsay MacDonald became Prime Minister again, this time as leader of the largest party but again without a majority; Labour had 288 seats against 260 Conservatives and the Liberals had risen slightly to 58 (probably because of Lloyd George's bold programme, "We Can Conquer Unemployment").

Financial Crisis. MacDonald's Second Ministry took over from the Conservatives in 1929 just when a financial crisis in the United States (the WALL STREET CRASH) signalled the end of the American boom of the 1920's and the onset of a depression that was to last for years. The causes of the GREAT DEPRESSION or "economic blizzard" of the 1930's are various and are considered more fully elsewhere. It was worldwide and left untouched scarcely any country except one with a closed economy like the Soviet Union. Britain had not been able to reduce her number of unemployed below the million mark since 1920. In the ten years before the war, over three millions had left Britain for America but that outlet for relieving unemployment was no longer open as the United States imposed restrictions after the war. The number of unemployed grew as the world depression became worse: it had been 1,178,000 in July 1929, a year later it was 2,070,000 and in July 1931, 2,806,000. The Labour Government started off with optimistic forecasts of a complete cure for the country's troubles but as more and more workless queued up at the Labour Exchanges, the Government seemed to drift helplessly along. One of their junior ministers, a wealthy young baronet, SIR OSWALD MOSLEY, resigned in disgust and later started the first Fascist party in Britain. The left-wing I.L.P. members, led by Maxton, criticized the Government for not introducing a socialist programme and were finally expelled from the Labour party. The Government did not have a majority over the two other parties but even if they had, there was little evidence that they would have acted very differently. Nor had their Conservative opponents any alternative to offer except to attack the mounting debt incurred by the Government on the payment of unemployment benefit (the unemployment insurance fund having long since become insolvent). It was over this question of unemployment benefit (or "the dole" as it was sometimes called) that the Government fell in 1931. The Americans, after the Wall Street crash in 1929, had ceased lending to Germany and had even called in some of their loans. The Germans, who were also seriously affected by the depression, were granted a year's moratorium on their reparation payments and began to borrow from London financiers, who made the mistake of lending for long terms to the Germans and Austrians (also in economic difficulties) and borrowing from Paris and New York financiers at lower rates but for shorter terms. Austria was also borrowing from the French; but when the Paris banks heard of a proposal for a customs union between Germany and Austria, they withdrew their money to force the Austrians to abandon the proposed union and the result was the collapse of the chief bank in Austria. The failure of many banks in Austria and Germany followed in the summer of 1931 and naturally led to a financial crisis in London, which had lent over £200,000,000 to Austria and Germany. Foreign investors began to make panic withdrawals of their deposits in London, and the Bank of England felt itself in danger as it could not stop the drain on its gold reserves. The financial crisis, it was thought, could only be solved by help from New York. One other grim alternative seemed to be to go off the gold standard and that, many felt, would mean opening the floodgates of inflation. American financiers looked askance at the requests for assistance from Britain, where a Labour Government paid a "dole" to the unemployed, while in the United States there was no state relief for the vast army of about twelve million unemployed, who had to depend on charity. Already the British Government had borrowed over £100,000,000 from other funds to maintain the payments to the unemployed and as a result were running into debt. The American banks made it clear that a loan to the Bank of England could only be made "if the Budget was balanced", which meant by cutting the expenditure on social services. An economy committee set up by the Government had recommended slashing cuts in expenditure such as unemployment benefit, civil servants' and teachers' salaries. MacDonald's Cabinet colleagues refused to accept these cuts, even although they were reduced by half, and the unhappy life of the second Labour Government came to an end.

National Government. When MacDonald announced the resignation of his Government to King George V, he was asked to form a National Government. The suggestion had come first from Sir Herbert Samuel, the Liberal leader at the time, and was approved by Stanley Baldwin, the Conservative leader, as it was felt that any such cuts would have a better chance of being accepted by the people from a Labour government or a government with Labour members. MacDonald thus became Prime Minister of a National Government which he was to lead for four years, but only a handful of his party followed him. An election was held soon afterwards in October 1931. The public were warned of the terrible consequences of inflation that would occur if Britain had to go off the gold standard, because of her refusal to accept the reductions in Government expenditure. Memories of the German inflation of 1923 (helped by Mac-Donald's waving of German 100,000,000 mark notes at election meetings and threatening that soon £1,000,000 would be needed to buy even a stamp) helped to rally supporters for the new National Government, which gained a record number of 547 seats in the House of Commons while the Labour representation was reduced to fifty-three. The National Government, which had gained such a sweeping victory in the election of 1931, was to remain in power (with another election victory in 1935) until the Second World War. Despite its name and the presence of Ramsay MacDonald as Prime Minister and a few Labour and Liberal members, it was for all practical purposes the Conservative party slightly enlarged. MacDonald did not at first seem to worry about the desertion of his former colleagues; according to Philip Snowden, the Chancellor of the Exchequer, MacDonald remarked when he became Prime Minister of the National Government: "Tomorrow every duchess in London will be wanting to kiss me." His hour of glory soon passed away. Even before the election of 1931, the gold standard had to be abandoned: the pound was now worth 3·49 instead of 4·86 dollars. This devaluation did not have the disastrous consequences predicted; British exporters were actually able to sell their goods more easily as foreigners found them cheaper to buy. The Government, along with the Bank of England, established an EXCHANGE EQUALIZATION FUND, to keep the foreign value of sterling steady by "pegging the exchanges". Although Britain thus benefited, Labour critics reminded MacDonald of the prophecies of inflation he had made. Unemployment nevertheless continued to increase through 1931 and 1932 till it was almost three millions or 20 per cent of the insured workers. In Germany, there were over six million unemployed and in the United States at least double that number. In some industries the figures were much higher, e.g. almost 60 per cent in shipbuilding and 34 per cent in coal-mining. Certain districts were very badly hit, such as Clydeside, South Wales and Tyneside; Jarrow, on the Tyne, was called "the town that was murdered". Later, some of these districts were called DEPRESSED AREAS and by a series of Special Areas Acts provision was made for welfare schemes and the attraction of new industries to industrial estates sponsored by the Government. The cuts in the "dole" or unemployment benefit and the imposition of what was called a MEANS TEST, to reduce the public assistance to an unemployed person if even one of the family was earning, called forth bitter protests from the working-classes. MacDonald particularly was abused and attacked by those who formerly admired him. He was unable to repeat his former success in foreign affairs: in 1932 and in the two succeeding years he attended the Disarmament Conference at Geneva, and like other national leaders put forward plans that the rest would not accept. By 1935, Hitler, in power in Germany, had denounced the Treaty of Versailles, and Mussolini, the Italian dictator, was attacking Abyssinia. Re-armament, rather than disarmament, then became the question of the day.

Tariffs. In imperial affairs, the National Government was responsible for certain radical changes so far as trade relations were concerned, although the results did not please the ardent Imperialists of the party very much. In 1932, the Chancellor of the Exchequer, Neville Chamberlain, was able at last to give effect to the proposals of his father, Joseph Chamberlain, for tariff reform by imposing TARIFFS of 10 per cent on all imports except food and raw materials. (Some of the duties were later raised to higher levels like 33⅓ per cent.) Agriculture was protected from the competition of cheap overseas food by introducing a quota system which guaranteed so much of the home market to British farmers and also by paying them subsidies on the price of wheat; a MILK MARKETING BOARD also guaranteed fixed prices and regular markets for the farmers. The end of free trade did not have the far-reaching consequences that were expected. Every country in the world was building higher tariff walls to protect its industries, thereby damaging similar industries elsewhere or, as it was said, "exporting unemployment". The idea of IMPERIAL PREFERENCE, which had been an important feature of Joseph Chamberlain's proposals, could not be carried out very effectively as it was mainly food and raw materials that Britain imported from the Dominions and Colonies. An Imperial Conference met at Ottawa in 1932, a year after Parliament had passed the STATUTE OF WESTMINSTER, incorporating the decisions of the Imperial Conference of 1926 about dominion status. The OTTAWA CONFERENCE tried, without much success, to evolve a system of imperial preference. But the Ottawa Duties on non-imperial imports caused much heart-burning in Canada and Australia, which felt that their trade with other countries was damaged by them; and unfortunately European countries, unable to trade with Britain, turned to Germany for a market and found themselves compelled to accept her terms for trading. In 1935, after the celebration of King George V's Jubilee, Ramsay MacDonald retired in favour of Baldwin as Prime Minister. In the general election which took place later in the same year, the National Government was returned with a reduced majority. MacDonald, whose health had been failing, was ignominiously defeated in his old constituency of Seaham Harbour in a straight fight with a Labour opponent, Emmanuel Shinwell, by a majority of over 20,000 votes. MacDonald was provided with a seat for the Scottish Universities but died not long afterwards on a voyage to South America. The Labour party never forgave him for his action in 1931, and in his last years he had cut a pathetic figure as the nominal head of a Government run by his former opponents.

Baldwin and the Abdication Crisis. Baldwin's Government of 1935–37 was overwhelmingly Conservative but it still retained the name of National Government, as also did that of his successor, Neville Chamberlain. Baldwin's ministry was his third; and although he had often been criticized for his tendency to drift, he had by 1935 earned the respect of all parties. His familiar pipe, his farm, his interest in pigs, his family background (the Baldwins had been ironmasters at Bewdley for generations), his knowledge of literature of ancient and modern times—all seemed to his fellow-countrymen to indicate someone fundamentally sound and reliable. His forthright replies to the attacks made on him by the newspaper "barons", Lord Beaverbrook and Lord Rothermere, in the *Daily Express* and *Daily Mail,* also earned him widespread sympathy. His reluctance to begin rearmament once Germany and Italy were obviously preparing for war was frequently criticized by Churchill, who during the 1930's remained out of office mainly because he opposed the Government's policy of granting more self-government to India. Baldwin's last year in office involved him in a controversy which at first seemed as if it would shake the British monarchy to its foundations. King George V died in January 1936, less than a year after the celebrations of his Jubilee. His reign (1910–36) had been the most disturbed for a century: the constitutional crisis of 1910–11, the threat of civil war over Ireland in 1913–14, the First World War of 1914–18, the Irish "Troubles" in 1919–21, the General Strike of 1926, the financial crisis of 1931 and the terrible depression of the 1930's—all presented him with very difficult situations. But at the end of the reign the prestige of the monarchy stood higher than before. He was followed by his son EDWARD VIII, who as Prince of Wales had earned popularity through his interest in sport and his many journeys throughout the Empire. In the summer of 1936 he announced to the Prime Minister that he intended to marry Mrs. Wallis Simpson, an American lady who had two divorced husbands living. Both Baldwin and his Cabinet were opposed to the match, even although King Edward was prepared to make it a morganatic marriage, whereby his wife would not be known as Queen and any children would be debarred from the succession to the throne. In this matter Baldwin felt that he had the public opinion of the country behind him; and he was confirmed in his views by the consultations he had with the Dominion Governments. As the King felt he had to choose between Mrs. Simpson and abdication, he decided to give up the throne. He was succeeded by his brother, Albert, Duke of York, who became King with the title of GEORGE VI. After a farewell speech over the radio in which he expressed his inability to carry on as King "without the help and support of the woman I love", Edward VIII left for the continent as DUKE OF WINDSOR and married Mrs. Simpson not long afterwards. What impressed Europe and the world about this ABDICATION CRISIS was that the British monarchy came out of it strengthened rather than weakened. It revealed also the importance of the constitutional dictum that the King must accept the advice of the Prime Minister and Cabinet even in a personal matter such as his marriage. Baldwin showed himself master of a difficult situation and was able to retire soon afterwards, conscious that he had by his actions earned the respect of the British people and preserved the monarchy as an institution.

Neville Chamberlain. Baldwin was succeeded in 1937 as Prime Minister by Neville Chamberlain. He had been Chancellor of the Exchequer since 1932 and was destined to hold the office of Prime Minister until the Second World War, when he was forced to resign after the British defeat in Norway in 1940. A son of "Radical Joe" Chamberlain (and a half-brother of Sir Austen Chamberlain, who had taken a prominent part in the negotations before the Locarno Pact), Neville Chamberlain had followed in his father's footsteps as Lord Mayor of Birmingham, where he had been the person chiefly responsible for establishing a municipal bank. He entered Parliament after the "Khaki

Election" of 1918 and rose very quickly in office, being appointed Chancellor of the Exchequer in 1923 in Baldwin's first Government. When Baldwin returned to power a year later, after the Labour Ministry of Ramsay MacDonald, Chamberlain could have taken the post of Chancellor of the Exchequer again but instead preferred the Ministry of Health as he had conceived an ambitious programme of SOCIAL REFORM, comprising twenty-five different Bills. Twenty-three of these he carried through himself in the years 1924-29 and the other four passed into law under his successors. The most important measure of reform was the Widows', Orphans' and Old Age Pensions Act of 1925, in which he completed the programme his father outlined as a Radical in 1885. By his other great achievement, the LOCAL GOVERNMENT ACTS of 1928 and 1929 for England and Scotland, he effected major changes in local administration. Among other measures he managed to place on the statute book were Acts relating to smoke abatement, housing, patent medicines and asylums. As Chancellor of the Exchequer in the National Governments of MacDonald and Baldwin (1931-37), he introduced six budgets, the most important of which was that of 1932, when he ended free trade by a 10 per cent duty on imports, thereby realizing part of his father's tariff reform hopes of 1903-06. He was strongly in favour of abolishing reparations and was responsible for repudiating Britain's war debts to the United States, one of the few occasions when Britain has refused to carry out her international obligations in modern times. As Prime Minister, Chamberlain concerned himself with foreign policy during much of the two pre-war years and became a familar figure to the European public because of his visits to Hitler, on which he carried a rolled umbrella. In Britain he never became popular except for a very brief period in September 1938 at the time of the Czecho-slovak crisis, and his reputation has been darkened by the failure of his policy of appeasement, which is dealt with elsewhere.

SOURCE EXTRACT
The Black-and-Tans in Cork

Half an hour before curfew, the streets were deserted. At about ten o'clock, Auxiliaries and Black-and-Tans set fire to two houses near

ECONOMIC DIFFICULTIES IN THE NINETEEN-TWENTIES. *Top:* French troops in the Ruhr in 1923 (see p. 195). *Bottom:* Volunteers unloading milk at Waterloo Station, London during the General Strike, 1926 (see pp. 88–9).

THE EMANCIPATION OF WOMEN (see pp. 368–9). *Top:* An arrested suffragette being led away from Buckingham Palace in May 1914. *Bottom:* A London bus conductress of 1917. In 1914 this photo would have seemed incredible.

Dillon's Cross and prevented attempts to extinguish the flames. At the same time Auxiliaries and Black-and-Tans began crowding the streets, shooting and yelling. Flames soon reddened the sky above the city as the central shopping district was systematically looted and destroyed by bombs and by arson. By midnight columns of black smoke, shot with flames, rose from the blazing buildings. Many of the Auxiliaries and Black-and-Tans were drunk and were shooting wildly, to the great danger of the fire-brigade. . . . In a night of frenzied disorder, soldiers, and even some Auxiliaries and Black-and-Tans, tried to fight the fire while others extended them. As the night advanced . . . uniformed figures were to be seen everywhere, staggering through the fire-lit streets, with valises bulging with loot. At two o'clock in the morning the incendiary forces of law and order broke into the City Hall and Carnegie Library and by four-o'clock, after one unsuccessful attempt, had them both blazing well with the use of bombs and petrol. A party of police guarded the hydrants and turned off the water every time the firemen turned it on. By five the clock tower of the City Hall was glowing as though it were floodlit and the clock went on striking the hour until six–fifteen, when it crashed into the ruins below. Few worshippers ventured out when the church bells rang for mass. The police had withdrawn at about five o'clock, but military patrols were still on the streets; some of them were also the worse for drink. As it became light, hundreds came out to see the damage: Patrick Street, the main street of the city, had been laid waste; twenty-one shops had been completely destroyed. In all, forty shops had been burned to the ground, twenty-four partially damaged and many more looted. The damage was estimated at £3 million.

Richard Bennett: The Black-and-Tans.

EXERCISES

1. What is meant by the phrase in the above extract—"the incendiary forces of law and order"?
2. Explain: "Coupon" election, "Red Letter" election, "Safety First" election, Sinn Fein.
3. Identify the authors of the following and explain where necessary:
   (a) "A fit country for heroes to live in."
   (b) "Executed by Order of the I.R.A.—Spies and Informers Beware."
   (c) "Things are being done in Ireland which would disgrace the blackest annals of the lowest despotism in Europe."

13

(*d*) "Tomorrow every duchess in London will be wanting to kiss me."
4. Write short notes on the following: Sankey Commission; Irish Republican Army; Black-and-Tans; Abdication Crisis, 1936.
5. Write notes on the following: The Irish "Troubles", 1919–21; Bonar Law; Financial Crisis of 1931.
6. Describe the work of the Labour Governments of 1924 and 1929–31.
7. Describe and account for the formation of the National Government in 1931.
8. Give an account of the career of *either* Stanley Baldwin *or* Ramsay MacDonald *or* Neville Chamberlain.

CHAPTER X

EUROPE BETWEEN THE WARS

Reparations and Disarmament. After the First World War, Britain and France emerged as the leading powers in Europe. The days of "splendid isolation" were over for Britain. She had been one of the founder-members of the League of Nations, and she was also committed to uphold the peace treaties, for which she had been, along with France and the United States, mainly responsible. Lloyd George's own interest in foreign affairs arose naturally enough from the part he played in the peace conference at Versailles. There was no French statesman who could compare with him for continuity of experience, as the French parliamentary system involved frequent changes of government. Partly because of this, the French appeared to the British as awkward allies, and attempts to solve the problems of post-war Europe nearly all broke down over this difficulty of Anglo-French co-operation. The main problems were those concerned with Germany's payment of REPARATIONS. Most Frenchmen were still bent on making Germany "pay for the war", regardless of the consequences to Germany. There were many difficulties about large-scale reparations, but the most important was that to exact a large amount meant the impoverishment of Germany and the creation of increased enmity between the nations. Lloyd George tried with little success to get the French to reduce their demands from the Germans. France was also difficult over the question of disarmament, which Britain was keen to carry out if only for the sake of reducing expenditure. A WASHINGTON CONFERENCE on disarmament met in 1921; but although all the naval powers agreed on limiting their fleets, France was unwilling to have any reduction of her army. When Germany's internal condition worsened, the Government in Berlin declared their inability to pay reparations and resorted to inflation, printing notes to pay off internal debts. Britain was willing to allow Germany a moratorium (or delay), but France, along with Belgium, in January 1923 sent troops into the RUHR valley, Germany's most important coal and iron producing district. The Ruhr miners adopted a policy of passive resistance, refused to work and told the French to "dig out the coal with their bayonets". The German Government, finding itself with over five million persons to support in the Ruhr, began even more serious inflation of the currency. The pound sterling had been worth about 20 marks before 1914; by 1921 it was worth about 1,300, in mid-June 1923 about 500,000 and by the end of the year about 20 billion marks. It was on November 9th of that year that an Austrian, Adolf Hitler, who had been a corporal in the German Army, attempted with General Ludendorff a *putsch* in Munich that proved a fiasco. This INFLATION had serious consequences for Germany of which we shall hear later; but it led to a new scheme for the payment of reparations, the DAWES PLAN (1924) called after the American Charles Dawes, later Vice-President of the United States. It was based on the slogan "Business not Politics" and aimed at reducing reparations to a level which Germany could pay, while providing for loans to Germany to set up her industries again. France through the influence of Ramsay MacDonald, accepted the Dawes Plan. The atmosphere of international affairs was helped by the policy of conciliation pursued by the men in charge of affairs in Western Europe, Stresemann in Germany, Briand in France, and Austen Chamberlain in Baldwin's second ministry. The signing of the LOCARNO AGREEMENTS (1925) was heralded as the dawn of a new era; and Germany was admitted to the League of Nations in the following year. At Locarno, the Franco-German and Belgo-German frontiers were guaranteed by Germany, France, Belgium, Britain and Italy, so that it was conceivable that aggression by France or Belgium would lead to Britain's going to Germany's aid. The Locarno spirit helped to ease tension in Western Europe for some time, although the Russians, whose government had been recognized by MacDonald in 1924, were again isolated and rebuffed when the Conservatives in 1926 withdrew British recognition. In 1928 the American Secretary of State (or foreign minister) Frank Kellogg joined with the French Premier Briand in a plan for the renunciation of war by all nations; this BRIAND–KELLOGG PACT was signed by 63 states in all. But although the nations' representatives solemnly promised "to abolish war as an instrument of policy", there was no provision for enforcing the pact on its signatories. Like the Locarno Agreements, however, it helped to lessen international tension.

Post-war Dictatorships. When Woodrow Wilson, President of the United States, asked Congress for a declaration of war against Germany in 1917, he declared that "the world must be made safe for democracy". Yet, looking back on the history of the years following the First World War, one is struck by the number of dictatorships which were set up during that time and which owed their origin in one way or another to the war itself or to the post-war settlement. The war left troubles in its wake. Even for the victors the consequences of the arrival of peace meant unemployment, heavy taxation, social and political unrest. After the war, a weak and ineffective government, unable to cope with the problems of peace, was apt to be overthrown by revolution. War upsets old ideas and traditions and creates new ones. After 1918 both Communism and Fascism grew in strength. The military class in many countries was reluctant to throw over the reins of power and, having learned to use force against the enemy outside the frontiers, was not averse to using it also against the enemy within. The fact that so many countries which had experienced democratic government should be willing to accept dictatorship has made some writers wonder whether the long struggle for democratic freedom was after all worth while. In nearly all the countries where dictatorship arose, however, there was little or no democracy previously, e.g. in Russia and Turkey, or it had not advanced very far, e.g. in Germany, which had a semi-autocratic government and a militarist tradition, and in Italy, which had not yet attained political maturity. Developments since the Second World War have been not unlike those after the First World War. One country which used to be called a "model democracy", Czechoslovakia, has become a Communist dictatorship, while the French, dissatisfied with the functioning of democracy, have entrusted large powers to their wartime leader, General de Gaulle.

Rise of Mussolini. The post-war years, 1918–22, were as difficult for Italy, which had been on the winning side, as they were for any of the defeated countries except Russia. The Treaty of Versailles disappointed the Italians, who had hoped for a bigger share of the German and Turkish territories. They had met with some severe reverses in the war and had suffered heavy casualties (over 600,000 deaths) but these sacrifices now seemed to them to have been in vain. To their disappointment and disillusionment were added grievances about economic conditions. Unemployment was widespread, food and fuel were scarce and dear, and inflation developed. As one Government succeeded another without any improvement in the affairs of the country, lawlessness and disorder became more common. In 1920, the workers occupied the factories in Northern Italy and tried to manage them. But there was a lack of leadership and the workers soon stood down. This failure weakened the Socialist party and strengthened the new Fascist party, run by a former Socialist, BENITO MUSSOLINI. Mussolini (1883–1945), a blacksmith's son, tried his mother's profession of teaching for a short time and then went abroad to Switzerland. He became a journalist, editing the Socialist paper *Avanti* (Forward) before the First World War and was actually imprisoned for his pacifist writings. He changed his opinions when war started, left the Socialists and joined the Army, rising to the rank of corporal. After the war he founded the *Fascio di Combattimenti*, a union of ex-servicemen. Many similar bodies were organized on a semi-military basis; the black shirt used by some Italian shock battalions during the war was chosen as a uniform and the old Roman salute of the raised hand was revived. The magistrates of ancient Rome used to be attended by officers carrying *fasces* (bundles of rods) and an axe, the instruments of punishment. The badge of the *fasces* was adopted by Mussolini, as it represented authority and the strength that came from union. In 1921, frequent clashes occurred between these Fascists (as they came to be known) and the rapidly-growing Communist party. It was in FIUME, a port on the Dalmatian coast, that the Fascists had their first success. A famous Italian poet, GABRIELE D'ANNUNZIO, had seized the former Austrian town of Fiume, which had been given to Yugoslavia in the peace settlement but which, according to the Italians, was an Italian city. At first the Italian Government refused to support D'Annunzio and after a year sent troops to expel him from Fiume; but in March 1922 it was seized again, this time by Fascist Blackshirts. In the summer of 1922 they had further successes. They took control of the cities of Bologna and Milan; and when a general strike was declared, the public services were kept going by them. In October, Fascists began to arrive in Rome in large numbers (later this was called "the March on Rome") and Mussolini demanded the resignation of the Government. When the King refused to support the Government, they resigned and Mussolini arrived by train from Milan to take over the leadership of a coalition government, in which at first only four out of fourteen were Fascists. By a combination of threats and promises, the Italian Chamber of Deputies was persuaded to grant Mussolini and his Cabinet full powers for one year. From then on, the Fascists took over the control of the Army and of the Government, both national and local. Their opponents were beaten up and their homes wrecked. One of the Socialist leaders, Matteotti, was murdered in 1924 and Mussolini was openly accused as the instigator of the crime. The murderers were later released after only two months' imprisonment. By 1926 all the other parties were outlawed, censorship of the press was rigorously imposed and freedom disappeared from Italy for a generation. The causes of the Fascists' success were similar to those in other countries where a revolutionary party achieved its ends:—(1) the weakness and incompetence of successive Governments; (2) the social and economic discontent following the war; (3) the political grievances about the peace settlement; (4) the existence of a strong political party, prepared to go to any length to achieve power.

Fascist Italy. Italy was the first totalitarian state in Western Europe. In a totalitarian state, the Government exerts its authority over the people and all their activities, there is only one political party and its function is to carry out the orders of the ruler or dictator. The motto of the Fascists was "No discussions, only obedience"; and Mussolini himself became known as *Il Duce* (the leader). In theory, the party was ruled by the Fascist Grand Council but all the members of the Council were nominated by Mussolini. The Chamber of Deputies was only a rubber-stamp for Mussolini's wishes as it was also an entirely Fascist body, chosen by the Grand Council. After 1938 it ceased to exist and its place was taken by the National Council of Corporations. These corporations represented the various industries, both employers and workers included. This idea of a CORPORATIVE STATE has been advocated by many writers, particularly Socialists, as a more natural basis for a Parliament than the usual method of election by constituencies. In Italy, however, it was completely under the control of the Fascist Government. Mussolini was to remain as dictator until 1943 during the Second World War. He did not attempt to abolish the monarchy, although the Italian King, Victor Emmanuel III, was only a figurehead. Mussolini was chiefly responsible for the famous CONCORDAT OF 1929, signed by the Pope Pius XI and the King and ending the quarrel which had gone on since 1870, when Rome became the capital of a united kingdom. Since then the Pope had been "the Prisoner of the Vatican", but from 1929 he was recognized as sovereign over the small state of the Vatican City, while in return the Pope recognized the Italian monarchy. This action helped Mussolini to obtain the support of the Catholics, who saw in him a bulwark against the Communists. Mussolini carried out an extensive programme of reconstruction: hydro-electric schemes were started, the railway trains were speeded up and made to run on time, great motoring roads were constructed, swamps were drained so that fertile land became available for cultivation, bandits in Sicily and Naples were suppressed. In a sense, therefore, Fascism could be said to have been successful but there was deep resentment among the lower classes, who felt exploited. In the depression of the 1930's Italy was badly hit, poverty and unemployment were rife, and it was partly in order to divert attention from troubles at home that Mussolini launched out on his aggressive foreign policy. Claims were made that the Mediterranean should be, as in the days of ancient Rome, *mare nostrum*; the return of Tunis, Corsica and Nice (all French possessions) was demanded at Fascist gatherings. The Italians, who have not in modern times been easily stirred by prospects of war, were encouraged by slogans painted on the walls of houses such as "Believe, obey, fight" and "Better one day as a lion than a hundred years as a sheep". In 1935, hoping for an easy conquest, Mussolini sent his armies to Abyssinia and, with only halfhearted opposition from the League of Nations, conquered it. The BERLIN–ROME AXIS, the collaboration of Germany and Italy after 1936, developed into a full military alliance in 1939, involving Mussolini's entry into the Second World War, with disastrous consequences to Italy and to himself.

Rise of Hitler. By the time Fascism and Mussolini had become established in Italy, a similar movement and a leader were to be found in Germany. ADOLF HITLER (1889–1945) was not born in Germany but in Austria. After an unhappy youth, when he failed to achieve his ambition to be a painter, he lived for some time by casual work in Vienna, where he is said to have acquired his hatred of the Jews. He then went to Munich in South

Germany, which he much preferred to Vienna as he considered it a more German city. When war broke out in 1914 he joined the Germany Army and, like Mussolini, rose to the rank of corporal. After the war he was employed as an agent by the German Army, which hoped one day to regain some of its former power. It was in Munich that he joined a small political group that formed itself into the National Socialist German Workers' Party. (The name was shortened to the first two syllables of the German word for "National", *Nazional*.) In 1923, along with the former

Swastika   Fasces   Hammer and sickle

EMBLEMS OF DICTATORSHIP

general Ludendorff, he tried a *putsch* in Munich but failed and was sentenced to five years' imprisonment. He served only eight months of his sentence, during which he wrote the first volume of his life-story, *Mein Kampf* (My Struggle), setting forth his political programme. His book, which was completed by 1927, contains dogmatic assertions about the superiority of what he called the Aryan or Nordic race, the leading representatives of which were the Germans. He condemned outright Jews, Bolsheviks and the French, ascribed the German defeat in the First World War to a "stab in the back" by Jews and Communists at home, and denounced the iniquities of what he called the Versailles *Diktat* or dictated peace of 1919. With Britain and Italy as allies, he claimed, Germany could destroy Russia and France. Hitler's first success came with the economic depression when his party won 106 seats in the Reichstag (or Parliament) in the 1930 election. As the depression worsened, Hitler's support grew. His propaganda machine, which was in the hands of DR. JOSEPH GOEBBELS, was easily the best in Germany. His private armies, the Brownshirts or Stormtroopers also called S.A. (abbreviation for *Sturm-Abteilungen*) and the Blackshirts or S.S. (*Schutz-Staffeln*) mustered over half a million men between them and used violent tactics to break up opponents' meetings. One of the Brownshirts, a young student called HORST WESSEL, whose death was blamed on the Communists, became a hero of the Nazi movement; and a song he had written about the S.A. was adopted as a second national anthem by Nazi Germany. In 1932 Hitler actually stood for the Presidency against the veteran Field Marshal VON HINDENBURG, who had been President since 1925, and polled over 13 million votes against Hindenburg's $17\frac{1}{2}$ million. Hitler's chance came in January 1933, when President Hindenburg was persuaded to appoint him Chancellor (a post like that of our Prime Minister) with a Cabinet composed partly of Nazis and partly of other German Nationalists. Those who helped him in the last stage of his rise to power were some of the nationalist landowning class who wished to see Germany strong and the industrialists who saw in Hitler's programme a chance to revive the dying steel industry of Germany. One of his first acts as Chancellor was to get rid of his enemies and rivals. When the Reichstag was set on fire by a Dutchman, Van der Lubbe, as a protest against the new Nazi regime, the Communists were blamed for the fire and hundreds were thrown into jail. The *Gestapo* or secret police, the S.A. and S.S. soon got to work and political opponents began to disappear into concentration camps. The Socialist wing of Hitler's National Socialist German Workers' Party was removed by having them arrested, accused of a plot and executed. Several hundreds died in this Nazi "Blood Bath" on June 30th 1934, "the night of the long knives" as it was called. When the old President Hindenburg died in August 1934, Hitler became both President and Chancellor with supreme power, and at the ensuing plebiscite when the people had to vote "*Ja oder nein*" ("Yes or no") the figures showed over 99 per cent in his favour.

Reasons for Hitler's Success. The rise of Hitler to power in Germany was due to a variety of causes, not unlike those responsible for the growth of Fascism in Italy. (1) Earliest in origin was the sense of grievance about the Treaty of Versailles felt by the Germans, so proud of their military past. It was not so vindictive a treaty as that of Brest-Litovsk, which they imposed on the Russians. But they complained that it was a dictated peace and not a negotiated peace. Apart from the loss of territories (including the few colonies they had), they also resented the occupation forces and the heavy reparations demanded. (2) The inflation of 1923 brought hardship and distress in Germany and helped the rise of new parties like the Communists and the National Socialists. When the depression came in the 1930's many Germans turned in despair to the parties which boldly offered to solve the problem of unemployment. (3) Wealthy industrialists saw that Hitler and his party were their strongest bulwark against Communism and would make possible the revival of the armaments industry. By contributions to Hitler's funds, they helped him to maintain a vast organization and a private army of Brownshirts, who crushed opposition by terrorist methods. (4) The leadership of the National Socialist party was fanatical, ruthless and efficient. Propaganda was controlled by the unscrupulous Dr. Goebbels, who thought that there was no lie so big that it could not be put over by forceful propaganda and who accused Jews, Americans and Bolshevists equally of enmity to Germany. Once established as the Government, Hitler and his colleagues suppressed all opposition parties, throwing thousands without trial into concentration camps and using the secret police (the *Gestapo*) to maintain a reign of terror. (5) In the late 1930's Hitler, by repudiating the Treaty of Versailles and by reducing unemployment, obtained the passive support of many who had never voted for him before 1933.

Hitler's Germany. In the six years between coming to power and launching war against Poland in 1939, Hitler was able to carry out a far-reaching programme in home and foreign affairs. (1) In furtherance of Hitler's ideas of anti-semitism, Jews were deprived of their German citizenship by the Nuremberg Laws of 1935; and those occupying official positions in the state or universities were compelled to resign, among them many world-famous figures such as Einstein the physicist. All people in official positions were obliged to produce evidence showing that they were of Aryan (i.e. non-Jewish) descent. Hitler seemed to believe genuinely in his anti-semitism but it was also a useful political trick to have the Jews as scape-goats for anything that went wrong. Naturally, many of them left Germany, and Palestine became crowded with refugees. In November 1938, following the assassination of a German diplomat in Paris by a young Polish Jew, hundreds of Jews in Germany were murdered, others thrown into concentration camps and a fine of almost £100,000,000 levied on the whole Jewish community. During the Second World War, when Germany conquered most of Europe, the Jews suffered terribly. Many were electrocuted or sent to their death in gas-chambers in Poland at the rate of 10,000 a day, while others, herded together in the dreadful "Ghetto" in Warsaw, died of starvation or typhus or other diseases. It is estimated that the Jewish population in Europe fell by at least five millions during the years 1939–45 for one cause or another; and for this terrible racial extermination Hitler must bear the chief responsibility. (2) In economic affairs, Hitler gained credit for the reduction of unemployment figures. This he achieved by recruiting some of them for his S.A. and S.S. troops, by compulsory military service and by the intro-duction of labour service for young Germans who were employed on projects like building larger motor roads or *Autobahnen*, useful in peace for the tourists and in war for the troops. The armaments and aircraft industries began to thrive on orders from the Nazi Government. The "little man" who had feared or hated the Nazis could not but feel grateful that he once more had a regular job and a full stomach. (3) As in other totalitarian states, only one party, the Nazi party, was permitted to function, and the Reichstag met merely to applaud a speech from the *Fuehrer* or leader, or his deputies. The principle of leadership (*Fuehrerschaft*) had been emphasized by Hitler in *Mein Kampf* as the only real basis of authority in a state and he was fond of attacking the "decadent democracies". With all political opponents removed to concentration camps, all books and newspapers critical of Hitler *verboten* (forbidden) and Germans unable to take more than a few days' holiday abroad, Nazi propaganda had every chance of success. Many of the older Germans still remained sceptical but the youth of Germany, indoctrinated in the Hitler Youth movement and in the schools, gave loyal and devoted support to Hitler. At the gigantic Nazi party rallies, Hitler received a most enthusiastic reception from his devoted followers, who would chant "*Ein Volk, ein Reich, ein Fuehrer*" ("One people, one Empire, one Leader") or "*Sieg Heil! Sieg Heil!*" ("Hail, Victory! Hail, Victory!"). All Nazis greeted one another with "Heil Hitler" and expected others to do the same. In addition, Nazis in schools, offices, workshops and dwelling-houses acted as spies on their neighbours, and anyone critical of the Government was likely to be taken away to a concentration camp by the *Gestapo*, who were often guilty of brutal treatment of their prisoners. In theory, these were only supposed to be in "protective custody" and were never brought to trial; but many thousands died of torture, starvation and overwork in camps like Dachau, Büchenwald and Belsen, the horrors of which were revealed to a shocked world in 1945 when Allied troops occupied Germany. The ordinary German, conscious that Hitler had overcome the depression and restored Germany's prestige, shut his ears to stories of Nazi brutality and found it easier to do nothing, as criticism of the Nazis would mean a visit from the *Gestapo*. But he had to pay for this acceptance of Hitler and the Nazis when the Second World War came and Germany was devastated.

Hitler's Foreign Policy. The chief aim of Hitler's foreign policy, was, as he often maintained, to abolish the Versailles Treaty. Soon after he came to power in 1933, he withdrew German representatives from the Disarmament Conference and from the League of Nations, which he regarded as the tool of the powers that had dictated the Versailles settlement. Reparations had ended with the depression; but Hitler insisted that Germany should be allowed equal rights with other countries in the matter of national defence and would never be content until the last German territories were restored to the Fatherland. Although the German Army was limited by the Treaty of Versailles to 100,000, it soon exceeded that figure after 1933 by the enrolment of volunteers. Germany was also prohibited from possessing an air force but nevertheless military airfields were constructed all over the country and military aeroplanes, disguised as commercial aeroplanes, were used to train men for an air force. In 1935 Hitler introduced conscription for COMPULSORY MILITARY SERVICE, publicly denouncing the Treaty of Versailles because of the way in which the Germans had been compelled to accept the dictated settlement and also because of the failure of the Allied Powers to disarm. France appealed to the League of Nations but Britain, her chief ally, was unwilling to take any action which would involve the use of force. Instead, she angered France by signing a NAVAL PACT with Germany, allowing her, despite the Treaty of Versailles, to build a navy of not more than 35 per cent of Britain's naval tonnage. Mussolini's defiance of the League of Nations over Abyssinia in 1935–36 received the support of Hitler, who seized the opportunity of the Abyssinian crisis to carry out the REOCCUPATION OF THE RHINELAND in March 1936, again contrary to the provisions of the Treaty of Versailles. In the same year, after the Spanish Civil War started, Hitler and Mussolini signed a pact establishing the BERLIN–ROME AXIS, and were soon helping the Spanish Fascist leader, Franco, with arms and men. By the end of 1936, Germany and Italy were linked with Japan in the ANTI-COMINTERN PACT against international Communism. Hitler had re-armed Germany despite the Treaty of Versailles, he had allied himself with Mussolini, and along with him had intervened in the Spanish Civil War. He was still determined to regain the German territories lost at Versailles and he made reference in his speeches at the great Nazi rallies at Nuremberg and elsewhere to the

German *Lebensraum* or living-space and to the ten million Germans outside the Reich. When the Germans of the Saar, whose mines had been run by the French for fifteen years, voted overwhelmingly in a plebiscite in 1935 for a return to Germany, beacon fires were lit on all the German frontiers as signals of hope to the German minorities in Poland, Czechoslovakia and France. It was, however, to Austria, his native country, inhabited by people of the same race as the Germans, that Hitler turned his attention in 1937. For years, some Austrians, conscious of the weakness of Austria as a state, had advocated ANSCHLUSS or union with Germany. Since Hitler came to power in 1933, the idea had not been so popular, particularly after some Nazis murdered the Austrian Chancellor, Dollfuss, in 1934. But the Austrian Government, lacking support from any of the Great Powers, was unable to stand up to pressure from Nazi sympathizers inside the country and to pressure from Hitler outside. The Austrian Chancellor, Schuschnigg, was summoned to meet Hitler in his Bavarian home at Berchtesgaden in February 1938. He tried to rally support at home but was unable to resist the Germans who invaded Austria in March. Hitler made a triumphal entry into the Vienna in which he had spent such a miserable youth and Austria became part of the greater German Reich or Empire. By March 1939 he was similarly installed in Prague, the capital of Czechoslovakia, after a year of bullying and threats which nearly led to war. It was over the German minority in the Polish Corridor that war finally came, but only after Hitler had secured himself from a two-front war by signing a Non-aggression Pact with the Russians whom he hated and despised.

Other Dictatorships. One of the first dictatorships set up after the First World War was that of KEMAL ATATÜRK in Turkey. As Mustapha Kemal Pasha he had been the leading Turkish general in the defence of the Dardanelles against the British in 1915. After the war, he was one of those who opposed the dismemberment of the Ottoman Empire by the Treaty of Sèvres (1920), and when the Greeks, in the name of the Allies, invaded Asia Minor to enforce the treaty settlement, Kemal defeated them and drove them out. Shortly afterwards Kemal led a nationalist revolt against the Government in Constantinople; the Ottoman Empire came to an end, the Sultan was deposed, and Kemal became President of the Turkish Republic with the capital at Angora, re-named ANKARA. From 1923 to 1938 he was dictator of Turkey. He overcame Muslim opposition to his policy of westernization, he abolished polygamy, banned the fez and discouraged the wearing of the veil. His idea was to break with the traditions, religious, social and political, of the decadent Ottoman Empire. He even introduced the Latin alphabet instead of the Arabic, and gave the first lesson to his own Cabinet. In 1936, when Turks were made to adopt surnames, he took the name Atatürk, meaning "Father of the Turks". Turkey, under him, went well on the way to becoming a modern state but the ruthlessness of the old Turks still survived: nationalist opposition by the Armenians and Kurds was suppressed in a manner that recalled the worst atrocities of the nineteenth century.

Poland was another country where the post-war troubles and confusion made a group of officers under MARSHAL PILSUDSKI seize power in 1926. This régime of the "Colonels", established to protect the interests of the Army and the wealthy landowners, lasted for nearly ten years, during which time the political opponents of the Government were imprisoned and often tortured. After Pilsudski's death in 1935, when he was succeeded by Marshal Smigly-Rydz, only one party was allowed in Parliament, although the other parties continued to exist in a kind of way outside Parliament. It was this Polish Government which made a non-aggression pact with Nazi Germany and which supported German aggression against Czechoslovakia only to find itself the victim of German aggression in 1939.

It was as a result of the Spanish Civil War (1936–39) that another soldier, GENERAL FRANCO, became dictator of Spain. There had been an earlier dictatorship under another General, Primo de Rivera, from 1925 till 1930 and when a revolution broke out in 1931, King Alfonso XIII was deposed. In 1936 another revolt started in Morocco, then in Spain, against the left-wing Socialist Government. The leaders were Army officers, among them General Franco, who wished to restore the former powers of the Catholic Church and the great landowners. With help from Germany and Italy, Franco finally defeated the Government forces, after he had besieged Madrid for over two years. During that time the Spanish Government forces, helped by Russian tanks and volunteers from all countries fighting in an International Brigade, resisted in determined fashion, with the slogan, "No pasaran" ("They shall not pass"). Franco, who was besieging Madrid with four columns, was helped by sympathizers in Madrid, where, he claimed, they formed a FIFTH COLUMN, a name still used for those organizing sabotage and espionage for a foreign power. Madrid fell in April 1939 and Franco, the *Caudillo* or dictator of Spain, set up a state modelled on Italian rather than on German lines. Spain's neighbour, Portugal, also lost its democratic government as far back as 1926 when a group of Army officers seized power, and in 1932 it was under the virtual dictatorship of DR. SALAZAR, a former university professor of economics. Although there was only one party as in other totalitarian states, yet it was a mild dictatorship compared with those already described and Dr. Salazar carried out a number of reforms, improving social conditions and promoting industrial development.

The Third Republic. How did the democracies survive the difficult post-war periods? The heavy casualties suffered by France in the First World War and the enormous amount of damage done to their towns and industries in Northern France left the French bitter and resentful. Their bitterness increased when it became clear as the years went on that they would not receive from Germany the reparations they had hoped for. The British seemed to them unable to realize the importance of keeping Germany weak and making her pay reparations: they had not suffered as much as the French nor were they so near to the German frontiers. Relations between the two countries were bedevilled by the difference in their attitudes to Germany. French Governments found the financial difficulties of the post-war period too much for them. The burden of the National Debt was increased by further loans to rebuild the devasted areas; and the occupation of the Ruhr in 1923 to force the German miners to produce coal only added to their financial troubles. In 1926 inflation had become so bad that the veteran minister, Poincaré, came back to office and helped to stabilize the nation's finances. The franc was, however, eventually devalued in 1928 at about 20 per cent of its pre-war value. People with savings were badly hit but not to the same extent that the German middle class suffered in their inflation of 1923. The world depression also affected France, but as it was not so industrialized as Britain, Germany and the United States, unemployment did not become so serious a problem. The 1930's were a period of great political strife and disorder. In 1934 there occurred the STAVISKY AFFAIR: the disclosure that Stavisky, a financier, had organized a large-scale swindle with bogus bonds and that Government officials were implicated led to a general strike and riots in Paris where over 200 were killed. Both Fascist and Communist parties grew in strength, and it seemed as if France might go the same way as Italy and Germany. To counter a possible Fascist *putsch*, the parties of the left (Radicals, Socialists, Communists) in 1934 formed themselves into a coalition called the POPULAR FRONT under the leadership of LEON BLUM, head of the Socialist party. Blum had to face tremendous difficulties in 1935 when "stay-in" and "sit-down" strikes became widespread; but he managed to establish collective bargaining for pay increases, holidays with pay, with a 40-hour week to please the workers and fixed prices of grain and other commodities to please the peasants. These measures did not help to solve France's economic problems, however, and, despite another devaluation of the franc, Blum was forced to resign in 1937. France was still in too weak a position to do much about German threats in 1938 and, relying on her defensive system called the Maginot Line, she fell after a few weeks' fighting when the Germans invaded in 1940. France's frequent changes of Government and multiplicity of parties did not help to achieve stability between the wars. These have often been blamed by foreign observers on the French character, which is said to be unstable and volatile. But the political instability was due primarily to the fact that the defeat of a

Government did not necessarily mean an election. The Chamber of Deputies was elected for a four-year term and deputies knew that they could make a Government resign without running the risk of a general election in which they might lose their seats. The average life of a French Government between 1871 and 1939 was eight months and some ministries lasted only a few weeks. The party boundaries were not so rigidly defined as in Britain and deputies frequently changed from one party to another. The looseness of the French party organization was such that in the Senate the parties were differently named and arranged. This instability of French ministries made government difficult, particularly in foreign affairs.

Czechoslovakia. The dismemberment of Austria-Hungary in 1919 led to the creation of a new state, Czechoslovakia, which was often cited between the wars as a model democracy. In all the "Succession States" (those set up in succession to the Austria-Hungarian Empire) dictatorships were established except in Czechoslovakia. The Czechs and Slovaks had for centuries been under the rule of the Austrians and Hungarians. During the war, many of them had deserted to the side of the Allies; and a Czechoslovak Legion, several thousand strong, gained the admiration of the world for an epic journey from Russia across Siberia to Vladivostok after the Revolution of 1917. The two Czechoslovak leaders during the First World War were THOMAS G. MASARYK, a university professor, and EDUARD BENEŠ, professor in a commercial college, both of whom were to become Presidents of the Czechoslovak Republic. The obvious frontiers of the new state in the west were the natural frontiers of the mountains surrounding Bohemia and these were the frontiers chosen at the peace settlement of 1919. But the Bohemian frontiers included many Germans, descendants of immigrants who had over the centuries settled down in the frontier lands. They were sometimes called the SUDETEN GERMANS, as they were strongest in the district of Sudetenland. This strong minority, numbering over three millions, presented Czechoslovakia with a thorny problem. As Czechoslovakia owed its origin to the Versailles recognition of the right to self-determination and as both the Czechs and Slovaks had been minorities for centuries, they were careful to give the German minority their full rights. Under the able leadership of President Masaryk, the new state settled down; the people were proud of the capital, Praha or

Expansion of Germany, 1935–9

Prague, one of the most beautiful cities of Europe and formerly the capital of the Holy Roman Empire, and also of their country's achievements in industry, agriculture, science and the arts. But the world depression hit the German industrial areas of Sudetenland badly and the German minority began to complain that the Czechoslovak Government gave priority to the interests of the Czechoslovaks. There were many minor pinpricks such as making Czech a compulsory language in all German schools. Nor was it easy for Germans who had been in a majority in the former Austrian Empire to accept the changed circumstances. When Hitler and the Nazis came to power, a German nationalist party was formed in Sudetenland. Beneš, who had been Foreign Minister since 1918 and succeeded Masaryk in 1935, foresaw the trouble that Hitler was to cause in Europe and signed treaties with France and Russia against Germany and with Rumania and Yugoslavia against Hungary. These treaties and the careful attention paid to the rights of the German minority, which enjoyed more freedom than any other similar minority in Europe, did not avail the Czechoslovaks when in 1938 Hitler began his campaign of propaganda against them and war was averted only at the last minute by the sacrifice at Munich. The Munich crisis of September 1938 was followed by the immediate occupation by the German armies of the frontier districts and later in March 1939 by the annexation of the rest of the country. A German "Protectorate" was declared over Bohemia and Moravia, the two western points of the Republic, while Slovakia was allowed to enjoy an uneasy independence for a few more years. The fact that Czechoslovakia had a democratic government had nothing to do with her falling a victim to Hitler's ambitions. Austria and Poland, which were semi-dictatorships, fell almost as easily. The Scandinavian states, Norway, Sweden and Denmark, the small countries of Belgium, Holland, Switzerland and Finland, all democracies, managed to function very well until they were engulfed in the Second World War. Czechoslovakia between the wars showed the danger that lurks for any state which encloses within its frontiers a large minority of the same race as that of a powerful neighbour.

Democracy and Dictatorship. In Britain we are so accustomed to our democratic form of government that we are reluctant to concede any merit in dictatorship. But there are some people in Britain who believe that the principles of leadership and authority in the state are more important than that of the freedom of the individual. A party called the British Union of Fascists was actually founded in the 1930's by SIR OSWALD MOSLEY, a wealthy ex-member of the Socialist party, who adopted the black shirt as a uniform, used a kind of Nazi salute with the upraised hand, sang the Nazi Horst Wessel song with an English text and openly sympathized with Germany and Italy. In 1940 he was, along with a Conservative M.P., Captain Ramsay, also of Fascist sympathies, interned for the duration of the war. It is certainly true, as Mosley claimed, that in most dictator states it was possible to achieve certain aims that could not have been reached had they remained democracies. An American once contrasted democracies and monarchies in words that could also be applied to democracies and dictatorships: "Monarchy" (or dictatorship) "is like a splendid ship with all sails set: it moves majestically on, then it hits a rock and sinks forever. Democracy is like a raft. It never sinks, but, damn it, your feet are always in the water." In democracies, a fairly low rate of progress is maintained because of the need to find a compromise between various points of view: in a dictatorship, progress may be spectacularly rapid or it may end suddenly in disaster. The contrast has been put in other words—freedom versus efficiency. But that phrase suggests that efficiency is bound to exist in dictatorships (which is not the case) and that it cannot exist in democracies. In a dictatorship, there is absolute power for the dictator to achieve his aims, regardless of other interests. The famous historian, Lord Acton, wrote: "Power tends to corrupt, and absolute power corrupts absolutely." The history of the inter-war period shows only a few cases, such as that of Dr. Salazar in Portugal, where Acton's dictum did not apply to the dictators. The troubles of the democracies were as nothing to the sufferings of the political opponents of Hitler and Mussolini and of the German and Italian nations when they were launched into war.

League of Nations. The League of Nations was set up in 1920 as part of the peace settlement. The fourteenth of President Woodrow Wilson's Fourteen Points had stipulated a League of Nations to guarantee "political independence and territorial integrity". Wilson was to suffer the humiliation of seeing his proposal rejected by the Congress of the United States. The first part of the Treaty of Versailles and of the other peace treaties contains the LEAGUE OF NATIONS COVENANT, a solemn contract of twenty-six articles, which form the constitution of the League. By this Covenant, the members of the League bound themselves (among other things) to respect and preserve against aggression each other's independence and territorial integrity, not to employ force in a dispute until arbitration had failed, and to reduce armaments "to the lowest point consistent with national safety". According to the Covenant, economic or military SANCTIONS (denial of important war materials or actual armed intervention) could be taken against any state committing aggression in defiance of the Covenant; but no country could be compelled to impose sanctions nor was the League to have any armed force at its disposal. The ASSEMBLY of the League met annually at Geneva in Switzerland, the country with the longest tradition of neutrality. Each of the fifty or more member states represented in the Assembly had a vote; the actual number of members varied as one state joined and another left. The Assembly was nominally responsible for the various German or Turkish lands mandated or handed over on trust to the victorious powers: thus German East Africa became the MANDATED TERRITORY of Tanganyika under the control of the British Colonial Office. Commissioners of the League of Nations were appointed to the Free City of Danzig, a German city surrounded by Polish territory, and to the Saarland. The COUNCIL, consisting of Great Britain, France and later, Russia along with twelve other elected members, met three times a year. In addition, the League was responsible for a PERMANENT COURT OF INTERNATIONAL JUSTICE, meeting at the Hague in Holland and thus continuing in the tradition of the body set up by the Hague Peace Conference of 1899. But no country could be compelled to accept a decision of this Court at the Hague. There was also an INTERNATIONAL LABOUR ORGANIZATION with its headquarters at Geneva to discuss and draw up agreements between nations about working hours, insurance, pensions, etc. There were some smaller organizations functioning under League of Nations auspices, such as the Nansen International Office for Refugees (who were given what came to be known as NANSEN PASSPORTS, called after the famous explorer Nansen, who was in charge of this office) and an Institute for Research on Leprosy, situated in Buenos Aires.

Weakness of the League of Nations. From the start, the League of Nations was weakened by the absence of some of the great powers. The United States, Germany and Russia were all absent from the first meetings. The Germans, who tended to regard the League as a body formed to preserve the Versailles settlement, joined in 1925 but left again in 1933, followed soon after by Japan. Russia did not join until 1934 but after the Abyssinian war, when Mussolini successfully defied the League, Italy left it also. There was a tendency to regard the League Assembly and Council as useless talking-shops; but they did achieve some small successes so far as preserving peace was concerned. The League Commissioners in Danzig and the Saarland were effective until Hitler's time. In 1920–21 a dispute arose between Finland and Sweden over the Aaland Islands in the Baltic and was decided by League arbitration in favour of Finland. When Germany and Poland quarrelled over Upper Silesia in 1922 the League arranged a partition settlement. In 1923, Greece appealed to the League of Nations over the Italian bombardment and occupation of Corfu and the Italians eventually evacuated Corfu. When the Greeks themselves invaded Bulgaria in 1925, following some frontier clashes, the League again settled the matter, imposing a fine on Greece. But all these disputes concerned only small powers; and even the two small South American states, Bolivia and Paraguay, defied the League by continuing their war over the Chaco region from 1932 to 1935. In the 1930's the great powers defied the League with impunity. The will of the League of Nations was, of course, no stronger than the wills of the states that composed it. The crisis of the League came in 1935 over Abyssinia. The League was already suffering from the resignation of Germany and Japan and from its failure to intervene effectively against Japan in the Manchurian affair in 1932. Despite the protestations of France and Britain, the two strongest powers left in the League, neither was prepared to enforce the economic sanctions decided upon by the League in a way that would stop Mussolini's aggression. When the United Nations Organization was set up after the Second World War some attempt was made, as we shall see, to avoid the weaknesses that had shown themselves in the League of Nations.

Failure of the League of Nations. During the 1930's international crises occurred every year or so until at last the nations of the world were at war again. Just before the DIS-ARMAMENT CONFERENCE of the League of Nations opened at Geneva in 1932 under the chairmanship of the British Foreign Secretary, Arthur Henderson, a war started in the Far East, where the Japanese invaded MANCHURIA in Northern China. Although the United States still remained outside the League of Nations, the American Secretary of State, Stimson, protested sharply to Japan and invited Britain and France to join with the United States in exerting pressure on her. Stimson's action, however, was one which the majority of Americans were most unlikely to approve; and neither Britain nor France was willing or prepared to stop the Japanese aggression. In 1932 the League of Nations tried to intervene in the Manchurian dispute but was rebuffed by Japan, which withdrew from the League—the first real blow suffered by the League since the United States had refused to join it. The Disarmament Conference (1932–34) spent a great deal of time in 1933 discussing Ramsay MacDonald's plan to reduce all European armies. But in that year Hitler came to power in Germany and as he very soon withdrew from the Disarmament Conference and the League of Nations, it was hardly worth while for other countries to continue the Confer-ence. Another conference met at Lausanne in 1932 to discuss REPARATIONS, which Germany had been unable to pay because of the depression and the financial crisis of 1931. MacDonald and the French Premier, Herriot, were willing to abandon reparations if the United States would agree to cancel her war debts. But the American depression was at its worst, a Presidential election was in the offing and the debts were not cancelled. Britain and France were finally forced to repudiate their obligations to pay their war debts—a step which made it easier for Hitler to refuse to pay reparations. After the Disarmament Conference adjourned in 1934, Russia joined the League of Nations, seeing danger in the new régime in Germany. In the following year, 1935, Hitler formally denounced the clauses in the Treaty of Versailles about German disarmament and introduced military conscription. France appealed to the League but neither she nor Britain was prepared to act. Baldwin was averse to taking any step that would lead to war, which he felt would destroy the nations involved. As he said in a moment of candour: "Whatever people may tell you, the bomber will always get through. The only defence is offence, which means that you have to kill more women and children than the enemy, if you want to save yourselves." In Britain, as in France, there was at this time a strong pacifist feeling, which led Baldwin at the 1935 election to proclaim his support for disarmament, while at the same time he and the National Government were so alarmed by the new mood of the German rulers that they determined to build up Britain's air force. In 1935 also, seeing that Germany was determined to break the Versailles Treaty by building a navy, the National Government signed a NAVAL PACT with Germany, allowing the Germans to build a navy of not more than 35 per cent of Britain's tonnage. But this Anglo-German Naval Pact annoyed France and all supporters of the League of Nations. France at the same time made an alliance with Russia, aimed against Germany. In the summer of 1935 Mussolini decided to invade ABYSSINIA. Warnings were given at the Council of the League of Nations at Geneva in September 1935 by the British Foreign Secretary, SIR SAMUEL HOARE, who declared that Britain stood for "the maintenance of the Covenant" (of the League of Nations) "in all its integrity, and particularly for the steady and collective resistance to all acts of unprovoked aggression". The French Foreign Secretary likewise announced: "Our obligations are inscribed in the Covenant; France will not evade them." But Mussolini's troops invaded Abyssinia and although the League of Nations imposed economic sanctions on the aggressor by denying Italy war materials, significantly enough, oil was not banned and Mussolini's troops fought on. A secret Anglo-French agreement called the HOARE–LAVAL PACT came to light in the French press and shocked all supporters of the League of Nations; it arranged for a partition of Abyssinia that would leave the Italians supreme. The two foreign ministers, Hoare and Laval, resigned but the Governments, which were involved as well, remained in power. The effect on public opinion was such that all confidence in the League of Nations was lost as the representatives of the chief nations there were only half-hearted in their support of it. Germany took the opportunity of the Italo-Abyssinian crisis to carry out the REOCCUPATION OF THE RHINELAND in March 1936 with only a formal protest from France and Britain. France was keen to take action but in Britain the general feeling was that the Germans could hardly be prevented from re-occupying their own country, if the Italians were allowed to occupy Abyssinia. The opportunity to call Hitler's bluff was lost, for the German generals had actually opposed the move, thinking that the weak, half-trained German army was quite inadequate to stand up against France and Britain. When the SPANISH CIVIL WAR started in the same year (1936), France and Britain decided on a policy of non-intervention; but both Germany and Italy intervened on the Fascist side and Russia on the Government side. The dictators in Germany and Italy came closer together by the establishment of the BERLIN–ROME AXIS, followed soon afterwards by agreements with the Japanese. The three "bad boys" who had left the League of Nations had now ganged up against it. By the beginning of 1937 the initiative in European affairs had passed to what were called the Fascist powers, while the western democracies France and Britain were limping behind, conscious that the League of Nations had failed and building up their armed forces.

Appeasement. Baldwin's Government had in their Naval Pact with Germany and in the Hoare–Laval Pact about Abyssinia undermined the authority of the League of Nations at the same time as they were paying lip-service to it. Sir Samuel Hoare's speech at Geneva in September 1935 and the appointment of Anthony Eden as Minister for League of Nations affairs had been hailed enthusiastically by the supporters of the League; but they had little effect on Mussolini and Hitler except to convince them that they had nothing to fear from Britain. Baldwin had taken little active part in foreign affairs but Chamberlain, who succeeded him in 1937, had his own personal views about other countries, often ignoring the advice of the Foreign Office experts. He brought to international affairs a business-man's outlook; but he made the mistake of thinking that in Hitler and Mussolini he had men on whose word he could rely. As a Conservative, he was naturally anti-Communist and he saw in Germany a bulwark against Communism, not realizing the menace to civilization that lurked in National Socialism itself. His policy of conciliating the Fascist powers has been called "appeasement", a word that gradually acquired a derogatory meaning by the time of the war. Chamberlain was genuinely interested in maintaining peace and was willing to go to any length to do so. Like Baldwin, he consistently underestimated the strength of the German armed forces, as he preferred to believe that they would not be used against Britain. Churchill, from his place in the House of Commons below the gangway, warned the leaders of his party during these years about German rearmament; but although Britain began to build up her own armed forces there was little in the foreign policy of these years to discourage the dictators of Europe. Chamberlain's determination to keep on good terms with Mussolini finally drove his Foreign Secretary, Eden, into resigning. Eden felt that there could be no Anglo-Italian pact so long as Mussolini was flouting the non-intervention agreement he had signed by sending his troops to help Franco and the Fascists in the Civil War in Spain. Italian submarines had also been attacking British merchant ships in the Mediterranean until British destroyers were sent to the area infested by submarines and the attacks ceased abruptly. This success had led Eden to feel that dictators should be treated with firmness rather than appeasement. A few weeks after Eden's resignation, Hitler's armoured cars swept over the Austrian frontier and on March 15th, 1938 Hitler returned to Vienna as Chancellor of Germany, in which was now forcibly incorporated

Austria, his native country. Success breeds success and it was not long before Hitler attempted another act of aggression.

Failure of Appeasement. Hitler's next move after Austria was against the small state of Czechoslovakia, which was almost surrounded by German and Austrian territory and in which there were over three million Germans living, he claimed, in intolerable conditions under the oppressive tyranny of the Czechs. In fact the German minority, living mainly in Sudetenland, on the German border, was probably better treated than any other in Europe; but nevertheless the leader of the SUDETEN GERMANS, Henlein, appealed to Hitler for protection. The Czechs had signed treaties of alliance with France and Russia for security against Germany, and if France were drawn into a Czech-German conflict it was hardly likely that Britain would keep out. The British Government therefore decided to play the role of mediator, and in the summer of 1938 LORD RUNCIMAN headed a mission of inquiry into the position of the Sudeten German minority. Lord Runciman's report in favour of re-drawing the frontiers to allow the Sudeten Germans to unite with Germany did not please the Czechs; but his proposal for negotiations to consider new Czech-German boundaries did not go far enough for Hitler. In a blustering speech at a Nazi rally at NUREMBERG he demanded that the Sudeten Germans should be allowed to decide for themselves and denounced Czech rule as intolerable. Did Hitler want war or expect war? Or was he just hoping by the threat of force to win another diplomatic triumph? The Czechs at any rate prepared for war and both Britain, France and Russia followed suit; it looked indeed as if hostilities were about to break out in September 1938. It was in this month that Chamberlain made three visits to Germany in order to save the peace. At his first meeting with Hitler at his mountain chalet in the Bavarian Alps at BERCHTESGADEN on September 15th, Chamberlain agreed to the Nazi leader's demand that all the German areas in which there was a majority for union with Germany should be handed over; and he also persuaded the Czechs to agree, although they did so with great reluctance. When Hitler a few days later demanded the immediate surrender of the Sudeten territories,

Chamberlain felt that he was going far beyond the terms of the Berchtesgaden agreement. He then made his second visit on September 22nd, meeting Hitler at GODESBERG on the Rhine, where the two leaders argued without coming to any agreement. The British Government then gave a promise to France to support her in case of war but no one in the French Government was willing to go the length of war with Germany over Czechoslovakia. The Russians offered their support to the Czechs, who ordered full mobilization. In Britain itself, trenches were dug in the public parks and gas-masks were issued for protection against air-raids; the fleet was mobilized and the Army and Air Force reserves were called up. In a broadcast on September 28th Chamberlain told the British people: "I see nothing further that I can usefully do in the way of mediation. . . . How terrible, fantastic, incredible it is that we should be digging trenches and trying on gas-masks here because of a quarrel in a far away country between people of whom we know nothing." The parallel with the Austro-Serbian crisis of 1914 must have impressed older people in Britain. On the following day he set out on his third journey to Germany, this time to Munich, at the special request of Mussolini, who was now after his Abyssinian victory posing as a mediator. Germany, Britain, France and Italy were all represented at the MUNICH CONFERENCE; the Russians were not invited and the Czechs were kept waiting outside. The only difference from Godesberg was that Germany was prepared to accept the surrender of the Sudeten districts in stages. The Czechs were told by Chamberlain and Daladier, the French Prime Minister, that if they did not accept these terms within twelve hours, they could receive no assistance from France or Britain. The Munich Agreement was signed and war was averted for the time being. Hitler's bullying tactics had been successful. As Winston Churchill said in the House of Commons: "£1 was demanded at the pistol's point (i.e. at Berchtesgaden); when it was given, £2 was demanded at the pistol's point (i.e. at Godesberg). Finally the Dictator consented to take £1 17s. 6d. (i.e. at Munich)." Chamberlain's reception on his arrival back in England was one of unbounded relief and enthusiasm. He himself claimed he had brought "peace with honour" (the words used by Disraeli after the Congress of Berlin). But the agreement was hotly attacked by some of his own party, not only by Churchill, who had been a constant opponent of the policy of appeasement, but also by the First Lord of the Admiralty, Duff Cooper, who resigned. Peace had been secured but only at the price of handing over to the mercy of the Germans a small state that had relied on Britain and France and that was now left with defenceless frontiers. Although Chamberlain has generally been held chiefly responsible for the Munich Agreement, it must be remembered that the French, who had committed themselves by treaty to defend the Czechs, were at least as culpable. Despite Hitler's assurance of peace—"I have no further territorial demands to make in Europe"—his troops marched into Prague in the following March, just a year after his entry to Vienna, the western parts of Czechoslovakia (Bohemia and Moravia) were declared a German Protectorate and Slovakia declared independent. Chamberlain realized that he had been deceived by Hitler and at once offered a guarantee of peace to Poland, which seemed to be the next in order of Hitler's victims. Again, Hitler posed as the champion of an oppressed minority, this time the Germans in the Polish Corridor. The problem of what the Russians might do in a German-Polish conflict was solved temporarily by a treaty between Russia and Germany in August 1939, a pact that Hitler was to break in less than two years. Despite British and French guarantees, the Germans invaded Poland on September 1st, and two days later Chamberlain announced that once again Britain and Germany were at war. We know enough now about the German dictator, who was in many ways abnormal, to doubt whether any other British policy in the years before the war would have stopped Hitler; but Chamberlain's own feeling and that of the country were that he had followed a policy which had failed. The name "Munich" and the word "appeasement" had an unpleasant sound for long afterwards.

SOURCE EXTRACTS
A   *Munich, 1938*
On September 28 Chamberlain gave the House an account of his

policy. . . . He closed his speech by the sensational announcement that he had sent "the last, last message" to Hitler, actually offering to discuss with him in Berlin an arrangement which could give him "all essentials without war and without delay", and that Hitler had invited him, with Mussolini and Daladier, to Munich next day. The scene that followed has been accurately described as an outburst of "mass hysteria". (The present writer witnessed this scene from a seat "under the clock", with a full view of the Conservative benches. He watched many members cheering and waving their papers, some actually weeping with emotion and relief. He will never forget the grim, set faces of three men—there doubtless were others—who held aloof from the demonstration, realizing the dire consequences which the House was preparing for itself: they were Mr. Churchill, Mr. Eden and Mr. Amery. He will remember the scene as the most humiliating in all his experience.) . . .

When the Big Four prepared their new "Diktat", the two Czech representatives, who reached Munich by air at 4.30 p.m. on Thursday, September 29, were met by Gestapo agents, escorted to their hotel, and kept waiting till 10 p.m., before Mr. Gwatkin (of the British Foreign Office) was able to show them a map indicating the new frontiers. "If you do not accept," he told them, "you will have to settle your affairs alone with Germany." Finally they were admitted, at 1.30 a.m. on September 30, to the presence of Chamberlain, Daladier and their discomfited officials. In the words of the Czech representatives' report, "The French were visibly embarrassed" and seemed to realize their loss of prestige. But Mr. Chamberlain, "who was constantly yawning, without the least sign of embarrassment, would hardly listen to Czech enquiries or objections." It at once transpired that there was no intention of submitting the plan to Prague or even listening to its views; the four statesmen regarded the plan as already accepted. . . . The Munich "Settlement" was described by Mr. Chamberlain as "Peace by Agreement" and "Peace with Honour". . . . No other than Mr. Churchill described it as "total and unmitigated defeat" and Mr. Duff Cooper reminded the House that Hitler had got away without fighting, "by well-timed bluff, bluster and blackmail . . .".

R. W. Seton-Watson: History of the Czechs and Slovaks.

B   *Hitler's Political Opinions*

(a) *Treaty of Versailles*

What a use could be made of the Treaty of Versailles . . . How each

THE MUNICH CRISIS, 1938. *Top:* The Chamberlain–Hitler Meeting at Berchtesgaden (see p. 221). From left to right: the interpreter, Chamberlain, Henderson (the British Ambassador), Ribbentrop, Hitler, Keitel (Chief of the German General Staff). *Bottom:* Digging air raid trenches in Hyde Park, London (see p. 222).

THE BATTLE OF BRITAIN, 1940. *Top:* Fighter pilots racing to their planes at an "alert" (see p. 235). *Bottom:* Londoners sleeping on the Underground "Tube" platform during a night attack (see p. 235).

one of the points of that Treaty could be branded in the minds and hearts of the German people until sixty million men and women find their souls aflame with a feeling of rage and shame; and a torrent of fire bursts forth as from a furnace, and a will of steel is forged from it, with the common cry: "*Wir wollen wieder Waffen!*—We will have arms again!"

(*b*) *Jews*

Was there any shady undertaking, any form of foulness, especially in cultural life, in which at least one Jew did not participate? On putting the probing knife carefully to that kind of abscess one immediately discovered, like a maggot in a putrescent body, a little Jew who was often blinded by the sudden light.

(*c*) *Politicians and Journalists*

All decent men who had anything to say said it point blank in the enemy's face; or failing this, kept their mouths shut and did their duty elsewhere. Uncompromising military measures should have been adopted to root out the evil. Parties should have been abolished and the Reichstag brought to its senses, at the point of the bayonet, if necessary.

(*d*) *Propaganda*

The receptive powers of the masses are very restricted, and their understanding is slight. On the other hand, they quickly forget. Such being the case, all effective propaganda must be confined to a few bare necessities and then must be expressed in a few stereotyped formulas.

(*e*) *Telling Lies*

In the big lie there is always a certain force of credibility; because the broad masses of a nation are always more easily corrupted in the deeper strata of their emotional nature than consciously or voluntarily, and thus in the primitive simplicity of their minds they more readily fall victims to the big lie than the small lie, since they themselves often tell small lies in little matters, but would be ashamed to fabricate large scale falsehoods. It would never come into their heads to fabricate colossal untruths and they would not believe that others could have the impudence to distort the truth so infamously.

Hitler: Mein Kampf.

EXERCISES

1. Explain: *Fasces, Duce,* totalitarian, corporative state, "Prisoner of the Vatican", *mare nostrum,* Berlin–Rome Axis, Versailles *Diktat, Mein Kampf,* Aryan, *Fuehrer,* protective custody, *Anschluss,* ghetto, *Reich,* fifth column, Popular Front, reparations.

2. Identify the authors of the following and explain where necessary:
   (a) "No discussions, only obedience."
   (b) "Better one day as a lion than a hundred years as a sheep."
   (c) "I have no more territorial claims to make in Europe."
   (d) "No pasaran."
   (e) "Power tends to corrupt and absolute power corrupts absolutely."
   (f) "Whatever people may tell you, the bomber will always get through."
   (g) "Britain stands for the steady and collective resistance to all acts of aggression."
   (h) "A quarrel in a far away country between people of whom we know nothing."
3. Write short notes on: D'Annunzio, March on Rome, Kemal Atatürk, Marshal Pilsudski, Locarno Agreements, General Franco, Léon Blum, Thomas G. Masaryk, Briand–Kellogg Pact, Hoare–Laval Pact.
4. Write notes on: German reparations, Spanish Civil War, French governments, 1918–39, the structure of the League of Nations.
5. Why was Mussolini able to gain power and hold it for so long?
6. Explain the rise of Hitler in Germany.
7. Trace the stages of Hitler's policy of defiance of the Treaty of Versailles.
8. What part did Czechoslovakia play in Europe between the two World Wars?
9. Give an account of the work of the League of Nations between 1919 and 1933.
10. Account for the decline of the League of Nations in the 1930's.
11. Explain what is meant by the word "appeasement" as applied to Chamberlain's foreign policy, 1937–39.

CHAPTER XI

THE SECOND WORLD WAR

"Blitzkrieg" and "Sitzkrieg". The Second World War started at dawn on September 1st, 1939, with the German

Luftwaffe launching a *Blitzkrieg* or lightning war against Poland. The Polish airfields were bombed and most of their air force destroyed on the ground, important railway centres were put out of action, and the German army with its mechanized transport was soon streaming across Poland. A heroic resistance was put up by the Poles but their air force was gone, and their army, still mainly dependent on horses, was no match for the Germans. In little more than a fortnight, the Polish war was over, the Russians marching in to claim their share of the spoils, as promised in the Non-aggression Pact of August 1939. In Britain, the declaration of war against Germany on Sunday, September 3rd was made known to the public by the Prime Minister, Neville Chamberlain, in a speech over the radio. During the broadcast, millions of listeners heard the wailing of sirens in London to indicate an air-raid warning (it turned out to be a false alarm) and assumed that the *Blitzkrieg* had also reached Britain. Already, the EVACUATION from the cities of school-children, carrying gas-masks and identity cards, had taken place in anticipation of heavy bombing at the very outset of the war. Some of these evacuees were to remain in country towns and villages for the duration of the war but many returned within a few weeks or months, as the *Blitzkrieg* failed to come. From September until the following May an uneasy quiet prevailed in France, where a British Expeditionary Force, composed mainly of Territorials and young militia-men, conscripted only a few months before, joined the French in expectation of a German attack. Both French and German military experts, aware of the superiority of the defensive in the First World War, had advocated before the war elaborate defence systems on the frontiers. The MAGINOT LINE in France and the SIEGFRIED LINE in Germany were not just trench lines in the 1914–18 sense but defence zones several miles in depth. In the "pillboxes" on the surface and the underground towns below, the armies settled down to a *Sitzkrieg* or "sit-down" war like the trench warfare of 1914–18.

Fall of Chamberlain. During this period of what was sometimes called the "phoney" war, both sides were arming and making preparations for the inevitable offensive. As Germany had started re-arming on a grand scale earlier, this delay was regarded as to Britain's advantage; and the Prime Minister, Chamberlain, declared, in a phrase that was to be thrown back at him later, that "Hitler has missed the bus". Five days afterwards, on April 9th, 1940, German troops occupied Denmark without resistance and began their invasion of Norway. Hitler had decided on this campaign to forestall a British attack and also to secure access to the rich iron-ore fields in Sweden. In another instalment of Hitler's *Blitzkrieg*, German paratroops were dropped in important centres and a pro-German "fifth column" of Norwegian Fascists seized airfields and ports. (Their leader, MAJOR QUISLING, provided the world with a new name for a traitor.) Fighting went on for some weeks, during which British and French expeditionary forces landed in Norway with little effect on the German advance. The allied failure to prevent the Germans overrunning Norway brought about the fall of the British and French Prime Ministers, Chamberlain and Daladier. Dissatisfaction with Chamberlain's lack of vigour, memories of his appeasement policy, and irritation about the revelations of muddle and mismanagement in Norway roused some of the Conservatives to oppose their leader. On May 7th, 1940, during an acrimonious post-mortem debate on the Norwegian campaign, a former Conservative Cabinet Minister, Amery, threw at the Prime Minister the words Cromwell addressed to the Rump Parliament in 1654: "You have sat too long here for any good you have been doing. Depart, I say, and let us have done with you. In the name of God, go!" On May 10th, Chamberlain resigned and a COALITION GOVERNMENT of all parties was formed by Winston Churchill, First Lord of the Admiralty in Chamberlain's Government. On the same day, the Germans had delivered their long-awaited attack on the west, their armies moving swiftly into Holland, Belgium and Luxembourg. Churchill, who came to office, like the Elder Pitt and Lloyd George, when things were going badly, was to remain in supreme charge of affairs until the war was won.

Winston Churchill. The new Prime Minister was sixty-six years of age when he achieved the ambition of his life—to be

Prime Minister of Britain in wartime. In many ways, it seemed, his previous career equipped him for this task. None in Parliament could vie with him in knowledge and experience of war and politics. Born in Blenheim Palace in 1874, grandson of the Duke of Marlborough and son of Lord Randolph Churchill, he was brought up in an atmosphere of politics. Both his father, Lord Randolph Churchill, the brilliant but erratic "Tory Democrat" who became Chancellor of the Exchequer at thirty-seven, and his mother's father, Leonard Jerome, an American newspaper proprietor, were men of forceful personality; and from his earliest days he showed an aggressiveness that led him into many an escapade. He was educated at Harrow, where he took little interest in any subjects but English and History, and went to Sandhurst, entering the Army in 1895. The tedium of a subaltern's life in India induced him to seek excitement as an observer with the Spanish forces fighting in Cuba. In 1898, he published his first book about an expeditionary force sent to Malakand in North-west India. In the same year, after he had failed to obtain a transfer to the Sudan, where Kitchener was nearing the end of his campaign, Churchill procured for himself the post of military correspondent to a London newspaper. Attached as an officer to the 21st Lancers, he took part in the famous cavalry charge at the battle of Omdurman. It was also as a war correspondent that he went during the Boer War to South Africa, where he was taken prisoner and escaped. Not long afterwards, he returned to England and entered Parliament in 1900 as Conservative M.P. for Oldham. During his first few years he still engaged in writing, producing a biography of his father, who had died at the early age of forty-six. His first speeches, despite careful preparation and memorizing of lengthy passages, were not very successful, partly due to an impediment in his speech. But he persevered and his brilliant qualities were recognized soon after he left the Conservative Party in 1905 by his being appointed to a junior post in the Liberal Government of Campbell-Bannerman. In 1908 he became President of the Board of Trade and in 1910 Home Secretary, a post which brought him some unpopularity through the sending of troops to deal with a miners' strike in Wales. These were the years of the People's Budget and the Parliament Bill. During the bitter party wrangle that dragged on for years, Churchill was an able lieutenant of Lloyd George, and both were fiercely attacked by the Conservatives, some of whom took a long time to forgive Churchill for his desertion of their party. In 1911, Churchill was appointed First Lord of the Admiralty to co-operate with Haldane, the Secretary for War, in preparing for hostilities against Germany. Along with Admiral Fisher he brought the Navy to fighting pitch by 1914. His energetic nature and his absorbing interest in warfare led him into what some of his colleagues termed interference in other departments. He was one of the first to appreciate the potentialities of the tank and forced the War Office to adopt it against their wishes. When the Dardanelles expedition, which he had proposed, failed in 1915, he was compelled to resign. He then spent some months in Flanders in command of the 6th Royal Scots Fusiliers. Through his friendship with Lloyd George, now Prime Minister, he returned to the Cabinet as Minister of Munitions in 1917 and at the end of the war became Secretary for War and for Air. His hatred of Communism made him one of the strongest advocates of allied intervention against the Bolsheviks in Russia. When he was defeated at Dundee in the election of 1922, he left the Liberal Party, which was then hopelessly split, and rejoined the Conservatives. From 1924 to 1929 he was Chancellor of the Exchequer in Baldwin's Ministry. He found time in the period after the First World War to pursue his hobbies of painting and writing and produced, in the six volumes of his *World Crisis*, one of the best histories of the war. He was out of office from 1929 to 1939, neither Baldwin nor Chamberlain being desirous of such a difficult, if brilliant, colleague. During the passage of the Government of India Act (1935), his opposition was so bitter and sustained that it seemed unlikely he would ever receive a Government appointment again. He constantly criticized Chamberlain also for his policy of appeasement and denounced the Munich settlement as a major defeat. Nevertheless, his ability and experience were such that he could not be kept out of office when war came, and in September 1939 he returned to his old post of First Lord of the Admiralty. When he became Prime Minister and head of the Coalition Government in May 1940, he was uplifted by the prospect of a hard struggle which he was confident Britain would win. He did not hold out any hopes of an easy victory. "I have nothing to offer but blood, toil, tears and sweat," he told the House of Commons. But all felt that this at least was an improvement on the faint optimism of his predecessor, Chamberlain.

The Fall of France. The German Army's invasion of Holland on May 10th, 1940, was preceded by the dropping of paratroops on airfields, bridges and other strategic points. Although the Dutch managed to flood some areas and mine bridges, the Germans took only three days to force them into surrender after a pitiless bombardment of Rotterdam in which over 30,000 persons were killed. The Belgians resisted for a few weeks but,

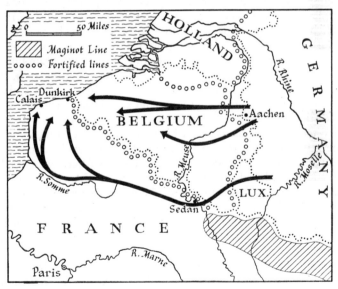

Invasion of France, 1940

by the end of May, King Leopold ordered his men to surrender. British and French forces in Belgium found themselves enveloped by German armoured divisions which had pushed rapidly through to Abbéville on the Channel after piercing the French defence lines. This break-through had occurred at Sedan to the north of the main section of the Maginot Line and had been preceded by dive-bombing that overpowered the weak French defences. The Germans moved so quickly that the Allied forces found themselves left with only one port for evacuation, DUNKIRK. When the port was destroyed by air attack, they were compelled to use the beaches near the town; from the town and the beaches, under constant bombing and machine-gunning from German aircraft, 215,000 British and 120,000 French soldiers were evacuated. This withdrawal was carried out not by the Navy alone but by calling on owners of all shallow-draught vessels in South-eastern England to help. Warships, passenger-steamers, fishing-smacks and motor-boats made up the strangest flotilla of modern times. Dunkirk meant a defeat for the British Army, which lost all its equipment in France and which would not return in strength for four more years; but the rescue of so many men from death or imprisonment was hailed by Churchill as "a miracle of deliverance". A fortnight later, on June 16th, the veteran Marshal Pétain, hero of Verdun and by this time eighty-four years of age, became Premier and asked the Germans for an armistice, the news of which request made Hitler dance with joy. The terms of the armistice, which was signed at Compiègne in the same railway carriage where the Germans had surrendered in 1918, were stiff indeed. All the French forces were to be drastically reduced and the greater part of France was to be handed over to German control; the remaining portion became known as VICHY FRANCE, as Pétain and his Government of collaborators had their capital at Vichy. Pétain and Laval, his deputy and successor as Premier, were both sentenced to death after the war, Laval being executed and Pétain's sentence commuted to life imprisonment. In London, a French general, CHARLES DE GAULLE, was recognized as leader of an army of "Free French" and later became head of the French Government in exile. The Germans had triumphed over their traditional enemy in little more time that it took them to defeat Poland. The French will to fight was certainly not strong: defeatism and pacifism, dating from the First World War when so many Frenchmen were killed, combined with a lack of leadership to give the powerful, efficient German military machine an easy victory.

Battle of Britain. Hitler had always hoped that Britain might come to terms with Germany. In his autobiographical *Mein Kampf*, he had expressed the opinion that the two were natural allies. He was also in 1940 probably under the impression that the policy of appeasement pursued by Chamberlain was still alive in Britain. His offers of peace were brusquely rejected by the new Prime Minister, Churchill, who announced to the world: "We shall not flag or fail. We shall go on to the end . . . We shall defend our island, whatever the cost may be, we shall fight on the beaches, we shall fight on the landing grounds, we shall fight in the fields and in the streets, we shall fight in the hills, we shall never surrender." He asked the people to brace themselves for the task so that posterity could say of them: "This was their finest hour." A German invasion seemed likely once Hitler's offers of peace had been rejected, but it would obviously take time to mount a large-scale offensive across even a narrow strip of water like the Channel. Barbed-wire entanglements and poles to prevent aircraft landing were erected on the beaches round Britain, concrete blocks were built on the roads, Home Guard units for local defence began to train, some of them with antiquated weapons, and the whole country was on the alert. We know now that the German naval leaders were most reluctant to undertake the cross-Channel operation "Sea-lion" (as it had been named), having neither the ships nor the landing craft for the large forces required. Air superiority over the Channel was also an indispensable pre-requisite for an invasion attempt; but the leader of the German *Luftwaffe*, GOERING, himself an air-ace of the First World War, was only too ready to prove the value of the *Luftwaffe* to Germany by driving the British out of the skies. The Battle of Britain that ensued was fought not only to make

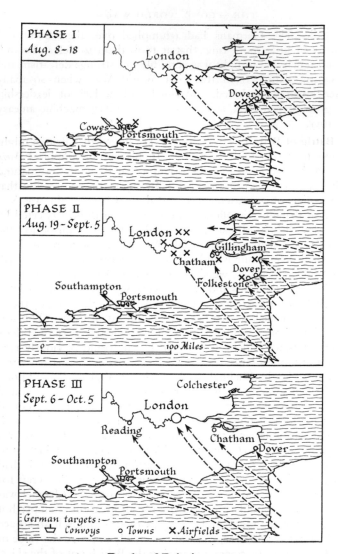

Battle of Britain, 1940

an invasion possible but also to enable Goering to claim credit for a decisive victory over Britain that would force them to surrender. In this hope he mis-calculated: he underestimated the strength of the R.A.F. and the fighting qualities of British airmen, and he did not know how effective was the warning system which RADAR provided against German aircraft. There were four phases in the Battle of Britain, which went on from early August to the end of October. (1) In the first phase, starting on August 8th, Goering sent mass formations of bombers, accompanied by fighters, against the shipping, the ports and coastal towns from Dover as far west as Portland. The Hurricane and Spitfire fighters of the R.A.F., although outnumbered, took heavy toll of the German bombers, on one day (August 15th) bringing down as many as 76 German aircraft. A few days later, at the end of this phase, Churchill paid his famous tribute to the young fighter pilots of the R.A.F.: "Never in the field of human conflict was so much owed by so many to so few." (2) In the next phase, from August 19th to September 5th, Goering used smaller bomber formations with increased escorts of fighters and switched his attacks to fighter airfields inland, perhaps thinking that he had destroyed Portsmouth and the airfields on the coast or perhaps merely keeping to a pre-arranged time-table. Again, losses were heavy on both sides but the R.A.F. still kept going. (3) On September 6th, Goering started on the third phase, attacking industrial targets, particularly those in or near London. London was heavily bombed again and again, and on September 12th a single raider, making use of cloud cover, bombed Buckingham Palace. The Germans were still losing heavily; from the beginning of August to the end of September their losses amounted to 1,244 planes and crews, the British radar system proving of invaluable assistance in the detection and interception of the enemy planes. (4) In the fourth phase, which lasted from the 6th of October to the end of the month, the tactics were again changed. The targets remained the same, that is, London and its environs; but instead of heavy bombers Goering used faster planes called fighter-bombers and raids were made at night in preference to daylight. The R.A.F. was still fighting back, conscious now that Goering could be defeated and bombers were even sent to raid German towns. On September 17th, Hitler had postponed the operation "Sea-lion" indefinitely but Goering continued the air battle throughout October, confident that he could crush British resistance by air power alone. The R.A.F., although badly weakened in the process, had proved Goering mistaken; and their victory in the Battle of Britain was to affect vitally the course of the war. If the British air force had suffered, so had the people of southern England. Over 14,000 had been killed in London alone, and thousands were sleeping night after night on Underground stations, while whole streets were deserted except for policemen and A.R.P. (Air Raid Precautions) wardens patrolling during the black-out.

North Africa and the Mediterranean. While the Battle of Britain was going on during the summer of 1940, Italian troops had been advancing from their colony of Libya towards Egypt. Mussolini's colonial ambitions had been whetted by his conquest of Abyssinia; and it also suited both Germany and Italy to cut Britain's chief artery of trade, the Suez Canal. The Italians, however, did not cover themselves with glory in North Africa or anywhere else during the war. A small British force under GENERAL WAVELL was able to counter-attack in December 1940 and chase the Italians for over 500 miles, capturing 130,000 Italians with little difficulty. Soon afterwards, British troops made a daring invasion of Italian East Africa (Eritrea and Somaliland) and went on to conquer Italy's new colony of Abyssinia. But these were not the only humiliations that Mussolini had to suffer. His troops were defeated when they invaded Greece in October 1940 and it required the assistance of German troops to defeat the Greeks. This they did, driving out British troops that had been sent to help and going on to seize Crete by a paratroop invasion. The British commander in Egypt, Wavell, was called upon to send troops not only to Greece and Crete but also to Iraq, where a pro-German *putsch* was nipped in the bud. In this weakened position Wavell found himself facing another attacking force from Libya, this time one consisting

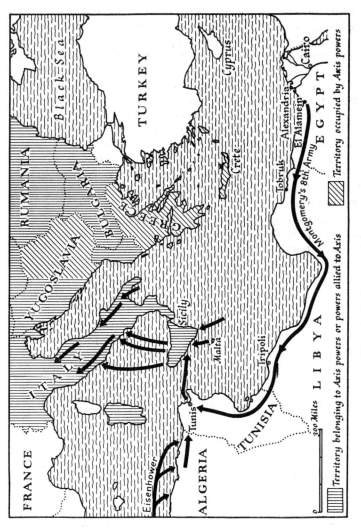

North Africa and Italy, 1942-3

Territory belonging to Axis powers or powers allied to Axis

Territory occupied by Axis powers

mainly of Germans under a brilliant commander, GENERAL ROMMEL. Rommel excelled in desert warfare, which was unlike the fighting in Europe in 1914–18: it was generally a war of movement depending for its success on tanks and armoured cars rather than on infantry. Rommel was able to drive the British back to the Egyptian frontier in May 1941, one isolated garrison holding out for months at TOBRUK with the help of the Navy. After a year of desert warfare, Rommel, who had been weakened by the withdrawal of some of his troops to fight in Russia, mounted another offensive in 1942 that brought the Germans and Italians to EL ALAMEIN, only fifty miles from Alexandria. It was there that, on October 23rd, the British 8th Army, now heavily reinforced and under a new commander, GENERAL MONTGOMERY, started a counter-offensive that after a week's hard fighting broke the German line. El Alamein was for Britain a turning-point in the war. Churchill, who was overjoyed at the news of the first major victory since he had taken office more than two years before, said: "Up to Alamein we survived: after Alamein we conquered." Montgomery, whose popularity with the troops won him the nickname "Monty", pushed on from El Alamein in pursuit of the German and Italian troops until he not only relieved Egypt of all threats but also drove the enemy out of Africa. His advance was helped by the invasion of French North Africa by a combined British and American force in November 1942. By the middle of May 1943, the resistance of the Axis powers in Africa had collapsed. Their total losses (killed, captured and missing) were almost a million men, mainly Italian. Mussolini was forced to resign in July 1943, soon after the British and Americans landed in Sicily, but the advance northwards up to the Italian peninsula was bitterly contested by the Germans. One of the fiercest and most prolonged battles of the war was fought at MONTE CASSINO, the site of St. Benedict's monastery. It was not until May 1944 that at last the Allies controlled the whole of Italy. During most of the campaign in North Africa the Mediterranean route had not been available for British ships because of the danger from German and Italian bombers. Gibraltar and Malta were bombed for months on end but held out, the island of Malta being awarded the George Cross, a unique distinction. But the Italian fleet was never a match for the British in the Mediterranean, where the British Admiral SIR ANDREW CUNNINGHAM had two early successes, one at Taranto in Southern Italy, the result of a bombing attack launched from aircraft-carriers, the other at Cape Matapan in Southern Greece, where he destroyed a number of Italian warships without loss to himself.

Invasion of Russia. In the early summer of 1941, Hitler decided on the invasion of Russia; although Britain was still undefeated, he felt that, except for air-raids, Germany had nothing to fear from the West for some time. The Balkans were firmly under German control, apart from resistance by the "Partisans" in Yugoslavia under two leaders, one of them the able TITO, later to be President of Yugoslavia. Hitler was actuated by two motives in his attack on Russia—his fanatical hatred of Communism, which he had not abandoned by forming the Non-aggression Pact with the Soviet Union in 1939, and his desire to gain control of the rich natural resources of Russia, e.g. her oil. Hitler was convinced he would succeed where Napoleon had failed; but it was probably only coincidence that his forces entered Russia on June 22nd, 1941, the anniversary of the day on which Napoleon had invaded Russia. Hitler regarded the Russian army, although numerous, as weak and the Communist system hopelessly inefficient. "We have only to kick in the door and the whole rotten system will collapse," he told one of his generals. He hoped, as his forces advanced, that the Russian armies would be enveloped and annihilated, but the Russians pursued the same tactics as in 1812, retreating and burning towns, villages and crops behind them. This "SCORCHED EARTH" policy meant that as Hitler's armies drove on and their lines of communication lengthened, it became more difficult for the Germans to supply their fighting forces. In October, Hitler, indulging in wishful thinking, announced: "The enemy is already broken and will never rise again." But the end of 1941 came with the Red Army still fighting and, far from being annihilated, launching a counter-offensive. The Germany army,

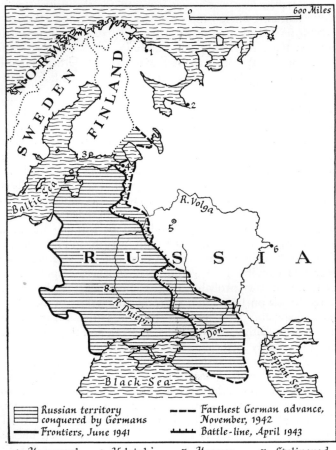

German Advance in Russia, 1941–3

unprepared for a winter campaign, was like Napoleon's army at the mercy of the Russian winter. Churchill, notwithstanding his hatred of Communism, had wasted no time in declaring his willingness to ally himself with Stalin. British and American supplies began to arrive by the sea-route through the White Sea to Murmansk and also by railway through Persia. In the summer of 1942, the Germans began a great offensive in the south through Ukraine, rich in corn, towards the Caucasus and the Russian oil-wells. By September they had reached the Volga at STALINGRAD, a large, modern, industrial town named after the Russian dictator, and there the Russians held them. Hitler would not hear of retreat and by the end of January 1943, 330,000 of the German army at Stalingrad had been killed or captured: the German Commander, VON PAULUS, later volunteered to give pro-Russian broadcasts to Germany, advising his fellow-countrymen to throw off the Nazi yoke. Stalingrad was a turning-point in the war in the east as El Alamein (fought at the same time) was in the west. The Russian army became stronger again as more industrial centres behind the Urals came into production and supplies arrived from Britain and the United States. A German offensive in July 1943 was their last in Russia and had little effect. By that time, the war losses of both sides were tremendous. The Russians admitted casualties of over four million and the German casualties were estimated at over six million. But the Russian resources of man-power far exceeded those of Germany and the Russian steam-roller, once it started moving westwards, went on inexorably. By the summer of 1944, when the invasion of Normandy was in full swing, the Russians entered Poland and were advancing on Germany.

Battle of the Atlantic. Despite the overall superiority of the British at sea, the early months of the war revealed, as in 1914, the danger of the German U-boat menace. A passenger liner, the *Athenia*, was torpedoed the day after war was declared; and the German U-boat commanders lay in wait at the "Western Approaches", ready to pounce on unsuspecting merchant vessels. Naval ships were also sunk, the aircraft-carrier *Courageous* and the battleship *Royal Oak* being among the victims

16

in 1939. The U-boat commander responsible for sinking the *Royal Oak* actually penetrated into the harbour of Scapa Flow and escaped again to the open sea after he had performed his task. A new German weapon, the magnetic mine, accounted for many British ships until the British found an answer to it by putting a "de-gaussing" girdle round the ship. One minor success which helped to restore British morale was the BATTLE OF THE RIVER PLATE in December 1939, when the German pocket-battleship *Graf Spee* was badly crippled by three British cruisers carrying much inferior armament (the heaviest guns being 6-inch as against the 11-inch guns of the *Graf Spee*). The German battleship made for the neutral port of Montevideo and then after three days put out to sea, where she was scuttled and the captain committed suicide. In 1940, when France fell and British naval strength was being overtaxed, the American President Roosevelt gave to Britain fifty old destroyers in return for the lease of some West Indian islands as naval bases. Britain was dependent on the Atlantic life-line for food and other supplies from America; and the U-boat menace was increased as by the German occupation of North-west France the range of U-boat activities was greatly extended. The Irish also refused to allow the use of any ports as British naval bases and maintained a strict neutrality in contrast to America's benevolent neutrality. The Irish refusal was a bitter pill for Churchill and the British to swallow, but De Valera and the Irish had not forgotten the long years of British supremacy and, more particularly, the partition of Ireland, which they regarded as a crime. Large armed convoys, long-distance flying-boats for spotting U-boats, bomber-raids on the well-defended U-boat concrete "pens" in North-west France, all helped to reduce the sinkings. But they continued to the end of the war, so that the lives lost in the Merchant Navy totalled more than those in the Royal Navy. In March 1941, by the ingenious LEND-LEASE ACT, President Roosevelt was authorized to use American resources on behalf of any state whose defence he regarded as vital to the defence of the United States. Not only Britain but other countries such as Turkey, Egypt, Iraq were declared eligible to benefit by this Act and in all the U.S.A. gave over £12,000,000,000 in aid by 1946. Britain itself later gave aid also at times to the U.S.A., in the form of munitions, vehicles, etc.; but it was in 1941 especially that Lend-Lease proved valuable to Britain and helped to see her through a difficult time. The Battle of the Atlantic gradually went more and more in favour of Britain, although in 1944 the Germans produced the "Schnorkel", a breathing-tube for submarines which did away with the necessity of surfacing to charge the batteries. The small fleet of German battleships and cruisers made occasional sorties; on one of them the battleship *Bismarck* sank the largest British warship, H.M.S. *Hood,* in Greenland waters before she was herself hunted down and sunk by British warships and aircraft in the Atlantic, 400 miles west of Ireland.

Pearl Harbor and After. As Hitler with his *Blitzkrieg* tactics had rapidly overrun Western Europe in 1940, so the Japanese in 1941–42 similarly made themselves masters of the Far East. Although there was no Japanese war-leader so unbalanced mentally as Hitler, there was among the Japanese military class an outlook not unlike that of the Germans. Each race felt itself competent and entitled to control other parts of the world, Germany in Europe and the Japanese in the Pacific, and each aimed eventually at world conquest. Each had been engaged in aggression for some years, each was thorough in its organization for total war, and since 1936 the two powers had been allied in the Anti-Comintern Pact. For both Japan and Germany, excessive ambition proved their undoing. All the Far Eastern empires of the British, the French and the Dutch were lying exposed to a possible Japanese attack, and it would have been a sufficient task for the Japanese to have conquered and occupied these territories. But, in her pride, she determined to attack also the American colony of the Philippines and drive the U.S.A. from the East Pacific. To make American defence of the Philippines more difficult, if not impossible, the Japanese decided on a bold stroke, aimed at the American base, PEARL HARBOR, near Honolulu in the Hawaiian Islands, 3,000 miles away from Japan. On the morning of December 7th, 1941, the Japanese *Blitzkrieg* began. From aircraft-carriers over 200 miles away, their planes bombed the airfields at Pearl Harbor and nearly every U.S. plane was destroyed on the ground. Eight warships (including two battleships) were sunk and eighteen others damaged by torpedo-carrying planes and midget-submarines. Two days after Pearl Harbor, Japanese dive-bombers and torpedo-carrying bombers sank the British battleships *Prince of Wales* and *Repulse* off the coast of Malaya and within two months Singapore, the chief British naval base in the East, had fallen. Pearl Harbor had far-reaching consequences. It prevented any American inter-ference with the Japanese plans for attacking the Philippines and other parts of East Asia and allowed them to make extensive conquests within the next year. But it destroyed the last traces of American isolationism and brought the United States into the war in a wholehearted resolve to avenge the disaster. From Pearl Harbor on, the Second World War was a "global" war— Germany, Italy, Japan ranged against Britain, Russia, U.S.A. and the rest of the free world. Pearl Harbor also marked the end of the era of the battleship and the beginning of the suprem-acy of the aircraft-carrier. Oddly enough, no aircraft-carrier was sunk at Pearl Harbor and the Americans were able to redress the balance of sea-power a few months later in the BATTLE OF THE CORAL SEA, between Australia and New Guinea (May 1942). This was the first great action at sea in which surface vessels did not exchange a single shot and in which aircraft-carriers decided the issue. The Japanese lost two carriers, three large cruisers and several other ships for a loss of only one American carrier. An even heavier defeat was inflicted upon the Japanese one month later on their way with a large fleet to attack MIDWAY ISLAND in the middle of the Pacific. By August 1942, American troops under GENERAL MACARTHUR had landed at GUADALCANAL in the Solomon Islands, north of Australia, and had begun to carry the war into what the Japanese called the "Greater Asia Co-Prosperity Sphere". Ultimate victory over the Japanese was to mean long and stubborn fighting, for they had overrun the Philippines, Indo-China, part of China, Borneo, Malaya, Burma, Java, Sumatra and other islands.

The Americans advanced by "island-hopping" and inflicted more
heavy defeats on the Japanese—the Battle of the Bismarck Sea
(March 1943), when the Japanese fleet opposing theirs was
annihilated by air attack, and the greatest naval battle in the
whole war, the BATTLE OF LEYTE GULF (October 1944), where a
decisive victory enabled General MacArthur to overcome
Japanese resistance on Leyte, one of the main islands in the
Philippines. It was in this last battle that the Japanese first used
Kamikaze suicide pilots who crashed their aircraft, loaded with
explosives, on the decks of enemy ships, but they did not prevent
an American victory. American submarines also took heavy toll
of Japanese warships and merchant ships, over half of the
Japanese merchant navy being sunk. During this time, British
forces in Burma fought in jungle warfare, at the mercy of the
monsoons and of tropical diseases, and slowly drove the Japanese
back. Early in 1945 they re-opened the BURMA ROAD, the supply
route to China, where a Nationalist army under Chiang Kai-
Shek was still holding out.

Air Raids. The Second World War was the first war in which
the civilian population, or some of it, were in the front-line for
much of the time. In the first two years of the war, casualties
were higher among civilians than in the armed forces. We have
already seen how the London "Blitz" began in the autumn of
1940 at the end of the Battle of Britain and continued throughout
the winter of 1940–41; on 82 out of 85 consecutive nights
during that period, bombers raided the capital city. In November,
the Germans carried their attack into the centre of England and
raided COVENTRY with a heavy force of over 500 planes. The
centre of the city, with the beautiful cathedral, was shattered but
most of the industrial plants on the outskirts escaped. Other
industrial towns in the Midlands and in the North received the
attention of the *Luftwaffe* but London continued to be the chief
target. On December 29th, 1940, thousands of small incendiaries
were dropped along with high-explosive bombs on the city of
London, and there resulted another "Great Fire of London",
much worse than that of 1666. The heaviest raid of all came at
the end of London's long spell of bombing on May 10th, 1941,

when the House of Commons was destroyed along with many other notable buildings. Before that happened, the *Luftwaffe* had made long-range raids on Clydeside on March 13th and 14th; losses were heavy as the Scots were taken by surprise and in Clydebank (where the famous Cunarders, *Queen Mary* and *Queen Elizabeth* were built) only eight of the 12,000 houses in the burgh were undamaged and 4,300 were destroyed or damaged beyond repair. From the summer of 1941 onwards, the Germans received more than they gave. Certain towns, mainly ports, continued to be raided at intervals; Hull, Bristol, Plymouth, Portsmouth, Southampton were among the worst-damaged. But life went on and people continued at their jobs. At first people with gardens depended for safety mainly on the ANDERSON SHELTER, a small corrugated iron hut embedded in the soil of the garden, while in London the "Tube" proved the most popular as it was the safest. Occasionally, by dropping delayed action bombs, the Germans caused the people to be evacuated from their houses until a Bomb Disposal Squad dealt with the bombs. Raids on Germany were undertaken by both British and American air forces, the former preferring night bombing and the latter daylight bombing. The increased weight of the bombs and the invention of new explosives made the later raids in the war terrifying in their effects. Some bombs of 10 tons (compared with the Germans' heaviest bomb of one ton at the beginning of the war) were called "block-busters" as they could flatten a whole block of houses. On some of the raids on Germany, more than 1,000 bombers were used and on one occasion over 2,500 tons of bombs were dropped on Berlin in one hour, an example of "saturation" bombing. The Germans in Berlin, Hamburg, Nuremberg and in the industrial towns generally suffered severely despite their effective deep shelters, as neither houses nor factories were left undamaged. In 1944–45, before and during the Allied advance into Germany, railway centres were smashed again and again, and the continual bombing made it very difficult for the Germans to supply their forces in France. It has been estimated that the total effect of the bombing—the destruction of factories and the houses of industrial workers, the death or disablement of Germans (over 300,000 were killed), the undermining of morale, the dislocation of communications—helped to shorten the war by two years. When the Allies advanced into the Ruhr, they found the towns just heaps of rubble and ashes. To keep up the morale of the German people in 1944, Hitler boasted of his "secret weapons" with which he would destroy Britain. First came a FLYING BOMB called V 1 (short for the German *Vergeltungswaffe* or "reprisal weapon") a pilotless plane travelling at about 400 m.p.h. and carrying a war-head with explosive equivalent to a one-ton bomb. These flying bombs or "buzz-bombs" were sent over London and the South-east of England from the middle of June 1944 (after the invasion of Normandy had started) and by the end of August had killed over 5,000 people. In September 1944, the Germans began to use their V 2, a ROCKET BOMB that travelled about 3,000 m.p.h. The Allied advance brought the V 1 and V 2 attacks to an end by December 1944, but it has been argued that had they been invented earlier, Hitler's chances of victory would have been much greater.

Invasion of Normandy. It was not until 1944 that the British and Americans returned with an invasion force to the France which had been left so hurriedly four years before. Stalin had been pressing for the opening of a SECOND FRONT in the West since 1942. He suspected that the British preferred to stand by while the Russians and Germans destroyed one another and he hoped for some relief from the pressure of the German attacks. It was the 6th of June (six days before the first "buzz-bombs" fell on London) that was chosen as the "D-Day" for the invasion of Normandy. Soon after midnight of June 5th, paratroops were dropped and 4,000 ships carrying five infantry divisions were grounded on the beaches. The Germans, who had been expecting an invasion near Calais, were taken by surprise, and the Allies managed to secure footholds or "bridge-heads" from which they were able to advance. Within a month, over a million men had been landed at prefabricated "Mulberry" harbours, which reached almost a mile out to sea. The Americans formed the right wing of the invasion force, which was under the supreme control of GENERAL EISENHOWER (later President of the United States); and the plan was for them to swing round first south, then east, while the British under MONTGOMERY acted as the "hinge". The fighting at Caen, the old Norman city at the hinge, was fierce and bloody, as the German tanks were at first too strong for the British. But while the BATTLE OF CAEN was in progress and more and more Germans were being sent to the Caen section, the Americans broke through the German lines and carried out the intended enveloping movement. Over 100,000 Germans were caught in the Falaise "pocket" and the rest retreated to the Seine. Soon afterwards, in mid-August, another invasion force, comprising American and "Free French" troops, landed in the south of France and pressed quickly north. Paris was liberated on August 24th, to the great joy of the French, who had given the Allies valuable help, both before and after the landings, through their "underground" movement, called the *Résistance* or the *Maquis*. While the Second Battle of France was in progress, an attempt was made on July 20th at Hitler's headquarters in East Prussia to assassinate the German Fuehrer, who narrowly escaped death when a bomb exploded under the table where he sat. The chief conspirator, Count von Stauffenberg, was a staff officer who had persuaded some of the German generals to come into the plot; after the failure of his Hitler bomb-plot, he was executed along with many others, Rommel, who was also involved, being allowed to commit suicide. Hitler's escape from death helped to confirm him in the idea that fate had destined him to continue the struggle until victory came: orders were given that there must be no withdrawal on any front, and as a result more German soldiers were killed or captured. With the British, American and French approaching from the west and the Russians from the east and south, Hitler gave instructions to make Germany into a fortified camp, *Festung Europa* (the fortress of Europe). In the autumn, Rumania and Bulgaria both surrendered to the Russians, and the Allies reached the Siegfried Line on the German frontier. A last German counter-offensive in the Ardennes forest surprised the Allies just before Christmas, but on March 23rd, 1945 the Rhine

THE SECOND WORLD WAR: THE YEARS OF DEFEAT. *Top:* The British surrender to the Japanese at Singapore, 1941 (see p. 244). *Bottom:* The torpedoing of the *Ark Royal* in the Mediterranean, November 1941.

THE SECOND WORLD WAR: THE YEARS OF VICTORY. *Top:* Winston Churchill (with Montgomery in beret) crosses the Rhine during the Allied advance, 1945 (see p. 249). *Bottom:* The American General MacArthur strides ashore on a Pacific island retaken from the Japanese (see p. 245).

was crossed in force and the advance towards Berlin was on. On April 13th the Russians took Vienna and a few days later were hammering at Berlin itself. From every front came terrible news to Hitler in his "bunker" or underground shelter in the Chancellery at Berlin. The German resistance in Italy, tough as it was, finally collapsed, and Mussolini, who had been under German

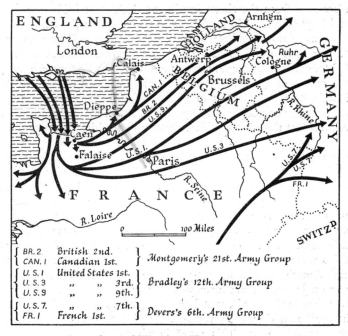

BR. 2	British 2nd.	
CAN. 1	Canadian 1st.	Montgomery's 21st. Army Group
U.S. 1	United States 1st.	
U.S. 3	„ „ 3rd.	Bradley's 12th. Army Group
U.S. 9	„ „ 9th.	
U.S. 7.	„ „ 7th.	
FR. 1	French 1st.	Devers's 6th. Army Group

Invasion of Western Europe, 1944–5

protection since 1943, was captured by some of the Italian "underground" movement, executed and his body hung up by the heels in a square in Milan to be spat upon by the passers-by. It was only two days later, on April 30th, after the Chancellery in Berlin had been heavily bombed, that Hitler committed suicide. Other Nazi leaders, Goebbels and Himmler, followed his example. An armistice was signed on May 7th, 1945, by Admiral Doenitz, head of the German Navy, who had been named by Hitler as his successor.

Surrender of Japan. When Germany fell in May 1945, the Japanese had already lost many of the islands they had seized in the Pacific and in the south-east of Asia. Their navy had not recovered from the shattering blows dealt it at Midway Island and Leyte Gulf. Their air force was no match for the Americans, who were now sending their heavy long-range bombers, the "Super-fortresses", to raid Japan. As Japanese houses were of lighter construction and more inflammable than European houses, the effects of the raids were immensely greater than those on Britain or Germany: on one occasion, March 9th–10th, 1945, almost 100,000 people in Tokyo were burned to death and over a million lost their homes. But, although the chief Japanese cities were lying in ruins, the Americans had still to face up to the last stage of the invasion and occupation of Japan. As a preliminary, General MacArthur, the American commander-in-chief, decided on the occupation of two islands, still a few hundred miles from Japan. The first, Iwo Jima, was taken after a desperate struggle. At the second, Okinawa, the Japanese depended too much on their Kamikaze pilots, almost 2,000 of whom committed suicide in their attacks on the American fleet; but although 36 ships were sunk, none was of any great importance. The British and Americans had been trying to persuade Stalin to declare war on Japan. He was interested in extending the Soviet Union's frontiers in the Far East at Japan's expense but he did not come in until two days after the first ATOM BOMB was dropped on August 6th, 1945. This atom bomb fell on Hiroshima, the headquarters of one of the main Japanese armies; 91,000, or almost one-third of the population, were killed and others maimed or blinded for life. On August 9th, a second atom bomb was dropped on Nagasaki, an important seaport of Japan, the casualties there numbering about 40,000 killed and as many wounded. On the following day, the Japanese Government sued for peace, laying down only one condition: that the Emperor's sovereignty must remain unimpaired. After some delay, they finally accepted the Allies' demand of unconditional surrender on August 15th, 1945, and the Second World War was over.

Home Affairs. We have already seen how the civilians at home suffered severely from the German bombing-raids in the early part of the war, 1940–41, and later from the V 1 and V 2 "secret weapons" of Hitler in 1944. In certain respects the British people were fortunate in comparison with other countries at war. Under a Ministry of Food, rationing was enforced from the beginning of the war, so that all were able to obtain a reasonable share of what was available. Children were given priority for milk, orange juice, etc., and by the end of the war, the average height and weight of school-children had actually increased. Full employment and high wages (there were also over four million serving in the Forces) contributed to this result. Wage-earners began to pay income-tax for the first time under a system called P.A.Y.E. (Pay as you earn), by which tax was deducted by the employers when wages were paid. Farmers were encouraged by grants and subsidies to increase their production, bringing into cultivation land that had not been ploughed for decades; and they began to enjoy prosperity for the first time since the previous war. Although the main interest of the Coalition Government was naturally in running the war, certain measures of permanent value were carried through. Chief among these were the EDUCATION ACTS for England and Wales (1944) and Scotland (1945). The minister responsible for these was R. A. Butler, a Conservative, who had long stressed the importance of social reform. In future, education in England and Wales was to be under a Minister of Education instead of the President of the Board of Education. The duties of education authorities were much enlarged to include community centres, youth service, etc., while all English and Welsh schools were placed under the education authorities, which were the education committees of county councils and county boroughs. (Before 1944 elementary or primary schools were under smaller bodies, the borough and urban district councils, while only secondary schools were under county councils.) The school-leaving age was to be raised from 14 to 15 at the discretion of the Minister of Education; this happened in 1950. The Scottish Education Act was along similar lines, although control of all public schools there had been in the hands of county education authorities since 1918 and the education committees of county councils since 1929. Following proposals for social security drawn up in 1943 by a distinguished civil servant, SIR WILLIAM BEVERIDGE, in what was called the BEVERIDGE REPORT, Churchill announced that national insurance would be made compulsory for all, to provide benefits in sickness, unemployment and other emergencies. A Ministry of National Insurance was set up in 1944 to look after the new schemes, which included family allowances for the first time. The Government was also considering the possibility of a National Health Service, which eventually came into existence after the war along with a much-enlarged scheme of social security. When the war in Europe ended in 1945, the Coalition broke up very quickly. Churchill had proposed that, after Germany's surrender, the Coalition Government should continue together until the Japanese were also defeated. But most people, before the atom bombs were dropped, expected that the conquest of Japan would mean at least two more years; and the Labour party were unwilling to remain in the Coalition Government for all that time. As a result, a general election, the first for ten years, was held in July 1945, and Churchill suffered the mortification of being defeated at the end of the war he had done so much to win. Clement Attlee, Deputy Prime Minister under Churchill, took over the reins of office and formed the first Labour Government to hold full power in the history of the country. Churchill had played a notable part as the country's leader in wartime. In 1940, he roused the people in his broadcast speeches from the apathy of the Chamberlain era, and he was soon the most popular man in Britain, being greeted with enthusiasm wherever he appeared, with his inevitable cigar and his two-finger sign, "V for Victory." Unlike Lloyd George, he was on the best of terms with the leading generals, admirals and air-marshals, and there was no major dispute on the strategy of the war between himself and the military and naval experts, although his ebullience made him at times a difficult colleague. Probably his most valuable contribution to the winning of the war was in the diplomatic sphere; by his friendship with Roosevelt he secured for Britain assistance on a massive scale even before Pearl Harbor, and he lost no time in forming an alliance with the Russian Communists (whom he detested) once Hitler launched his attack on the Soviet Union.

SOURCE EXTRACTS

A *From Viscount Alanbrooke's War Diary*

August 6th, 1942.—Cairo.

One of the most difficult days of my life, with momentous decisions to take as far as my own future and the war was concerned. Whilst I was dressing and practically naked, the P.M. suddenly burst into my room. Very elated, and informed me that his thoughts were taking shape and that he would soon commit himself to paper. I rather shuddered and wondered what he was up to! Ten minutes later he burst into my room again and invited me to breakfast with him. However, as I was in the middle of my breakfast by then, he asked me to come along to his bedroom as soon as I had finished. . . . When I went round he made me sit on the sofa whilst he walked up and down. First of all, he said, he had decided to split the Middle East Command in two. . . . He went on to say that he intended to remove the Auk (General Auchinleck) to the Persian-Iraq Command as he had lost confidence in him. And he wanted me to take over the Near East Command with Montgomery as my Eighth Army Commander. This made my heart race very fast! He said he did not require an answer at once, and that I could think it over if I wanted. However, I told him without waiting that I was quite certain it would be a wrong move. . . . Another point which I did not mention was that, after working with the P.M. for close on nine months, I do feel at last that I can exercise a limited amount of control on some of his activities and that at last he is beginning to take my advice. I feel, therefore, that, tempting as the offer is, by accepting it I should definitely be taking a course which would on the whole help the war the least.

Bryant: The Turn of the Tide, 1939–43.

B *Bombs on Buckingham Palace, September 1940*

We went to London and found an Air Raid in progress. The day was very cloudy and it was raining hard. We were both upstairs with

Alec Hardinge [the King's Private Secretary] talking in my little sitting room overlooking the quadrangle; (I cannot use my ordinary one owing to the broken windows). All of a sudden we heard an aircraft making a zooming noise above us, saw 2 bombs falling past the opposite side of the Palace, and then heard 2 resounding crashes as the bombs fell in the quadrangle about 30 yds. away. We looked at each other and then we were out into the passage as fast as we could get there. The whole thing happened in a matter of seconds. We all wondered why we weren't dead. Two great craters had appeared in the courtyard. The one nearest the Palace had burst a fire hydrant and water was pouring through the broken windows in the passage. 6 bombs had been dropped. The aircraft was seen coming straight down the Mall below the clouds, having dived through the clouds, and had dropped 2 bombs on the forecourt, 2 in the quadrangle, 1 in the Chapel and the other in the garden. The Chapel is wrecked and the bomb also wrecked the plumber's workshop below in which 4 men were working, 3 of them were injured and the fourth shocked. Looking at the wreckage how they escaped death is a wonder to me.

From King George VI's diary, quoted in
J. W. Wheeler-Bennett: King George VI.

EXERCISES

1. (*Source Extract "A".*) What decision was finally taken about the Near East Command?

2. Explain: *Blitzkrieg, Sitzkrieg, Luftwaffe,* quisling, Vichy France, Operation "Sea-lion", Home Guard, Radar, A.R.P., partisans, scorched earth policy, Schnorkel, Kamikaze, Greater Asia Co-Prosperity Sphere, Anderson shelter, block-buster, buzz-bomb, V 1, V 2, Mulberry harbour, *Maquis, Festung Europa,* bunker, Super-fortress, P.A.Y.E.

3. Identify the authors of the following and explain where necessary:
   (*a*) "Hitler has missed the bus."
   (*b*) "Depart, I say, and let us have done with you. In the name of God, go!"
   (*c*) "We shall defend our island whatever the cost may be, we shall fight on the beaches, we shall fight on the landing grounds, we shall fight in the fields and in the streets, we shall fight in the hills, we shall never surrender."
   (*d*) "This was their finest hour."

(e) "Never in the field of human conflict was so much owed by so many to so few."

(f) "We have only to kick in the door and the whole rotten system will collapse."

(g) "The enemy is already broken and will never rise again."

4. Write short notes on: Maginot Line, Siegfried Line, Evacuation from Dunkirk, General Wavell, General Rommel, General Montgomery, Sir Andrew Cunningham, General Eisenhower, General MacArthur, Bomb-plot of July 1944, Atom bombs of 1945, Education Acts of 1944–1945, Beveridge Report.

5. Write notes on: Battle of Britain, Battle of ? Alamein, Battle of Stalingrad, Battle of the Atlantic, Pearl ?or, Invasion of Normandy.

6. Sketch the career of Winston Churchill up ? 9. What was his contribution to winning the Second World ?

7. Give some account of the war at sea, 1939–?

8. What part was played by air-power in the Sec? World War?

CHAPTER XII

TWO WORLD POWERS

Great Powers. At the beginning of the twentieth century, it was possible to speak of as many as six "Great Powers". Britain, Germany, France, Austria-Hungary, Russia and the United States were then given that rank, either for the size of their populations, the extent of their territories, their military and naval strength or the volume of their industry and trade, or a combination of all of these. Britain, Germany and the United States surpassed the rest in economic strength, on which military power is based. Germany's challenge to Britain's economic leadership collapsed in the First World War, during which the United States pulled ahead of all the rest. The dramatic rise of Russia (or the Union of Soviet Socialist Republics as it is called today) has taken place since the First World War and is without doubt the result of the Communist revolution of 1917 and the series of five-year plans put into effect afterwards by Stalin. This does not necessarily imply, as some think, that Communism is the best political system. It may be so for a very backward country, used to a despotic régime, and possessed of great potential wealth in natural resources like Russia. The main reasons why both the U.S.A. and the U.S.S.R. have become the two leading powers in the world are similar: both are large states with large populations, both have rich natural resources and are largely self-sufficient, both have been able to exploit the resources with which nature has endowed them, and both aspire to world leadership. The rapid expansion of the U.S.A. and the U.S.S.R. has taken place in different atmospheres, in the first case, one of free enterprise and in the second, one in which priority was given to the interests of the state and of the Communist Revolution. But in each state, the mood of most of the people has been buoyant, optimistic and self-confident, inspired by the belief that their political system and way of life are definitely the best. Of the remaining Great Powers in the world, Britain is in a specially important position, not to be measured only by reference to her population, volume of her industry and trade and extent of her territories. As the leading country in the British Commonwealth and as one of the chief victorious powers in the two World Wars, she has a prestige unparalleled by any of the other Great Powers. France, although it lacked the empire and industrial wealth of Britain, at one time sought to emulate it; but her defeat in the Second World War, like that of Japan, lost her much prestige. On the other side of the world are two large states, China and India, possessing huge populations and vast resources but at present backward in industry and agriculture. None of these four, Britain, France, China or India, is capable of independent military action on a scale comparable to what the U.S.A. or the U.S.S.R. could accomplish. Status as a world power then can be said to depend on the desire and ability to intervene independently and effectively in world affairs.

Causes of Russian Revolution, 1917. In order to understand the modern Russian state, it is necessary to know something of the Revolution of 1917. The causes of it may be summarized briefly:—(1) The Government of the Tsar, Nicholas II, inefficient enough before the war, showed itself grossly incompetent in its conduct of the war and by 1917 was held in contempt by almost the whole Russian people. Soldiers were sent to the front-line, ill-clad and often without weapons, to receive rifles from those whose places in the trenches they took over. Russia had no armaments industry, and supplies from the West, after the failure of the Dardanelles campaign, could come only by the Trans-Siberian railway or by the White Sea. But guns and vehicles, vital to the Russian war effort, lay rusting at Archangel, the White Sea port. As the Tsar had taken over command of the Army himself, he was blamed for the defeats and the enormous casualty lists. The Tsaritsa (Empress) Alix, had fallen under the influence of a disreputable monk, RASPUTIN, who had been able to save the life of the young prince, the Tsarevitch; and rumour had it that the Tsaritsa, of German birth, had favoured the Germans by revealing to them military secrets. The hatred felt for Rasputin was such that a group of nobles in Petrograd murdered him in December 1916. He was first poisoned, then shot, and finally his body was thrown into the water under the ice of the frozen river Neva. A few months later the Tsarist régime, despotic and inefficient, collapsed. (2) The second cause of the Revolution was the widespread social and economic discontent. The emancipation of Russian serfs had taken place as late as 1861 but the peasants lived in grinding poverty on small plots of land, weighed down by debt and taxation. In the towns, the factory workers had to put up with conditions like those in Britain a hundred years before. As far back as 1905, after the Russo-Japanese War, the workers throughout the country had declared a general strike because of what they called the intolerable conditions of their daily life. In 1917, because of food shortages, workers in Petrograd staged a general strike and started street demonstrations that were to lead to the Tsar's abdication. (3) Political grievances constituted a third factor. The Tsarist Government was a dictatorship and critics of the Government were generally exiled to the salt mines of

17

Siberia. One extreme leads to another, and it is not surprising that the despotic Russian state produced in the late nineteenth and twentieth centuries more Anarchists, Nihilists, not to mention Communists, than the rest of Europe together. After the 1905 troubles, the Tsar had allowed a DUMA, or parliament, to meet but, as it had no real powers, the opposition to the Government was only encouraged to seek more violent methods. (4) The fourth and most vital factor in the Revolution was the group of Bolsheviks, prepared to undertake the leadership of the Revolution, to organize the discontented working-classes, to seize power and to establish themselves as a revolutionary government. The BOLSHEVIKS (or Communists, as they are now called) were originally the majority at a Social Democratic conference in 1903, who voted in favour of revolutionary socialism as opposed to moderate reformist socialism, advocated by the Mensheviks. ("Bolsheviks" and "Mensheviks" stand for "the majority" and "the minority".) The man who, without doubt, inspired the other Bolsheviks to this achievement was LENIN (1870–1924). He had spent most of the time since 1907 in exile and was sent back to Russia in April 1917 in a sealed carriage of a special train by the Germans, who hoped that he would thereby bring about the collapse of the Russian Government.

Lenin and the Bolshevik Revolution, 1917–24. Earlier, in March 1917 when the workers of Petrograd staged a general strike because of the food shortage, women had joined them in demonstrations, and red flags were flown in houses in the main streets. The troops sent to deal with the demonstrations had refused to obey orders, many of them going over to the side of the workers. Messages were received from the generals at the front, complaining that soldiers were deserting wholesale or forming themselves into "soviets" or councils. A soviet of workers' deputies was formed in Petrograd on March 12th and on the same day a PROVISIONAL GOVERNMENT was set up. It consisted of left-wing Liberals and one Socialist, a young lawyer, KERENSKY. Three days later the Tsar abdicated. He and his family were arrested and, after a year's imprisonment at Ekaterinburg in the Urals, were all shot by local Communists and their bodies thrown down a disused mine shaft. (It was long afterwards claimed that one of the princesses, Anastasia, had escaped and was still alive forty years later.) The Provisional Government, of which Kerensky had become head, tried to continue the war against the Germans but neither the soldiers nor the people at home wanted more war. Throughout the summer of 1917, Lenin and another Bolshevik, TROTSKY, a Russian Jew who had returned from internment in Canada, organized workers, soldiers and sailors in readiness for revolution. By October 1917, the Bolsheviks were in a majority in the Petrograd Workers' Soviet or Council and on November 7th they struck. Railway stations, post offices, military headquarters were occupied by Bolshevik soldiers and sailors and the Kerensky Government collapsed. (The day, November 7th, was October 25th by the old Russian calendar, which was thirteen days behind the rest of Europe, and for this reason the revolution is still called the "October Revolution".) One of Lenin's first actions was to bring the war to an end, and a peace-treaty was signed in March 1918 at BREST-LITOVSK, where the Russians surrendered extensive territories and were forced to promise vast sums in reparations. But this treaty did not mean the end of fighting in Russia. For the next two years there was civil war between the "White" or anti-Bolshevik armies and the "Red" armies of the Bolshevik or Communist Government (as it was now named). Troops were also sent by Russia's former allies, Britain and France, and even by the U.S.A. to help restore the Tsarist régime. The Red Army, organized by Trotsky, was able to defeat the White armies, which never managed to co-ordinate effectively; and by the end of 1920 the Communists had re-conquered the Ukraine, surrendered by them at Brest-Litovsk. The years 1919–20 were years of great hardship and suffering for the Russian people. Those who opposed the new Communist régime fell victims to the "Red Terror" exercised by the "Cheka" or secret police, which had such a bad reputation that in 1922 it was re-organized and re-named the Government Political Office or G.P.U. (sometimes also known as the O.G.P.U.). Thousands of priests, schoolmasters, doctors, officers, land-owners and business people were "liquidated" or shot, as well as workers and peasants who criticized the new Government.

N.E.P. Soon after the Tsar had abdicated, some of the peasants seized the lands and burnt the mansion-houses of the nobility, many of whom were murdered while others fled from the country to Western Europe. By a decree of November 8th, 1917, all the large estates were confiscated and placed under soviets or councils of peasants. Workers' soviets also attempted to run the industries, which were gradually nationalized. By 1921 both industry and agriculture were in a state of collapse. Industrial output was as low as 17 per cent of that of 1913, and the yield of corn was less than half of the pre-war figures. Famine was widespread in 1920–21 and the typhus epidemic which swept across Europe after the war claimed thousands of victims. Finally, when the sailors at Kronstadt, the naval base near Petrograd, mutinied in March 1921 and were only suppressed after terrible bloodshed, Lenin decided on a temporary "retreat from Communism". In order to increase production he initiated the NEW ECONOMIC POLICY (N.E.P.), by which private concerns were permitted to engage in trade and manufacture, while the peasants were to pay a fixed levy of grain which would leave them with a surplus to sell. As a result, some improvement took place in economic conditions. During all the time that elapsed since the Revolution Lenin had worked with amazing energy but the strain was beginning to tell. In 1918 he had been shot at by a woman belonging to a rival party, a bullet remaining in his neck till his death, and in 1922 he had a stroke which left him for a time paralysed and unable to speak. He died in January 1924 and his embalmed body was placed in a glass coffin, in a mausoleum built in Moscow's Red Square in front of the Kremlin. Petrograd, which had been called St. Petersburg before the war of 1914–18, was re-named LENINGRAD after him; and the Communist dictator, whose career had involved so much violence and bloodshed, is today revered in Russia almost as a saint. Few men have had such influence on history in modern times and yet his main work was performed in the short space of five years.

Stalin and Trotsky. Lenin's successor, STALIN (1879–1952), was not a Russian but a native of Georgia near the Caucasus. He had been educated for the priesthood in a seminary at Tiflis but left it under a cloud at the age of nineteen. He engaged in revolutionary activities for many years, was sent to Siberia, from which he escaped, and on one occasion arranged a hold-up by bomb-throwing in order to replenish the funds of the local Bolshevik party. His name, Stalin ("Man of Steel") was a pseudonym adopted when he was managing editor of *Pravda* ("The Truth"), the official paper of the Bolsheviks. He was appointed Secretary of the Communist party before the death of Lenin, who had expressed doubts about Stalin's fitness for the post, as he felt he might prove too ruthless. It was this office which gave him a controlling position in the Communist movement and in the state itself. Although not officially a member of the Government, he gradually became a dictator, ousting all possible rivals from power. His greatest rival was TROTSKY, who had won a notable reputation as War Commissar during the troubled years, 1917–21. Trotsky believed in helping to create Communist revolutions in other countries and he had been one of the chief organizers of the Third International or COMINTERN, whose aim was to co-ordinate Communist activities in the different countries of the world. Stalin, on the other hand, advocated "Socialism in one country", concentrating on making Communism effective in Russia first and was prepared to pursue a foreign policy of "co-existence" with capitalist states. Trotsky lost his post as War Commissar in 1925, was exiled in 1928 and went to live first in Turkey, then in Mexico, where he was assassinated in 1940. Stalin was always ready to denounce anyone who disagreed with him as a Trotskyite and unfaithful to Lenin.

Five-Year Plans. Stalin's internal policy of building up the Soviet Union's economic strength was carried out in a series of FIVE-YEAR PLANS. The first (1927–32) was intended to industrialize the U.S.S.R., by constructing steel plants, giant motor-car and tractor factories and a huge hydro-electric scheme on the Dnieper, while at the same time increasing the agricultural output. Naturally, ordinary domestic comforts were not to be expected during this time and even necessities like clothing were obtained only with much difficulty. The finished plan, although it did not reach all the ambitious targets set, was still a wonderful achievement and made possible the later industrial expansion of the Soviet Union. It was carried through at a time when the rest of the world was suffering from a severe economic depression and millions of workers in capitalist countries were unemployed. Workers were roused to emulate the achievements of

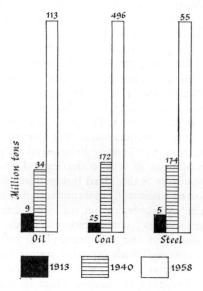

Soviet Production, 1913–58

A. Stakhanov, a coal-miner, and specially selected workers, called STAKHANOVITES, were encouraged to produce double the normal output in order to set high targets for the other workers. The Communists' plans for agriculture led them into tremendous difficulties. When the Government tried to "collectivize" the peasants' farms (turning them into "collective farms" of several hundred peasants) they were met with opposition from the better-off peasants or KULAKS. They had become keen property-owners since the Revolution, particularly after N.E.P. had allowed them some private trading. The kulaks tried to defeat the Government's plans, slaughtering their livestock and letting their grain rot in the fields rather than hand it over to the collective farms. It was estimated that about 50 per cent of the livestock in the Soviet Union were thus destroyed. The Government took forceful measures against the kulaks, who were labelled as "capitalist farmers" and "class enemies". Almost a million of them were "liquidated"—sent away to prison camps and compelled to labour on canals and railways. But, in addition to these measures, Stalin ordered a slowing-down in the pace of collectivization. The Second Five-Year Plan (1933–37) was, like the first, aimed at increasing the number of factories and, in particular, those for armaments manufacture, because of the new threat from Hitler's Germany. Although, according to the plan, it was hoped that all land would be cultivated by collective farms, the peasant was allowed to keep certain private stock and property, like cattle, goats, kitchen garden and orchard. The greatly increased number of tractors in the country made possible a vast expansion of agriculture so that in 1935 it was possible to bring the rationing of food to an end. In 1929 there had been only 45 combine harvesters in the Soviet Union and by 1938 there were 137,000. The Third Five-Year Plan was started in 1938 and, because of the threat of a European war, the emphasis was on armaments; and new factories were placed east of the Urals, far away from the western frontiers. When the Germans invaded Russia in 1941, they found then a country, very much unlike the Russia of 1917, with modern industries, mechanized transport and agriculture, capable of resisting and finally defeating the invaders.

Communist Dictatorship. Communist writers like Marx, Engels and Lenin had forecast that in order to establish Communism, revolution would be followed by a temporary "dictatorship of the proletariat", leading eventually to a classless society in which there would be no need for a state to function. The temporary dictatorship, however, has lasted for a long time after the Revolution in Russia; and the state, instead of "withering away" as forecast, seems as strong as ever. The threat of war with its western neighbours, and, in particular, with Germany after 1933, gave the Communists an excuse for strengthening their control over all the activities of the people. In theory, the Soviet Union is not one state but several, its full name being the Union of Soviet Socialist Republics (Russia and fourteen other republics). Although, by a constitution promulgated in 1936, all over eighteen years were to be allowed to vote at elections, in practice there was only one legal party, the Communist party, and only a single candidate was nominated for each constituency. In theory, the Supreme Soviet was the highest body in the State; but in practice the Communist party (which numbered just over 1 per cent of the total population) ruled the country. The political bureau of the party (known as the POLITBURO) consisted of thirteen men who decided on policy; and, as the members of the Politburo were selected by the Secretary of the party, Stalin, it was not surprising that he became the dictator of the country. Stalin showed himself increasingly jealous of the older Communists and gradually got rid of them. When in 1934 his best friend and likely successor, Kirov, was assassinated, Stalin started on a "purge" of the Communist party that reduced it from over two millions to 1,650,000. The G.P.U., the Russian secret police, became as hated and feared as the old Tsarist police had been. Many ordinary members of the Communist party were sent away to forced labour camps, which were under the control of the G.P.U. Public trials were staged in 1936 and several "Old Bolsheviks" like Zinoviev confessed their "crimes" and were executed. The Commander-in-Chief of the Red Army, Marshal Tukhachevsky, was likewise executed for alleged plotting with the Germans. Although some allowance must be made for the effect upon Stalin of Kirov's murder, this reign of terror was one of the great blots upon his reputation. It was not until twenty years later, at a secret session of the Communist Party Congress in 1956, that, at last, three years after his death, Stalin was denounced for the tyranny he had exercised at the time. Up to 1956 he had been hailed by the Communists of the Soviet Union as "the greatest leader of all ages and peoples"; but at this Congress he was accused of having "abolished collective leadership" and was called a sadist, a mass-murderer, a coward and a military bungler. Like Lenin, however, Stalin cared not what means he took to promote his aims, and these were the establishment and consolidation of a Communist state with himself as head of the state. Nor did this mean merely the setting up of a "police state": in education, in medicine, in science and in social services, great advances were made under Stalin's rule so that Russia could compare favourably in these respects with most Western states.

Woodrow Wilson and the Isolationists. One of the great tragedies of the peace settlement after the First World War was the withdrawal of the United States from European affairs. The two great American political parties, the Republican and the Democratic, had always favoured the policy of isolation from Europe, which was regarded as a corollary of the MONROE DOCTRINE, enunciated by President Monroe in 1823, when he made his famous stand against European intervention in American affairs. Although the United States had entered the First World War in 1917 under the leadership of the Democratic President Woodrow Wilson, there was a strong isolationist element even in his own party, which is natural enough when one considers that there were millions of people of German and Irish origin who had no reason to favour the Allies. The elections of 1918 resulted in a Republican majority (that is, for isolationism) in both Houses of Congress, the Senate and the House of Representatives. As a result, the Treaty of Versailles was not ratified by Congress, while the newly-constituted League of Nations, of which Woodrow Wilson was so proud, came into existence without the United States as a member. The isolation from Europe was not complete. During the war, the United States had forged ahead of her rivals in trade, Britain and Germany, and as time went on, American products flooded into British and other markets until people began to complain of the Americanization of the world. The United States during the war had advanced loans to most of the Allies, who found it difficult to repay; and Britain, much to the Americans' disgust, tried to make repayment of her loans conditional on her receiving payment of German reparations and war debts owed by other countries. Two American plans, the DAWES PLAN of 1924 and the YOUNG PLAN of 1929, went some way to settling the problems of war debts but still left the Americans unpopular in Europe.

Return to "Normalcy". The presidental election of 1920 was a victory for the Republican candidate WARREN HARDING, who had campaigned for a return to "normalcy"; by this he meant the end of intervention in European affairs and the end of interference with "big business". It has been said by a modern American historian that "no more pitiable incompetent had ever occupied the President's chair" and Harding certainly had little influence on affairs. He did not complete his term of office, being succeeded in 1923 by another Republican President, CALVIN COOLIDGE, who held office till 1928. As elsewhere in the world, a post-war depression developed and lasted till 1923, after which things gradually improved. The 1920's were the era of PROHIBITION in the U.S.A. By the Eighteenth Amendment to the American Constitution, the manufacture or sale or transport of intoxicating liquors was declared illegal in 1920. The results of Prohibition were very different from what the sponsors of the Eighteenth Amendment had fondly hoped. Whisky, gin and rum were smuggled in by "bootleggers", who landed their illegal cargoes from fast motor-boats along isolated parts of the coast. Fortunes were made by the owners of "speak-easies", where spirits of doubtful origin were sold at fancy prices. The control of the illegal liquor trade fell into the hands of gangsters; and they had little compunction in "bumping off" rival gangsters who had tried to "muscle in" on their territories. A favourite weapon of the gangsters of this period was the Thompson sub-machine gun or "tommy gun". The system of Prohibition had become a farce long before 1933 when, by the Twentieth Amendment to the Constitution, the Eighteenth Amendment was repealed. Another challenge to law and authority at this time came from the Ku-Klux-Klan, a secret organization of the nineteenth century revived during the First World War. It was anti-negro, anti-Jewish and anti-Catholic, and was responsible for the lynching of negroes in the Southern States. The 1920's saw a vast expansion of the automobile industry, mainly through the agency and example of HENRY FORD, at whose giant factory in Detroit cheap mass-produced cars were turned off the assembly line and workmen of little skill could earn high wages. The FILM INDUSTRY also became big business at this period with its centre at Hollywood, a suburb of Los Angeles in California, and films of Charlie Chaplin, Douglas Fairbanks, Al Jolson went all over the world. The last-named featured in the first "talkie", *The Jazz Singer*, produced in 1927 in the U.S.A. (and shown in 1928 as *The Singing Fool* in Britain). BROADCASTING started in 1920 and by 1922 was already on a commercial basis, programmes being sponsored by firms in order to advertise their products. The 1920's also saw the beginning of the craze for JAZZ, helped by the cinema, broadcasting and the gramophone: composers like Irving Berlin, George Gershwin and Jerome Kern made fortunes that composers of classical music had never dreamed of. Sport, like everything else, was commercialized on a large scale, and Babe Ruth, the baseball player, Jack Dempsey, the heavyweight boxer, and Bobby Jones, an amateur golfer, were heroes of the "roaring twenties". Films, radio, advertising, all tended to emphasize the importance of women, even more than the grant of the franchise in 1920 by the Nineteenth Amendment. The idea of labour-saving devices to reduce the housewife's drudgery became popular with housewives and manufacturers. As workers' pay-packets bulged with piece-work bonuses, the standard of living rose considerably. Buying by instalments made it easier to acquire expensive goods, and many ordinary working-men considered a motor-car a necessity. One result of the boom in industry and the increased standard of living was that thousands began to engage in speculation on the Stock Exchange for the first time. During the orgy of speculation of 1928–29, some shares quadrupled in value, so great was the demand for them. The Government had successively reduced income-tax so that more idle money was available and the Americans had not learned, like the British, to invest their capital overseas. To many Americans, although shocked by the excesses of the gangsters, it seemed that they had never been so prosperous when in 1929 the boom collapsed, heralded by what is known as the WALL STREET CRASH, Wall Street being the site of the New York Stock Exchange.

The Great Depression. When the Wall Street crash came in October 1929, shares that stood at high prices slumped drastically. On one day, October 29th, over 16 million shares were sold at throw-away prices. Many men who had financed their investing by borrowing were ruined overnight and some saw no alternative to suicide. Banks which had given loans too freely to borrowers closed their doors; and factory-owners, finding that orders were cancelled, were compelled to dismiss their employees. Farmers, in difficulties because they depended so much on loans, which were no longer available, faced disaster when a prolonged drought ruined their crops and livestock had to be destroyed. In other countries, also, the boom of the mid-twenties collapsed and large-scale unemployment developed. The decision of President HERBERT HOOVER in 1930 to increase tariffs in order to protect American industries did not help matters either in the U.S.A. or elsewhere, as other tariffs were raised in reprisal. When the Austrian and German financial crises occurred in 1931, however, Hoover arranged for a year's moratorium on war debts and reparations. By 1932, the depression had become world-wide, affecting not only manufacturing countries but also those producing primary commodities—raw materials, food and fuels. In Canada and the United States, grain prices were so low that wheat was burned in stacks as it was not worth while paying for transport to the elevators, while in Brazil, as coffee prices dropped to record low levels, coffee beans were actually used as fuel for the railway engines. Unemployment figures soared to over ten millions in the U.S.A. in 1932 and to at least thirteen millions in 1933 (according to some estimates over seventeen millions). There was no unemployment insurance scheme as in Britain and state authorities were slow and niggardly in providing relief. The sufferings of the workless, tramping the country in search of jobs and begging for food or money, were worse than in Europe, particularly during the severe American winter. For a proud nation, which had just enjoyed such a wonderful spell of prosperity, the depression was hard to bear; their self-pity found expression in a popular "hit"—*Brother, can you spare a dime?* The Presidential Election of 1932, not unexpectedly, brought about the defeat of the Republican President, Herbert Hoover, and the return of a Democrat for the first time since Woodrow Wilson. The new President, FRANKLIN D. ROOSEVELT, was to be elected to the White House four times in all—a record for American Presidents. When he took over office in March 1933, the condition of the country could hardly be worse. Most of the banks had closed their doors and business was at a stand-still in many districts. Farmers, who were fearful of losing their farms because they were so much in debt, stood on guard with rifles to prevent eviction. It was a national emergency that called for leadership of a high order and fortunately Roosevelt was able to provide it.

The New Deal—First Stage. Franklin Delano Roosevelt (1882–1945) was born of a rich and aristocratic family at Hyde Park in the state of New York. Another famous American President, Theodore ("Teddy") Roosevelt was a distant cousin. He was educated at an exclusive school, Groton, and at Harvard University, later taking a law degree at Columbia University, during which time he married his cousin, Eleanor Roosevelt. He was elected to the Senate in 1910 as a Democrat and was for a time Assistant Secretary to the Navy under President Woodrow Wilson. In 1921 he was struck down by infantile paralysis but helped by his patient and understanding wife he bore his affliction with courage. Although he never regained full power over his legs, he was able to return to politics, stronger in mind and character than ever. He held the office of Governor of New York from 1928 to 1932, when he was elected President with a large majority over Hoover, having pledged himself to give "a new deal for the American people". Roosevelt's NEW DEAL was in reality several different "new deals". He had announced before the election that he was prepared to try any kind of experiment that would help to bring about the recovery of the nation. With the help of a body of professors and financial experts, called the "BRAINS TRUST", he set to work on a programme,

which he put before Congress in a memorable session of a
hundred days in 1933. The first New Deal (1933-34) aimed at
recovery from the depression by helping business, labour and
farming. By the National Industry Recovery Act (usually called
the N.R.A.) the President was given far-reaching powers over
business and industry. Almost all American banks were either
closed or on the verge of closing at the beginning of 1933, and
by a series of Acts they were forced to accept various reforms,
restricting their lending and compelling them to adopt new
standards. The activities of the Stock Exchange were also regulated and new companies were obliged to give prospective
investors the fullest information. In order to help external
trade, which was stagnating at the time, the gold standard was
abandoned, the dollar was devalued to 59 per cent of its former
value. A Public Works Administration, with a fund of 3,300
million dollars, financed projects, such as new houses, afforestation, etc., which meant more employment not only on the sites
but also in the factories providing materials. The expenditure of
public money in this way during a depression is called "priming
the pumps" of industry. Obviously, a million men at work are
able to buy more food, clothing and furniture than the same
number of unemployed; and more men, in turn, will be
required in the industries producing food, clothing and furniture
and eventually in other industries also. Relief for the vast army
of unemployed was provided by distributing 500 million dollars
to the state authorities. A new labour code was laid down for
relations between masters and men: workers were given the right
to form trade unions, child labour was abolished, hours were
reduced to about 40 a week and wages kept at a minimum of
40 cents an hour. By the Agricultural Adjustment Act (A.A.A.),
the farmers received help in the form of loans and subsidies in
return for cutting down their acreage of crops, while the prices
of farm products were regulated. The TENNESSEE VALLEY
AUTHORITY (T.V.A.) was set up in 1933 to bring new life to the
Tennessee Valley, one of the most depressed areas in the United
States. Early settlers had been careless in their cultivation and
had ruined the soil; woods had been cut down and the rivers

frequently flooded the adjacent land. Irrigation, afforestation, hydro-electricity, malaria control, national parks were all parts of a vast regional plan which raised over three million people from the poverty line to a standard of living comparable with other parts of the United States. Roosevelt's New Deal was not carried out without considerable opposition. Certain Acts of Congress were declared unconstitutional by the Supreme Court (something which could not happen in Great Britain) and a long-drawn-out battle ensued between President and the Supreme Court. Roosevelt was the object of the bitter hatred of the employers, who thought of him as a traitor to his class and who resented the increased taxation, the new labour regulations and Government interference generally. The poorer classes, on the other hand, regarded him with something akin to worship. His "New Deal" and his radio "fireside talks", in which he managed to put over in a simple, intimate style a few home-truths, brought him a respect and admiration that no other President ever achieved. The elections to Congress in November 1934 showed that the country was behind Roosevelt and he was encouraged to go ahead with other measures.

New Deal—Later Stages, 1935–38. The second New Deal was mainly a programme of social reform. In Roosevelt's first speech to the new Congress in 1935, he declared that "we have not weeded out the overprivileged and we have not effectively lifted up the underprivileged". "The right to work to earn a decent livelihood," Roosevelt claimed, was to have priority over "the appetite for great wealth and great power". These words and his subsequent actions made many people label Roosevelt as a Liberal or a Socialist and gained for him rebukes from members of his own party. Roosevelt was accused of "soaking the rich" and, in effect, he was aiming at redistributing the wealth of the rich among the needy. Taxes on large incomes and estate duties were increased. More public works schemes were started (roads, bridges, flood control, etc.) and a National Youth Act provided for work for young people who since leaving school had never learnt a trade. Unemployment insurance, old age pensions, relief for the blind were introduced in a Social

Security Act. Employers were forbidden by the Wagner Act to interfere in any way with their employees' unions; this Act has been called the Magna Carta of the American trade unions. Roosevelt was in the middle of a long struggle with the Supreme Court, which was holding up various measures as unconstitutional, when the Presidential Election in 1936 gave him victory again with a handsome margin. In his first four years he had achieved what amounted to an economic and social revolution in the United States. The New Deal entered a third phase in 1938, when the Republicans gained some seats for the first time in ten years and the Democrats in the south (the so-called "Dixiecrats") showed more opposition to their party leader. Roosevelt was still faced with the problem of unemployment (the roll of unemployed stood at over eight million); and his policy from 1938 onwards was one which could be called "permanent pump-priming". This meant spending public money on projects in areas where unemployment was still giving concern. In addition, he guaranteed fixed prices for farmers and granted subsidies, where necessary, to maintain the prices. The hatred of the business world grew as more and more public utilities (gas, electricity, water supply concerns) came under Federal control and new corporations were formed for shipping, railways, banking, etc. Trade unions were given even more rights. The two large combinations—the Committee for Industrial Organization (the C.I.O.) and the Associated Federation of Labour (the A.F. of L.)—waxed stronger than ever under trade union bosses like John L. Lewis. The approach of war from 1938 onwards gave a fillip to the armaments industry but there were still seven million unemployed when the United States went to war in 1941. In the previous year, 1940, Roosevelt had been elected President for the third time, thus breaking a tradition going back to Washington that no President should stand for election a third time. His New Deal had revolutionized the American economy by the large-scale intervention of the Government in industry, thus ending the long period of *laissez-faire* and free enterprise. He had also by his protection of the workers introduced the elements of a Welfare State. At the same time, although unemployment still existed, he had brought new hope and life to millions of workless and raised America out of the slough of despond in which it had lain in 1932.

American and British Constitutions. The American constitution differs from the British constitution in many respects. It is the constitution of a presidential republic, and Britain's that of a limited monarchy. It is federal, the fifty states (Alaska was added in 1958 and Hawaii in 1960) each possessing its own administration and legislation and the right to send representatives to Congress, whereas Britain is a United Kingdom with only one parliament. The American constitution is a document drawn up in 1789, and changes are effected by a long and complicated process, only twenty-one amendments having been passed in the first 150 years. (The first ten amendments, which safeguard the liberty of the subject, are called the American BILL OF RIGHTS.) The American constitution is thus an entirely written one and is described as rigid because of the difficulty of changing it. The British constitution includes not only laws passed at different times over the centuries but also certain customs and conventions; changes can and have been made without the necessity of passing an Act of Parliament, e.g. most of the developments in the office of Prime Minister. The British constitution is thus both written and unwritten; and, as changes can be effected so easily, it is described as flexible. Of the three main parts of the constitution—the executive, the legislature and the judiciary—the first is most important as it wields the powers of government. The head of the executive in the United States is the PRESIDENT and in Britain the Prime Minister. The President, nominally elected by an electoral college but in fact elected by popular vote, himself chooses his ministers, who must not be members of the legislature, Congress. The Prime Minister is appointed by the monarch, who generally selects the leader of the majority party in the House of Commons; the ministers whom he chooses are, unlike the Americans, members of the legislature, either of the House of Commons or of the House of Lords. The American judiciary is of more importance in the constitution than the British judiciary: the SUPREME COURT OF JUDGES in the United States can determine whether the Acts passed by Congress are in accordance with the constitution or not. In Britain, the judges interpret the laws passed by Parliament but have no power to reject them as unconstitutional. The elections to the legislature differ in the two countries. The 435 members of the HOUSE OF REPRESENTATIVES are elected afresh every two years on the basis of the population of the various states, while the 100 members of the SENATE (two members for each state) are elected for six years, one-third retiring every two years. Elections to the House of Commons must take place at least once every five years but may occur at shorter intervals if a Government is unable to command a majority in the House of Commons; for example, there were three elections in Britain in three successive years, 1922–23–24. No elections are necessary for the Upper House of the British Parliament except for the Scottish peers, sixteen of whom are elected at each general election; the other peers attend by hereditary right except for a few life peers. The separation of the various functions—the executive, the legislative and the judicial—was intended by the framers of the American constitution in 1789 to provide a system of checks and balances and to prevent any one side of government gaining too much power at the expense of the others. Sometimes a difficult situation arises when President and Congress do not see eye to eye. This may happen in the second half of a President's four-year term, when after the biennial elections the majority in the House of Representatives and the Senate are of a different party from the President. This was the reason why President Woodrow Wilson's plans for a League of Nations were not accepted by Congress in 1919–20. During such a period of deadlock, the President is unable to pursue his policy without having his measures defeated in Congress, while the Bills passed by Congress can be vetoed by the President. A deadlock of a similar kind used to exist formerly in Britain also until 1911 when by the Parliament Act the absolute veto of the House of Lords was restricted to one of two years (and still further reduced in 1949 to one year). The flexibility of the British constitution made it

possible, however, for the Government, if it so desired, to alter
the majority in the House of Lords by asking the King to create
more peers.

Stalin and the Second World War. Neither the Soviet Union
nor the United States entered the Second World War until 1941.
In the case of the Russians, they felt they had been slighted when
the Munich Conference over Czechoslovakia was held in 1938
without them. Stalin abandoned his policy of "collective security"
and co-operation with the west and startled the world by signing
in August 1939 a Non-aggression Pact with Hitler. There is
little doubt that this RUSSO–GERMAN PACT led directly to Hitler's
invasion of Poland for he was thereby secured from the danger of
fighting a two-front war as the Germans had done in 1914, a
mistake he constantly criticized in *Mein Kampf* and in his speeches.
To Stalin, the pact offered a free hand in dealing with the Baltic
states, Estonia, Latvia and Lithuania, which he promptly
annexed, and also a share of Poland once Germany had conquered
it. These acquisitions of territory were obviously intended to give
Russia greater depth in defence and therefore greater security—
against Germany. As a Communist, Stalin must also have
derived some satisfaction from the prospect of remaining neutral
while the great capitalist states set about destroying one another.
Both Stalin and Hitler were quite cynical about this NON-
AGGRESSION PACT, which they would observe only so long as it
suited them. The signing of the pact added to the detestation
of Communism felt in Western Europe and the United States;
and when the Russians, after seizing the Baltic states and taking
their share of the defeated Poland, declared war on FINLAND in
November 1939, sympathy for the Finns and hatred of Russia
were world-wide. Stalin had shown that the new Communist
Government had imperialist ambitions no less than the old
Tsarist régime. The Finns defended themselves heroically for
three months but were forced to surrender territory which would
afford the Russians greater security for Leningrad in the case of a
German attack. The German invasion started on June 22nd, 1941,
less than two years after the signing of the NON-AGGRESSION
PACT between Germany and the Soviet Union. Russia had been

rearming steadily for some time, and Hitler, like Napoleon, was to find that Russia and the Russian winter were too much for him, finally meeting defeat and death in the two-front war he had always tried to avoid. The Soviet Union emerged from the war, shattered, her western towns and villages destroyed, millions of Russians dead or missing, but victorious and master of Eastern Europe. Rumania, Bulgaria, Hungary, Poland, East Germany, East Austria were all under her occupation forces with Communist governments in power, while Czechoslovakia was sympathetic and after 1948 directly under Soviet influence. These "SATELLITES" of the Soviet Union did not so much provide the Soviet Union with additional fighting strength as with a protective defence zone against the Western Powers. From Germany was taken a vast amount of industrial equipment as reparations to make good some of the damage caused by Germans. In the Far East, where Stalin joined in the war against Japan only two days before she surrendered, Russia regained Port Arthur, which she had lost to the Japanese forty years before, and the Kurile Islands to the north of Japan. The effect of the Second World War was to make the Soviet Union one of the two leading world powers and once again an instigator of world revolution. She had shown her fighting strength in the struggle against the German invaders, she had surrounded herself with satellite states, and in many of the other chief countries of the world there were Communist parties or sympathizers ("fellow-travellers", as they were called) who considered loyalty to the Soviet Union as having priority over allegiance to their own country. In China, also, a strong Communist movement was making what was to be a successful bid for power. Stalin could well afford to regard with pride his achievements in the war and in the peace negotiations in which he had invariably got his way in anything that was important. The Communist aim of world revolution, which had been abandoned in the 1920's, was now a principal factor in Soviet foreign policy and therefore a threat to all the capitalist countries of the world, including the United States.

U.S.A. at War. There were many similarities between the parts played by the Americans in the First and Second World

Wars. In both, entry was made well after the start, although in the Second there were still three years to run as against just over one in the First. Democratic Presidents were chiefly responsible in both wars for the break with the traditional American policy of isolation—Woodrow Wilson in 1917 and Roosevelt in 1941. In both cases, declaration of war was preceded by a friendly neutrality so far as Britain and her allies were concerned. But there were differences as well as similarities. There were for the Americans in the Second World War two important zones of warfare—the Pacific and Western Europe—instead of only one in 1917–18; and in each zone they were much more deeply involved than in the earlier war. Further, in 1945, in contrast to 1919, the Americans did not shake themselves free of European entanglements. This was due to various reasons:—(1) Their longer and fuller participation in the fighting, which made them more conscious of the issues involved; (2) The personality of Roosevelt, who had taken an interest in European affairs long before the war and who realized that the United States as a world power could not afford to ignore the other half of the world; (3) The personality of Churchill, who used all his skill of diplomacy to bring the United States into European affairs; (4) The existence of the very much stronger Soviet Union, which, with Communism spreading over half of Europe, seemed to threaten the American way of life; (5) The existence of the United Nations, which like the League of Nations was mainly the creation of the United States but was from the first firmly based on American support (the headquarters being at New York instead of Geneva). Roosevelt saw himself as holding the balance between Churchill and Stalin; but at the conference held in February 1945 at YALTA in the Crimea, he allowed Stalin to realize every one of his important demands and establish himself as supreme on the continent of Europe. When the war was over, therefore, the United States was a leading member of the United Nations and American armies of occupation remained in Europe. In 1947, President Truman (who succeeded Roosevelt on his sudden death in April 1945) intimated a major change of foreign policy, the so-called TRUMAN DOCTRINE, by which the United States would "support free people who are resisting attempted subjugation by armed minorities or outside pressure". This was a radical departure from the previous policy of isolation from European affairs and in practice involved intervention in Europe or aid to countries like Greece and Turkey, in order to resist Communist pressure. The Americans, having defeated Japan, also realized that with the Soviet Union on her border and a strong Communist bid for power in China, there was every chance that Japan also might fall into the orbit of Communist states if she were left to herself. As a result, the United States set about restoring Japan's industries and trade, spending large sums of money in a way that few victors have ever done for the vanquished. The war and the peace settlement after it had thus brought the two leading world powers into rivalry with one another in Europe and in the Far East for the first time. It is not surprising that the post-war years proved to be years of tension and crisis and that the former allies seemed to be on the brink of war on various occasions.

SOURCE EXTRACTS

A   *Lenin on Democracy*

. . . On the basis of all that has been said above, it is possible to determine more precisely how democracy changes in the transition from capitalism to communism. In capitalist society, under the conditions most favourable to its development we have more or less complete democracy in the democratic republic. But this democracy is always restricted by the narrow framework of capitalist exploitation, and consequently always remains, in reality, a democracy for the minority, only for the possessing classes, only for the rich. Freedom in capitalist society always remains the same as it was in the ancient Greek republics: freedom for the slave-owners. Owing to the conditions of capitalist exploitation, the modern wage-slaves are so crushed by want and poverty that "they cannot be bothered with democracy," and "they cannot be bothered with politics"; in the ordinary peaceful course of events the majority of the population is debarred from participating in social and political life. . . . Marx grasped this *essence* of capitalist democracy splendidly when he said that the oppressed were allowed, once every few years, to decide which particular representatives of the oppressing class should misrepresent them in parliament.

But from this capitalist democracy—inevitably narrow, tacitly repelling the poor, and therefore hypocritical and false to the core— development does not proceed simply, smoothly and directly to "greater and greater democracy", as the liberal professors and petty bourgeois professors would have us believe. No, development— towards communism—proceeds through the dictatorship of the proletariat: it cannot do otherwise, for the *resistance* of the capitalist exploiters cannot be *broken* by anyone else or in any other way.

But the dictatorship of the proletariat, i.e. the organization of the vanguard of the oppressed as the ruling-class for the purpose of crushing the oppressors . . . imposes a series of restrictions on the freedom of the oppressors, the exploiters, the capitalists. We must crush them in order to free humanity from wage-slavery; their resistance must be broken by force; it is clear that where there is suppression there is also violence, there is no democracy.

Lenin: The State and Revolution.

B   *Amendments to the American Constitution*

    I Congress shall make no law respecting an establishment of religion, or prohibiting the free exercise thereof; or abridging the freedom of speech, or of the press; or the right of the people peacefully to assemble, and to petition the Government for a redress of grievances.   (1791)

    V No person shall be held to answer for a capital, or otherwise infamous crime, unless on a presentment or indictment of a Grand Jury, except in cases arising in the land or naval forces, or in the Militia, when in actual service in time of War or public danger; nor shall any person be subject for the same offence to be twice put in jeopardy of life or limb; nor shall be compelled in any criminal case to be a witness against himself, nor be deprived of life, liberty or property, without due process of law, nor shall private property be taken for public use, without just compensation.   (1791)

XIII Neither slavery nor involuntary servitude, except as a punishment for crime whereof the party shall have been duly convicted, shall exist within the United States, or any place subject to their jurisdiction.   (1865)

XIV   All persons born or naturalized in the United States, and subject to the jurisdiction thereof, are citizens of the United States and of the State wherein they reside. No State shall make or enforce any law which shall abridge the privileges or immunities of citizens of the United States. . . .   (1868)

XVIII   After one year from the ratification of this article the manufacture, sale, or transportation of intoxicating liquors within, the importation thereof into, or the exportation thereof from the United States and all territory subject to the jurisdiction thereof for beverage purposes is hereby prohibited.

(1919)

XIX   The right of citizens of the United States to vote shall not be denied or abridged by the United States or by any State on account of sex.   (1920)

EXERCISES

1. Explain: Bolshevik, G.P.U., N.E.P., *Pravda*, Comintern, "liquidation" of kulaks, Monroe Doctrine, boot-legger, speakeasy, tommy gun, Ku-Klux-Klan, Brains Trust, T.V.A., Dixiecrat, American Bill of Rights, satellite state, "fellow-traveller".

2. Identify the authors of the following and explain where necessary:
   (a) "Freedom in capitalist society always remains the same as it was in the ancient Greek republics: freedom for the slave-owners."
   (b) "No more pitiable incompetent ever occupied the President's chair."
   (c) "Brother, can you spare a dime?"
   (d) "The right by work to earn a decent livelihood must have priority over the appetite for great wealth and great power."

3. Write notes on: Rasputin, Kerensky, Treaty of Brest-Litovsk, Trotsky, Stalin's "purges", Wall Street crash, Tennessee Valley Authority, Russo-German Pact of 1939, Truman Doctrine.

4. What were the main causes of discontent in Russia in 1917? Account for the success of the Bolshevik Revolution.

5. Give an account of Stalin's Five-Year Plans. What difficulties had he to overcome?

6. Describe the situation in the United States when F. D. Roosevelt became President. What is meant by the New Deal?

CHAPTER XIII

THE BRITISH EMPIRE AND COMMONWEALTH

The British Empire. In an earlier chapter we have seen how the British dealt with the problems that faced them in Africa. There, in the "Scramble for Africa" they acquired in the 1880's and 1890's a number of colonies in the tropical zone, where the inhabitants were generally of primitive races. In South Africa, the chief problem was that of her relations with the Boers of Dutch origin, and a settlement only came, after two unfortunate wars, by the formation of the Union of South Africa. In North Africa, the British interest was primarily that of securing the Suez Canal. Although Egypt was up to 1914 nominally part of the Ottoman Empire, she was under British government and the main problem the British had to face was the rise of Egyptian nationalism. Outside Africa, there were other colonies administered by the British Colonial Office—in the West Indies, in Malaya and in various islands scattered throughout the oceans of the world. In addition, there was the problem of the relations between the self-governing colonies and the Mother Country. These problems did not engross the attention of the British and indeed most of the people were indifferent to them. They were certainly proud of the vast Empire but only one or two far-sighted men in the 1880's were aware of the problems of Empire. The feeling that Britain and the self-governing colonies were in a sense a commonwealth or federation was strengthened by the periodic meetings of overseas Prime Ministers and the participation of overseas troops in the South African war. We shall see in this chapter how self-government developed in the colonies and how the relations between the self-governing colonies and Britain were cemented very slowly, until they could properly be called a Commonwealth of Nations.

Opening up the Prairies. It was in 1867 that there began the federation of the provinces of Canada into one state, the DOMINION OF CANADA, although it did not possess what we today call dominion status. British Columbia joined the Dominion in 1871 with a promise that a railway would be constructed across the Rockies within ten years. The project for a transcontinental railway went slowly for some time but at last it was completed in 1885. Donald Smith and George Stephen, both natives of Speyside, Scotland, and later known as Lord Strathcona and Lord Mount Stephen, formed a syndicate to finish off the last stretch, the actual construction being carried out by an engineer of Dutch origin, Van Horne. At a place called Craigellachie (the name of a village in Speyside near to the birthplaces of Smith and Stephen) Smith drove in the last spike on the CANADIAN PACIFIC RAILWAY, one of the great railways of the world. Two other railways, the Canadian North Railway and the Grand Trunk Pacific, were to be built across Canada; but troubles also developed and they were not completed until after the First World War, when the Government took them over as parts of the state-controlled system, Canadian National Railways. The Canadian Pacific and other railways opened up the prairies and the Rockies to new settlers and new industries, grain-growing in the prairie provinces and lumbering and mining further west. The great wheat lands of Manitoba, Saskatchewan and Alberta did not, however, begin to compete with the Middle West States of the U.S.A. until the twentieth century. Up till 1898 the total wheat crop even in the best years never exceeded 50 million bushels; by 1905, it was over 100 million bushels and in 1915 nearly 400 million bushels. The Canadian prairie wheat is of a hard, dry quality and is preferred by British millers to all others for making the flour that goes into British bread. Like other wheat farmers throughout the world, the Canadians suffered severely during the depression of the 1930's when prices droped so low that they would not pay for the freights to the elevators. Immigration reached its height in the period before the First World War. The rate had never exceeded 45,000 a year in the nineteenth century but it steadily increased until in the years 1912-13-14 over a million immigrants

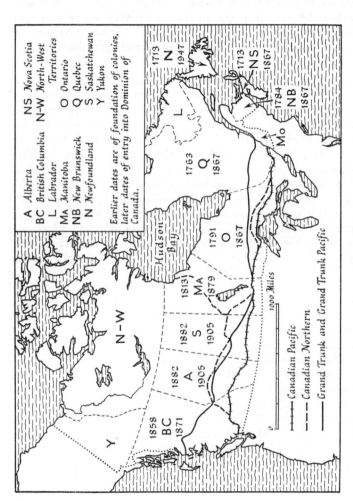

Dominion of Canada

arrived, most of them from Britain but some also from Scandinavia and Central Europe. In the forty years from 1871 to 1911, the population almost doubled itself (from 3,690,000 to 7,207,000) but Canada still remained sparsely populated in many regions.

Canadian Prime Ministers. The chief architect of Canadian federation (and the first Prime Minister of the Dominion of Canada) was SIR JOHN A. MACDONALD (1815–91). He was born in Glasgow, where his parents had settled temporarily after being evicted from their home at Lairg during the Sutherland clearances. He was a skilful politician, adept in the handling of men, and held office for almost twenty years. It was by his promise of a trans-continental railway that British Columbia was persuaded to join the Dominion in 1871. In politics a Conservative, MacDonald was strong for maintaining the connection with Britain and also for a high tariff policy, which was started by him in 1878. When the Conservatives were defeated by the Liberals in 1896, the new Prime Minister was a French Canadian and a Catholic, WILFRID LAURIER (1841–1919), later knighted. He was to remain at the head of affairs until 1911 and during his long term of office Canada enjoyed general prosperity. Saskatchewan and Alberta were organized as provinces in 1905, wheat production in the prairies was increasing by leaps and bounds, and immigrants were arriving each year in larger numbers. In addition to the traditional occupations of farming, lumbering and fishing, Canadians were now exploiting the rich mineral resources of their land—coal in Nova Scotia and Vancouver, silver, gold, copper and nickel in Ontario (90 per cent of the world's nickel comes from Sudbury in North-west Ontario). Although a Liberal, Sir Wilfrid Laurier was not like the British Liberals in favour of free trade; nor was he willing to join with the other self-governing colonies in 1907 in a scheme of imperial preference, as he felt Canada would be better off with a trade agreement with the United States. Laurier, however, was keen to preserve the links with the Mother Country; and during the South African War (1899–1902) he sent troops to help the British despite French-Canadian criticism. Laurier's successor,

SIR ROBERT BORDEN (1854–1937), Conservative Prime Minister from 1911 to 1920, was notable for his contribution to Britain's war effort. In 1912, he had proposed to build three battleships to help increase Britain's naval strength. It was the time of keen naval rivalry between Britain and Germany, and New Zealand, Australia and the Federated Malay States had each volunteered to construct a battle-cruiser. Borden's proposal was defeated in the Canadian Senate, mainly through the opposition of Laurier and other Liberals. In the First World War, however, the Canadian forces played a conspicuous part; their storming of Vimy Ridge in North France in 1917, when over 10,000 lives were lost, is commemorated in a massive memorial there. The Canadian Prime Minister with the longest period in office was W. L. MACKENZIE KING (1874–1950), grandson of the Scottish-born William Lyon Mackenzie, political reformer and rebel of 1837. Mackenzie King was Liberal Prime Minister from 1921 to 1949 with one or two gaps when Conservative Governments were in office. Although prepared to co-operate with the other dominions, he was determined to uphold the independence of Canada and preferred a loose federation to any kind of centralization in London. The Statute of Westminster of 1931, based on the findings of the Imperial Conference of 1926, which he attended, defined the relations of the Commonwealth countries more or less in terms of Mackenzie King's attitude. In 1939, he deliberately delayed Canada's declaration of war against Germany for a week to assert Canada's independence in foreign affairs. Once again, as in the First World War, the Canadians were able to render valuable assistance to Britain not only in soldiers, sailors and airmen but also in food, munitions and other supplies.

New Zealand. A Federal Parliament existed in New Zealand from as early as 1852 and self-government, with ministers responsible to Parliament, from 1856. For over twenty years, the two islands had six provincial councils but these were abolished in 1876, so that federation, which came early in New Zealand, also disappeared early. During the Maori war in North Island (1860–70), discoveries of gold in Otago and Westland led to a short-lived gold rush to South Island. Railway construction started during this period, from the first under the ownership and control of the Government. New Zealand trade benefited from the opening of the Suez Canal in 1869 and the improvements in marine engines, which almost halved the time for the voyage to Britain. Of great significance to New Zealand was the beginning of the trade in frozen mutton in 1882, when the *Dunedin* arrived in London from Port Chalmers in South Island with 4,410 sheep and 449 lamb carcasses in prime condition. Within a few years the trade in CANTERBURY LAMB was booming and dairy produce soon found its way to the British market also. It was at the end of the nineteenth century that sweeping political and social reforms were introduced in New Zealand. The person chiefly responsible was RICHARD J. SEDDON (1845–1906), commonly called "King Dick". He became Prime Minister in a Liberal-Labour coalition in 1893 and held office until his death. By a heavy land tax he broke up large undeveloped estates; and with the revenue obtained from steeply graduated death duties and income-tax (some people in New Zealand were paying 7s. 6d. in the £ when the rate in Britain was under 1s.) he was able to carry out many reforms to help the poor, such as old age pensions. Women were given the franchise as early as 1893, an 8-hour working day was established, and conciliation boards were set up for industry. This reforming policy Seddon combined with a strong feeling of patriotism. The New Zealanders were among the earliest colonial forces sent to fight in the South African war. The same spirit was shown in 1909, after Seddon's death, when the New Zealand Government offered to pay for a battle-cruiser to be added to the British Navy. When war came in 1914, the New Zealanders along with the Australians formed the Australian and New Zealand Army Corps (A.N.Z.A.C.), which earned the admiration of the world by its bravery in the Gallipoli campaign of 1915. The depression in the 1930's brought much suffering to New Zealanders and the Government of the United (or Liberal) party was driven to take drastic measures such as reduction of salaries, pensions, etc., that were very unpopular. When in 1935 a Labour Government under MICHAEL J. SAVAGE came into power for the first time, an ambitious programme was attempted. The Reserve Bank was nationalized, the railways were placed under Government control again and road transport regulated to prevent competition with the railways; farmers were promised guaranteed prices for their products, any deficits to be met by state subsidies. The industrial arbitration system was restored and made compulsory, while a minimum wage was laid down in 1936 of £3 16s. for a man with a wife and three children. (In Britain at that time the average wage for an unskilled worker was 43s., with nothing extra for wife or children.) The Labour party remained in office (in a coalition with the National party during the war) until 1949, when it was replaced by the National party under SIDNEY G. HOLLAND, who was returned to power with a programme to encourage private enterprise and initiative. New Zealand is the smallest of the British Dominions, with only a little over two million inhabitants; but it is fortunate in its natural resources, its climate and the character of its people.

Australia. An interest in social and political reform was also early evident in New Zealand's neighbour, Australia. There was a long-standing Radical tradition in the country, going back to the days when Chartists and trade union leaders had been transported to Australia. Wage boards for sweated industries were set up in the state of Victoria as early as 1885 and later introduced into other states. In 1889, over £30,000 was subscribed by Australian trade unionists to help the dockers in the Great Dock Strike of that year. The first Labour Government in the whole of the British Empire was set up in Queensland in 1899. Manhood suffrage, women's suffrage, vote by ballot, payment of M.P.s, all came earlier in Australia than in Britain. The Labour party is strong in Australia to this day. During the First World War a split developed in the party, then in power, over conscription. The party leader and Prime Minister, WILLIAM M. HUGHES, was in favour while some of his colleagues were against it. Twice the issue was put to the public to decide by popular vote— the method of REFERENDUM, used not only in Australia but also in Switzerland, U.S.A. and other countries to decide questions affecting the constitution or other important issues. Although the referendum showed that the public was against conscription, large numbers of Australian volunteers went to Europe; the heroism of the ANZACS in Gallipoli has been referred to above. The advent of refrigerator ships meant as much to Australia as to New Zealand. No longer was it dependent on the wool

1	Port Darwin	4	Adelaide	7	Canberra	10	Hobart
2	Perth	5	Ballarat	8	Sydney		
3	Coolgardie	6	Melbourne	9	Brisbane		

Commonwealth of Australia

trade and the gold mines of Victoria and Western Australia. The arrival of the Clyde-built *Strathleven* in London from Melbourne in 1880 with 40 tons of frozen beef and mutton heralded a trade which was to grow vastly in the future. The FEDERATION of the various states in Australia came slowly. It was a much larger country than New Zealand and the interests of the states were different and sometimes conflicting. It was the fear of

German expansion in the Pacific and, in particular, their ambition to annex New Guinea that led in the 1880's to united action on the part of the Australian states. In 1884 New Guinea was actually annexed by order of SIR THOMAS MACILWRAITH, the Ayrshire-born Prime Minister of Queensland. Gladstone's Government, unwilling to risk any more colonial adventures after their troubles in the Transvaal, Afghanistan and Egypt, quickly disavowed the Queensland action. They were shocked, however, when soon afterwards the Germans did annex the north-eastern portion of New Guinea, leaving the remainder to the British. A conference of the Australian colonies to consider the question of New Guinea had already met in 1883 and, after the annexation by the Germans, a Federal Council of Australasia was set up in 1885. This was to meet only on special occasions to discuss common problems. Unfortunately, New South Wales was unwilling to join the Council. In 1895, after a meeting of Australian Prime Ministers, an attempt was made to draw up a federal constitution, but this time Queensland hung back. There had been a good deal of criticism throughout the rest of Australia of the terrible treatment of the Kanakas, South Sea Islanders employed on Queensland sugar plantations in conditions akin to slavery, thousands of them dying each year. The traffic in Kanakas was prohibited in 1906, five years after the COMMON-WEALTH OF AUSTRALIA came into being, all the states (New South Wales, Victoria, South Australia, West Australia, Queensland and Tasmania) at last agreeing in 1901. When the Commonwealth of Australia was formed, considerable powers were still left in the hands of the states. The state Governors are appointed by the Queen on the advice of the state Governments (that is, their nominations are accepted by the Queen) while in Canada the Lieutenant-Governors of the provinces are appointed by the Governor-General. It seemed at first that there would be keen rivalry between Sydney and Melbourne to be the capital of the new Commonwealth; but it was decided to build a new capital at CANBERRA in New South Wales. Until the Parliament House was opened there in 1927, Melbourne functioned as capital. Among the first problems the Federal Parliament had to face was

19

that of Japanese immigration in the north, especially in Queensland. Australians were keen to preserve the British character of their country and, in order to maintain a "White Australia", compelled all intending immigrants to pass a test "in any prescribed language", which allowed the immigration authorities to bar anyone they pleased.

India, 1876–1914. The story of self-government in India is very different from those of Canada, New Zealand and Australia, all of which enjoyed a fair measure of autonomy from early on in the century. In 1876, when Disraeli created the Empire of India, the Indians in British India were ruled by the British, acting (it may be added) generally in the interests of the Indians. Britain created for herself most of the problems she had to face in India in the last hundred years. Many beneficial reforms were introduced during the viceroyalty of LORD RIPON (1880–84) but their main effect was to increase Indian nationalism. He gave full freedom to the Indian press, set up elected councils in the towns and rural districts under the supervision of British officials, and made possible a great expansion of education, both in schools and colleges, under Indian management. Unfortunately too many young men were attracted to colleges for the number of posts available; and among the unemployed "intellectuals" there were naturally discontent and frustration that often led to political agitation, now made easier by the lack of press censorship. The British also, by the use of English as a language of instruction, made it possible for Indians to get together and discuss affairs. In 1885 the first Indian NATIONAL CONGRESS met and passed resolutions claiming self-government. This first meeting of Congress was not anti-British and indeed paid tribute to the great service rendered by the British to India in bringing the light of free civilization to a land where despotism had reigned. From this time, National Congresses met regularly to proclaim the same demand. Most of the 72 delegates at the first Congress were lawyers, journalists or teachers and almost all were Hindus. As the Congress movement developed, it became influenced not only by Western political ideas but also by Hindu religious ideas. One of the popular Bengali prophets of the

time taught that "the world must be conquered by India"; and
Indian nationalists tended to believe in the superiority of India
with its long-established religion and ancient civilization over
the modern industrial democracies of the western world.
But in addition to the Hindus there were millions of Muslims in
India. At first they remained aloof from the movement for self-
government, but in 1906 the ALL-INDIA MUSLIM LEAGUE was
formed. Before that time the Indian Councils Act of 1892 had
made possible another step towards self-government. The
provincial councils, which were nominated by the Governors,
were to be allowed to discuss financial and other matters, although
they were still not allowed to vote on them; and, further,
to the nominated members were to be added certain other members on the recommendation of outside bodies like universities
and religious communities. The Indians were more interested in
the second point: here, according to them, was the principle of
election. The Conservative MARQUESS OF CURZON, Viceroy from
1898 to 1905, was a zealous administrator who did much to
restore Indians' pride in their past by his restoration of ancient
monuments. Unfortunately, at the very end of his viceroyalty,
the partition of Bengal was carried out for the sake of more
efficient administration and created a wave of Hindu agitation.
For the first time since 1857 Indians resorted to violence
and British people were killed. The Japanese victory over the
Russians in 1904–5 also helped to raise the hopes of an Indian
victory one day. In South Africa, Indian immigrants were being
treated by white South Africans as an inferior race and the
Indians naturally resented this. During the period 1905–11, when
the Liberal, John Morley, was Secretary for India and the Earl of
Minto was Viceroy, an attempt was made to conciliate the Indians
in what came to be known as the MORLEY-MINTO REFORMS.
In the Viceroy's Council there would still be a majority of officials
over others, but in the provincial councils the unofficial members
would be in a majority and some of the unofficial members were
not to be appointed by the Governors but elected. The method of
election, decided upon because of the agitation of the All-India
Muslim League, was to be by religious communities. These

councils, however, still had no real power but were merely to advise the Governors. If this were not bad enough, Lord Morley made matters worse by explaining to the Indians frankly that he did not consider them fit for Parliamentary government. Notwithstanding the nationalist agitation, the Indians responded well in 1914 when the First World War broke out, and over a million volunteered for service overseas.

Gandhi's Early Career. It was at the beginning of the war that there returned to India after years abroad the man who was to become the leader of the Indian nationalist movement, M. K. GANDHI (1869-1948). He had been born at Porbandor on the western coast of India and as a boy had been nervous and averse to games and exercise. He was married at thirteen and although his marriage was a happy one, he later did what he could to stop the practice of child-marriage. After studying at London University, he was called to the Bar. He practised first of all in Bombay and then went to South Africa, where there was a large Indian population engaged mainly in trade. During the South African War (1899-1902) he formed an Indian Red Cross unit and about this time he began to correspond with the Russian author, Tolstoy, whose doctrines of pacifism and non-resistance to evil influenced him. He had always been religious and in time he was troubled by thoughts that his profession as lawyer was immoral. Nevertheless, it was because, as a lawyer, he was often called to defend Indians in the South African courts that he became their leader. They felt that they were unjustly treated by the race laws forbidding them to move from one part of the country to another without permits; and in 1906 Gandhi led 3,000 Indians across a state boundary in defiance of the law, advising his followers not to resist arrest. His tactics of PASSIVE RESISTANCE (which he was later to practise on a large scale in India) drew public attention to the unjustness of this racial discrimination. He repeatedly suffered arrest himself but won the respect and loyalty of the Indian people by his example.

Gandhi in India. In the First World War Gandhi returned to India and set to work organizing an Indian ambulance corps. At the end of the war, the British Government through their

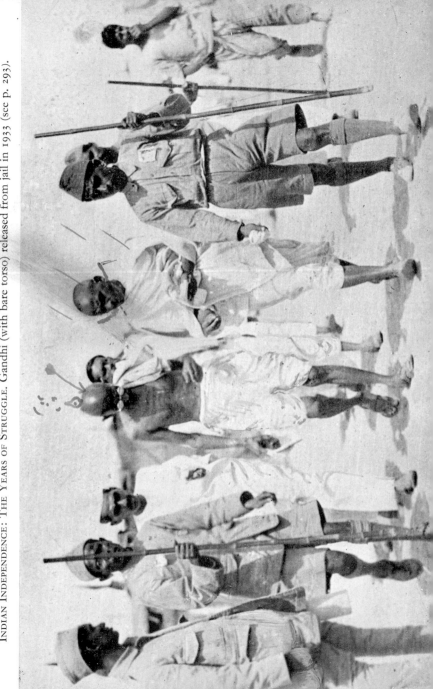

INDIAN INDEPENDENCE: THE YEARS OF STRUGGLE. Gandhi (with bare torso) released from jail in 1933 (see p. 293).

INDIAN INDEPENDENCE: THE TRANSFER OF POWER. Admiral Lord Mountbatten, the last British Viceroy of India, greets Mr. Rajagopalachari, the First Governor General of the independent Republic of India in 1947 (see p. 294).

Secretary for India, Montagu, and their Viceroy, Chelmsford, recommended in 1918 that India should be encouraged towards the goal of dominion status by making the Governments in the provinces responsible to their Assemblies, although certain powers (e.g. police, law and order) were "reserved", that is, still under British control. A central Legislative Assembly was also to be set up but only a small percentage of Indians were to be allowed to vote at elections to the Assembly; and, finally, the Viceroy could ignore the Assembly's decisions. The "dyarchy" (or dual rule) of the MONTAGU–CHELMSFORD REFORMS did not go nearly far enough to please the Indian Nationalists, who now looked on Gandhi as their leader. So far as the Montagu–Chelmsford proposals were concerned, he advocated NON-CO-OPERATION and a complete stoppage of work throughout India for one day in protest. Despite his appeals to use only passive resistance and to avoid violence, some Europeans were killed; and in April 1919, at Amritsar in the Punjab, a large unarmed crowd of Indians was fired on by order of Brigadier-General Dyer, 379 Indians being killed. The Indian Nationalists never forgave the British for this AMRITSAR MASSACRE, which rendered the chances of co-operation between British and Indians very slight indeed. Strikes and riots were common in the next few years, despite Gandhi's pleas for peaceful methods. In 1921 he again started a CIVIL DISOBEDIENCE campaign, which involved refusing to pay taxes, but abandoned it when some of the Nationalists resorted to violence. During the twenties he was imprisoned more than once, and his sufferings, religious outlook and saintly, ascetic life (he had given up western clothes and dressed in the simplest of garments woven by himself) won him the respect of millions of Hindus, who gave him the title MAHATMA ("Great Soul"). In 1930 he started another civil disobedience campaign, asking the people to refuse to buy salt, which was a Government monopoly. He led a march of his followers from Ahmedabad down to the sea, a hundred miles away, and there made salt from sea-water. He was again imprisoned but released in order to attend a Round Table Conference in London. More than once, during his terms of imprisonment, he announced that he would fast to death, and the Government found itself compelled to release him. On one occasion, he started a fast to death in order to bring the outcasts (millions of Hindus who were also called "UNTOUCHABLES" and the "DEPRESSED CLASSES") back into the Hindu fold. His enemies among the Muslims claimed that this was done to strengthen the Hindu chances at elections; but he had always been disturbed about the position of the "Untouchables" in the Hindu community. He kept in the background for some time in the thirties, while Congress still opposed and criticized the British Government. In 1935 a new GOVERNMENT OF INDIA ACT was passed, giving more self-government to the Indian provinces, and setting up a central Federal Government for British India and the native states. Congress objected to the latter proposal as the rulers of the native states in India were generally considered reactionary, while the Indian princes themselves were hesitant about any co-operation with members of Congress. In the British provinces, however, Congress did accept the new proposals and formed the Governments in seven of the provinces. But no one felt any confidence in the new system of government, and clashes between Hindus and Muslims were still unfortunately only too common.

End of the Indian Empire. When war came in 1939, the Viceroy of India immediately proclaimed India to be at war with Germany. Congress, although wholeheartedly against Hitler and the Nazis, criticized the Government for declaring war without the consent of the Indian people. Congress members resigned in protest from the Central Assembly at New Delhi and from the Provincial Governments until India should receive a satisfactory statement of war aims (some of them described the war as imperialist) and an immediate grant of Dominion status. In 1942, Sir Stafford Cripps, representing the British Government, arrived in India with an offer of Dominion status immediately after the war, the constitution to be drawn up by the Indians themselves, and the provinces to have the right to join the Dominion or not as they pleased. Again, Congress refused, claiming Dominion status right away. Gandhi went even further by demanding that the British Army should withdraw and that the

Japanese, then in the process of conquering the Far East, should be allowed to enter India and make peace with the non-resisting people. When Congress decided on another campaign of "mass obstruction" to the British war effort, Gandhi, Nehru and other Congress leaders were imprisoned. When war ended in 1945, a Labour Government under Clement Attlee came into power in

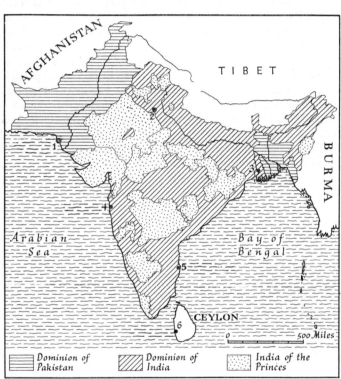

Most of the Princes' States have subsequently adhered to India or Pakistan.

1	Karachi	3	Calcutta	5	Madras
2	Delhi	4	Bombay	6	Colombo

India after 1947

Britain. One of their main aims was to give India its independence. Wrangling between Hindus and Muslims over the form of the constitution would have gone on for a long time, but Attlee announced that the British intended to leave India by June 1948. Led by Winston Churchill (who in 1942 had said with reference to India: "I haven't become the King's First Minister to preside over the liquidation of the British Empire") the Conservative Opposition criticized Attlee's proposal as a betrayal of the Indian minorities such as the Muslims and the depressed classes. Attlee and the Labour Government persisted in their plan, which seemed to them preferable to interminable wrangling; and under the Viceroy, EARL MOUNTBATTEN, a plan was drawn up to partition India into mainly Hindu and Muslim areas. The British Empire of India came to an end on August 15th, 1947; after this the letters "IND. IMP." no longer appeared on British coins. In its place there came into existence two Dominions—INDIA, a mainly Hindu area with the capital still at New Delhi, and PAKISTAN, a mainly Muslim area with the capital at Karachi. The population of India in 1951 was 357 million of whom 303 million were Hindus, 35 million were Muslims, 8 million were Christians and 6 million were Sikhs. Pakistan, which actually consists of two areas, one in North-west India and the other in North-east India, in 1951 had a population of 76 million, of whom 65 million were Muslims, 10 million were Hindus and over half a million were Christians. India's first Prime Minister was Pandit JAWAHARLAL NEHRU, a high-caste Hindu, educated at Harrow and Cambridge, and qualified in England as a barrister, while Earl Mountbatten became the first Governor General. Pakistan's first Prime Minister was LIAQUAT ALI KHAN, also qualified as a barrister in England, and the Governor General MOHAMMED ALI JINNAH, who had been President of the Muslim League for many years. Although partition seemed the only practical solution, there were great difficulties. Generally, Muslims were predominant in the north and west of India but there was a strong Muslim element in North-east India. The partition left many people on the wrong side of the frontiers; riots and mass emigrations took place, and it was estimated that over half a million were killed in the Punjab alone. The worst trouble arose over KASHMIR, an Indian native state, in which Nehru was born but in which 80 per cent of the population were Muslims while the ruler, the Maharajah, was Hindu. When the Maharajah decided in 1947 to join the Dominion of India, fighting broke out and continued, with assistance from India and Pakistan, for two years. The Security Council of the United Nations recommended a plebiscite for the people to decide which Dominion they should join; but Nehru and the Government of India have refused on several occasions to hold the plebiscite. Gandhi was heart-broken at the strife and at the division of India into two states. When everyone else was rejoicing on Independence Day, he excalimed: "I feel little joy, only sorrow that my country should be dismembered." He was assassinated in 1948 by some Hindu extremists who regarded him as a traitor to India and Hinduism. It was also under Attlee's Government that BURMA was declared an independent state in October 1947 (it rejected the offer of Dominion status) and CEYLON became a Dominion in February 1948. Another Dominion in the Far East came into existence in August 1957, when MALAYA became a sovereign and independent state of the British Commonwealth.

Africa. The story of the British in Africa up to the beginning of the twentieth century has already been told above. EGYPT, which had nominally been under Turkish suzerainty but under British administration, was declared a British Protectorate in 1914, when Britain and Turkey went to war and the pro-German Khedive was deposed. In 1922, the British Protectorate was ended and the Khedive Fuad proclaimed King at a time when Egyptian nationalism was again becoming strong. It was not until 1936 that the British recognized Egyptian sovereignty and undertook to evacuate their troops except from the Suez Canal zone; according to the Anglo-Egyptian Treaty of 1936, Alexandria and Port Said could also be used by the British as naval bases and British troops could be moved across Egypt in case of war or a threat of war. During the Second World War, Egypt had plenty of British troops in it, as it contained the British bases for their campaigns against the Italians and Germans in the

Western Desert. After the war, nationalist discontent with the continued British occupation, aggravated by the poor showing of the Egyptian army in the troubles in Palestine, grew as economic conditions failed to improve. In 1952, after a *coup d'état* by some officers, KING FAROUK was deposed and in 1953 Egypt was declared a republic with General Neguib as Prime Minister. In 1954, the British Government under Sir Winston Churchill agreed to evacuate all troops from Egypt including the Canal Zone by June 1956. The agreement about the Canal Zone was negotiated by Neguib's successor as Prime Minister, COLONEL NASSER, who two years later, after the British troops had left, seized the Suez Canal, declaring it Egyptian property. Despite a combined British and French attempt in November 1956 to re-take the Canal (an attempt which was denounced by an over-whelming majority of the United Nations) the Canal remained in the hands of Egyptians. SUDAN, which had been a British and Egyptian condominium since 1899, became independent in 1956. Other British territories in Africa have achieved independence since the Second World War. The Gold Coast became an independent state within the Commonwealth in 1957 with the name of GHANA. A neighbouring colony, NIGERIA, also became self-governing in stages—East and West Nigeria in 1957 and Northern Nigeria in 1959, when a Federal Council of Nigeria was formed. Demands for self-government have also been made in other colonies, for example in Uganda and in Kenya, where an African secret society, MAU MAU, terrorised both Africans and white settlers. SOUTHERN RHODESIA, in which there was a comparatively high proportion of white settlers, was a self-governing colony as early as 1923; and in 1953 it was joined with Northern Rhodesia and Nyasaland in a FEDERATION OF RHODESIA AND NYASALAND. A plebiscite was held in Southern Rhodesia before federation but in the other two colonies the decision to join was taken only by the Legislative Council, in which the native Africans were in a minority. The natives of Nyasaland, who fear that the Federation would be dominated by the white settlers of Southern Rhodesia, have since 1953 started a move-ment to leave the Federation. Further south, in the UNION OF

SOUTH AFRICA, the outstanding personality in the first half of the twentieth century was JAN CHRISTIAAN SMUTS (1870–1950). He was a brilliant student at the University of Cape Town and Cambridge, where he studied law. A Boer general in the South African War, he helped the first Prime Minister of the Union, another Boer general, Louis Botha, to co-operate loyally with the British after 1910. In the First World War, Botha and Smuts conquered German South-west Africa and German East Africa after having dealt with a rising by pro-German Boers inside the Union. Smuts became a member of Lloyd George's War Cabinet in 1917 and attended the Peace Conference at Versailles. After the First World War, he tried to exercise a moderating influence on South African opinion, which still tended to be anti-British. He was Prime Minister from 1919 to 1924 and Deputy Prime Minister from 1933 to 1939, when he again became Prime Minister after General Hertzog, his predecessor, had recommended neutrality. Smuts held office throughout the war, and his advice on political and military matters was highly regarded in Britain. After the war, he was displaced in 1948 by DR. MALAN, leader of South Africa's Nationalist party. Before his death in 1950, Smuts strongly criticized the Malan Government's policy of race-segregation of APARTHEID (an Afrikaans word for "separateness"). The whites in South Africa were outnumbered by coloured races (in 1957 over 11 million of them as against 3 million white people). The Nationalist Government, therefore, decided on a policy of *apartheid* as a way of protecting South Africa against the eventuality of a government of coloured people. *Apartheid*, as practised by the Nationalist Government, involves separate schools, separate suburbs and the compulsory carrying of passes by those Africans who leave their own district. As the whites are very much dependent on Africans for labour, both factory and domestic, the carrying of passes became an intolerable grievance and led to riots in 1960. The solution of the colour problem is not easy but the South African method of *apartheid* is inevitably bound to lead to repercussions in a continent where, as the British Prime Minister, Harold Macmillan, said, "a wind of change" is blowing and where African Governments, as in

Ghana and Nigeria, are acquiring a status equal to that of the South African Union.

British Commonwealth. The idea of a British commonwealth or federation of free nations goes back to the 1880's, when it was advocated by some Liberals and Conservatives. In 1887, on the occasion of Queen Victoria's Jubilee, the first COLONIAL CONFERENCE was held. This meeting of the Prime Ministers of the self-governing colonies did no more than discuss trade and defence problems in a general way. It was Joseph Chamberlain who did most to foster the idea of imperial federation at the end of the nineteenth and the beginning of the twentieth century. He was impressed by the colonies' interest in imperial trade preference at the second Colonial Conference, held in London at the time of Queen Victoria's Diamond Jubilee in 1897, and at the third Colonial Conference at the time of Edward VII's coronation in 1902. His idea of a Federal Council had been turned down by the colonial Prime Ministers as likely to encroach on the independence of the colonies. They were prepared to give British goods preference but they were keen to have some arrangement that would give the colonies preference in British markets. This was possible only if Britain had tariffs and it was for this reason that Chamberlain put forward his programme of tariff reform, which failed, however, to gain the approval of the British public. Although the self-governing colonies were unwilling to sacrifice their independence by joining a federal council, they had sent troops over to help Great Britain in the South African War. It might be thought that the issue of Boer independence would have rallied the other colonies against Britain but there was a strong feeling of affection for the Mother Country, right or wrong. It was a Canadian statesman who referred to Britain at the time of the Jameson Raid (January 1896) as "the great Mother Empire standing splendidly isolated in Europe". (This is the origin of the expression, "splendid isolation", used to describe Britain's foreign policy.) Whenever there was a war, Britain was able to depend on support from overseas—in 1899, 1914 and 1939. In the 1907 Colonial Conference, it was decided to adopt the name DOMINION for the self-governing colonies (Canada had already used the word to designate the federation of provinces set up in 1867). A proposal to form an Imperial Council was again rejected but it was agreed that the Prime Ministers of the Dominions should meet every four years in what was in the future called an IMPERIAL CONFERENCE. During the war of 1914–18, the peoples of the Empire drew more closely together; and Lloyd George took the opportunity of forming the IMPERIAL WAR CABINET, which included the Dominion Prime Ministers or their representatives, a representative from India, the Colonial Secretary as well as five members of the British Cabinet. At Versailles in 1919, representatives of the Dominions took part in the negotiations and signed the peace treaty, entering the League of Nations as separate states. After the Imperial Conference of 1926, a memorandum was issued, declaring the United Kingdom and the Dominions to be "autonomous communities within the British Empire, equal in status, in no way subordinate one to another in any aspect of their domestic or foreign affairs, though united by a common allegiance to the Crown, and freely associated as members of the British Commonwealth of Nations". The principle of this memorandum was embodied in the STATUTE OF WESTMINSTER (1931), which recognized the absolute sovereignty of the Dominions. From 1931, it was usual to refer to the BRITISH EMPIRE AND COMMONWEALTH OF NATIONS, the Empire comprising India and the colonies under British rule, and the Commonwealth of Nations the Dominions and the United Kingdom. Dominions resent any discussion at Imperial Conferences of what they consider internal affairs, e.g. the *apartheid* question in South Africa. Dominions are also sensitive about their rights to be consulted. As we have seen above, on the outbreak of war in 1939, the Canadian Prime Minister, Mackenzie King, delayed the Canadian declaration of war for a week in order to assert Canadian independence in foreign affairs. In 1956, at the time of the Suez crisis, no prior consultation between the British and Dominion Governments took place; and it was the Canadian representative in the United Nations who took the lead in criticizing the British invasion of Egypt. With the end of the

Indian Empire in 1947, the opportunity was taken to leave out the word "Empire" as too reminiscent of colonial days, so that the official title became the BRITISH COMMONWEALTH OF NATIONS. The developments of the first half of the twentieth century can be seen by comparing the list of countries whose Prime Ministers attended the Imperial Conference of 1911 (Canada, Australia, New Zealand, Newfoundland, Union of South Africa) with those represented at the Commonwealth Conference of 1960 (Canada, Australia, New Zealand, Union of South Africa, India, Pakistan, Ceylon, Malaya, Ghana, Federation of Rhodesia and Nyasaland).

Secessions. While co-operation between most self-governing units of the Commonwealth has been growing, a few have severed relations altogether. NEWFOUNDLAND is the only country that surrendered its Dominion status voluntarily. In 1933, at the time of the world depression, Newfoundland was in such grave financial difficulties that its Dominion status was suspended. It was governed by a Commission of three members from Newfoundland and three members from the United Kingdom until 1948 when, by a referendum, the people voted to surrender their Dominion status; in 1949 Newfoundland became a province of the Dominion of Canada. The Irish Free State, set up in 1922 as a Dominion, adopted a new constitution in 1937, renaming the country EIRE. When De Valera, after a long abstention from the Irish Parliament because of unwillingness to take the oath of allegiance, at last came to power in 1932 as head of the republican party, Fianna Fail, he began a gradual process of separation from Britain. In 1936, he stopped the payment to Britain of the land annuities, the interest on the loans made to Irish peasants for land purchase. By the new constitution of 1937 the Irish Free State was declared a republic and given the name EIRE (in theory it was applied to the whole of Ireland). During the Second World War, a strict neutrality was officially observed although thousands joined the British forces or went to work in Britain. In 1948, all connection with Britain and the rest of the Commonwealth was severed and the official name became the REPUBLIC OF IRELAND. After the First World War, PALESTINE, which had formerly been

Turkish territory, was handed over to Britain to administer as a mandated territory by the League of Nations. Under the British, it became a "national home for the Jews" between the wars, in accordance with the BALFOUR DECLARATION of 1917, made by the British Foreign Secretary, Balfour, who had also, however, promised protection for the rights of the Arabs in Palestine. Hitler's persecution of the Jews drove thousands to seek refuge in Palestine in the 1930's. After the Second World War, when the British insisted on continuing in Palestine, there was strong opposition from the Jews, particularly the Zionist movement, and outbreaks of terrorism occurred. The neighbouring Arab states, Egypt, Iraq, Jordan, Lebanon and Syria, all made it clear that if Palestine became a Jewish state, there would be war. Britain was unwilling to offend the Arab states (so important to the western world because of their oil) but was mindful of her obligations to the Jews under the Balfour Declaration. Unable to produce a solution, the British Labour Government handed over the problem to the United Nations General Assembly, which recommended partition. The British left Palestine in 1948, a new independent state of ISRAEL was proclaimed and was at once attacked by her Arab neighbours, all of which failed to make any impression on the small but efficient Israeli army. Israel was thus able to carry out its own partition, more favourable to her than the United Nations plan but not recognized by the neighbouring states, with which a state of war still continued to exist. BURMA, which had been under Japanese occupation during the war, set itself up as an independent state in 1948, and their left-wing Socialist Government decided to leave the Commonwealth. CYPRUS, which had been occupied by the British since the Treaty of Berlin (1878), became a British colony in 1925 when the Turks, the previous rulers, ackowledged British sovereignty. A strong movement for *Enosis* or union with Greece existed for a long time in Cyprus, where four-fifths of the population are Greek-speaking and the rest are Turkish. Riots took place in 1931, when the Legislative Council was suspended and two bishops were exiled. The Enosis movement, under the leadership of the Ethnarch of the Greek Orthodox Church,

ARCHBISHOP MAKARIOS, became more active in 1954 when Cyprus was made the headquarters of British military forces in the Middle East instead of the Suez Canal Zone. A campaign of terrorism by E.O.K.A., an underground organization led by Colonel Grivas, forced the British Government in 1956 to send Archbishop Makarios to the Seychelle Islands for complicity in some of the E.O.K.A. outrages. In 1959, after talks between the Greek and Turkish Governments, an agreement was signed by Britain, Greece, Turkey and representatives of the Greeks and Turks in Cyprus. By this agreement, Cyprus was to become an independent republic with British sovereignty over the military bases there. Despite these secessions, the most remarkable phenomenon in the development of the Commonwealth since 1945 has been the willingness of colonies which receive self-government to remain in the Commonwealth.

SOURCE EXTRACT

Gandhi on Civil Disobedience (April 1919)

Before one can be fit for the practice of civil disobedience one must have rendered a willing and respectful obedience to the State laws. For the most part we obey such laws for fear of the penalty for their breach; and this holds good particularly in respect of such laws as do not involve a moral principle. A *Satyagrahi* (one who practises truth-force or soul-force) obeys the laws of society intelligently because he considers it to be his sacred duty to do so. It is only when a person has thus obeyed the laws of society scrupulously that he is in a position to judge as to which particular rules are good and just, and which unjust and iniquitous. Only then does the right accrue to him to undertake civil disobedience of certain laws in well-defined circumstances. My error lay in my failure to observe this necessary limitation. I had called upon the people to launch upon civil disobedience before they had thus qualified themselves for it; and this mistake of mine seemed to me to be of a Himalayan magnitude. As soon as I entered the Kaira district (where I heard reports of a large number of people having been arrested for acts of violence) I wondered how I could have failed to perceive what was so obvious. I realized that before a people could be fit for offering civil disobedience they should thoroughly understand its deeper implications.

C. A. Andrews (ed.): Mahatama Gandhi—His Own Story.

EXERCISES

1. What was the tragic event in 1919 that resulted from the failure of Gandhi's followers to use only passive resistance? What consequences did it have for India?

2. Explain: Anzac, White Australia, passive resistance, dyarchy, Mahatma, Untouchable, IND. IMP., *Apartheid*, Mau-Mau, Dominion status, Enosis, E.O.K.A.

3. Identify the authors of the following and explain where necessary:
   (*a*) "The world must be conquered by India."
   (*b*) "I haven't become the King's First Minister to preside over the liquidation of the British Empire."
   (*c*) "I feel little joy, only sorrow that my country should be dismembered."
   (*d*) "The great Mother Empire standing splendidly isolated in Europe."
   (*e*) "Autonomous communities equal in status and in no way subordinate to one another."
   (*f*) "A national home for the Jews."

4. Write short notes on: Canadian Pacific Railway, Indian National Congress, All-India Muslim League, Amritsar Massacre, Pandit Nehru, M. A. Jinnah, Imperial Conferences, Colonel Nasser, Balfour Declaration, Archbishop Makarios.

5. Write notes on: Sir John A. MacDonald, Sir Wilfrid Laurier, W. L. Mackenzie King, Richard J. Seddon, Morley–Minto Reforms, Montagu–Chelmsford Reforms, Jan C. Smuts, Statute of Westminster.

6. Trace the events leading to the formation of the Commonwealth of Australia.

7. Give an account of the career and estimate the importance of Gandhi.

8. Trace the events that led to the end of the British Empire in India. What difficulties resulted from the partition of 1947?

9. What colonies or dominions have left the Commonwealth since 1945 and why?

20

CHAPTER XIV

THE POST-WAR WORLD

Election of 1945. The result of the British general election of
July 1945 was a surprise to the world. Churchill, the great war
leader, was rejected by the British people who so much admired
him. There were, however, two points about this result which
foreigners (and some British people) ignored:—(1) Churchill's
success in the war was regarded by many as an argument against
his continuing in office in peacetime. He himself, in his autobiographical book, *My Early Years,* had expressed the same
opinion: "Those who can win a war well can rarely make a good
peace, and those who could make a good peace would never
have won the war." (2) The public still distinguished between
Churchill and the Conservatives who had kept him out of office
for nine years before 1940 and who were identified with the policy
of appeasement he had criticized so strongly. CLEMENT ATTLEE
(b. 1883), the new Prime Minister, was a middle-class Socialist,
educated at Haileybury and Oxford, and he had taken up social
work among the poor as Secretary of Toynbee Hall in 1910.
After the First World War, in which he served with the rank of
major, he was a lecturer in the London School of Economics and
became Mayor of Stepney. He was Leader of the Opposition when
war broke out and in 1940 became Leader of the House in
Churchill's Coalition Government. He never became a popular
figure to compare with Churchill, and his position as Prime
Minister was like that of Asquith and Baldwin, one of a chairman
of committee (which is, of course, what a Cabinet is). Attlee's
Cabinet was a mixture of men in the middle class and upper class,
like Dr. Hugh Dalton and Sir Stafford Cripps, and men of
working-class origin like Ernest Bevin, Aneurin Bevan,
Herbert Morrison and Emmanuel Shinwell. The resounding
victory Labour gained at the polls (396 seats out of a total of
640) gave the new Government confidence to carry out their
ambitious legislative programme.

Labour in Power. In addition to nationalizing industry and transport, the Labour Government went boldly ahead with the scheme outlined in the Beveridge Report in wartime. The WELFARE STATE, the foundations of which had been laid nearly forty years before by Lloyd George, was now to attain full growth. In 1946, NATIONAL INSURANCE became compulsory, with benefits to cover sickness, unemployment, retirement, maternity and also funeral expenses. To the weekly contribution paid by each employee (in 1960 it was 9*s.* 11*d.*) were added contributions from the employer and from the State. Alongside the National Insurance scheme was set up in July 1948 a NATIONAL HEALTH SERVICE, which provided medical, dental and ophthalmic treatment for everybody. Some of the expenditure of this National Health Service was recouped from the National Insurance Fund but the rest was met by the Government—in other words, it came from ordinary taxation. The doctors and dentists protested at first, not because of the principle of the Health Service, which they had themselves advocated, but because they were afraid that a Socialist Government would interfere with the service too much. There was an appalling lack of housing accommodation in the country, particularly in the large towns, as a result of war damage and the stoppage of building during the war. Priority was given to building of local council houses, and subsidies were paid by the Government and local authorities to keep rents down. The cost of living was prevented from going too high by food and farming subsidies, which rose to nearly £500,000,000 in 1948–49. As food shortages (which were world-wide) continued despite the ending of the war, rationing was still enforced; and in 1948 it was found necessary to ration even bread, which had been unrationed during the war. Workers benefited by the gradual introduction of the five-day week in coalmining and most industries; paradoxically, there was also regular overtime working, usually on two evenings a week and on Sundays, which helped to increase the bulk of the weekly pay packet. A new TRADES DISPUTES ACT was passed in 1946, reversing the provisions of the Conservative Act of 1927 about the political levy; and a REPRESENTATION OF THE PEOPLE ACT ended plural voting (the university and business franchises) and redistributed constituencies. Another PARLIAMENT ACT, passed in 1949 after being twice rejected by the House of Lords, reduced the Lords' veto from two years to one year; by this Act the Labour Government were able to complete their programme of nationalization by the inclusion of the iron and steel industry to which the Lords had objected.

Nationalization. Since 1918, the British Labour party had been a Socialist party, whose aims, according to their constitution, were to be achieved "on the basis of common ownership of the means of production, distribution and exchange". Nationalization (i.e. bringing industry and transport under public ownership) was advocated by the Labour party and condemned by Conservatives and Liberals on many grounds, moral, economic and political. It must be said, however, that it has not proved either so beneficial as Socialists made out or so harmful as Conservatives argued. First on the list for Attlee's Government was the BANK OF ENGLAND, which had been suspected of an anti-Labour policy ever since the financial crisis of 1931. The coal industry was placed under the NATIONAL COAL BOARD on January 1st, 1947. It had long been in need of reconstruction, and nationalization had been proposed by a Royal Commission as far back as 1921. Electricity and gas supply services (most of which were already under public control, but often in small units, belonging, e.g. to a town council) were placed under the BRITISH ELECTRICITY AUTHORITY and the BRITISH GAS AUTHORITY, with regional boards for the different parts of the country. CIVIL AVIATION was nationalized and inland transport (canals, railways, roads) came under a British Transport Commission. BRITISH RAILWAYS henceforth became a national undertaking, replacing the four railway systems, L.M.S., L.N.E.R., G.W.R. and S.R., that had existed since the amalgamation of 1921. The iron and steel industry was also nationalized, but only after a struggle in Parliament, the House of Lords rejecting the nationalization Bill, which was only passed by the insertion of a special clause in the new Parliament Bill. In the first few years after being taken over by the Government, nearly all of the nationalized industries and services were subjected to criticism. There seemed to be far too many employed in administration or management in comparison with those engaged in producing coal or iron or steel or operating the services. Expenditure also rose steeply after nationalization, partly because of wage increases and partly because of interest charges on the sums paid in compensation to the previous owners. Despite higher prices for coal, gas and electricity and higher

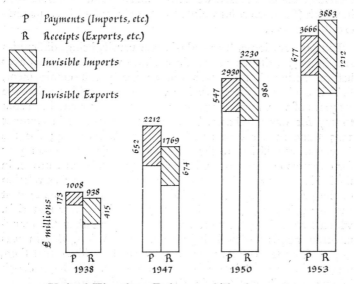

United Kingdom Balance of Trade, 1938–53

fares for transport, annual deficits occurred. Coalmining was the key industry on which electricity, gas and railways depended. In the years before the war, wages and working conditions were so poor that fewer recruits were entering the industry each year; the number of miners which had stood at nearly 1,250,000 in 1913 had shrunk to less than 700,000. Increased mechanization made up to some extent for the loss of manpower, and the Government tried many schemes to help recruitment—high

wages, a five-day week, bigger food rations in mining areas, introduction of foreign labour. The figures for coal production, however, climbed up very slowly, much to the disappointment of some
of the Labour M.P.s., who had expected that nationalization would
quickly improve output. Conservative criticism of the National
Coal Board was naturally stronger still but when they came into
power they left coalmining under public ownership. The only
industries de-nationalized were iron and steel and road transport,
in which (Labour critics pointed out) owners had been making
excellent profits.

Export Problems. The end of a war usually brings difficulties
and in 1945 Britain's economic position was weaker than ever
before. Although there was full or nearly full employment,
Britain could no longer pay her way in the world. During the
six years of war, most of her overseas investments had been sold
to pay for war purchases. The end of Lend-Lease in October
1945 came as a severe shock to Britain's economy; for the
Government still had to face a bill of over £400,000,000 a year
for overseas expenditure, what with large armies in Europe, in
the Middle East and Far East. The TERMS OF TRADE (the relation
of the prices of imports to prices of exports) had gone against
Britain; primary commodities such as food and raw materials,
which Britain bought, were scarcer and dearer than the manufactured goods which Britain sold. In addition, Britain was
buying from the U.S.A. much more than she sold, so that there
was a "dollar gap" in our trading accounts. The large deficit
in our trade budget (nearly £300 millions in 1946) could be
wiped out either by reducing imports or increasing exports. SIR
STAFFORD CRIPPS, President of the Board of Trade, stressed the
urgency of the situation with his slogan "Export or die!"
Restrictions were placed on imports, visible and invisible (the
latter including travel abroad for which a British tourist was
allowed to take only a small sum of money out of the country).
Every encouragement was given to industries to export, particularly those producing goods which sold well in America, e.g.
motor-cars, whisky, harris tweed from the Hebrides, fine woollen
cloth from the West Riding, and knitted garments from the

Border mills. Manufacturers of motor-cars and distillers of whisky who could have disposed of all their annual output in Britain were allowed to sell only a quota based on what they exported overseas.

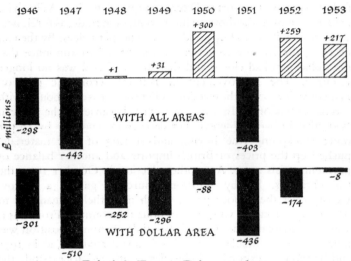

Britain's Export Drive, 1946–53
Trade Deficits and Surpluses

American Aid. A dollar loan worth £1,000 millions was negotiated with the U.S.A. by Lord Keynes at the end of 1945 just before his death; it was to be repaid by 2001 but it was all exhausted within two years. One condition of the loan was that sterling should become freely convertible with any currency instead of a merchant or banker requiring special permission from the Bank of England. When that happened in July 1947, there was an immediate run on sterling and Britain's gold reserves sank dangerously low. Imports from the U.S.A. (food, films, tobacco, etc.) had to be cut, new and higher export targets were set, and the convertibility clause of the loan agreement was suspended. Fortunately for Britain, the MARSHALL PLAN for helping the recovery of Europe was proposed in 1947, and the United States began to provide, through the Organization for European Economic Co-operation (O.E.E.C.), millions of dollars for re-equipping industries in Britain and the rest of Europe. In 1949, another dollar crisis developed and it was found necessary to resort to DEVALUATION of sterling. As in 1931, devaluation brought about an improvement in trade, as foreigners were more willing to buy goods at the cheaper prices. By the end of 1950, the Labour Government was proud to announce that the dollar gap had closed and that Marshall Aid was no longer required. The improvement in Britain's economic position helped Attlee to win the election in February 1950, although with a reduced majority. In 1952, however, because of the Korean War, Britain had to increase her defence expenditure by 50 per cent; stockpiling (the buying and storing of war materials) pushed up the prices of British imports and another balance of payments crisis arose. At another election in October 1951, the Conservatives, led by Winston Churchill, gained a narrow victory over the Labour party, which nevertheless managed to poll a larger total of votes throughout the country. From 1953, when the Korean War stopped, Britain's economic position was much more favourable, although crises still recurred, as in 1955 and 1957. Her exporting industries continued to expand, the terms of trade went in her favour with the fall in the prices of primary commodities, and through N.A.T.O. America began to spend large sums in Britain on bases, etc. It has often been asked why Britain in the post-war period of full employment should have so many balance of payments crises in comparison with the previous post-war period in the 1920's when there was constant unemployment. There are various reasons, but the most important are that in the earlier period Britain still had a "cushion" in her income from overseas investments made before 1914 and that for most of the time she enjoyed favourable terms of trade.

End of Old Imperialism. In the chapter, "The British Empire and Commonwealth", the story has been told of the break-up of Britain's Empire in the post-war years. The Indian Empire came to an end in 1947 and in its place there were set up the two Dominions of India and Pakistan, while Ceylon also achieved Dominion status. Burma and Palestine both left the Commonwealth when they were given their independence, and Ireland severed all relations with the Commonwealth in 1948, the year in which the name "Empire" was given up. Other European powers also found that they were no longer able to control their overseas possessions as formerly. ITALY's empire in Africa was, of course, lost by reason of her defeat in the war: Abyssinia (Ethiopia) and Libya were given their independence, Eritrea was allowed to join with Ethiopia in a federation, and Somaliland was promised its independence in 1962. FRANCE also lost parts of her colonial empire, Syria and Lebanon declared their independence during the war, when France was occupied by the Germans. In 1946, the French tried to satisfy the nationalist aspirations of the North Africans by announcing that Tunisia and Morocco were to belong to the French Union, while Algeria, in which there is a strong minority of French settlers, was part of Metropolitan France. But changing names was not enough for the strong Arab and Islamic movement in North Africa. After a great deal of unrest, Tunisia and Morocco became independent in 1956, and an Algerian rebellion kept almost half a million French soldiers occupied continuously from 1954. Indo-China also broke away from France, an independent republic of Viet-Nam being set up ten days after the surrender of the Japanese in 1945. It was not until 1954, after years of guerrilla warfare, that the defeat of the French at Dien Bien Phu convinced them of the futility of continuing the struggle. The French left the Far East, their former empire being split up into independent states—Laos, Cambodia and North Viet-Nam under Communist rule and South Viet-Nam under Nationalist rule. The DUTCH EMPIRE in the Far East also collapsed after the war, the islands of Java, Sumatra, most of Borneo and the Celebes forming themselves into the independent republic of INDONESIA, although it was not officially recognized by the Dutch till 1949. In tropical Africa, movements for self-government made headway in most of the British colonies, while in South Africa the white Nationalist Government started on a policy of *apartheid* or race segregation in 1948. In the 1950's, the Arab world in the Middle East began to assert itself with far-reaching consequences, because of the importance of the area as the source of most of the world's oil supplies. In 1951, the Persian Government nationalized the oil industry and took over the property and installations of the ANGLO-IRANIAN OIL

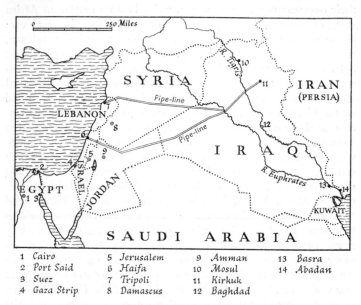

1	Cairo	5	Jerusalem	9	Amman	13	Basra
2	Port Said	6	Haifa	10	Mosul	14	Abadan
3	Suez	7	Tripoli	11	Kirkuk		
4	Gaza Strip	8	Damascus	12	Baghdad		

Middle East, 1951

COMPANY, in which the British Government was a large shareholder. As the Labour Government, then in power, had itself just completed a vast programme of nationalization it was placed in a difficult position; and its defeat in the election of 1951 was partly due to its troubles in the Middle East. Negotiations went on for a long time between Churchill's Government, which succeeded Attlee's in October 1951, and the Persians, the

Americans using their good offices to reach a settlement. By a new agreement drawn up in 1954, the British were given certain rights along with the other great oil companies of the world (mostly American) while Persia received 50 per cent of the earnings. The Egyptian Government also began to press in the early 1950's for the evacuation of all British troops from Egypt, including the Canal Zone, and in 1956 the Egyptian dictator, Nasser, went on to declare the Suez Canal nationalized. Various factors combined to bring about the end of the old Imperialism:— (1) the upsurge of nationalism in the Far East, due partly to the ousting of Europeans by the Japanese in 1941–42 with their slogan "Asia for the Asiatics", and, later, to national resistance to Japanese occupation troops; (2) the revelation during the war of the weakness of the European Imperialist Powers, France, Holland and, to a lesser extent, Britain; (3) the influence of Western teachings, particularly their ideas of democracy and self-determination; (4) the spread of Communism among colonial peoples. In 1955 there was held at Bandung in Indonesia the AFRO–ASIAN CONFERENCE, "the first inter-continental conference of the so-called colonial peoples in the history of mankind", as the President of the Indonesian Republic pointed out. Almost all the twenty-nine countries represented at Bandung had been colonial possessions of European powers at one time or another, and among the resolutions passed was one opposing colonialism. The day of the old Imperialism was over.

Churchill's Last Ministry (1951–55). The Conservatives won the election in October 1951 by a narrow majority and Winston Churchill returned to No. 10 Downing Street, where he had spent five memorable years in wartime. He was to remain there till 1955, when he retired at the age of eighty-one. His duties as Prime Minister, he said when taking office, were to give the British people a rest from the hectic legislative activity of the Labour Government and to "set the people free" from controls and restrictions. One of the first Acts of Churchill's Government was one of DE-NATIONALIZATION: the iron and steel industry and road transport were restored to private ownership. This move was fiercely contested by the Labour Opposition and they threatened to nationalize them again when they returned to power. By the HOUSING REPAIRS AND RENTS ACT, landlords were permitted to increase the rents of their tenants, provided sufficient money was spent on repairs. Rents had been kept low for years by a series of Rent Restriction Acts, while the cost of repairs had mounted higher and higher, so that landlords were unable to maintain their properties or were losing money on them. Council houses were not affected by this Act, and the subsidies paid by councils to maintain the rents at a low level became so burdensome that in some areas the councils decided to raise the rents of council tenants despite strong protests from Labour members, who claimed that housing should be considered a social service and subsidized as such. In an endeavour to reduce taxation, the Government abolished or lowered the food and farming subsidies. Unfortunately, higher rents and dearer food led to demands for increased pay and strikes became more common as the cost of living, which had been held down under the Labour Government, began to rise higher. The difficulties over the balance of payments which had given so much trouble to the Labour Government were eased considerably after 1953 when the Korean War ended. The TELEVISION ACT of 1954, which was passed after heated debates in the House of Commons, provided for the setting up of an Independent Television Authority, under which television programmes would be sponsored by firms wishing to advertise their products. It was during Churchill's last ministry that KING GEORGE VI died. He had undergone an operation for a cancerous lung and had seemed to be recovering well when he died in his sleep at Sandringham in 1952. He had earned the respect of all by his conscientiousness and his friendly relations with all classes (he had, for many years before the war, run a camp where boys from factories and public schools mixed easily on equal terms). His daughter ELIZABETH was crowned at Westminster Abbey in a ceremony seen for the first time on television by millions of British people. One of her first actions was to make the Prime Minister, who is said to have declined the offer of a dukedom in 1945, a Knight of the Garter; and it was as Sir Winston Churchill he spent his last years in office. In 1955, he retired in favour of the Deputy Prime Minister, SIR ANTHONY EDEN. He had spent more years in office than anyone of his generation and his career surpassed that of any other British statesman in its variety and in its importance.

Birth of United Nations. In August 1941, after the Lend-Lease Act had been passed by the Congress of the United States but before Pearl Harbor, the British Prime Minister, Winston Churchill, and the American President, Franklin D. Roosevelt, met on a battleship off Newfoundland and agreed on a statement of their aims for a peace settlement after the War which became known as the ATLANTIC CHARTER. (Churchill had already stated Britain's war aims to be "the complete destruction of Nazi tyranny", and Roosevelt was later to use the phrase "unconditional surrender" of Germany and her allies to describe the war aims of the U.S.A. and Great Britain.) The Atlantic Charter laid down the principles of self-determination and international co-operation, and gave an assurance that after the war all men should have a chance "to live out their lives in freedom from fear and want". The eight points of the Atlantic Charter had a strong resemblance to the Fourteen Points of President Wilson in the First World War, and they afforded good propaganda for the Allied cause. On January 1st, 1942, a few weeks after Pearl Harbor, representatives of the U.S.A., Great Britain and U.S.S.R. and twenty-three other "United Nations" met at Washington and signed a declaration of support for the aims of the Atlantic Charter and for a common effort against Germany, Italy and Japan. In October 1944, when the end of the war was in sight, proposals were put forward at a conference at DUM-BARTON OAKS in Washington, attended by representatives of China, the Soviet Union, Britain and the United States, to set up a permanent organization of the United Nations, whose aims were fairly similar to those of the Atlantic Charter—the preservation of world peace and security. But the United Nations organization did not come into existence until the end of the war when delegates of fifty nations met at the SAN FRANCISCO CONFERENCE (April–August 1945) to draw up the Charter of the United

Nations and the Statute of the International Court of Justice. Membership of the United Nations was to be open to all peace-loving nations which accept and are willing to carry out the obligations of the Charter. (Some Asiatic countries, North Korea, South Korea, North Viet-Nam, South Viet-Nam, Outer Mongolia have been denied admission because of disputes about the rights of their Governments to represent their peoples.) The aims of the United Nations, as set out in the Charter, were:— "To save succeeding generations from the scourge of war, to reaffirm faith in fundamental human rights, in the dignity and worth of the human person, in the equal rights of men and women and of nations large and small, and to establish conditions under which justice and respect for the obligations arising from treaties and other sources of international law can be maintained, and to employ international machinery for the promotion of the economic and social advancement of all peoples." The permanent headquarters of the United Nations are in New York in a magnificent new building on a site made available by the City of New York and by the millionaire of Standard Oil Company, John D. Rockefeller, Jr. The League of Nations suffered through being abandoned by the Americans at the end of the First World War: the United Nations is firmly based on American support and there has been little serious talk of isolationism since the Second World War.

United Nations Organization. All the member states (81 in 1958) are entitled to be represented in the General Assembly, which begins its annual meeting in New York on the third Tuesday of September, although special meetings are also held if need be. Each member can be represented by five delegates but it has only one vote; decisions in the General Assembly are taken by a two-thirds majority of members present and voting. The official languages are English, French, Russian and Spanish, and the working languages English and French. Interpreters are available to carry out immediate translation of speeches for delegates from the different member states. There is a permanent central administrative staff called the Secretariat, under the SECRETARY GENERAL, who is appointed for a period of five years by the General Assembly on the recommendation of the Security Council. This post, which is one of the most important and onerous in the world, was held first by Trygve Lie, a Norwegian lawyer, from 1946 to 1953, when he was succeeded by a Swedish banker, Dag Hammarskjöld. The SECURITY COUNCIL is on duty all the time in order to be prepared for any act of aggression. Of the eleven members, five are permanent members, Great Britain, the United States, France, U.S.S.R. and China, and the other six are elected by the General Assembly for two-year terms. Any decision (except on procedure) needs the approval of at least seven members, including all of the "Big Five". The use of the veto by the Soviet Union so weakened the Security Council that in 1949 the NORTH ATLANTIC TREATY ORGANIZATION (N.A.T.O.), consisting of the U.S.A., Canada and all the states in Western Europe except Spain, was set up "to safeguard the freedom, common heritage and civiliza- ation of their peoples, founded on the principles of democracy, individual liberty and the rule of law". N.A.T.O. was obviously aimed at the Soviet Union, which was then engaged in the "cold war" against the western powers. When the Korean War started in 1950, it happened that the Soviet Union was then boycotting meetings of the Security Council, so that for once it was possible to take decisive action. The Soviet Union soon came back to the Security Council; but because of continued Russian obstruction (the Russian word "Nyet", which means "No", became familar to all Americans at this time) the General Assem- bly decided that if the Security Council failed to *order* action, the Assembly itself could *recommend* action. The INTERNATIONAL COURT OF JUSTICE meets like its predecessors at the Hague in Holland; about forty states have undertaken to accept decisions of the Court as binding in questions of international law and in the interpretation of treaties.

Functional Co-operation. By Article 55 of the United Nations Charter, the member states undertook to promote "higher standards of living, full employment and conditions of economic and social progress and development, the solution of international economic, social, health and related problems, and international cultural and educational co-operation". Under the Economic and Social Council of the United Nations, there are certain bodies which perform very valuable work among the nations of the world. Some of them were in existence (in certain cases with different names) long before 1945, e.g. the UNIVERSAL POSTAL UNION, founded in 1874 with its headquarters at Berne in Switzerland, and the INTERNATIONAL LABOUR ORGANIZATION (I.L.O.), dating from 1919, with its headquarters at Geneva in Switzerland. The WORLD HEALTH ORGANIZATION (W.H.O.) has probably achieved more notable successes than any of the other bodies of U.N.O. E.g. in 1947 when a cholera epidemic broke out in Egypt, W.H.O. acquired cholera vaccine supplies from all over the world and inoculated about 20 million people. Over 20,000 died but the epidemic might easily have been much worse were it not for the prompt action taken by W.H.O. Disease knows no frontiers, and it is only by international co-operation that epidemics of this kind can be dealt with effectively. After the First World War, millions died of typhus, spread from one country to another by refugees; but after 1945 W.H.O. worked hard among the refugees to prevent the spread of typhus, tuberculosis and other diseases. W.H.O. has devoted special attention to dealing with age-old scourges of humanity such as leprosy, yaws and malaria. The FOOD AND AGRICULTURAL ORGANIZATION (F.A.O.), which has its headquarters in Rome, aims at promoting better health by encouraging the growing of food. Some of the enterprises of F.A.O. have been on a large scale, e.g. their locust-fighting campaign, and some on a small scale, such as the teaching of Afghan hill farmers to use scythes instead of sickles. The UNITED NATIONS INTERNATIONAL CHILDREN'S EMERGENCY FUND (U.N.I.C.E.F.) is used to give relief to children in distress, as e.g. when a volcanic eruption devastated the countryside in Ecuador in 1949 and after the earthquakes in Greece in 1953 and in Morocco in 1960. The UNITED NATIONS EDUCATIONAL, SCIENTIFIC AND CULTURAL ORGANIZATION (U.N.E.S.C.O.) does most valuable work among backward peoples, setting up schools, providing mobile libraries. Since the war between Israel and her neighbours in 1948–49, the plight of Arab refugees was terrible till U.N.O. took a hand. U.N.E.S.C.O. set up 300 schools for the Arab children; and W.H.O. and U.N.I.C.E.F. looked after their health and arranged for free milk and other foods. But U.N.E.S.C.O. also brings scientists of different countries together on projects such as their Arid Zone Research scheme, which is intended to develop lands throughout the world. Lack of finance has often hindered progress on some worth-while project. The INTERNATIONAL MONETARY FUND, which has its headquarters at Washington, provides short-term loans to Governments faced with difficulties in their balance of payments (it did not, however, prevent France devaluing its currency in 1948 and Britain in 1949). The International Bank for Reconstruction and Development, known as the "WORLD BANK", provides long-term loans for major projects, but it does not function automatically: Egypt's failure to obtain a loan in 1956 for the Aswan High Dam because of American and British opposition in the "World Bank" provoked Nasser into nationalizing the Suez Canal. All this "functional co-operation" (as it is called) helps to promote peace in two ways:— (1) The work of co-operation helps people of different nations to know one another better; (2) By combating ignorance, famine, disease, U.N.O. helps to raise the standard of living.

Germany after the War. When Germany surrendered in May 1945, the country was devastated and chaos prevailed. Many Germans had nowhere to sleep and little food to eat, and one of the first actions of the British and Americans was to bring relief to those who had been their enemies for six years. The United Nations Relief and Rehabilitation Administration (U.N.R.R.A.) had been set up as far back as 1943 to bring relief to the liberated countries of Western Europe, but its main work was done in enemy territory. As the Allies took over control of Germany, the horrors of the Nazi concentration camps were revealed to the world. When the German economy was breaking down in the winter of 1944–45, ordinary civilians were suffering badly enough but the conditions of the prisoners in the concentration camps were almost incredible. At Büchenwald, near Goethe's

Weimar, the number of deaths per day in the spring of 1945 was about a hundred; the 80,000 inmates found there by the Americans were living in the utmost squalor and many of them were hopelessly ill. From them were obtained accounts of the horrible brutalities performed by the Nazi jailers at the camp; and pieces of hide made into articles like lampshades for the commandant's wife were identified as human skin. At another camp, BELSEN, near Celle in Hanover, the Allied troops found emaciated prisoners lying huddled together, covered with ulcers of filth and disease, unable to move, over a thousand ill with typhus and another thousand ill with typhoid. It was found that 17,000 bodies had been cremated by the Germans just before they abandoned the camp in March. Eleven of the former camp staff were sentenced to death for their crimes. The worst concentration camp of all was in Poland near Cracow at Auschwitz or Osviecim. The commandant of the camp was executed in 1947 at Warsaw for the murder of four million people, and he actually admitted that 1,500,000 Jews were put to death in the gas-chambers there. Other Nazis of higher rank were accused of "war crimes" at the NUREMBERG TRIALS (1945–46) and twenty-two of them were put to death. Of Hitler and his circle, he himself, Goebbels, Minister of Propaganda, and Himmler, chief of police, all committed suicide just at the end of the war, while Goering did so on the morning before his intended execution.

Occupation of Germany. Germany was divided into four occupation zones, for British, American, French and Russian forces, the line between the Russians and the rest having been decided beforehand at the Yalta Conference. The Russian zone included the capital, BERLIN, which was, however, divided into four sectors under the control of the occupying powers. The Western Allies set about through U.N.R.R.A. helping the Germans to make a fresh start and trying to do something for the "displaced persons", refugees mainly from East Germany and Poland, which were under Russian occupation. The Russians themselves were keener on making the Germans pay reparations for the war and damage they had caused. Mindful of the mistake

made in trying to extract large indemnities from Germany after
the First World War, the Allies decided in 1945 that reparations
should be paid not in money but in capital goods. Industrial
equipment and machinery were taken away to be used in restoring
the damaged towns and countryside of the Soviet Union.

Partition of Germany, 1945

Difficulties among the occupying powers early developed and
made the prospects of a peace treaty for Germany a remote one.
When the three western zones were combined in one economic
unit, the Russians in June 1948 tried to drive the Western
Powers from Berlin by blocking all the roads, railways, and
canals leading to the British, American and French sectors.

This blockade was sustained for almost a year, during which time the British and Americans managed through the BERLIN AIR-LIFT to keep West Berlin supplied, and at length the blockade was given up. A few days before (May 1949), the western zones were formed into the FEDERAL REPUBLIC OF GERMANY, usually known as West Germany, with its capital at Bonn in the Rhineland and with DR. KONRAD ADENAUER, former Mayor of Cologne and an opponent of the Nazis, as the first Chancellor. The Russian zone in East Germany was set up by the Russians as the GERMAN DEMOCRATIC REPUBLIC. The partition of Germany, which many had advocated for years as a means of destroying her potential for making war, had thus come about because of the rift that had developed between the Soviet Union and the West. West German industry, financed by Marshall Aid and re-equipped with up-to-date plant, was able to begin an economic recovery that made her in ten years the most prosperous country in Europe. As for a peace treaty, even in 1960, fifteen years after the war, negotiations for it could scarcely be said to have begun. Austria was more fortunate because it was less important: in 1955, the four occupying powers agreed to evacuate their zones and Austria became an independent state again.

The Settlement of Europe. When Churchill and Eden, the British Prime Minister and Foreign Secretary, met with Stalin at the Kremlin in Moscow in October 1944, they tried to arrange a division of Europe after the war into "spheres of influence". This involved the partition of Germany into zones of occupation, as mentioned in the last paragraph. Churchill was alarmed at the prospect of Communism, which he hated, spreading over Europe after the war. He was prepared to see the Soviet Union paramount in Hungary, Rumania, Bulgaria and Yugoslavia, but not in Turkey, Greece, Austria or Czechoslovakia. He tried to obtain a promise that Poland's independence would be respected; but the Soviet armies already occupied Poland and Stalin only gave vague promises. In the summer of 1944, the signal had been given to the Polish independence movement to start a rising in Warsaw as the Russian armies were so near; but the Polish revolt was suppressed with terrible bloodshed, while Stalin's armies waited outside the city. Various explanations have been given for this refusal to help the Poles; but it certainly suited Stalin to have the leaders of the Polish national movement out of the way and made it easier for him to set up a puppet Communist Government in Poland. At YALTA, in the Crimea, where the "Big Three" (Churchill, Roosevelt, Stalin) met in February 1945, not long before Roosevelt's death, most of the arrangements at Moscow were confirmed, and plans were discussed for setting up the United Nations Organization, for holding trials of war criminals, and for the entry of the Soviet Union to the war against the Japanese. Churchill tried to extract a promise that the puppet Government in Poland would accept some of the exiled Poles in London as colleagues and that free elections would be held, but Stalin paid no attention after the war was over and went on to set up other puppet Governments in Bulgaria, Rumania and Hungary. At the POTSDAM CONFERENCE, held at Potsdam, near Berlin, in July of 1945, only Stalin remained of the "Big Three" of Yalta. Roosevelt had died, to be succeeded by the Vice-President, TRUMAN, and Churchill had been replaced as Prime Minister by the Labour leader, ATTLEE. Apart from dealing with reparations, it was decided to leave a settlement of Germany to a peace conference later (but in 1960 it had still not taken place). Poland's fate was finally sealed. As its eastern frontier had been altered in 1939 by the Russo-German partition, the western frontier was moved further west to incorporate a large area of German territory, and the Germans there either fled or were expelled by the Poles. In addition, the Germans in Czechoslovakia, whose 1939 frontiers were restored to her, were also expelled so that the Sudeten problem of 1938 would not recur. These transfers of population involved countless personal tragedies, and camps for "DISPLACED PERSONS" had to be set up to accommodate stateless people. Peace treaties were not signed with the defeated countries for some time after hostilities had ended. The first treaties were signed in 1947 at Paris. ITALY lost her African colonies (which became independent), some islands to Greece, and territory on the Adriatic coast to Yugoslavia, while Trieste was made a Free Territory under British and American control. (In 1954, Trieste was handed back to the Italians, who undertook to maintain it as a free port.) Hungary, Rumania and Bulgaria all lost certain territories and were restricted in their production of armaments and the size of their armed forces. What was more important than the territorial settlement was the political division of Europe into East and West. Behind the IRON CURTAIN, the frontiers of the most westerly Communist countries, lay the Soviet Union and her SATELLITE STATES—Poland, East Germany, Bulgaria, Rumania, Hungary, in which ruled Communist Governments obedient to Moscow. Yugoslavia, which also had a Communist Government, was ruled by Tito, former head of the Partisans, the Yugoslav resistance movement, and a man who was unwilling to toe the Moscow line. Most of the other countries in Europe, ruled by democratic Governments, with the exception of Spain and Portugal, were by 1948 dependent on Marshall Aid from the U.S.A. to keep going. In that year, Churchill wrote:—"After all the exertions and sacrifices of hundreds of people and in spite of the victories of the Righteous Cause, we have still not found Peace and Security, and we lie in the grip of worse perils than those we have surmounted."

Cold War. The ambitions of Stalin to dominate Europe were not restricted to the countries in which there were Communist Governments. In Italy and France, there were strong Communist parties, the members of which felt that their first allegiance was to the Soviet Union rather than to their own Government. The former allies became more suspicious of each other's intentions. The Americans' attempt to restore Germany's economy by large-scale relief through U.N.R.R.A. and by loans to finance industry were regarded by the Russians as inspired by a desire to build up Germany as a barrier against Communism; and undoubtedly the Americans were afraid that a ruined Germany might fall a prey to Communism. In 1947, it became obvious that Britain could no longer afford to keep her troops in Greece, which was at that time troubled by Communist guerrilla bands. President Truman decided that, to prevent further Russian expansion in an area so near the important sources of oil in the Middle East, the Americans must send aid to Greece and, in addition, to Turkey, also on the borders of Russia. When Truman announced his intention of supporting "free peoples who are resisting attempted subjugation by armed minorities or outside pressure", he had obviously in mind outside pressure from the Soviet Union. By this intervention in European affairs, he created a revolution in American foreign policy, the so-called TRUMAN DOCTRINE, which meant a radical departure from the previous tradition of isolation from Europe in peace-time. It was in 1947 also that the American Secretary of State (the equivalent of the British Foreign Secretary), General Marshall, made an offer of financial help to Europe. Marshall realized that Europe faced economic collapse and that a weakened Europe would lead to disorder and chaos, of which the Soviet Union could take advantage. Marshall had learnt the lessons of the troubles in Europe in the 1930's; as he said in his speech announcing the proposals, "Without a return of economic health in the world, there can be no political stability and no assured peace." The British Foreign Secretary, Ernest Bevin, was quick to respond; and although the Russians and her satellites refused the invitation, nearly all the other states of Europe decided to participate in the MARSHALL PLAN. The Organization for European Economic Co-operation (O.E.E.C.), set up to carry out the Marshall Plan, was naturally composed only of non-Communist states; and thus another gulf developed between East and West. It was in this year and in 1948 that the Russians tried to drive the American, British and French forces out of Berlin by imposing a blockade that was, however, defeated by the Berlin air-lift. The COMINFORM (or Communist Information Bureau) was also formed in 1947 to co-ordinate and organize propaganda and activities of the Communist parties in the satellite states of East Europe and also in the democracies of the West. It had its headquarters at first in Belgrade, the capital of Yugoslavia, and after 1948, when Tito quarrelled with Stalin, at Bucharest, capital of Rumania. The greatest shock to the West came in February 1948, when the democratic Government of Czechoslovakia, which included

Communists, was overthrown by a Communist *coup d'état*. There was no bloodshed (although the Czechoslovak Foreign Minister, Jan Masaryk, committed suicide) and Czechoslovakia thus became another satellite of the Soviet Union. In the Far East, the Chinese Communists under MAO TSE-TUNG compelled the Nationalist forces under Chiang Kai-Shek to retreat to the island of Formosa in 1949. As the U.S.A. still recognized Chiang Kai-Shek as head of the Chinese Government and the Soviet Union recognised Mao Tse-Tung, there was constant friction in the meetings of the United Nations. This state of affairs in which the United States and the Soviet Union seemed to oppose each other in everything has been called the "Cold War". Neither power wanted war, and the Soviet Union constantly proclaimed its desire for peace, encouraging Communists in Western countries to wage peace campaigns. The atmosphere grew worse, particularly after Klaus Fuchs, a brilliant German-born physicist, employed by Britain, was found guilty in 1949 of giving secrets about the atomic bomb to the Soviet Union. In the United States, hatred of Communism rose to such heights that anyone who had the faintest connection with a Communist was likely to be treated as a traitor. Under the rabidly anti-Communist SENATOR MCCARTHY, a campaign was started against many persons in Government posts and public life; he at one time claimed that there were over 200 Communists in the State Department (equivalent to the British Foreign Office). Eleven Communist party officials were sentenced to five years' imprisonment. Those who tried to defend the men accused of "un-American activities" were branded as "fellow-travellers". McCarthy was acting from mixed motives (he was a Republican Senator and wished to embarrass the Democratic Government for allowing such subversive activities) but the effect of his campaign was to embitter relations between the United States and the Soviet Union. At the same time, the Soviet Union, having learned the secret of the atom bomb, made their first atomic explosion in 1949, the U.S.A. decided to begin work on the hydrogen bomb in 1951, and it seemed that five years after the end of the war another world war might be just around the corner.

Korean War (1950–53). When the Russians declared war on Japan in August 1945, one of their first moves was to enter the peninsula of Korea, which had been under Japanese control since 1905. Korea has rich mineral resources (gold, copper, iron, coal, graphite, tungsten), particularly in the northern part, which had been industrialized under the Japanese. The peninsula was partitioned in 1945 along the 38th parallel of latitude (a line on the map corresponding to no geographical feature like a mountain range or a river), the northern part being under Soviet control and the southern part under American. Relations between North and South Korea gradually deteriorated and there were numerous incidents along the frontier in 1948 and 1949. After the American forces withdrew in 1950, the North Koreans, well equipped and well trained by Chinese Communists, invaded South Korea, which was totally unprepared for war. The South Korean forces retreated, abandoning their capital, Seoul, to the advancing North Koreans. When the matter was referred to the Security Council of the United Nations, the Russians were at the time boycotting the meetings; and as there was no Russian veto to prevent action, it was immediately decided that North Korea had been the aggressor and that all member states of the United Nations should send aid to South Korea. The Russians quickly returned to the meetings of the Security Council but too late to stop United Nations intervention, the first of its kind. Most of the troops and equipment in the United Nations army were American. In a short time the North Korean army had collapsed but as soon as the United Nations forces, under the American GENERAL MACARTHUR, reached the border between Korea and Manchuria, Mao Tse-Tung sent over 200,000 Chinese troops into Korea. MacArthur, who had such brilliant success against the Japanese during the Second World War, was compelled to retreat in face of a fierce Chinese offensive in mid-winter. The United Nations forces, however, counter-attacked and, making use of their naval power and air superiority, were able to advance till they were back across the 38th Parallel. Some Americans were eager, like General MacArthur, to extend the war to China; but Truman and Attlee were afraid that war with

China (which might well be prolonged) would allow Stalin a free hand in Europe. An armistice was at last, after two years of negotiations, signed in July 1953, settling the frontier roughly along the 38th Parallel. In one sense, the Korean War had been just another phase of the "Cold War" for the Russians; but over 300,000 Americans and a much smaller number of British had taken part. The war was a test for the United Nations, which by the accident of the Russian abstention in 1950 was able to act quickly. Because of later obstruction by Russians, the General Assembly of the United Nations decided to accept a proposal of the American Secretary of State, Dean Acheson, that it could recommend action against aggressors in cases where the Council failed to order action. Another result of the Korean War was that the United States was compelled by the threat of a war on two fronts in Asia and Europe to become even more deeply involved in Europe by strengthening their alliance, N.A.T.O., set up in 1949.

Balance of Power. In 1953, at the end of the Korean War, the position in Europe and in the world was one of a balance of power between the Soviet Union and her allies on the one side and the United States and her allies on the other. In 1952, President Truman had been succeeded by GENERAL DWIGHT D. EISENHOWER ("Ike" as he was popularly called), who although a Republican made it clear that he would not revert to the traditional Republican policy of isolationism but would continue in the policy started by his predecessor in 1947. Eisenhower's experience as Supreme Commander of the Allied forces in 1944–45 and of the N.A.T.O. forces from 1950 to 1952 made it easier for him to appreciate that Europe's difficulties were also America's difficulties. A Conservative Government had been in power in Britain since October 1951 under Sir Winston Churchill and no one was more conscious than Churchill of the importance of keeping N.A.T.O. going. It was estimated that east of the Iron Curtain the Soviet Union had 175 divisions ready; and the awareness of the danger in Eastern Europe was sufficient to bring the countries of Western Europe together. In 1953, the European Coal and Steel Community began to function, France, West Germany,

Italy, Belgium, the Netherlands and Luxembourg having agreed to abolish their tariffs so far as coal, iron and steel were concerned. (This was later to be known as the COMMON MARKET, when it was extended to cover all other goods and commodities in 1958.) By the end of 1953, the nations in N.A.T.O. had managed to

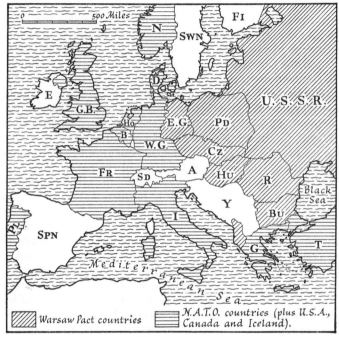

Europe, 1955

build up forces equal to 75 divisions, and attempts were being made to bring West Germany into a European Defence Community. Many people in France, Britain and, of course, the Soviet Union were strongly opposed to the re-arming of Germany. At last, the occupation of Germany was brought to an end in 1955; West Germany joined N.A.T.O. and there was formed a WESTERN EUROPEAN UNION, consisting of Britain, France, Italy, Belgium, the Netherlands, Luxembourg and West Germany. As a member of this new body, which was linked with N.A.T.O., Britain undertook to maintain four divisions and a tactical air force on the continent, the most serious military commitment ever made by Britain in peace time. Before then, in 1953, Stalin had died without leaving any obvious successor to fill his place. By that time, the Americans had carried out some experiments in preparation for exploding a HYDROGEN BOMB; but it was the Russians who were first with the hydrogen bomb, in the summer of 1953, not long after Stalin's death. The Americans followed with theirs in 1954. It was not long before people all over the world began to realize the implications of the "H-bombs". One of the American bombs tested at BIKINI, a coral atoll in the South Pacific, developed an energy of 17 megatons of T.N.T. explosive, the equivalent of 850 Hiroshima bombs. Almost incalculable is the effect of the radio-active dust or "fall-out"; after the first American H-bomb (which developed an energy of 3 megatons) exploded, Japanese fishermen over a thousand miles away became dangerously ill and the fish they caught became radio-active. The possession of hydrogen bombs by the United States and the Soviet Union gave to the rulers of these countries a frightening responsibility: but it also made them pause lest any aggression should lead to the launching of a "nuclear" war. The most wonderful achievement of the twentieth century, the release of the energy in matter, made it possible to have a war that would mean the end of the human race. The alternative to war, a balance of power resting on the possession of nuclear deterrents (as the hydrogen bombs have been called) demands restraint and statesmanship on both sides, of which, fortunately, there have been some encouraging signs in the 1950's. It is possible indeed that the existence of the most dreadful weapon of all time may be the strongest reason for peace, and that, as Sir Winston Churchill has said, "When the advance of this destructive weapon enables everyone to kill everybody else, nobody will want to kill anyone at all".

SOURCE EXTRACTS

A   *The work of W.H.O.*

Its immediate tasks were self evident, though intimidating. The world,
as in 1918, was faced with the threat of diseases that follow the
malnutrition of war, the movement of armies and the scattering of
millions of refugees. One of the worst threats was tuberculosis. A mass-
inoculation campaign was undertaken, using B.C.G. This is the
Bacillus Calmette-Guerin, a live vaccine with a bacillus too weak to
cause active infection but enough to mobilize the resistance in the body
to withstand invasion by more virulent types. From the war-ravaged
countries, this protection was extended to millions in the under-
developed countries. Syphilis and the kindred affliction, yaws, could
now be dramatically cured by just one injection of penicillin. W.H.O.
and the Children's Fund co-operated in the campaign against those
diseases until tens of millions had been successfully treated.

D.D.T., with its power to kill mosquitoes, meant that malaria
control could be undertaken. Whole areas were cleared of the disease
until, with the appearance of D.D.T.-resistant mosquitoes, W.H.O.
made bold to launch a world wide campaign of *eradication* instead of
control, i.e., the malaria parasite has to be got out of the blood of
human beings so that there is no reservoir of the infection on which
the mosquitoes can draw. This, to-day, is possible by the combined
use of insecticides and of treatment drugs. This campaign, above all
others, demonstrates the need for essential internationalism.

Ritchie Calder: After Ten Years.

B   *The H-Bomb*

Already in the summer of 1952 some preparatory experiments were
carried out on the small island of Eniwetok in the centre of the
Pacific, but the outside world was told next to nothing. It was all the
more amazed, therefore, when in the summer of 1953 Stalin's successor,
Malenkov, announced that the Soviet Union had the so-called hydrogen
bomb. A week later, the seismographs of the Western world recorded a
powerful explosion in the area of Wrangel Island, in the Arctic Ocean.

The implications were obvious. The Russians were in possession of a
transportable, "dry" hydrogen bomb; the American device at Eniwetok
—it had been given the nickname of "Lulu"—had been in a much less
developed stage; it was liquid and stationary, which meant that it was
not yet a practical weapon. The Russians were clearly ahead in the
nuclear race.

In March 1954, however, America was again in the spotlight. Her
first transportable H-bombs were successfully exploded at Bikini.
Reports and calculations on the new weapon made Hiroshima pale into
insignificance. One such "device", it was said, could reduce the
major part of London or New York to ashes.

The excitement over the H-bomb reached its climax when the
Japanese trawler *Lucky Dragon* returned from its fishing grounds
1000 miles from Bikini. The fishermen were dangerously ill from burns
caused by radio-active dust—the "fall-out" of the bomb. The fish they
had caught were still radio-active. A panic seized all Japan, whose
staple food is fish. And the world knew that from now on it would
have to live under the cloud of the new bomb.

Egon Larsen: Atomic Energy.

EXERCISES

1. Explain: Terms of trade, dollar gap, O.E.E.C., I.L.O., W.H.O.,
   F.A.O., U.N.I.C.E.F., U.N.E.S.C.O., U.N.R.R.A., displaced
   person, sphere of influence, Iron Curtain, satellite state, Cominform,
   fellow-traveller, N.A.T.O., Common Market, B.C.G., D.D.T.,
   fall-out.
2. Identify the authors of the following and explain where necessary:
   (*a*) "Those who can win a war well can rarely make a good peace."
   (*b*) "Export or die."
   (*c*) "Asia for the Asiatics!"
   (*d*) "The first inter-continental conference of the so-called coloured
          peoples in the history of mankind."
   (*e*) "All men should have a chance to live out their lives in freedom
          from fear and want."
   (*f*) "We have still not found Peace and Security, and we lie in the
          grip of even worse perils than those we have surmounted."
   (*g*) "When the advance of this destructive weapon enables every-
          one to kill everybody else, nobody will want to kill anyone at
          all."
 . Write short notes on: C. R. Attlee, National Health Service,
   World Health Organization, concentration camps, Nuremberg
   Trials, Berlin Air-lift, Truman Doctrine, General Marshall, Senator
   McCarthy.
4. Write notes on: Germany after 1945, the settlement of Europe
   after the Second World War, Korean War.

5. Give an account of the Labour Government's programme of nationalization, 1945–51. What other measures were passed during this time?
6. How did the United Nations Organization come to be set up? Describe the work of two of its chief constituent bodies.
7. Compare the United Nations and the League of Nations from the following aspects—(a) aims, (b) organization, (c) effectiveness.
8. What is meant by the term "Cold War"? Give a brief account of international affairs, 1947–53.

CHAPTER XV

ECONOMIC CHANGES, 1914–55

Farming, 1914–55. We have seen in an earlier chapter how British farmers at the beginning of the twentieth century were adapting themselves to the changed conditions brought about by the importation of cheap grain and meat from overseas. Stockbreeding, potato-growing, dairy-farming, large-scale poultry-keeping, fruit-farming, market-gardening took the place of the arable farming which had fallen on such evil days. During the First World War, because of the German U-boat blockade, Britain became more dependent on home producers, who were able to enjoy prosperity for the first time for many years. To replace the young men called up to serve in the forces the WOMEN'S LAND ARMY was started in 1917; 1,800 "land girls" (of varying ages) worked on the farms in the First World War and over 80,000 in the Second World War. Two other developments of the earlier war that were to be of much greater significance in the later war were the payment of subsidies when the price of wheat fell below a fixed minimum and the granting of powers to the Board of Agriculture to enforce proper cultivation. In 1919, after it was seen how dependent Britain was on imported timber, the FORESTRY COMMISSION was set up: it took over poor land for afforestation, adding year by year to the acreage of woodland. Between the wars, farmers had a lean time. One new crop, SUGAR BEET, for which the first British factory had been opened in Norfolk in 1912, was encouraged by subsidies, a new development in peace-time. Certain improvements were carried out by go-ahead farmers during this period. The practice of storing green grass in pits or SILOS was very old, but it only became popular in Britain in the inter-war period, when it was found that, by adding molasses to the silage, the result was a very much improved feeding-stuff on which the cows gave plentiful milk. MECHANIZATION increased on the farms: tractors, which had made their appearance during the First World War, became more common and milking machines took the place of dairy-maids. A MILK MARKETING BOARD was set up in 1933, and a slogan "Drink more milk" encouraged the consumption of milk, while schoolchildren received it daily, at first at half-price and later free of charge. Pasteurization of milk had been adopted to destroy the bacteria of tuberculosis; and extra payments were given to farmers who owned herds of tuberculin-tested cattle in order to produce fresh, germ-free milk. During this inter-war period, great progress was made in agricultural RESEARCH in the fourteen new agricultural colleges set up in England and Wales (as also in the three Scottish colleges on which the English and Welsh were modelled) and in experimental and research stations such as the research station at Rothamsted near St. Albans, founded as far back as 1843.

Farming in the Second World War. The coming of war in 1939 not only brought prosperity to the farmers but also great improvements in almost every respect. The need for more food forced the Government to acquire more powers over farmers and farming. Instructions were given as to the crops and the acreage for each season. County War Agricultural Executive Committees, composed of local farmers and landowners, had powers to evict any bad farmers; they also gave advice on rotations and fertilizers, however, and supplied machinery. Before the war, British farmers produced only two-fifths of the nation's food: by the end of the war they were producing four-fifths. Millions of acres of grassland were brought under cultivation, and the wheat, barley and potato crops were more than doubled. The milk yield increased by 40 per cent during the war; and thousands of town-dwellers grew vegetables for themselves and others in their allotments. All this was achieved with many farm-labourers in the forces, although 80,000 of the Women's Land Army helped to take their places. The loss in man-power was also made up by increased mechanization: by the end of the war there were 175,000 tractors in Britain and combine-harvesters were becoming common. One of the most interesting developments of the war period was LEY-FARMING. This involves sowing mixtures of grasses and clovers (to be cut for hay and also to serve as pasture for as long as six years) and sowing root or green crops. Ley-farming is the basis of good grazing for dairy and beef cattle. It had been popular for generations in Scotland, but it was as a result of the experiments of SIR GEORGE STAPLEDON at Aberystwyth that it was practised scientifically in England and Wales. At the end of the war, the land of Britain was in better heart than it had been for a century. The improvements continued after the war. Farmers were more prosperous and therefore able to afford new mechanical aids. Electricity brought improvements to the cowshed as well as to the farmhouse. The combine-harvester ceased to be a rarity, and the tractor was so popular that fifteen years after the end of the war the horse was seldom seen on some lowland farms. A scheme of guaranteed prices and subsidies, introduced by Attlee's Labour Government, enabled the farmer to plan ahead. In addition to the Milk Marketing Board, there were also set up boards for marketing wool, eggs, bacon, etc. Life on the farm has changed almost completely in the last half century. Just as the coming of mechanization brought an end to the old drudgery of farmwork, so wireless, television, the country bus, the motor-car (for the older ones), the motor-bicycle (for the younger ones), the community centres, the young farmers' clubs have all added to the variety and interest of life outside working hours.

Difficulties in Trade. Of Britain's two main rivals in the

22

economic sphere in 1914, Germany and the United States, the first was ruined by the war and the second made such strides forward that there was never afterwards any doubt that it was the wealthiest country in the world. Britain, of course, had four years' fighting compared with the one year of the U.S.A. She had acquired an enormous burden of war debts, which necessitated heavy taxation. Her overseas investments had shrunk so that there was less income from interest and dividends. She had lost markets (and continued to lose them) in the Far East, where Japan, because of low wages, was able to undersell Britain in cotton goods and machinery. In Europe, too, the war had forced countries to be self-sufficient, to produce steel, to manufacture goods, to build ships for themselves. Britain's industrial equipment (factories, mines, machinery) tended to be older and therefore less efficient than those of recently industrialized countries. Belgian coalmines and Dutch shipyards could thus produce more cheaply than those in Britain. New sources of power, electricity and oil, meant that other European countries were no longer so dependent on British coal as in 1913, when over 70 million tons were exported. It is, therefore, not surprising that the British coal industry was in the doldrums in the decade following the First World War. London was no longer regarded as the chief financial centre of the world: with Britain off the gold standard, London gave place to New York. The only redeeming factor in the changed situation was that the TERMS OF TRADE suited Britain: the relation of the prices of exports to those of imports improved by at least 40 per cent in 1921. The immediate post-war boom was short-lived and was succeeded by a depression which hit the coalmining and shipbuilding industries badly; and many mines and shipyards closed down in the early 1920's never to re-open. Emigration was no longer so easy as in the days before 1914 since the U.S.A. had restricted it by a quota system. Unemployment became chronic, with a figure never less than a million and sometimes nearly two million.

World Depression. In the late 1920's (called "the roaring twenties"), trade improved generally, and in the United States a boom developed that led to an inordinate amount of speculation on the stock exchange. The WALL STREET CRASH of 1929 was the signal for the onset of a slump or depression that became world-wide and lasted for years. The succession of boom, slump, boom, slump was nothing new in the nineteenth century; and economists had come to describe this fluctuation as the TRADE CYCLE. In the period 1873–93, although there had been some temporary improvements, trade was so poor and unemployment so common

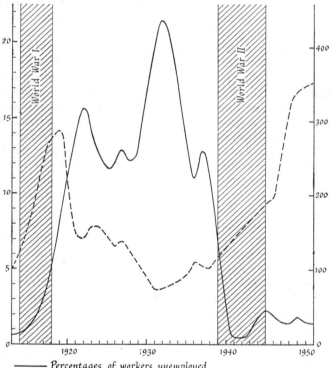

———— *Percentages of workers unemployed*
– – – *Wholesale prices as percentages of 1913 figures*
Left-hand scale represents unemployment percentages.
Right-hand scale represents wholesale prices percentages.

Unemployment Percentages and Wholesale Prices, 1913–51

that historians have called it the period of the "Great Depression". Why was the "World Depression" or "Economic Blizzard" of the 1930's so much worse than any previous depression? (1) The dependence of world trade on the United States was bad for the United States and the rest of the world. America was almost self-sufficient and did not need to import from Europe, and her high tariffs made it difficult for countries to export to her. She exported her surplus to Europe, however, by making loans on short terms to countries like Germany and Austria, but could only be paid in gold as she did not receive imports from these countries. As a result, gold accumulated in the U.S. Federal Reserve Bank, even when unemployment figures began to soar in the 1930's. Because of the dependence of Europe on the United States, the Wall Street crash had repercussions in Europe almost as disastrous as those in America. (2) Agriculture throughout the world was also at a low ebb. Increased mechanization and new fertilizers meant bigger crops but low prices for wheat in the prairies of the mid-west, coffee in Brazil, sugar in the West Indies. Unfortunately, the only way farmers tried to improve their lot was by producing more, which pushed prices lower still. Some economists and politicians spoke of the farmers over-producing, but at the same time many of the industrial workers of Western Europe and America were unemployed and under-nourished, not to mention the starving millions in Asia. (3) Once the depression developed, it tended to become worse in a kind of vicious circle. As revenue from taxation fell with growing unemployment, a government normally tried to reduce expenditure, which meant cutting the purchasing power of government employees and those engaged on government contracts and thus creating more unemployment. Tariffs were pushed up to protect home industries (even Britain, the home of free trade, joined the rest in 1932); but the total effect was to restrict trade further. In 1934, the volume of world trade had fallen to one-third of what it was in 1929. As the farmers of the world were poverty-stricken, they could not afford to buy machinery so that there was less work in industrial countries, which were thus less able to buy from abroad. In each country, the inability of the unemployed to buy anything but the bare necessities of life meant unemployment in the industries that produced consumer goods and also in the industries making capital equipment (machinery, etc.) for the manufacture of consumer goods. And so the vicious circle continued until by 1933 there were over 30 million unemployed in Europe and at least half of that number in the United States. The political consequences of the "World Depression", which have been mentioned in earlier chapters, were far-reaching. It contributed to the rise of Hitler in Germany, to Mussolini's colonial adventures in Africa, and thus indirectly to the Second World War.

Full Employment. The most striking contrast between conditions before and after the Second World War is in the unemployment figures. The percentage of registered workers unemployed in Britain in 1932 was 21·9 (59 in shipbuilding, 28·7 in cotton manufacture and 34 in coalmining): when the unemployment percentage in 1959 went up as high as 2·8 for the whole country (it was almost double that in Scotland), the Cabinet was alarmed and began to take steps to improve matters. The total number of registered workers had also grown considerably, from nearly 13 millions in 1932 (9,324,000 males and 3,506,000 females) to nearly 24 millions in 1959 (16,128,000 males and 7,863,000 females). Re-arming before the war and the demands on man-power during the war obviously helped to alleviate unemployment. It was during the period 1936–45 that men began to accept the theories put forward by J. M. KEYNES (later Lord Keynes), a Cambridge economist. In 1934, he had advocated a large development loan for housing, roads, and other public works as a means of dealing with unemployment. Private investment had dried up for lack of confidence; but with labour plentiful and materials cheap, the Government, Keynes maintained, could "prime the pumps" of industry by such a public works programme. His book, *The General Theory of Employment, Interest and Money* (1936) has been compared in its influence with Adam Smith's *Wealth of Nations* (1776) and established him as the world's leading economist. Keynes felt that unemployment was too serious a problem to leave to the free operations of the market to put things right, and he advocated control of all forms of investment and more careful timing of public expenditure to maintain employment. In effect, President Roosevelt in his New Deal policies was carrying out a kind of Keynesian policy. In 1944, the British Government, in an official White Paper on economic policy, accepted its obligation to ensure adequate public spending in order to maintain FULL EMPLOYMENT. When depressions occurred after the Second World War, they were small affairs and were termed "recessions". They were taken as warnings for the Government to make spending easier by lowering the rate of interest required by the banks for loans to industry (as had been done before the war) and to initiate public expenditure, by loans if necessary, to "prime the pumps" of industry. Full employment also brings its difficulties. It means that there is nearly always a boom in industry, a controlled boom but nevertheless one that brings with it inflation, rising prices and a tendency to speculation. The £1 of 1960 was worth only 7s. 4½d. in comparison with the £1 of 1939. The Government exercises control over spending by employing what is called a "credit squeeze", making it more difficult to borrow money for expansion. Along with full employment has come a higher standard of living for the workers, who enjoy higher wages and the five-day week, although it has often been sought by trade unionists not for the sake of increased leisure but in order to swell the weekly pay packet by working more overtime.

Modern Industrial Developments. Since the beginning of the century, Britain has gone over from almost complete dependence on coal to the utilization of many sources of fuel and power —electricity, oil and more recently nuclear energy. Increased MECHANIZATION has relieved workers of much of the drudgery. Dockers, for example, may work for weeks without doing what was called at one time manual labour. Stoking furnaces is only one of many jobs, formerly drudgery, that are now done mechanically. Giant excavators, bull-dozers, pneumatic drills have replaced the navvy's pick and shovel. Mechanization has been succeeded by AUTOMATION. Automatic or semi-automatic machines have existed for a long time, e.g. spinning and weaving machines, engineering lathes, but they needed to be under the supervision of the human operator. ELECTRONICS have made possible automatic processes that appear wonderful to the ordinary person. With electronic control gear, one or two operators can control from a distance the complicated processes of a factory. Electronic computers have made the processing of information rapid and automatic. They are used to do routine clerical work such as accounts; e.g. J. Lyons and Company in 1954 installed an electronic computer which prepared the pay-roll for 10,000 employees in about four hours instead of 37 full-time clerks working for a week. A new industrial revolution is taking place in the twentieth century that should mean more efficient production and more leisure for the workers.

Transport by Land and Sea. The greatest change in the past half century so far as transport is concerned has been brought about by the internal combustion engine. Since 1914, when a few motor-cars and charabancs might be seen occasionally, motor traffic has increased tremendously. The coming of the cheap car made this expansion possible. A two-seater Rover car with a 6-h.p. engine had been put on the market in 1914 but the First World War interfered with production. It was the American Ford car, nicknamed the "Tin Lizzie" and mass-produced at Detroit, that was the first cheap popular car in the 1920's. Soon it had British competitors. William R. Morris, later LORD NUFFIELD, built his first motor-car in 1911, opening a small factory a year later, and he produced a car to sell at £165 at a new factory at Cowley near Oxford before the war broke out in 1914. It was not until after the war that he made a name for himself with a mass-produced car, selling 50,000 cars a year by 1925. Another famous cheap car of the 1920's was the Austin Seven, produced at the Austin works at Birmingham. Britain also produced expensive, comfortable, fast cars of which the best known was the Rolls-Royce. In the First World War, more than half of the aero-engines in British planes came from the Rolls-Royce works at Derby; and in the Second World War they again turned out first-class aero-engines on a large scale. Long-distance lorries, with diesel engines, were preferred by many firms to the railways from the early 1930's, as it meant cutting out loading and unloading at stations. With the increase in traffic has come an improvement in the roads. But British motorists complain that their roads are not to be compared with the German *Autobahnen* or the American trunk roads with their fly-over crossings and broad carriage-ways. In the 1920's the first British roads with dual carriageways were made, sometimes with separate tracks for cyclists. In 1959 there was opened the first stretch of a new motorway, M 1, from London to Yorkshire, designed for fast traffic only, with fly-over junctions and dual or three-lane carriage-ways. In 1958, there were in Britain over 4,549,000 private cars, 1,520,000 motor-cycles and three-wheelers, 1,613,000 vans, lorries and tractors. But, unfortunately, with increased traffic and higher speeds, accidents have multiplied. Various devices, such as zebra crossings, have been used to help pedestrians; but despite these, nearly 6,000 were killed on the roads in 1958. On RAILWAYS, the main improvements have been brought about by electrification. Many of the London surburban lines were electrified by 1932; but Britain, the pioneer of the steam locomotive, remained faithful to it and it was not until 1960 that the first electrification scheme in Scotland was completed on the Airdrie–Helensburgh line. Britain's preference for the steam locomotive lost her most of the speed records to the United States, Germany, France and Italy, where diesel-electric locomotives were introduced between the wars. In Britain, the change-over from steam to diesel locomotives was only begun in 1955. A similar change has taken place at sea but earlier. The British Navy adopted oil fuel instead of coal just before the First World War. Motor vessels became more common after the war; and diesel engines were installed in vessels where speed was not important, e.g. in fishing boats. A more recent development has been the fixing of STABILIZERS on ships to reduce rolling. Both passenger and merchant ships are fitted with these devices, so that better speeds as well as increased comfort can be achieved. Although air travel is preferred by many people to long sea voyages, large liners are still being built. The two giant Cunarders,

Queen Mary (81,237 tons) and *Queen Elizabeth* (83,673 tons) were launched from John Brown's shipyard in Clydebank in 1934 and 1938 respectively. They are the world's largest ships and follow a weekly schedule, crossing the Atlantic usually in four days.

Flying. The First World War gave a tremendous fillip to aviation. Before the war, Blériot's flight across the Channel in 1909 had caused a sensation in Britain. Ten years afterwards, in June 1919, the first TRANSATLANTIC FLIGHT was made by Captain John Alcock and Lieut. Whitten Brown in a Vickers Vimy biplane from St. John's, Newfoundland, to Clifden in Galway in Ireland, about 1,880 miles in 16 hours, 12 minutes. A few weeks later, the British airship R.34 made a double crossing of the Atlantic. The first solo transatlantic flight was made in 1927 by an American, Charles Lindbergh, who flew from New York to Paris, 3,000 miles in 33½ hours. In the inter-war years, a number of long-distance flights were made from Britain to South Africa, India, Australia, by aviators like Sir Alan Cobham, Jim Mollison and Amy Johnson. AIRSHIPS were used on the Atlantic route by the Germans, whose zeppelin *Hindenburg* could carry up to a hundred on board and achieved a speed of nearly 180 m.p.h. on its trials in 1926. Unfortunately, the *Hindenburg* was destroyed by fire in 1937 when about to land near New York. The Germans were unable to obtain the non-inflammable helium (the main source of which was in Canada) and had to depend on the highly inflammable hydrogen to keep their airships in the air. A sister airship, *Graf Zepplin,* continued to keep up a regular Atlantic service until 1938. Before then, the British had given up building airships after a terrible disaster that befell the R.101 in 1930, when it crashed in France and nearly all aboard were killed. In the Second World War, as in the first, great improvements were made in aeroplanes, the fighters becoming faster and the bombers heavier as the war continued. The most important development was that of JET PROPULSION. As early as 1930 the idea of using a gas-turbine to produce the air-flow necessary for jet-propulsion had been conceived by FRANK WHITTLE, then a cadet in the Royal Air Force. But it was not until just before the outbreak of war that he was given official encouragement, and the first successful British jet-plane flight was made in 1941. The German firm of Heinkel had been busy with the same idea and actually produced the first jet fighter a few days before war started in 1939. German planes were in operation before the British but were not so reliable. Aircraft speeds soon passed the pre-war record of 469 m.p.h. put up in 1939 by a German Messerschmitt. The first SUPERSONIC FLIGHT (at a speed greater than that of sound, 746 m.p.h.) was made in 1947 by Captain C. Yeager of the U.S. Air Force in a Bell X1 research aircraft. SUPERSONIC SPEEDS are now regarded as normal for fighter aircraft. In 1956 the first flight at over 1,000 m.p.h. was made by the Englishman, Peter Twiss, in a Fairey Delta 2 aeroplane at 1,132 m.p.h. Much faster speeds have been attained by ROCKETS. The scientists engaged during the war in research on ballistic missiles turned their attention to the possibilities of space flight. In October 1957, the first man-made earth SATELLITE went into orbit. It was a metal sphere of 180 lbs., fired by a three-stage rocket launched by Soviet scientists and engineers, and received the name SPUTNIK, the Russian word for "satellite", and also for "fellow-traveller". On September 12th, 1959, a Russian rocket was fired at the moon and, after a 36-hour journey at 25,000 m.p.h., hit its target. The next stage in man's conquest of the air will be space travel; but that involves other factors than that of firing a rocket into the air. Much less speedy but potentially more useful are the HELI-COPTER, the aircraft which has a vertical take-off and which was first produced in Germany in 1937 (American helicopters designed by SIKORSKY, an engineer of Russian origin, were much used for rescuing wounded during the Second World War) and the HOVERCRAFT, a vehicle resting on a cushion of air; it was invented by C. S. Cockerell, an English engineer, and made a successful flight across the Channel in 1959.

Communications. It was just prior to the First World War that the importance of wireless came to be appreciated by the ordinary man. Everyone knew that the fact that the murderer Dr. Crippen was on board a Canadian Pacific liner in 1910 had been transmitted by the captain to the police by wireless, and that the drowning of over 1,500 passengers and crew of the *Titanic* in 1912 might have been averted if the wireless operators on the nearby *Caledonia* had not turned in to sleep soon after the White Star liner had struck the iceberg. It was in 1920, two years after the war, that BROADCASTING on a large scale began in America; and almost from the start it was being organized on a commercial basis, the programmes being sponsored by advertisers of toothpaste, cereals, motor-cars, etc. Britain was the first country to run broadcasting as a public service. The British Broadcasting Company was formed in 1922 with stations at London, Manchester, Birmingham and Newcastle, and a fifth station at Glasgow in the following year. In the early days of broadcasting, most people had cheap "crystal" sets with earphones; but soon valve sets with loud-speakers made it possible to dispense with earphones. In 1926, the B.B.C. became the British Broadcasting Corporation, a semi-independent public body. Two years before this the first successful TELEVISION experiment had taken place. JOHN L. BAIRD (1888–1946), the inventor of television, was a son of the manse and was educated at Helensburgh and at the Royal Technical College, Glasgow. When still at school, he rigged up a private telephone system in order to communicate with his school chums. He was only eighteen when he set up a small laboratory to investigate the possibilities of seeing by wireless. He had a long and difficult period of waiting and hoping before his experiments proved successful. (At one time he ran a small shoe polish factory and at other times he acted as a salesman in order to raise sufficient money to keep going.) Baird's pictures were not at first very clear, and it was the cathode-ray tube invented in 1925 by Zworikyn, a Russian living in America, that made it possible to produce satisfactory pictures by wireless. In 1932 the B.B.C. started television tests, using Baird's low-definition system. When a regular television service from London opened in 1936, the systems of Baird and Marconi were used for a year, after which Baird's was abandoned. Baird has an honoured place as the pioneer of television, although his method is not that used today.

Some time after the Second World War, during which television was discontinued, the B.B.C. set up stations in different parts of the country, until in 1959 only the extreme north and west were unable to obtain reliable reception. Scotland began to receive regular television programmes in 1953; and commercial television, which had been introduced in the U.S.A. in 1941, was started in the following year. In sound broadcasting, great use has been made of recordings on magnetic tape since the 1930's. Programmes are recorded before the actual time of broadcasting, and the TAPE RECORDER reproduces concerts, interviews or talks of months or years before. Since the Second World War, police cars and taxis have been connected with their headquarters or head offices by mobile radio systems using HIGH FREQUENCIES. The substitution of TRANSISTORS for valves has made possible tiny transmitters and receivers, some of which are so small that they can be worn like a watch. Transmitters and other devices have been installed in the rockets fired into space so that information collected can be sent back to earth. At the beginning of the Second World War, both British and German scientists were working on what was then called radio location or RADAR, by which distant objects were located by means of wireless wave echoes reflected back. SIR ROBERT WATSON WATT (b.1892), a native of Brechin in Angus, was able in 1939, after research in the National Physical Laboratory, to establish a radar system to meet the threat of German air attacks. Although the Germans were also engaged in similar research, they never matched the British success with their radar system. It was used not only against air attacks but also in submarine detection and in surface warfare at sea; and it can be claimed with justice that radar was one of the decisive factors in the British victories in the Battle of Britain and the Battle of the Atlantic. RADIO TELESCOPES like the giant instrument, 250 ft. in diameter, at Jodrell Bank near Manchester, have enabled astronomers to study the universe in a more exact and detailed way than was ever thought possible before.

SOURCE EXTRACT
The First Solo Transatlantic Flight

At 10.22 on Saturday night Captain Charles Lindbergh, the lone American aviator, arrived at Le Bourget aerodrome, Paris, after a record-breaking journey of 3,000 miles from New York, which was performed in 33½ hours.

The Paris airport has never in its history witnessed such scenes as those of Saturday night, when a crowd estimated at between 100,000 and 200,000 swept down the iron barriers and, despite the efforts of a force of five hundred troops and police, swarmed on to the landing-ground as soon as Lindbergh's machine was sighted.

Shortly after ten o'clock there arose a murmur of long-suppressed excitement as the Ryan monoplane swung into the field of light created over the aerodrome by the searchlights and arc lamps. Twice the pilot made a circuit of the landing-ground, and then, having carefully chosen his point of descent, came down with a neatness and precision which astonished the observers. "Hullo, boys, I'm here!" said Lindbergh as he thrust his head out of the cockpit, and then, as though he could not quite believe that he had succeeded, he said "I'm Lindbergh. Where am I?"

While Lindbergh rested in the headquarters of the aerodrome, on a mattress stretched across three chairs, a section of the crowd had stormed the machine, and before this could be stowed in a hangar under a strong guard of troops, it had suffered considerable damage at the hands of souvenir hunters, who had torn off large pieces of the wing covering, chipped off lumps of aluminium, and even broken stays in their eagerness to secure a relic of the record-breaking achievement.

It must be realised that, once in his machine, Lindbergh, owing to the features of its construction, could never look out straight ahead directly, but only by means of a periscopic arrangement. To the left and to the right his view was uninterrupted through the windows. He carried no lights on board, but all the dials of his instruments were luminous.

His steering—this is what surprises the experts—was done entirely by means of one small compass. His route was marked out on maps on a scale of 1 in 1,000,000, besides those for the British Isles and France on a very much bigger scale. Lindbergh wore for his flight, breeches, thick woollen stockings and shoes, a moleskin waistcoat under his coat, and over this an overcoat, for he was not entirely enclosed.

Behind him in the cockpit of his machine was a chronometer, and on one side a bag of provisions and a tin of water, but there was no parachute and no wireless apparatus. A large knife, a pair of pliers, and the sealed barograph completed the equipment.

Daily Telegraph, May 23, 1927.

EXERCISES

1. Explain: Ensilage, ley-farming, terms of trade, trade cycle, "priming the pumps" of industry, insulin, supersonic, sputnik, transistor.
2. Write short notes on: Women's Land Army, J. M. Keynes, automation, Lord Nuffield, *Hindenburg*, Sir Frank Whittle, John L. Baird, Sir Robert Watson-Watt.
3. Write notes on: Road transport in the twentieth century; Sea transport in the twentieth century.
4. What are the reasons for the prosperity enjoyed by farmers during and since the Second World War?
5. Explain the reasons for the World Depression of the 1930's.
6. What are the main developments in flying since 1900?

CHAPTER XVI

THE TWENTIETH CENTURY

Twentieth-Century Materialism. In mid-Victorian times, there was a general feeling of optimism and a belief in progress: by the end of the century, although these feelings remained with some, there was also a pervasive scepticism that affected people's attitudes not only to religion but also to culture generally. The confident faith of the Victorians in the inevitability of progress, their highly moral and religious outlook on life and their idealism were replaced in the twentieth century by a cynicism and materialism which deepened as the century advanced. The poetry of the Victorian giants, Tennyson and Browning, is often inspired by a moral earnestness that is seldom found in twentieth-century verse. Browning's lines—

"A man's reach should exceed his grasp,
Or what's a heaven for?"

today seem old-fashioned. The prevailing tone of *The Waste Land* of T. S. Eliot, the most popular poet of the first half of the twentieth century, is that of a cynical commentary. George Bernard Shaw, who exposed popular prejudices and social abuses at the turn of the century in his witty and provocative plays had a conscious social purpose; but in the plays of Somerset Maugham, one of the leading playwrights of a generation later, there is little more than a mordant criticism of the weaknesses of mankind. Two world wars that spread such devastation and caused such terrible loss of life left many people embittered. The inter-war period included what is known in the United States as the "roaring twenties", when pleasure-seeking and a "good time" were given priority by those who could afford it, and also the World Depression, when misery and distress undermined any faith in the future. Religion generally has suffered a decline, the chief complaint of the churches today being about the apathy of their members; and sport, recreation and entertainment are regarded by many people in the twentieth century as more important to them than religion.

Scientific Revolution. The twentieth century has seen a revolution in science: what men in the nineteenth century deemed improbable has been accomplished—the splitting of the atom and the transformation of matter into energy. ALBERT EINSTEIN, a young German Jew, who was a technical expert in the patent office in Berne, challenged many of the traditional theories of physics in a book on a new theory of relativity published in 1905. In it, he expressed the relationship between matter and energy in his famous equation, $E = mc^2$. (In other words, the energy in matter is equal to the mass of that matter multiplied by the square of the velocity of light, 300,000 km. per second.) The experimental work that led to the modern use of nuclear energy and the demonstration that Einstein was right was undertaken by scientists in many countries, but the man who dominated all the rest was LORD RUTHERFORD. It was at the Cavendish Laboratory in Cambridge that Ernest Rutherford (1871–1937) began to make a name for himself as a physicist. Born in New Zealand, he was educated first at Canterbury, New Zealand, which he left in 1895 to work under Sir J. J. Thomson at the Cavendish Laboratory. Thomson, who discovered the electron in 1897, gathered round him the most brilliant scientists of his day, seventy of whom became professors, and Rutherford was later to have an even greater influence. Rutherford was professor in McGill University, Montreal and Manchester before returning to Cambridge in 1919 to succeed Thomson as head of the Cavendish Laboratory. At McGill University, Rutherford began to work out a theory that radio-activity depended on transformation of the elements, that when an element emits radiation it is being transformed into another element. During the First World War, he was engaged in experiments in underwater acoustics to counter the U-boat menace. In his first year as head of the Cavendish Laboratory, he concentrated his attention on splitting the atom, which feat he achieved in that year, 1919. His words when he demonstrated this experiment to his assistants were: "We are entering no-man's land". Shortly before his death in 1937, he could see little prospect of using nuclear energy for any industrial purpose. By that time, scientists all over the world, many of them former students of Rutherford, had been splitting atoms by different methods. It was in 1938 that OTTO HAHN, professor at Berlin University, found in an experiment in which he had "bombarded" a uranium nucleus with neutrons that there were two nuclei afterwards; in other words, he had produced NUCLEAR FISSION. Scientists in Germany, Sweden, Denmark, France and America, communicating their results to one another, were responsible for producing chain reaction by nuclear fission of U-235, an isotope of uranium. The first practical use that was made of chain reaction by nuclear fission was the manufacture of the atomic bomb, the story of which is told elsewhere. But scientists were keen to see the development of nuclear energy for peaceful purposes. The tremendous heat developed by nuclear fission was utilized by having a "coolant" (water or some other liquid) carry the heat out of the atomic pile or reactor; then, having turned to steam, it was used in a steam-turbine to generate electricity. Britain has played a prominent part in developing atomic or nuclear energy for peaceful purposes. The first nuclear power station in the world, CALDER HALL, in Cumberland, was opened in 1956. The electricity produced from a nuclear power station is still dearer than the electricity produced in an ordinary power station. The Americans in 1953 completed the building of the first nuclear powered ship, a submarine called *Nautilus*, which steamed over 60,000 miles on a single charge of fuel. Mankind stands on the threshold of a new age full of wonderful developments for the benefit of all if only it is possible to control this source of energy for peaceful use.

Medical Improvements. The story of medical science in the twentieth century is almost as marvellous a tale as that of atomic energy. Sir F. Gowland Hopkins, Professor of Biochemistry at Cambridge, was the first to show, in 1914, that there were present in food certain "accessory factors" unknown to the chemist but necessary for life. These were afterwards called VITAMINS and research has established that they are present in fresh food. They are designated by letters, vitamin C, the anti-scorbutic vitamin which prevents scurvy, being present in fresh fruit and vegetables, so that Captain Cook was making use of vitamins on his voyages without knowing of their existence. In 1921, a Canadian doctor, F. G. Banting, prepared INSULIN, which makes it possible for people suffering from diabetes to live a fairly normal life. The most notable development in twentieth-century medicine has been the production of ANTIBIOTIC drugs, which destroy the bacteria causing a disease. In 1935, a German chemist, Domagk, found that the aniline dye, prontosil, was able to destroy bacteria in the body, and in the following year chemists in the Pasteur Institute in Paris proved that the active constituent of prontosil was sulphanilamide. Within a short time a number of SULPHONAMIDE drugs were being used effectively to treat various diseases and illnesses, the most striking success being in the treatment of pneumonia, hitherto regarded as a very dangerous illness. Before the sulphonamide drugs were known, ALEXANDER FLEMING, a farmer's son from Darvel in

23

Ayrshire and Professor of Bacteriology at St. Mary's Hospital, London, had taken the first steps towards the production of one of the most useful drugs discovered. He had been experimenting in 1928 with a green mould or fungus called PENICILLIUM and had noticed that certain cultures of bacteria near the mould had ceased to grow. In one sense, this discovery could be said to have been accidental but it was due primarily to the skill and experience of the trained observer. It was not until the Second World War that PENICILLIN, a stable and reliable form of the mould, was produced by Oxford research workers. It saved thousands of lives during the war and Fleming was knighted for his services in 1944. Penicillin was an improvement on the sulphonamide drugs as it was an effective destroyer of bacteria that was not harmful when taken in large doses, although like the sulphonamides it sometimes had side-effects with certain people. Other products from fungi which have become available since the Second World War are streptomycin, produced in 1944 also and extremely valuable in dealing with some kinds of tuberculosis, and chloromycetin, useful in scrub typhus and other diseases. Among more recent advances in medicine has been the isolation, in 1949, of the virus of poliomyelitis (or infantile paralysis), which was followed by the preparation of a vaccine by the American DR. SALK that was given to millions of children in the U.S.A. in 1954. Unfortunately, some children died but later vaccines have proved successful and harmless. Inoculation and vaccination have become normal practices in preventive medicine, most children thus receiving protection from smallpox, diphtheria, tuberculosis and poliomyelitis. Social health (or public health) has also improved enormously by the provision of water supply to houses and also by the vast programme of house building undertaken since the war. Better food and better knowledge of food values, e.g. vitamins, have also contributed to better health. It has been said that the infant mortality rate (that of the deaths of infants under one year) is one of the clearest indications of the living conditions of the people. The following table shows clearly the advance in the last seventy years.

INFANT MORTALITY RATES

(per 1,000 live births)

	Scotland	England & Wales	Holland	Sweden	New Zealand
1886–90	121	145	175	105	84
1906–10	112	117	114	—	70
1936–40	76	55	37	42	32
1950	39	30	25	20	23
1957	29	23	17	16	20

Certain diseases seem to be on the increase, probably because people are no longer prone to so many illnesses as fifty years ago. Smallpox, scarlet fever, typhoid, diphtheria, tuberculosis account for very few deaths today. Among the illnesses which are more common are coronary thrombosis (which has been attributed to the strain of modern living), lung cancer (which is often associated with heavy smoking) and bronchitis (which is particularly bad in Britain because of the polluted atmosphere).

Exploration. It was in the first decade of the twentieth century that men were at last able to stand at the North and South Poles. In 1909, an American expedition under COMMANDER PEARY was successful in reaching the North Pole. It was in the same year that a British expedition, brilliantly organized and led by SIR ERNEST SHACKLETON, journeyed to within a hundred miles of the South Pole. Shackleton was compelled to turn back because of terrible blizzards, and managed to lead his party back to their base, keeping up their energies with strictly rationed cups of cocoa. He became a national hero in Britain, was knighted and awarded £20,000 by the Government. A Norwegian explorer, ROALD AMUNDSEN, who had himself been planning an Arctic expedition, heard of Peary's achievement and sailed south to the Antarctic in the *Fram*, the ship built for Nansen many years before. Amundsen had a straightforward and speedy journey to the South Pole, which he reached in December 1911. He had sent word of his intentions to another British explorer, CAPTAIN ROBERT F. SCOTT, who had been planning a similar expedition since 1909. Scott's expedition consisted of 59 men, some dogs and ponies, and three motor sledges. Scott, hampered by many difficulties (some of them of his own making), reached the South Pole more than a month later to find the Norwegian flag flying. The story of Scott's tragic return journey is one of heroic endurance on the part of Scott and his four companions. The bodies of three of the explorers, who had been overwhelmed by a blizzard and had died for lack of food, were found over a year later in a tent only eleven miles from a food depot. Scott wrote in his diary shortly before his death: "How much better has all this been than lounging in too great comfort at home!" These words sum up the spirit of the adventurous throughout the ages, and the story of Captain Scott has been an inspiration to many since his death. Shackleton, whom many regard as a greater explorer than Scott, undertook another expedition to the Antarctic at the beginning of the First World War; when the ice floes broke up, he managed, after a voyage in a small boat through terrible seas, to rescue the main party which had been stranded for two years. Antarctica has been explored since the First World War by Americans, Russians, Norwegians as well as British, using airships and aeroplanes; and a base was established by the Americans at the South Pole as part of their research activities during the International Geophysical Year of 1957-58. Since the North and South Poles have been conquered, the chief interest of explorers has been in mountaineering. Once all the Alpine peaks had been climbed, new and more difficult routes were explored. Often the conquest of a new ridge or face became a matter of international rivalry, as on the north face of the Eiger in Switzerland, where several climbers, German, Austrian and Italian, died in their attempts to make the first ascent before it was at last climbed in 1938. Several British expeditions were organized to scale MOUNT EVEREST, which was finally conquered in 1953 with the help of oxygen apparatus to overcome the difficulty of breathing at such a high altitude. The two climbers who actually reached the summit were SIR EDMUND HILLARY, a New Zealand bee-keeper, and TENZING, one of the Sherpa porters. Other Himalayan peaks have been climbed since then, including Kangchenjunga, not so high as Everest but a much more difficult mountain.

Religion. Since the beginning of the twentieth century, interest in religion in Britain has generally been on the decline. The scepticism of the late nineteenth century and the controversies about evolution tended to undermine the faith of many. In the First World War, when millions of servicemen were overseas, far from churches, and millions of workers in Britain were working on Sundays, the traditional routine of Sabbath observance was broken and never again restored. The "Continental Sunday" (in Catholic countries, people are allowed to engage in recreation after attending morning service) became popular in England in the 1920's, although in Scotland and Wales the change was resisted for a long time. Golf, swimming, tennis, polo were played regularly in England and, occasionally, in southern Scotland on Sundays. Cinemas were allowed to open on Sunday evenings in some places, at first for charities and, later, on a normal commercial basis. Broadcast religious services provided some kind of salve to the consciences of those who went for a Sunday's sport or recreation; but a service which could be cut short by turning a switch did not help to promote respect for religion. Only in some parts of Wales and in the Scottish Highlands and Islands was the Sabbath Day strictly observed: the FREE CHURCH OF SCOTLAND, which is still strong in the north and west of Scotland, remained the chief guardian of the Puritan tradition of respecting the fourth commandment by permitting only works of necessity and mercy on Sundays. Members of other churches in Scotland and England generally tended to satisfy themselves with a morning attendance at church, and gradually lapsed into visiting perhaps once a month or even less frequently. Apathy is difficult to conquer but the clergy in most churches have set themselves the task of attracting younger members by running youth clubs and similar organizations. In the CHURCH OF ENGLAND, the ANGLO-CATHOLIC MOVEMENT continued to be strong in the twentieth century. Clergy with High Church sympathies have introduced innovations in the ritual that occasionally provoked outbursts from some of their parishioners. When certain changes in the PRAYER BOOK were proposed in 1927, the National Assembly of the Church of

England approved of them by a large majority, as also did the House of Lords. On two occasions, however, in 1927 and 1928 the House of Commons rejected the proposed changes on the grounds that they savoured too much of High Church ritualism. Many of the M.P.s were, of course, Presbyterians who strongly opposed the changes. It was suggested at the time by some Anglicans that the Church of England would do better if it were disestablished from the state, as there would then be no need for parliamentary approval of a new Prayer Book. But the Church of England remains the established church, and in many churches the new Prayer Book, despite Parliament's rejection, was quietly introduced and accepted. The ROMAN CATHOLIC CHURCH differs from the Protestant churches in that there is little sign of decline in the twentieth century. The continued immigration of Irish Catholics has strengthened the Roman Catholic Church in the areas where they settled, e.g. the south-west of Scotland and Liverpool. In addition, there has been a small but significant stream of converts from the Church of England. Some of these were men of high ability such as G. K. Chesterton, Ronald Knox, Sir Arnold Lunn, Graham Greene, whose conversion influenced others to follow their example. MONSIGNOR RONALD KNOX (as he became) carried out a new translation of the Bible which was given the approval of the Pope. Another translation of the Bible into modern English was completed in 1924 by the REV. JAMES MOFFAT. Like all the recent translations of the Bible, however, it has been criticized by some scholars; and the Authorized Version of 1611 is still preferred because of its associations and traditions.

Architecture. The architecture of Queen Victoria's reign was almost entirely one of imitations. Most popular was the Gothic style, used not only for churches and castles but also for hotels and railway stations. In Scotland, the country houses of the wealthy were invariably built in the Scots Baronial style, complete with corbelled turrets and crow-stepped gables; and the same adornments were to be seen on town halls and schools. The most important new building of the twentieth century has been LIVERPOOL CATHEDRAL, the construction of which began in 1908.

It was designed by SIR GILES GILBERT SCOTT in Gothic style but with certain revolutionary innovations: the nave and chancel are the same length on opposite sides of the preaching space under the tower, the focal point of the cathedral instead of the altar as in medieval churches. As reactions to the monopoly of Victorian Gothic, at the end of the century came the simple cottage style, preferred by those who followed William Morris's teachings on art and politics, and the rather florid semi-Baroque style of the large banks, hotels and public houses. It was at the beginning of the twentieth century that the idea of the GARDEN CITY was carried out by the establishment of Letchworth Garden City in Hertfordshire in 1903. It had been conceived by Sir Ebenezer Howard as part of his scheme of land reform. This completely new and planned town was built on land owned by a joint stock company, any improvement in the value of the land to be for the benefit of the community. There was ample space for gardens and parks within the town, and it was surrounded by a green belt of farming land. Welwyn Garden City, also in Hertfordshire, was established in 1920. Since that time, in some housing estates such as Wythenshawe Estate near Manchester, an endeavour has been made to emulate the attractiveness of the garden cities. So far as dwelling houses are concerned, the twentieth-century tendency has been to prefer houses with gardens to flats in large blocks or tenements. The rows and rows of semi-detached houses on the outskirts of every large town mean a healthier life for the inhabitants although it very often has involved the loss of good farmland. There is a great variety of styles in housing estates, sometimes in the same road; one of the commonest has been the HALF-TIMBERING of the Tudor period. This can be seen even in Scotland, where bricks replaced the traditional stone as the building material except for parts of the north-east. The craze for the antique even led to the procuring of old beams from derelict country cottages, the thatching of the roof, weather-boarding, leaded glass panes, and inside the house low ceilings, wainscoting and log fires (sometimes imitation log fires lit by electricity). Public houses and tea-rooms in Tudor style became common sights between the wars; and not infrequently the passing traveller would alight from his motor-car to visit "Ye Olde Tudor Tea Shoppe". In the cities, the use of steel frames made possible very tall buildings like the Shell Mex building in London but not so high as to compare with the American skyscrapers. Since the beginning of the century, some firms had given attention to the lay-out and appearance of their factories, particularly the chocolate factories of Rowntree, Cadbury and Fry, these employers, as Quakers, taking a more enlightened interest in their employees than the average factory-owner. In the INDUSTRIAL ESTATES, the first of which were built just before the Second World War, the amenities provided in the factories and the pleasant surroundings are a marked contrast to "the dark Satanic mills" of Blake's England. In factories, schools, colleges, office buildings, libraries generally there has been evident in the last twenty years or so a tendency towards FUNCTIONALISM, which considers that the design and decoration should be functions of the purpose for which the building will be used.

Sport. The greatest change in the sphere of sport over the past fifty years has been the decline of Britain from its position of pre-eminence in the world. The occasional defeats at cricket by their Australian cousins the British did not find too difficult to bear after the first agonizing loss of "The Ashes" in 1882. It was different when defeats were administered by teams from the continent of Europe in sports distinctively British, like football. In the sphere of athletics, too, the British have had to yield to the superiority of foreign athletes, particularly in field events, although Britain has usually produced middle-distance runners to compare with the best in the world. The OLYMPIC GAMES, started hopefully in 1896 with the object of promoting harmony among the nations, unfortunately led to bickering. Athletes and officials were sometimes accused of bad sportsmanship in trying to further the interests of their country, as at London in 1908, when the Scottish runner, Lieut. Wyndham-Halswell was "boxed in" by the three other finalists, all American, in the 400 metres race. The Olympic Games have been held twice in Britain, in 1908 and 1948. On the first occasion, the marathon race ended with the disqualification of the Italian, DORANDO PIETRI, who entered the stadium first, collapsed and was helped over the finishing line by officials. He later received, however, a gold medal from Queen Alexandra, and the distance of the race, which had hitherto varied from 22 to about 25 miles, was fixed at 26 miles, 385 yards, the distance from Windsor Great Park to the White City Stadium. At the Paris Olympic Games in 1924, the Scottish runner, Eric Liddell, later a medical missionary in China, caused a sensation by declining to compete in the final of the 100 metres, as it was to be run on a Sunday, but managed to win the 400 metres in record time. The Berlin Games of 1936 saw the unique performance of the American negro, J. C. Owens, of winning four events (100 metres, 200 metres, long jump, 110 metres hurdles) to the discomfiture of Hitler and the Nazis, who rated negroes as belonging to an inferior race. It was after dropping a baton in a relay race at the Berlin Games, while her team was in a winning position, that a German woman committed suicide, an indication of the exaggerated importance with which success in the Games was regarded. It was not only over athletics that international squabbles arose: in 1933 the use of body-line bowling by the English cricketer, Larwood, led to heated controversy between Australians and Englishmen. What was once considered as impossible, the running of a mile inside four minutes, was first done by DR. ROGER BANNISTER at Oxford in 1954 in 3 minutes, 59·4 seconds. When CAPTAIN MATTHEW WEBB swam the Channel in 1875, the first man to do so, he took 21 hours, 45 minutes. Webb used the breast-stroke, the principal swimming stroke of the Victorians. In the twentieth century, new strokes like the trudgen and the crawl made possible much higher speeds, and in 1950 an Egyptian swimmer, H. ABD EL REHIM, actually recorded the fast time of 10 hours, 50 minutes. The most popular sport of the twentieth century, at any rate so far as the number of spectators is concerned, is ASSOCIATION FOOTBALL. Britain was the home of football: it had football clubs in every large town, it had the largest football grounds in the world (Hampden Park in Glasgow and Wembley Stadium in London) and from it went football coaches to help foreign clubs to improve their game. In time, the other countries were able to match the best from Britain and defeat them. In 1954, when the World Cup tournament was played for the first time, no British team survived to the final, in which West Germany defeated Hungary. In other sports, such as golf, tennis, rowing and boxing, the honours go round, the United States generally providing the majority of the winners. It has sometimes been asked whether the British are not becoming a nation of spectators; and comparisons have been drawn with the Roman people in their period of decline when they used to clamour for "bread and circuses". Increased urbanization, full employment with higher wages, more facilities for travel such as the motor-car, the increased professionalism and specialization in sport have all contributed towards making the modern youth prefer other things (including spectating) to participation in sport, which he can at any rate view more easily on television.

Leisure Time. Today there is much more leisure for the ordinary person than ever before. The five-day week, holidays with pay and higher wages have given people not only increased leisure but the money to spend in their leisure time. Holidays abroad are no longer the exclusive privilege of the well-do-to. Each summer, coach parties leave Britain to tour the Continent; and by contributing small amounts to a holiday fund, a man and his wife find the financial burden involved not too heavy. Caravans, camping, youth hostels all became popular in the 1930's and made cheap touring possible. There can be little doubt that the people of this country have travelled much more about Britain and the world than their grandparents did. Increased leisure has also been secured for the housewife. Relief from the drudgery associated with household tasks has only come to this country on a large scale since the Second World War, although the American housewife had for years before considered herself entitled by natural right to LABOUR-SAVING DEVICES in the home. Electricity has made the greatest difference to the housewife. Only in a few isolated places is paraffin now used for lighting; and yet, even in country districts where there is no electricity, the housewife has benefited by the coming of calor gas. Carpet sweepers, washing machines, dish-washing machines, cake-mixers, refrigerators, electric or gas fires, central heating—all help to make the housewife's lot an easier one. The widespread use of the HIRE PURCHASE SYSTEM has brought all these devices within the reach of almost everyone. In the workshops and in the offices, also, automatic or semi-automatic machines have eliminated the drudgery of former days. Buses or motor-cars make the journeys to and from work less arduous, but this saving of time has often been negatived by slum clearance schemes which removed whole communities to housing estates some miles away. What use is made of this increased leisure time? There is more general interest in sport, although often it takes the form of mere spectating. Young people, sometimes called "TEENAGERS" (the term, it seems, may be applied to those from sixteen to about twenty-four years of age), with more money than their elders had at their age, spend much of their time listening to "pop" music on their record players or dancing to it in the local dance-halls. Cinemas for the younger ones and television for the older ones also absorb much of their time. MOTORING, especially at weekends, has become so popular that motorists, keen to get away from the towns into the country, may spend six or more hours on a Sunday, bumper to bumper, in queues on busy roads. NEWSPAPERS also have exploited the increased leisure and incomes of the British people. The first cheap, popular newspaper was produced in 1881 by George Newnes: it was the weekly *Tit-Bits* and its success with the vast new reading public created by the extension of public education prompted ALFRED HARMSWORTH, later Lord Northcliffe (1865–1922) to start the *Daily Mail* in 1896. Although the Prime Minister, the Marquess of Salisbury, contemptuously described it as "written by office-boys for office-boys", it met an obvious demand. The circulations of the two largest national dailies in the 1950's, the *Daily Express* and the *Daily Mirror*, have soared to over four millions. The banner headlines, the abundant pictures, the gossip columns, the sensation-mongering in many of the national dailies offer a marked contrast to the newspapers of the late nineteenth century; and critics of what is called the "gutter-press" sometimes wonder whether the vast increase in the number of newspapers has been good for the country or the newspaper readers. Even with the more serious newspapers, like the *Sunday Times* and *Observer,* however, the circulations have quadrupled since before the war. Women's magazines multiply every year, the large advertising revenue enabling them to maintain their attractive, glossy appearance. Even LIBRARIES throughout the country report each year on increases in the number of books borrowed, so that not all the reading of the modern housewife is of ephemeral journalism. Many who failed to take advantage of their years at school have sought to make good the leeway in their education by attending evening classes, usually called ADULT EDUCATION CLASSES, run by the University Extension Movement, the Workers' Educational Association or by local education authorities in community centres. The twentieth century has thus seen a vast expansion of opportunities for all kinds of leisure.

SOURCE EXTRACTS

A   *Wembley Stormed*

Never before in all the wonderful history of our sports has anything been seen like the occurrences associated with the battle for the Football Cup, in the new and mighty Stadium of the British Empire Exhibition at Wembley on Saturday. There were amazing and incredible scenes, the result of failure to control crowds such as have never before gathered in so small an area in this country.

Some thousand people were injured—men, women, boys and girls. What happened should never have been. The assurance was given that "no longer need the public remain at home because they do not care to read the unwelcome announcement over the turnstile entrances, 'Gates closed'". But the gates were closed; at a modest estimate more than 60,000 people were shut out; thousands of ticket-holders were turned away. What we had been led to suppose was a perfect organisation was beaten and broken.

Gates were rushed, iron railings were bent and twisted and trampled down. The crowd poured in, and before the rush was over something like 200,000 people were packed into the arena and at the most there was but room for 125,000. . . .

What seemed to be but a handful of police accepted the inevitable; they could do nothing; they were lost in the crowd. Against iron railings, against cement walls, men and women were crushed and bruised; the whistles of overwrought, overworked, hot, tired, badgered ambulance men were blowing frantically; a casualty here, a casualty there, casualties everywhere.   *Daily Telegraph, April 30th, 1923.*

B   *Hillary's Account of the First Ascent of Everest*

At 6.30 a.m. we crawled out of our tents into the snow, hoisted our 30lbs. of oxygen gear on to our backs, connected up our masks and turned on the valves to bring life-giving oxygen into our lungs. A few good deep breaths and we were ready to go. The ridge was now all bathed in sunlight and we could see our first objective, the South Peak, far above us. We reached it at 9 a.m. The virgin ridge was certainly impressive, even rather frightening.

We cut a seat for ourselves just below the South Peak and removed our oxygen. Once again I worked out the mental arithmetic that was one of my main preoccupations on the way up and down the mountain. . . .

As my ice-axe bit into the first steep slope of the ridge, my highest hopes were realized. The snow was crystalline and firm. We moved one at a time. I would cut a forty foot line of steps, Tenzing belaying me while I worked. Then in turn I would sink the shaft of my ice-axe and put a few loops of rope round it and Tenzing, protected against a breaking step would move up to me. Then once again I would go on cutting.

After an hour's steady going we reached the foot of the most formidable looking problem on the ridge—a rock step some forty feet high. The rock itself, smooth and almost holdless, was here a barrier beyond our feeble strength to overcome. Fortunately, another possibility of tackling it still remained: a narrow crack running up the full forty feet of the step. I jammed my way into the crack. Taking advantage of every little rock-hold with all the force I could muster, I literally cramponed backwards up the crack.

As Tenzing paid out the rope I inched my way upwards until I finally dragged myself out of the crack on to a wide ledge. For a few moments I lay regaining my breath and for the first time felt the fierce determination that nothing could stop us reaching the top. As I heaved hard on the rope Tenzing wriggled his way up the crack and collapsed at the top like a giant fish just hauled from the sea. . . .

I went on cutting steps on the narrow strip of snow. The ridge seemed never-ending. Our original zest had now quite gone and it was turning more into a grim struggle. . . . I looked upwards to see a narrow snow ridge running up to a snowy summit. A few more whacks of the ice-axe in the firm snow and we stood on top.

Sir John Hunt: Our Everest Adventure.

EXERCISES

1. Football spectators and mountaineers are often criticized by other people: would you criticize either one or the other and, if so, why?
2. Explain: Continental Sunday, antibiotics, infant mortality rate, half-timbering, functionalism.
3. Identify the authors of the following and explain where necessary:
    (*a*) "We are entering no-man's land."
    (*b*) "How much better has all this been than lounging in too great comfort at home!"
    (*c*) "Written by office-boys for office-boys."
4. Write short notes on: Prayer Book revision in the twentieth century, Modern translations of the Bible, Ascent of Everest, Garden City Movement.
5. Write notes on: Lord Rutherford, Sir Alexander Fleming, Sir Ernest Shackleton, Captain Robert F. Scott, Olympic Games in modern times.
6. Give an account of the chief improvements in medical science in the twentieth century.
7. In what ways, other than in the manufacture of bombs, has nuclear energy been utilized?

CHAPTER XVII

PARLIAMENT

Franchise Extensions. The history of parliamentary government in modern Britain used to be considered mainly as the story of the extension of the franchise. The advance of democracy, it was thought, could be measured by the number of persons who had the right to vote. Today, it is not so readily assumed that democracy, which is often defined in Lincoln's words as "government of the people for the people by the people", can be achieved in a country by the mere granting of universal adult suffrage or even that it can be achieved at all in any large state. From the time of the Chartists (1838–48), however, manhood suffrage was a goal which reformers aimed at, not as an end in itself but as a means towards other ends, social equality and justice. In 1868, by the passing of the SECOND REFORM ACT of the previous year, the electorate was more than doubled but at 2,500,000 was still only about 10 per cent of the adult population. Women had no vote and the bulk of the population outside the large towns, that is in the rural areas and the many small industrial towns, was still unenfranchised. The Second Reform Act, by which the artisans or working-men in the large towns were enfranchised, revealed at once some of the weaknesses of the existing system. Bribery, corruption and intimidation were worse than before. In Gladstone's second ministry (1880–85) there was passed a CORRUPT PRACTICES ACT (1883), which prevented unauthorized payments at elections and helped the process of cleaning up British elections, begun by the Ballot Act (1872). It was in this ministry that the THIRD REFORM ACT of 1884 extended to the county constituencies the provisions of the Second Reform Act of 1867; that is, it enfranchised all male householders and lodgers, so that about 80 per cent of the male adults in the country could now vote. This reform had been pressed by Joseph Chamberlain and the Radicals for some time but his Whig colleagues had been reluctant to agree. There was also difficulty over the House of Lords, which Chamberlain castigated in aggressive speeches, describing the Conservative leader, Lord Salisbury, as the spokesman of the wealthy aristocrats "who toil not neither do they spin". At last, after the Conservative peers had insisted on the passing of a REDISTRIBUTION BILL also (to make the electorates in constituencies of more or less equal size) the Franchise Bill became law. This Act, which increased the electorate from 2,900,000 to over 5,000,000 had, along with the Redistribution Act, important results. Many of the two-member constituencies were abolished, thus helping to end the practice of Whig and Radical running in double harness at elections. This change, coupled with the large increase in working-class voters, led to the gradual disappearance of the Whigs except in the House of Lords. The extension of the franchise almost trebled the Irish electorate, assuring Parnell and the Irish Nationalists of victory everywhere except in the north-east. Women, however, still remained without the franchise, and equality with men at elections was not to be gained for almost fifty years.

Women's Suffrage. By the end of the century, education for women and girls was well established, many women possessed university degrees and held responsible posts in the professions. Women householders had been allowed to vote in muncipal elections since 1869 and in county council elections from 1888. By Forster's Education Acts of 1870 and 1872, women could both vote for and sit on parish school boards, and in 1894 they were given the same rights for parish councils. But in 1900 most men (and many women) believed it was wrong to allow women, however well educated, to vote in parliamentary elections, even although the right was granted to illiterate men. The gross injustice of this state of affairs at length provoked a violent reaction. In 1903 Mrs. Emmeline Pankhurst, widow of a Dr. Pankhurst who had been one of the founders of the I.L.P., started the WOMEN'S SOCIAL AND POLITICAL UNION, to press for women's suffrage or franchise at parliamentary elections. Parliament, however, took no notice of their polite and moderate requests, and they decided to use stronger methods to convince the male legislators at Westminster. Some of them padlocked themselves to the grille of the gallery in the House of Commons and interrupted the debates below with cries of "Votes for women!" Others broke up political meetings with similar outbursts; at a meeting in the Albert Hall in 1909, when Asquith addressed an audience of 10,000 men (women being expressly excluded to prevent any interruptions), one ardent young supporter of Mrs. Pankhurst concealed herself in the organ beforehand. As time went on, their actions became more violent: letter-boxes were burned, pictures in public galleries were slashed, the Coronation Chair in Westminister Abbey nearly destroyed by a bomb, the Jewel Case in the Tower smashed, policemen and cabinet ministers assaulted. When the SUFFRAGETTES (as they were called) were imprisoned, they went on hunger-strike, and the Government, faced with the responsibility for their deaths and being unwilling to make martyrs of them, had an Act passed allowing the suffragettes to be released and re-arrested later at will. This "CAT-AND MOUSE" ACT was much criticized and caused more exasperation and violence, the tactics of "the wild, wild women" leading many of their own sex to oppose the suffragette movement. Efforts made in Parliament by M.P.s sympathetic to the suffragettes proved fruitless. One young suffragette on Derby Day, 1913, threw herself in front of the King's horse when it was coming round Tattenham Corner and was killed; the procession of women at her funeral was one of the largest ever seen in London. But in the following year, 1914, when war broke out the suffragettes dropped their agitation and patriotically devoted their energies to helping the war effort. In nursing services, in offices, in factories, in farm-work the women played such important parts that there were few to cavil at Lloyd George's proposal in 1917 to extend the franchise to women. The RREPRESENTATION OF THE PEOPLE ACT (1918) gave the franchise for the first time to women over thirty years of age, provided they were either university graduates, house-holders or married to householders, and also to all male adults with the exception of peers, criminals and lunatics. (Those last, along with civil servants and clergymen of the Churches of England and Scotland and the Roman Catholic Church, were also excluded from the Commons.) The Act added nearly two million men and six million women to the electorate, making it sixteen millions in all, but still left a large number of women (about four millions) unenfranchised. The last step to full adult suffrage was taken under the Conservative government of Stanley Baldwin in 1928 when the EQUAL FRANCHISE ACT extended the franchise to women between twenty-one and thirty years of age

24

(the "flappers" as they were called at that time) and also to women over thirty who were not householders or wives of house-holders. The electorate as a result jumped by over five millions to 26,750,000; and in 1951 the number of electors had risen to over 34,000,000. The first woman elected to the House of Commons was an Irish Sinn Feiner, a Countess Markiewicz, who refused to take her seat after the election of 1918; but it was Viscountess Astor, elected in 1919, who was the first woman M.P. to appear in the House of Commons. Ten years later, Margaret Bondfield became the first woman Cabinet Minister on her appointment as Minister of Labour in Ramsay MacDonald's Government (1929–31). A few changes in the franchise have been made since the Second World War. In 1948 PLURAL VOTING was completely abolished. The Equal Franchise Act of 1928 had put an end to voting in two constituencies where voters had residences or business premises and an Act of 1948, passed during Attlee's Labour ministry, withdrew the extra vote of university graduates by abolishing the university constituencies. The principle of one adult, one vote was finally established.

House of Commons. Parliament has changed its character along with the electorate but not nearly to the same extent. The changes have naturally been most noticeable in the House of Commons. From being a house of landlords, as it was before 1832, it has come to include more and more of other classes. Working-men were slow to reach Parliament, the first two, Alex MacDonald and Thomas Burt, being elected in 1874. By the end of the century a number of trade unionists had become M.P.s with the help of Liberal party and trade union funds. These funds made possible a salary of about £200 per annum, which compared favourably with the wages of that time (about 35s. per week for a skilled tradesman). The Osborne Judgement of 1908, which declared the trade unions' political levy illegal, made it difficult for working-men to be M.P.s; but their position was eased by an Act of 1912 which allowed the payment of £400 per annum to M.P.s and another Act of 1913 which restored the trade unions' right to levy for a political fund. The salaries of M.P.s have been raised since then to £600 in 1937, to £1,000 in

1946, and in 1957 stood at £1,000 plus a tax-free expenses allowance of £750. The number of M.P.s has also altered during this century as can be seen from the following table.

NUMBER OF M.P.s

	1901	*1918*	*1922*	*1955*
England	461	492	492	511
Wales	34	36	36	36
Scotland	72	74	74	71
Ireland	103	105	13	12
Totals	670	707	615	630

(The highest total, 707 in 1918, included the Irish M.P.s, few of whom attended Parliament; and from 1922 the only Irish M.P.s have been from Northern Ireland. The abolition of university constituencies in 1948 accounts for the Scottish figures declining from 74 to 71 and the Irish figures from 13 to 12.) To the outsider, the main business of the House of Commons seems to be that of LEGISLATION or making laws. The procedure involved in making an Act of Parliament is a long one, intended to ensure that, by thorough discussion and debate, the weak parts of the Bill are deleted and necessary improvements made. There are three "readings" of the Bill (the word "reading" only means nowadays that, as members have printed copies of the Bill in front of them, the Bill is taken as read); and each reading represents a definite stage in the Bill's progress. The FIRST READING serves merely for the introduction of the Bill, and there is invariably no debate or voting at this stage. The SECOND READING follows a general debate on the principles of the Bill; should it survive this stage, there is every reason to expect the Bill to become an Act in due course. After the second reading comes the COMMITTEE STAGE, when the Bill is considered, clause by clause, by a Committee of the House, usually comprising forty to sixty members and meeting upstairs in a committee room above the House. (The SCOTTISH GRAND COMMITTEE, for consideration of Scottish Bills, is larger than the other committees, as it includes all the seventy-one Scottish members and enough English and Welsh members to have the parties in the Committee in the same proportion as in the House itself.) Much time is spent on the committee stage, and it is at this stage that the Bill is carefully scrutinized and amendments moved. After the committee stage comes the REPORT STAGE, when the amendments are considered by the whole House, and finally the THIRD READING, when the Bill is debated again in its latest form and voted upon. The Bill then goes through a similar process in the House of Lords but occasionally the reverse happens,

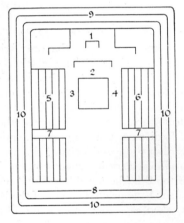

1 Speaker's Chair
2 Clerks' Table
3 Government Front Bench
4 Opposition Front Bench
5, 6 Back Benches
7 Gangways
8 Bar of the House
9 Press Gallery
10 Galleries

House of Commons

the Bill being initiated in the Upper House. The House of Lords may delay the passing of the Bill for a year by exercising its VETO; but finally the Bill becomes an Act by the signature of the Sovereign, which is nowadays never withheld. Various devices have been invented for shortening and controlling debates. The CLOSURE, by which a debate can be terminated by a simple motion being carried, goes back to 1881, the heyday of Irish obstruction, when a succession of all-night sittings and marathon debates nearly paralysed the work of the House. The

GUILLOTINE, first used in 1887 (also in a debate on Ireland) is a kind of closure by compartments: if the Government feels that the Opposition is taking too long with its amendments to a Bill, a certain number of amendments are allotted to each day and the amendments that are not reached by the end of the day are "guillotined". Not all the time of the House of Commons is spent on discussing Bills. There may be protracted debates on specific motions perhaps involving censure of the conduct of a minister, and at the beginning of each session after the QUEEN'S SPEECH, which is a statement of the Government's policy prepared by the Prime Minister and Cabinet, the moving of an Address to the Queen gives the Opposition the chance to criticize the Government's policy. A good part of the session is also spent in discussing finance, when the whole House goes into Committee, the COMMITTEE OF SUPPLY for the expenditure side and the COMMITTEE OF WAYS AND MEANS for the revenue side. Every day of the session starts with prayers and then generally goes on to QUESTION TIME, when members can question ministers about grievances or complaints that have been brought to their notice. It may be that in asking about an alleged grievance a member makes a statement which would be regarded as slander if uttered outside the House; but he is protected from legal action by his PRIVILEGE as M.P. Many people consider that the ventilation of grievances is one of the most important functions of Parliament, as it provides a check on the abuses of government powers by officials; in countries where this is not possible, a bureaucracy develops powers which are akin to dictatorship. Newspapers often give as much space to parliamentary questions as they do to debates. There is also a daily official report of all the proceedings in Parliament; this report, called Hansard after one of the early printers, T. C. Hansard, is available in most public libraries.

Political Parties. Last century there were two great parties in Parliament, the Conservative and the Liberal; today there are also two, the Conservative and the Labour parties. To what extent is it true, as is often said, that British parliamentary government favours the two-party system? Certainly, the experience of the first half of the twentieth century, which has

BRITISH PARTY POLICIES IN 1951

	CONSERVATIVE	LIBERAL	LABOUR
Defence	Champion of strong defence forces, including nuclear weapons.	For reduction of defence expenditure to minimum possible; some Labour M.P.s against nuclear weapons.	
Foreign Policy	All more or less similar but Liberal and Labour more in favour of U.N.O. than Conservatives.		
Imperial Policy	British security given priority; maintenance of empire if possible, but prepared to grant self-government by slow degrees.	Both strongly opposed to racialism and more ready to grant self-government.	
Finance	Keen to reduce taxation. Prefers not to cut defence expenditure.	Prefers not to cut expenditure on social services.	Believes in taxation as a form of redistribution of wealth.
Industry (*Nationalized*)	Accepts nationalization of 1945–51 except for steel and road transport; against bureaucratic control.	Against bureaucratic control.	In favour of more public control.

Industry (Private Sector)	Favours management and ownership as against trade unions; against controls and restrictions.	Favours profit-sharing by employees.	Favours controls where necessary, e.g., in directing new industries to depressed areas.
Agriculture	Fairly similar, in favour of guaranteed prices for a period of years; Labour more favourable in matter of subsidies.		
Social Services	Urges economy in administration.	Stresses importance of private individual's wishes.	In favour of expansion; less concerned about finance.
Education	Maintenance of grammar schools and of fee-paying.	Like Cons., but with more financial assistance for education.	Favours comprehensive schools; against fee-paying schools.
Scottish and Welsh Home Rule	Against.	For.	Against but formerly for.

seen the decline of the Liberal party as the Labour party gained in strength, would seem to support this view. Up to the First World War there were for a long time three, and for a short time four, parties—the Conservative or Unionist, the Liberal, the Irish Nationalist parties and the Labour party. One of the usual features of a parliament where there are several parties is that the government is a COALITION and as such pursues a policy which is based on a compromise between the parties in the coalition. As neither party can afford to offend the other party and so break up the coalition, the result is likely to be a policy that is indecisive. In Britain, successful coalitions have been formed in the two world wars, when the national emergency has enabled the parties to co-operate more easily; but the only peace-time coalition government of this century, Lloyd George's ministry of 1918–22, was always in difficulties, partly because of the numerous political and economic problems that confronted them but also because of the strain involved in holding Liberals and Unionists together. In 1931 a National Government was founded under the Labour Prime Minister, Ramsay MacDonald, but it was so predominantly Conservative, with only a handful of Labour M.P.s, that it could hardly be considered a coalition government. Sometimes, two parties work together without forming a coalition government. This happened when the Irish Nationalists supported the Liberals over the Parliament Bill in 1910–11 in return for a promise to pass the Irish Home Rule Bill. The decline of the Liberal party was due to a number of reasons, mainly connected with the split in the party that developed in the First World War when Lloyd George ousted his leader, Asquith, from the office of Prime Minister. Although a reunion of the two small Liberal parties came about in 1922, it no longer had the support of the working-classes, which Lloyd George had tried before the war to retain but which gradually passed to the Labour party. The Liberals also lost favour with other electors for the part they played in 1923–24 when they put the Labour Government in office and helped them to stay there for almost a year. A centre party like the Liberals can lose supporters to both the right and the left, the Conservative and the Labour parties. An American observer once remarked that in Britain there are three "centre" parties, whose policies overlap; and thus the Liberals are left with little ground in their party programme that is not already covered by the Conservative and the Labour parties. Once the decline began it was difficult to stop. A party may poll fairly well in all the constituencies and even finish in second place in most of them, but its share of seats in the House of Commons may be disappointingly low, as can be seen from the accompanying table.

PARLIAMENTARY ELECTION, 1924

Party	Votes polled		Seats gained	
	No. (approx.)	Percentage	No.	Percentage
Conservative	7,500,000	47	382	68·5
Labour	5,500,000	34	142	25·5
Liberal	3,000,000	19	34	6

(There were also 57 uncontested seats, mainly Conservative.)

There comes a stage when some supporters of a small third party feel that a vote for a party with no chance of forming or even influencing a government is a vote wasted. Sometimes the Liberals have done comparatively well at by-elections, which provide an opportunity for electors to voice their protest on some issue without bringing the Government down. It was at by-elections that representatives of other small parties (such as the Commonwealth and Scottish Nationalist parties) have won seats; but they, like the Communists, who have occasionally won a seat and in 1945 two seats, normally lose their deposits of £150 at general elections. The system of PROPORTIONAL REPRESENTATION, by which the number of seats gained is in proportion to the votes cast, is practised in many countries on the continent and to some extent in New Zealand and South Africa.

It would give the Liberals and other small parties a chance to make their voices heard; but it could only be introduced if it were supported by one of the two major political parties, and neither is likely to support a measure which would affect its power adversely. A voter today may have the choice of voting for one or other of two parties neither of which has a policy that appeals to him or leaders in whom he has confidence. Sometimes, therefore, his vote may be given against the party for which he has the greater distrust rather than for the party for which his vote is cast. Sometimes also the position is more complicated when the personality of the candidates is taken into account; the vote then may be for the man rather than the party. But in the long run, although there are a few exceptional M.P.s of independent mind, it is the party not the individual member that counts. Since the organization of the parties in national federations, the control of the party over its members has become increasingly strong. A too independent attitude in parliament may mean the withdrawal of official approval and support at the next election. Resignation from the Government or party or opposition to the party policy on one issue need not be so damaging to a member's prospects of promotion: three Conservatives have done so this century and have later become Prime Ministers—Sir Winston Churchill (twice and once also from the Liberal party), Sir Anthony Eden (over Italy) and Harold Macmillan (over Abyssinia).

Parliament Act. The position of the House of Lords has altered considerably since the Victorian age when it frequently rejected legislation passed by the Commons, notably the Irish Home Rule Bills. Since the resignation of the Marquess of Salisbury in 1902, no peer has been chosen as Prime Minister; and the Cabinet shows nowadays a predominance of members of the Lower House, whereas in Gladstone's Cabinet of 1880 half of the members were peers and in Salisbury's Cabinets generally more than half. It was the prolonged struggle over the PEOPLE'S BUDGET in 1909, a climax to the Lord's rejection of several Bills in the early years of the Liberal ministry, that led to a settlement of the constitutional issue between Lords and Commons. The

House of Lords, which a Unionist M.P. had called "the watchdog of the constitution", had become, it seemed to the Liberals, "Mr. Balfour's Poodle". This phrase, coined by Lloyd George, referred to the claim of A. J. Balfour, the Unionist leader, that his party, although defeated in the 1906 election, "would continue to control the destinies of the Empire" (through their large majority in the House of Lords). The People's Budget, whether they so intended it or not, became the battleground for a struggle between Lords and Commons in which the Liberals felt that popular sympathy was on their side. In the first election of 1910, in January, they were returned to power with a reduced majority; but the Lords, bowing to the will of the electorate, passed the 1909 Budget without a division just on the eve of the introduction of the 1910 Budget despite a speech by Lord Milner to reject it and "damn the consequences". The reform of the House of Lords and its power now became the issue. Some Unionists, seeing the writing on the wall, produced plans which would have diminished the hereditary element and made the House of Lords more like the Senate in the United States and in other countries. The Liberals were afraid that a reformed House of Lords would still reject their Bills, and were thus inclined to leave the Upper House unreformed but with curtailed powers. During 1910, conferences were held between the leaders of the two parties at the request of the new King, George V, who succeeded his father, Edward VII, on his death in May of that year. The party leaders were unable to agree as the Liberals, with their reduced majority, were dependent on the Irish vote and felt obliged to re-introduce a Bill for Irish Home Rule, which the Unionists would never accept. At length Asquith and the Liberals produced the PARLIAMENT BILL to restrict the powers of the Lords. This was to be effected in three ways:—(1) Bills certified by the Speaker of the House of Commons as "money bills" were to become law without being considered by the House of Lords at all; (2) Any other Bill passed in three successive sessions by the House of Commons and rejected by the House of Lords would go straight to the King for his signature; (3) The maximum duration of Parliament would be five instead of seven years.

Another election was held in December 1910; there was sur-
prisingly little public interest and the total poll fell by over a
million but the balance of parties was almost unchanged. The
Prime Minister, Asquith, had taken some time to make up his
mind and his stock answer to questions on the subject for some
time had been, "Wait and see!" But before the election he had
received from King George a pledge that if the Unionist peers
threw out the Parliament Bill, he would exercise the royal
prerogative to create sufficient Liberal peers to pass the Bill,
as William IV had similarly promised the Whigs in 1832 in
connection with the Reform Bill. The debates in the House of
Commons were protracted and acrimonious, with a brief lull
for the King's coronation in May. Another international crisis
blew up in this year over Morocco but did nothing to deaden
the conflict at home. On one occasion Asquith tried for half an
hour to make himself heard against the interruptions of the
Opposition and eventually had to sit down—a scene unparalleled
in the history of the House. It was not until mid-August (in
one of the hottest summers ever known in Britain—a record
temperature of 100°F. was registered at Greenwich Observatory
on August 9th) that at last the Bill passed through the House of
Lords and reached the King for his signature. The Unionist
peers were divided, over a hundred "Die-hards" voting against it,
the majority abstaining, and about 30 voting with the Liberals,
as they preferred the Bill to the alternative of being swamped
by some 300 newly-created peers. The effects of the Parliament
Act were to strengthen the hands of the Commons, who thereupon
used the new procedure for the passing of two Bills long delayed
by the Lords—the Irish Home Rule Bill and the Welsh Church
Disestablishment Bill. Since 1911, the House of Lords, shorn of
absolute veto, has occupied a humble place in the constitution.
The Labour Government of Clement Attlee (1945–50) went
further in curtailing the Lords' powers. By the PARLIAMENT
ACT (1949) the Lords' veto was reduced from two years to one
year: a Bill which was passed by the Commons in two successive
sessions would thus, despite rejection by the Lords, go to the
Sovereign for signature. This Act was itself introduced as a Bill

in 1947 and passed in three successive sessions by the Commons. Two Bills of Attlee's Ministry were rejected by the Lords on the grounds that they had not been among the proposed measures included in the Labour party's election manifesto: these were the Bills for nationalizing the steel industry and the Parliament Bill itself. The proposal to suspend capital punishment was also rejected by the House of Lords in 1948 on the grounds that it had passed through the Commons by only a small majority and that it lacked public approval.

House of Lords. The House of Lords has had its powers considerably curtailed in this century but it is still a useful part of the constitution. Although there are over 900 peers, the average attendance is about 50, but the debates are of a high standard. Among the regular attenders are some of the 25 Lords Spiritual (the bishops, led by the Archbishop of Canterbury), the 16 elected Scottish peers, the life peers and peeresses created under the terms of the Life Peerages Act (1958), and the Labour peers, who are so few in number that they have to put in an appearance more frequently than the Conservatives. The LORD CHANCELLOR, who sits on the Woolsack, combines three important functions: he presides over the debates of the House of Lords, he is the highest judge in the English law-courts, and he is a member of the Cabinet. The post usually goes to a leading lawyer who has given some years of faithful political service to the party with a majority in the House of Commons. The Lord Chancellor is one of the Lords of Appeal who decide law suits that go to the House of Lords, the supreme court of appeal for civil cases. Appeals are heard before at least three Lords of Appeal, who are law lords holding life peerages and must include a Scottish Lord of Appeal in Scottish cases. By the LIFE PEERAGES ACT (1958) two minor changes were effected by Macmillan's Conservative Government: life peerages were conferred on persons other than judges, and women were permitted to enter the House as life peeresses. Various other proposals have been made to alter the composition of the House of Lords, e.g. by reducing the proportion of hereditary peers and inviting representatives of the professions, trade unions and other bodies to become members of the House. But the Labour party, like the Liberal party before it, is more interested in restricting its powers than in making it more representative of the nation. A reformed House of Lords would probably still be Conservative in character and might be given more powers that would detract from those of the House of Commons.

Home Rule Movements before 1914. The Irish Home Rule question loomed so large in British politics in the nineteenth century that it is dealt with in a separate chapter elsewhere. It was partly responsible for the birth of the Scottish and Welsh Home Rule movements. At one time it was envisaged that there would be four parliaments in the British Isles—one at Westminster and the other three for Ireland, Scotland and Wales. There had been discontent for a long time with the way in which Scottish affairs had been administered. In principle, they were controlled by the Home Secretary with the help of the Scottish Lord Advocate but in practice they were left to the latter, who was normally too busy in his work in the law-courts to bother much about other matters. Agitation in the early 1880's led to the appointment by Gladstone in his second ministry of a Scottish Under-Secretary for Home Affairs; the office was given to the young Liberal peer, the Earl of Rosebery, who had himself been one of the strongest advocates for a separate department for Scottish affairs. In 1885, a Secretary for Scottish Affairs was appointed with a seat in the Cabinet but the office was given to an Englishman, Sir George Trevelyan, and in the following year (which saw the introduction of the first Irish Home Rule Bill) a Scottish Home Rule Association was formed. The chairman was Dr. G. P. Clark, Liberal M.P. for Caithness, and the secretary was R. B. Cunninghame Graham, Liberal M.P. for Lanarkshire and one of the founders of the Scottish Labour party. From this time on, nearly all Scottish Liberal and, later, Labour M.Ps were in favour of Home Rule for Scotland. English Liberals, who supported Irish Home Rule, also tended to favour Scottish Home Rule. But, although the Liberals were always in a large majority in Scotland from 1880 to the end of the century, the Conservatives and Unionists were in control at Westminster for most of the time. The motions put forward almost annually from 1889 to 1900 in favour of a separate Scottish Parliament were unsuccessful except for one occasion in 1894 when the Liberals were in power under Lord Rosebery. In the previous year, when Gladstone was Prime Minister, a SCOTTISH GRAND COMMITTEE was set up to deal with Scottish Bills. This committee did not become a standing (or regular) committee until 1907; it contained English M.P.s to maintain the balance of the parties as Scotland's proportion of Liberal M.P.s was much higher than in England. Earlier, in 1889, when COUNTY COUNCILS were set up in Scotland during Salisbury's ministry, it was hoped that the grant of some local government powers would help to damp down Home Rule agitation; and in 1894 the process was carried a step further by the setting up of parish councils. No Bill for Scottish Home Rule was introduced until 1908, by which time the Liberals were in power with a commanding majority. From 1908 to 1914 five Bills passed the first or second readings and a motion that Irish Home Rule should be followed by Scottish Home Rule was also carried. But each session came to an end without the later stages of the Bills being considered; and when war broke out in 1914, the debate on the latest Scottish Home Rule Bill stood adjourned. The support received from the Government, who alone could provide time for consideration of a Bill, was at best lukewarm. Their attention was certainly taken up with the bitter struggle over the Irish Home Rule Bill, which passed into law in the spring of 1914; and it is conceivable that had war not broken out, Asquith, the Liberal Prime Minister, would have redeemed the promise he made in 1912 to follow up Irish Home Rule with Scottish Home Rule. The movement for WELSH HOME RULE started also in the 1880's under the inspiration of the successful Irish Nationalist campaign. It was closely linked with the movement for Welsh Disestablishment, that is, for disestablishing and disendowing the Anglican Church in Wales, where the Nonconformists were strong in their opposition to what they considered an alien church. The movement for Disestablishment absorbed most of the nationalists' energies for many years. It was not until 1920 that the Welsh Disestablishment Bill was finally passed, after being rejected by the House of Lords in two successive sessions at the beginning of the First World War. Some motions for Scottish Home Rule before the war had also contained proposals for Welsh Home Rule; but after the war the agitation for separate Parliaments in both countries died down for some time.

Devolution. When the question of Home Rule was discussed after the First World War, it was mainly as a means of relieving the congestion of business in the Parliament at Westminster. The steps taken towards devolution of government—the appointment of a Secretary for Scotland (a title changed to that of Secretary of State for Scotland in 1926), the setting-up of county councils and parish councils—had done nothing to reduce the amount of time spent on Scottish affairs in Parliament but rather the reverse. The Scottish Grand Committee had helped a little to ease the congestion of business by considering Scottish Bills at the committee stage before the third reading. But on nine occasions after 1918 when motions or Bills proposing Home Rule in one form or another were presented to the House of Commons, with large majorities of Scottish M.P.s in favour, they were crowded out by pressure of other business. No Government of course is seriously interested in getting rid of the chronic congestion of business at Westminster, as it would thereby lose a good reason for not accepting awkward Bills. The frustration felt by Home Rulers about the reception of their proposals in Parliament led to the formation in 1921 of two groups in Scotland, both seeking fairly similar measures of self-government, the National Party and the Scottish Party, which united in 1934 as the SCOTTISH NATIONAL PARTY. But although several candidates stood for Parliament, they won only one seat, at a by-election in 1945 when Dr. Robert Macintyre was returned for Motherwell. There were many reasons for expecting the party to gain strong support in the 1930's: in particular, there was a strong feeling that the state of employment, housing and health (which were very much worse than in England) pointed to a neglect of Scottish affairs. After the Second World War, the nationalization of industries added another cause for grievance, as more and more it seemed that Scottish affairs were being determined in Whitehall. In 1949, a SCOTTISH COVENANT was drawn up and signed by over two million people who thereby pledged themselves to press for a Scottish Parliament; and a sensation was caused at Christmas 1950 when, as a gesture of protest, the Coronation Stone (the so-called "Stone of Destiny") was removed by some young Scottish Nationalists from Westminster Abbey. But the signatories of the Covenant have almost invariably voted Labour or Conservative or Liberal at elections, and a separate Scottish Parliament seems no more likely than before. The attitudes of both major political parties to Scottish Home Rule are now similar, although the Labour party supported the idea until it gained power in 1945. Scottish M.P.s maintain that separation would deprive Scotsmen of the opportunity of contributing to the solution of world problems, as defence, foreign and imperial affairs would not be considered by a Scottish Parliament. Conservative M.P.s regard the close links between English and Scottish industry and trade as obstacles to Home Rule, while Socialist M.P.s emphasize the benefits of international co-operation and planning on a large scale. Each of the major political parties also tends to attribute the ills of Scotland to the policy of the rival party, while the Liberal party, which has had no experience of government since the days of the Coalition in 1922, is alone in thinking that these ills can be remedied (or partly remedied) by Home Rule. Some devolution of government has been granted but the final control remains with the Parliament and Treasury in London. In 1939 the Scottish Office was transferred from Whitehall to ST. ANDREW'S HOUSE in Edinburgh; and new appointments were made in 1951 and 1952—a Minister of State, normally resident in Scotland, and a third Under-Secretary of State. Since 1948, also, the Scottish Grand Committee has been able to debate Scottish Bills at the second reading stage, while it discusses Scottish estimates for six days each session, its only opportunity for a general review of Scottish affairs. As with Scotland, so with Wales. After many years of campaigning by the small but vigorous Welsh Nationalists, who have demanded a separate

25

Welsh Parliament, the greatest concession so far has been the creation in 1954 of a separate MINISTRY FOR WELSH AFFAIRS. But it has been linked usually with some other ministry, e.g. the Home Office in 1954 and the Ministry for Housing and Local Government in 1959. It is interesting to note that all these small changes in administration have been made by the Conservatives, who have always been opposed to Home Rule in principle.

SOURCE EXTRACTS

A   *The Prime Minister to the Leader of the Opposition*
                                    10, Downing Street,
                                    July 20, 1911.

DEAR MR. BALFOUR,

I think it courteous and right, before any public decisions are announced, to let you know how we regard the political situation.

When the Parliament Bill in the form which it has now assumed returns to the House of Commons, we shall be compelled to ask the House to disagree with the Lords' amendments.

In the circumstances, should the necessity arise, the Government will advise the King to exercise his prerogative to secure the passing into law of the Bill in substantially the same form in which it left the House of Commons, and His Majesty has been pleased to signify that he will consider it his duty to accept and act on that advice.

                                    Yours sincerely,
                                    H. H. ASQUITH.

B   *From My Diary, July 24th, 1911*

The Speaker's Gallery was closely packed, and excited ladies were standing up on their chairs. My husband got a deafening reception as he walked up the floor of the House; but I saw in a moment that the Opposition was furious and between the counter-cheers I could hear an occasional shout of "Traitor!" When the hubbub had subsided he rose to move the rejection of the Lords' amendments: at this Lord Hugh Cecil and Mr. F. E. Smith (later Lord Birkenhead) led an organized and continuous uproar which kept him on his feet for over thirty minutes. "Divide! Divide! 'Vide! 'Vide!!!" was shouted by the Opposition in an orgy of stupidity and ruffianism every time he opened his mouth. The Speaker tried in vain to make them listen, but the

House was out of hand and the uproar continued. Looking at the frenzied faces from above, I realized slowly that Henry was being howled down. Edward Grey got up from his place four off from where my husband was standing, and sat down again close beside him. His face was set. I scrawled a hasty line from our stifling gallery and sent it down to him. "They will listen to you—so for God's sake defend him from the cats and the cads!" Arthur Balfour followed, and when Grey rose to speak the stillness was formidable. Always the most distinguished figure in the House, he stood for a moment white and silent, and looked at the enemy: "If arguments are not to be listened to from the Prime Minister there is not one of us who will attempt to take his place," he said and sat down in an echo of cheers. Mr. F. E. Smith rose to reply, but the Liberals would not listen to him and the Speaker adjourned the House on the ground of grave disorder. I met Edward Grey for a moment afterwards alone, and when I pressed my lips to his hand, his eyes filled with tears.

Margot Asquith, Autobiography.

C   *Question Time in the House of Commons*

MR SIDNEY MARSHALL (Sutton and Cheam, Cons.) asked the Minister of Education whether ample supplies of one-third pint bottles are now available for school milk distribution; and to what extent in London and the home counties supplies are still being distributed by the teaching staffs in all sorts and kinds of odd containers from bulk. MISS WILKINSON (Minister of Education): I regret that ample supplies of one-third pint bottles for school milk distribution are not yet available, but all possible steps are being taken to increase the supply and a gradual improvement in the position is expected. I am informed that in all but a few schools in London and the neighbouring areas milk is now being delivered in bottles and delivery in churns has been discontinued.
MR MARSHALL; Is the Minister aware that in January she said the supply of bottles would get better and that up to now there has, in fact, been no improvement? It is a very serious matter that teachers' time should be taken up distributing this milk from bulk and can she do anything in this regard?
MR PETER FREEMAN (Newport, Lab.): May I ask the Minister to consider the use of carton containers for this purpose? They are in supply and much more hygienic than this present system and would do away with washing bottles.

MISS WILKINSON: I am fully aware of all the uses of cartons, but they are available only in a few places and the Ministry of Supply cannot give us the amount of wax paper necessary for the job.

MR JAMES HUDSON (Ealing W., Lab.): Could not the Minister divert some of the beer bottles to this purpose?

Hansard, April 11th, 1946.

D   *Examples of Political Vocabulary*

1. (*a*) Your party "indulges in opportunist shilly-shallying".
   (*b*) Our party "displays the requisite flexibility".
2. (*a*) Your party "resorts to rash make-shifts".
   (*b*) Our party "meets the emergency with prompt resourcefulness".
3. (*a*) Your party "shows its usual stubbornness in face of the facts".
   (*b*) Our party "has pursued a consistent policy throughout a difficult period".
4. (*a*) Your party "is emotional in its outlook".
   (*b*) Our party "shows a warm and sympathetic understanding of the nation's problems".
5. (*a*) Your party "indulges in irresponsible criticism".
   (*b*) Our party "exposes the fallacies of the opposition's policy".

(Adapted from list originally published in *Manchester Guardian* and quoted in Denys Thompson's *Between the Lines*.)

EXERCISES

1. Explain the connection between the first two extracts given above.
2. Explain: "Cat-and-Mouse Act", flappers, plural voting, committee stage, report stage, veto, closure, guillotine, Committee of Supply, Committee of Ways and Means, proportional representation, devolution.
3. Identify the authors of the following and explain where necessary:
   (*a*) "Government of the people by the people for the people."
   (*b*) "Damn the consequences!"
   (*c*) "Wait and see!"
4. Write short notes on the following: Ballot Act; Mrs. Pankhurst; Representation of the People Act, 1918; Equal Franchise Act, 1928; Scottish Grand Committee; Parliament Act, 1949; life peerages.
5. Write notes on the following: Third Reform Act; Parliament Act, 1911; Scottish Home Rule movement.
6. Give an account of the extensions of the franchise since 1880.

7. Trace the steps by which women have achieved political equality with men.
8. How does a Bill become an Act of Parliament?
9. Is it true to describe the British parliamentary system as a two-party system?
10. Compare and contrast the programmes of the three main political parties in the mid-twentieth century.

CHAPTER XVIII

LAW AND GOVERNMENT

Constitutional Monarchy. Britain has had a constitutional monarchy since the Revolution of 1688–89. The British Sovereign "reigns but does not govern". In law, however, the monarch is not only head of the government of the country but is also one of the three elements in the process of legislation. Every Act of Parliament passed under a King begins with the phrase—

> "Be it enacted by the King's most Excellent Majesty by and with the advice and consent of the Lords Spiritual and Temporal, and Commons, in this present Parliament assembled, and by the authority of the same" . . .

In practice, the assent of the monarch is now never withheld. This assent is signified in Parliament by the Clerk at the table of the House of Lords using the phrase "Le Roy le veult" (old French for "The King wills it"). The alternative "Le Roy" (or "La Reine") "s'avisera" ("The King will consider it") has not been used since Queen Anne's reign. The King or Queen, however, is not a mere figurehead. Although it is the duty of the Queen to accept the advice of her constitutional advisers, the Prime Minister and the Cabinet, it is also their duty to pay heed to the advice of the Queen. Whether a Prime Minister does so or not depends on the characters of the Sovereign and the Prime Minister. In Queen Victoria's reign, royal advice was freely given: it is reckoned that during the Bulgarian crisis that led to the Congress of Berlin in 1878 the Queen was at certain times sending telegrams hourly to the Prime Minister, Beaconsfield. Where a Prime Minister or Government, however, decided to act contrary to her wishes, all her letters and telegrams were of no avail: for example, Gladstone pursued his Irish policy despite her bitter opposition. Since Victoria's time, none of the British Sovereigns has attempted to wield so direct and active an influence in politics. Even in the creation of PEERAGES, which is supposed to be part of the royal prerogative power, it is in the last resort the Prime Minister's will that prevails, e.g. in the constitutional crisis of 1910. In 1922, during Lloyd George's Coalition Government, there was an outcry in the press about the wholesale disposal of peerages and some of the new peers were openly criticized. The King, George V, was most distressed about his personal position, and later his Private Secretary informed a Royal Commission that the King never conferred a peerage except on the advice of his responsible ministers. All the important prerogative powers of the Queen are, in fact, wielded by the Prime Minister or one of his colleagues. The Queen may be SUPREME GOVERNOR of the Church of England; but it is the Prime Minister (whether an Anglican like most Premiers or a Presbyterian like Campbell-Bannerman, Bonar Law or Ramsay MacDonald or a Baptist like Lloyd George or a Unitarian like Neville Chamberlain) that makes the appointment of the Archbishops and Bishops of the Church, in consultation with certain ecclesiastical advisers. The PREROGATIVE OF MERCY (a relic of the dispensing power which James II was charged in the Bill of Rights with having abused) is exercised by the Home Secretary or the Secretary of State for Scotland; it is for them alone to decide on a reprieve in the case of a death sentence. George VI is known to have discussed appeals for a reprieve with his Home Secretary, Herbert Morrison (later Lord Morrison); but when he differed from the Home Secretary, he accepted the latter's decision on the case.

The Sovereign and the Prime Minister. The most important political function of the Sovereign is the selection of a new Prime Minister. In most cases this is automatic: if it follows an election, then the leader of the majority party is invited to form a Government. When a Prime Minister resigns his office during the life of a Parliament, the question of a successor is sometimes difficult. When Bonar Law was forced to resign in 1923 because of the cancer that caused his death a few months later, the Marquess of Curzon, deputy leader of the Conservative party, confidently expected to succeed as Prime Minister. But King George V, taking the advice of his Private Secretary that a Prime Minister in the House of Lords was no longer acceptable to the British people, sent for the Chancellor of the Exchequer, Stanley Baldwin, to the disgust of Curzon, who once referred to Baldwin as "a man of the utmost insignificance". In 1940, when Britain was facing defeat in France and Norway and Neville Chamberlain was compelled to resign, King George VI wished to appoint Lord Halifax as Prime Minister. But when Chamberlain told the King that Halifax himself thought the appointment of a peer unsuitable, the King decided on Winston Churchill. In 1957, when Sir Anthony Eden resigned for health reasons, Queen Elizabeth's choice was not the Deputy Prime Minister, R. A. Butler, but the Chancellor of the Exchequer, Harold Macmillan. When the Prime Minister has been appointed, he becomes in effect the ruler of the country. The Prime Minister occupies his position as leader of the majority party in the House of Commons, however, and plays an important part in the ordinary day-to-day business of the House at question time and in debate. Until 1942 he was also LEADER OF THE HOUSE OF COMMONS but the position is now occupied by one of the chief ministers to relieve the Prime Minister of the strain of constant attendance at the House. Since the Second World War, also, it has been customary for a senior member of the Government to be recognized as DEPUTY PRIME MINISTER, although the post is not regarded as one that automatically entitles the holder to succeed the Prime Minister, as was seen in 1957 when Sir Anthony Eden resigned. When Sir Anthony himself became

Foreign Secretary in 1951, Sir Winston Churchill wished him to be designated as Deputy Prime Minister, but King George VI objected on the grounds that it would restrict his choice of Prime Minister. This right to choose the Prime Minister is exercised only very occasionally but the King or Queen does not stand aloof from the daily business of government. The Sovereign still, as in the nineteenth century, has the prerogatives which Walter Bagehot defined as "the right to be consulted, the right to encourage and the right to warn". During both World Wars, these prerogatives imposed heavy burdens upon the conscientious George V and his son George VI; and indeed it has been suggested that the early death of George VI in 1952 was due mainly to the strains of his wartime duties. Finally, the Sovereign is the main link between Britain and other parts of the Commonwealth. In the Dominions, the Governor-General represents the Sovereign and plays a similar part in relation to the Dominion Governments. Even in the case of India and Pakistan, which are republics, the Queen is regarded as Head of the Commonwealth.

The Cabinet. The Prime Minister is in reality head of the Government although it is still styled "Her Majesty's Government". He presides over the Cabinet, the members of which he personally chooses, so that the Government can with justice be called "Gladstone's Government" or "Salisbury's Ministry" or "Churchill's Cabinet". The members of the Cabinet are collectively responsible for the decisions taken. By this doctrine of COLLECTIVE RESPONSIBILITY, a Cabinet Minister must resign if he feels he cannot accept responsibility for a Cabinet decision. The Cabinet meets weekly in normal times (perhaps even daily during wartime) at No. 10 Downing Street, the Prime Minister's official residence in London. On occasions the Cabinet has met elsewhere—at Chequers, the Prime Minister's country house in Buckinghamshire, and once, during the Irish negotiations in 1921, in Inverness Town Hall, as Lloyd George was on holiday in the Highlands. The number of ministers in the Cabinet has varied considerably, generally under twenty in Queen Victoria's reign but ranging from twenty to twenty-five in the twentieth century. In both World Wars there have been small WAR

CABINET CHANGES

1886

First Lord of the Treasury (and Prime Minister)	Marquess of Salisbury
Lord Chancellor	Lord Halsbury
Lord President	Viscount Cranbrook
Chancellor of the Exchequer ·	Lord Randolph Churchill
Home Secretary	Henry Matthews
Foreign Secretary	Earl of Iddesleigh
Colonial Secretary	Hon. Edward Stanhope
Secretary for War	W. H. Smith
Secretary for India	Viscount Cross
Chief Secretary for Ireland	Sir Michael Hicks-Beach
First Lord of the Admiralty	Lord George Hamilton
President of the Board of Trade	Lord Stanley
Chancellor of the Duchy of Lancaster	Lord John Manners
Lord Chancellor of Ireland	Lord Ashbourne

1959

Prime Minister and First Lord of the Treasury	Harold Macmillan
Home Secretary (and Deputy Prime Minister)	R. A. Butler
Lord Chancellor	Viscount Kilmuir
Chancellor of the Exchequer	D. Heathcoat Amory
Foreign Secretary	Selwyn Lloyd
Lord President of the Council and Secretary for Commonwealth Relations	Earl of Home
Secretary for Scotland	J. Maclay
Lord Privy Seal and Minister in charge of Science and Technology	Viscount Hailsham
Minister of Aviation	Duncan Sandys
Secretary for Colonies	Iain Macleod
Minister of Defence	Harold Watkinson
Minister of Housing and Local Government and Minister for Welsh Affairs	Henry Brooke
Minister of Education	Sir David Eccles
Paymaster-General	Lord Mills
President of the Board of Trade	Reginald Maudling
Minister of Agriculture, Fisheries and Food	John Hare
Minister of Labour	Edward Heath
Chancellor of the Duchy of Lancaster	Dr. Charles Hill
Minister of Transport	Ernest Marples

CABINETS of five to seven ministers for the sake of conducting the war more expeditiously. The Prime Minister himself has generally held the office of First Lord of the Treasury, but the Marquess of Salisbury, during his thirteen years as Prime Minister, was First Lord of the Treasury only for a few months, the office being given by him usually to the Conservative Leader of the House of Commons. Some of the Cabinet offices have had their names altered during the last fifty years. In 1924, the Colonial Secretary became the Secretary for the Dominions and Colonies; then because of the growing importance of the Commonwealth the office was split in 1929, and there were two Secretaries, one for the Colonies and one for the Dominions, the latter becoming the Secretary for Commonwealth Relations in 1947. During the Second World War, the Prime Minister, Winston Churchill, acted as MINISTER OF DEFENCE in order to co-ordinate and direct the work of the three defence ministries. Since the end of the war, the Minister of Defence has become a regular member of the Cabinet, to the exclusion of the First Lord of the Admiralty and the Secretaries for War and for Air, who have been relegated to the body of members of the Government outside the Cabinet of whom there are about twenty. Among the latest additions to the Government are the MINISTRY FOR SCIENCE AND TECHNOLOGY, an office combined with that of Lord Privy Seal in 1959, and the MINISTRY FOR WELSH AFFAIRS, combined with the Ministry for Housing and Local Government. With all the junior ministers such as Parliamentary Under-Secretaries added, Government officials number about a hundred. One, whose official title is Parliamentary Secretary to the Treasury, is better known as the CHIEF WHIP; it is his duty to see that members of the Government party attend and vote at divisions, and the Opposition have also a Chief Whip with similar duties. Another M.P. who receives a special salary is the LEADER OF THE OPPOSITION, an office that often puzzles foreigners. To be paid to criticize and oppose the Government seems paradoxical and absurd to a person from a country like Russia or Spain where only one party is permitted to function. It is one of the healthiest features of British democracy and if sometimes the criticism of the Government seems to be rather factious, it should be remembered that it is the function of the Opposition to oppose and to criticize and that the Leader of the Opposition is actually paid extra to do so.

Central Government. Cabinet Ministers are the political heads of the various departments of the central government. They are responsible to Parliament and to the electorate for the government of the country. They themselves are seldom experts in the particular branches of administration of which they are the nominal heads. A politician who has never been in the Army or Navy may find himself in charge of the War Office or Admiralty. Sir Winston Churchill, who had been soldier, journalist and author before he entered Parliament, first gained Cabinet rank as President of the Board of Trade, from which he passed to the Home Office, and then to the Admiralty—all in the brief space of three years. How, it may be asked, can the country's government be carried on when it is entrusted to the direction of amateurs, however brilliant they may be? The answer lies in the existence of a permanent CIVIL SERVICE. At the head of each Department is a PERMANENT UNDER-SECRETARY, who is an acknowledged authority, with a long experience of the problems of his Department; and below him are various other officials, each an expert in one branch or another. Cabinets come and cabinets go but the Permanent Under-Secretary may remain the same. What effect, if any, does a Cabinet Minister have on his Department? The answer will depend mainly on the personality of the Minister: if he is an energetic, go-ahead man, with ideas about possible changes, he is likely to lead the civil servants of his Department rather than be led by them. It will depend also on whether party policy is involved: a Labour Colonial Secretary is likely to differ from a Conservative Colonial Secretary in his way of dealing with the problems of his office. With many ministers and many departments, *plus ça change, plus c'est la même chose*; or, as was often said in the nineteenth century, when the Liberals formed the Government they turned Conservative, and when the Conservatives went into Opposition they became Liberals. To have an amateur as the head of a government department may seem an odd way of running the affairs of a country, but over the past hundred years it has been shown to work very well. There are various reasons for this:— (1) The British Civil Service has a very high standard of efficiency and honesty, whereas in many other countries the same cannot be said. (2) The danger that an efficient Civil Service may become a bureaucracy ruling the country without respect for the rights of individuals is safeguarded by the presence of the political head, the Secretary of State or the Minister, who is bound to be questioned in the House of Commons and held responsible for the misdemeanours or shortcomings of his Department. (3) There is a very strong feeling in Britain against bureaucracy, and the newspapers are always prepared to ventilate publicly the grievances of any citizen. In a position of control over all the other departments is the TREASURY, which, as it provides the money, must approve of a project before the money is made available. Naturally, this Treasury control often leads to an argument in the Cabinet and has been responsible for various resignations of Cabinet Ministers. Lord Randolph Churchill resigned from the post of Chancellor of the Exchequer in 1886 over a dispute with the Secretary for War, who received the backing of the Prime Minister and the Cabinet, and in 1958 another Chancellor of the Exchequer, Peter Thorneycroft, resigned after a similar dispute.

National Boards. Since the Labour Government of 1945–50 carried out its programme of NATIONALIZATION, a large section of the country's industry and transport has been under public ownership and control. But, although it might have been possible to create a Minister of Mines responsible to Parliament, as the Postmaster-General is responsible for the Post Office and all its departments, there was set up instead the NATIONAL COAL BOARD, which has full authority for the management of the mines. There are various similar bodies such as the British Electricity Authority, the British Transport Commission, the Atomic Energy Authority. There are certain questions connected with finance and the general policy of the nationalized industries which are sometimes raised in Parliament and for which a Minister in the Cabinet, such as the Minister for Transport,

Fuel and Power, is called upon to answer. An opportunity is given each year for Parliament to have a general debate on the work of each Board or Corporation when the annual report is submitted. The members of these national bodies are appointed by the Cabinet Minister responsible. Even before the nationalization of 1945–51 there were certain public bodies, which had been set up to control a national service or industry, e.g. the B.B.C. or British Broadcasting Corporation dating from 1926 (originally the British Broadcasting Company, which was formed in 1922), the Forestry Commission, first set up in 1919. Much criticism has been directed by Conservatives against the nationalized concerns as top-heavy, over-staffed and wasteful. But they themselves have maintained the national boards except that for the steel industry, which was denationalized in 1952, while they have also handed back road transport to private ownership. The accountability of the national boards and corporations to Parliament offers an opportunity to the public to see that the nationalized industries and services are run efficiently and economically.

Finance. The financing of Government activities has changed considerably over the past century. A Government nowadays has to find money on a much vaster scale than in the nineteenth century when comparatively little was spent either on defence or on social services. In addition, the two world wars have left a heavy burden of debt to be repaid. As a result, taxation has had to be greatly increased. Gladstone, the most famous Chancellor of the Exchequer of the nineteenth century, used to aim at reducing taxation to a minimum in order to allow the money "to fructify in the pockets of the people". Other Chancellors were of like minds, and under the Conservative ministry of Disraeli in 1874 the income-tax was brought down to 2d. During the Second World War it was at 10s. for much of the time. The greatest change in the country's fiscal policy came with Lloyd George's "People's Budget" of 1909, which aimed at redistributing the wealth of the country by heavy taxation of the rich and increased expenditure on social services for those in poorer circumstances. The Government's revenue is obtained by direct or indirect taxation. DIRECT TAXATION includes both income-tax, either on individuals or on companies, and death duties. Since the early part of the Second World War, income-tax has been deducted from the weekly or monthly pay packets by the employers and remitted by them to the Collectors of Inland Revenue. This system, called P.A.Y.E. ("Pay as you earn"), was started when so many wage-earners were paying tax that it would have been difficult to collect the tax in half-yearly instalments as had been done before the war. SURTAX is a form of income-tax on large incomes and is a successor of the supertax introduced by Lloyd George in 1909. On a very large income the rate of surtax is high: in 1959 on an income of £50,000 per annum the income-tax and surtax together amounted to over £40,000. The principal DEATH DUTY today is the estate duty, which is a tax on capital; formerly there were various other death duties such as legacy duty and succession duty. ESTATE DUTY is levied on the estate left by a dead person, not merely on landed property (as the name might imply) but also on his house, his stocks and shares, the money deposited in the bank, etc. The estate duty is a graduated tax: on an estate of £5,000 only £40 (or 1 per cent) is levied while on an estate of £1,000,000 the duty would amount to £750,000 (or a rate of 75 per cent). To pay such an amount of money is for some heirs almost impossible without disposing of a large portion of the estate; and where one death in a family is followed fairly closely by another, the family might find itself compelled to sell off almost all its property. The estate duty was introduced in 1894 by the Liberal, Sir William Harcourt, at a fairly low rate; the sharp increase in the rate of the duty this century has been described as the main cause of the ruin of the large landed estates of Britain. INDIRECT TAXATION can be simply defined as taxation on spending: it is levied on articles bought by the people rather than upon their incomes. Indirect taxes are mainly EXCISE DUTIES of one kind or another and are supposed to be taxes on articles which are not necessities of life. The most important ex-cise duty (from the point of view of the collection of revenue) is that on tobacco but alcoholic liquor, oil and motor duties come

BUDGET 1959

Revenue

	£
Taxes on Income and Capital	
Personal Incomes—Income-tax and Surtax	1,693,000,000
Companies—Income-tax, Profits Tax, etc.	900,000,000
Death Duties	195,000,000
Taxes on Spending	
Tobacco (Import and Excise Duties)	750,000,000
Alcoholic Liquors (Import and Excise Duties)	376,000,000
Entertainments, Television, Betting	54,000,000
Purchase Tax	471,000,000
Oil (including Petrol) (Import and Excise Duties)	355,000,000
Motors	104,000,000
Stamp Duties	68,000,000
Import Duties (other than those on Alcoholic Liquors, Tobacco, Oil)	144,000,000
Non-Tax Revenue	
Miscellaneous (including broadcast licences)	215,000,000
Total	5,325,000,000

Expenditure

	£
National Debt Interest (on Government Stocks, etc.)	639,000,000
Defence	
Army	441,350,000
Navy	370,700,000
Air Force	492,800,000
Ministry of Supply	191,800,000
Ministry of Defence	17,485,000
Social Services	
Health	560,000,000
Personal Payments (Family Allowances, War Pensions, National Assistance, etc.)	543,000,000
Agriculture—Subsidies	245,000,000
Assistance to Local Services (Education, Housing, Health, Police, Roads, etc.)	840,000,000
Miscellaneous	
Atomic Energy, Universities, Trunk Roads, Broadcasting, etc.	882,000,000
Surplus (used for loans to colonies, nationalized industries, etc.)	102,000,000
Total	5,325,000,000

fairly close after. In addition, PURCHASE TAX, which was introduced only during the Second World War, brings in a considerable revenue. CUSTOMS DUTIES are levied at the ports on imported articles. In the second half of the nineteenth century, when Britain boasted of its free trade, there were no customs duties. Chamberlain's tariff reform campaign of 1903-06 was unsuccessful but it helped to make the Conservative party favour protection of industry and agriculture by customs duties. Some duties were imposed by the Coalition Government during the First World War but it was not until 1932 that the British Government finally abandoned free trade by imposing an all-round tariff of 10 per cent. On the expenditure side, the main item has always been DEFENCE, which, along with the payments on the National Debt (that is, for defence during the two world wars) accounts for almost half of the country's annual bill. The other main item was a very small one in the nineteenth century—SOCIAL SERVICES (education, health, housing, pensions, national insurance, etc.). It includes grants to local authorities, which also raise revenue by local taxes called rates. The surplus of revenue over expenditure is used today to provide loans to nationalized industries and services and also to colonies overseas. The preparation of the Budget, the statement of the country's estimated revenue and expenditure for the forthcoming year, is the duty of the Chancellor of the Exchequer; and the Commons' debates after the introduction of the Budget in April are among the most important of the parliamentary session. To ensure that the national revenue has been spent properly as estimated, there exists a system of auditing of the public accounts under the Comptroller and Auditor-General. His reports are submitted to the House of Commons Committee of Public Accounts; and in addition a Select Committee of National Expenditure reports from time to time on means of effecting economies.

Local Government—(a) Urban. Of the two main branches of local government, that of the towns is the older. Some English boroughs and Scottish burghs have royal charters dating from the early Middle Ages. In the nineteenth century, the administration of the towns was improved by the Scottish Municipal

Reform Act of 1833 and a similar Act for England in 1835. These Acts gave to householders the right to elect the town councils and provided for a public audit of accounts each year. They brought to an end the system of corruption that had prevailed for so long in both countries, where self-elected councils or corporations, responsible to no one but themselves, were able to do as they pleased about the town's property and finances. The towns which were represented in Parliament after 1832 became known as "parliamentary" boroughs or burghs, some of them possessing charters of old and others having grown large as a result of the industrial revolution. In both countries there is a municipal election each year, formerly held in November but since 1948 in May. The electors were from 1833 in Scotland and 1835 in England only male householders, until 1869 when women householders were also allowed to vote. Since 1948 the franchise for local government elections, both urban and rural, has been the same as that for parliamentary elections, that is, adult suffrage. There were and still are differences between Scotland and England so far as municipal government is concerned. In the Scottish burghs, one-third of the council or corporation members are elected each year for a period of three years, after which they can seek re-election. The councillors elect the various office-holders, also for three-year periods—the head of the council or PROVOST (or in a city Lord Provost); the magistrates or BAILIES, who preside in the Burgh Police Court; the TREASURER, who fixes each year the "rate" to be levied on all occupiers of property in order to meet the town's expenditure; and the DEAN OF GUILD, who controls through his court the erection of buildings in the town. In England, some senior members are elected from the councillors— ALDERMEN, who hold office for a period of six years, half of them retiring after three years, and the head of the council, the MAYOR (or Lord Mayor in seventeen of the largest or most important towns), who is elected annually but is eligible for re-election. The Scottish burghs are of three types:— (a) SMALL BURGHS, some of them with a population under 1,000, are restricted in their powers to housing, cleansing, lighting, parks,

26

etc. (*b*) LARGE BURGHS with populations of 20,000 or over, exercise all the functions of local government except education and, in some cases, police, which come under the county councils. (*c*) Edinburgh, Glasgow, Aberdeen and Dundee are designated as COUNTIES OF CITIES, and have all the functions of county councils. Perth, although lacking this county status, is also called a city and its chief magistrate is called the Lord Provost. Elgin and Brechin, both cathedral towns, are also sometimes called "cities" (after the English fashion); but although Elgin's chief magistrate carries the title of Lord Provost, the title is not recognized at state functions and is disregarded by some other burghs. The term "ROYAL BURGH" in Scotland denotes a burgh founded by royal charter. The royal burghs were the only burghs represented in Parliament up to 1832, but some of them are very small, with populations under 1,000, like Inveraray, Dornoch, Fortrose, Culross. The CONVENTION OF ROYAL BURGHS has met annually for hundreds of years to discuss matters of common interest and to make representations, when necessary, to the Government. In England, boroughs with more than 50,000 inhabitants, were designated as COUNTY BOROUGHS in 1888 by the Local Government Act setting up county councils. The councils of these county boroughs (of which there were eighty-three in England and Wales in 1955) have the same status and functions as county councils. Until 1926, boroughs automatically became county boroughs once they had a population of 50,000; but from that date till 1945 75,000 was the required population and since 1945 100,000. The name "CITY" is applied in England and Wales to many very large boroughs like Birmingham, Sheffield, Bradford, Manchester, Liverpool, and also to cathedral towns, some of them, Lichfield and Wells, being comparatively small, with populations of 11,000 or less. London differs from all the other towns and cities in the country. By the Act of 1888, which set up county councils, the administration of Greater London, which had become a vast congeries of boroughs, came under the LONDON COUNTY COUNCIL, the head of which is a chairman as in other county councils. The METROPOLITAN BOROUGHS within that area have their own councils with mayors and aldermen;

one of them is the City of Westminster, which includes many of the best-known buildings in London. The CITY OF LONDON covers a relatively small area, that of the old medieval city, and contains today the financial and business centre of Britain. It has very ancient rights, and the LORD MAYOR OF LONDON, who is elected annually in November, occupies one of the most important offices in the country. Although mainly a figurehead like the Sovereign, he represents the wealth and glory of the capital of Britain, one of the oldest and largest cities of the world.

Local Government—(b) Rural. In rural England and Scotland formerly, it was the parish rather than the county that was the unit of administration; the first local taxes were levied in parishes, the poor rate in England and the school rate in Scotland. The new poor laws passed in 1834 and 1845 for England and Scotland introduced the idea of groups of parishes under Boards of Guardians in England and Parochial Boards in Scotland. The English squires and Scottish lairds carried out for centuries a number of functions as Justices of the Peace, Commissioners of Supply (in Scotland) or (later) Commissioners of Police for the county. There was no unified county administration or system of popular election until 1888 in England and 1889 in Scotland when COUNTY COUNCILS were set up. At first the duties of the county councils were confined mainly to public health, police and the upkeep of roads. But in 1902, by the Education Act of that year, the English parish school boards, which were in charge of elementary education, were abolished, and both elementary and secondary education in England were placed under the control of the county councils, which thus became the LOCAL EDUCATION AUTHORITIES. In Scotland, with its older traditions in education, the parish school board was still responsible for all education till 1918, when separate *ad hoc* Education Authorities were elected for each county area; in 1929 the control of education in Scotland also passed into the hands of the county councils, whose education committees also include certain co-opted members, e.g. ministers and university professors. PARISH COUNCILS came into existence by the Local Government Act of 1894, which was notable in that it gave to all women ratepayers, married or single, the right both to vote for and sit on parish councils. But parish councils had very little power, as they were normally permitted to levy only a 3d. rate; and the words "parochial" or "parish-pump politics" are generally used to refer in a derogatory sense to a restricted outlook on affairs. The parish councils disappeared in Scotland in 1929 but in England they still exist, their duties being confined to the provision of parks, the maintenance of rights of way, etc. URBAN AND RURAL DISTRICT COUNCILS were set up in England as a result of the 1884 Act; in Scotland there were District Committees of the County Councils from 1889 and these were re-named District Councils in 1929, when the Scottish parish councils were abolished. The LOCAL GOVERNMENT ACTS of 1929 for England and Scotland were the first real attempts to work out a systematic scheme of local government from the patchwork of administration that had developed over the previous forty years. These Acts are still largely the basis of our present local government with some amendments in another Local Government Act of 1948. The 1929 Act for Scotland was responsible for bringing Scotland more into line with England, the control of education by county councils being the outstanding example of the process of assimilation. In addition, poor relief, which for centuries had been administered on a parish basis, became in 1929 the duty of the County Council Public Assistance Committee (in 1948, it was transferred to the National Assistance Board). The other main change in 1929 for both England and Scotland was the introduction of government grants to local councils (both in towns and counties), mainly to make up for the loss of rates from farms and industrial concerns, which were allowed by a Derating Act to pay only one-quarter of their former rates. Elections to county councils and district councils are held once every three years in the month of April in England and May in Scotland. The councillors elect as their chairman, the CONVENER, and various committees, under Chairmen, for education, housing, health, roads, etc. The main feature of the county council elections, as also, to an increasing degree, of town council elections is the apathy of the electors; often the total poll is less than 20 per cent of the electorate. The franchise, so hard fought for and so dearly won, is now regarded as hardly worth using.

Criminal Courts. The maintenance of law and order is one of the duties of the Government. This is done ordinarily through the agencies of the police and the magistrates in the various courts. Formerly. before police forces were organized, the Government had to depend on the use of soldiers and they still have to do so occasionally, as for instance during a serious strike. Breaking the law involves committing an offence or a crime and if the person concerned is detected and arrested, leads to his appearance in a CRIMINAL COURT. The names of the courts and the judges are given in a table elsewhere. There are in addition to the main courts JUVENILE COURTS for young offenders. The "Children's Charter" Act of 1908, which started the system of probation instead of imprisonment for those under seventeen, also laid down that children should not be tried in the ordinary courts and that their identities should not be disclosed in the public press. In 1932, it was further enacted that a juvenile court should be held in a different building or room from the ordinary court, or, if it were held in the same place, that it should be on a different day. The idea behind the Acts of 1908 and 1932 was to give a youthful offender a chance to make good without being forced to consort with older, hardened criminals. The ordinary practising lawyer who would defend a man in a local court or draw up a will for him or help him dispose of property is called a SOLICITOR, but in Scotland he may also be known as a "writer". Lawyers who, after passing examinations, are "called to the Bar" and allowed to practise in the higher courts of law are known as BARRISTERS in England and ADVOCATES in Scotland. Those barristers or advocates who are appointed Queen's Counsel (Q.C.s) are said to "take silk" because of their special gowns of silk. The LORD ADVOCATE in Scotland and the ATTORNEY-GENERAL in England are M.P.s whose offices are Government appointments. They or the Solicitors-General often undertake important prosecutions. In the lower courts the Scottish PROCURATOR FISCAL and the

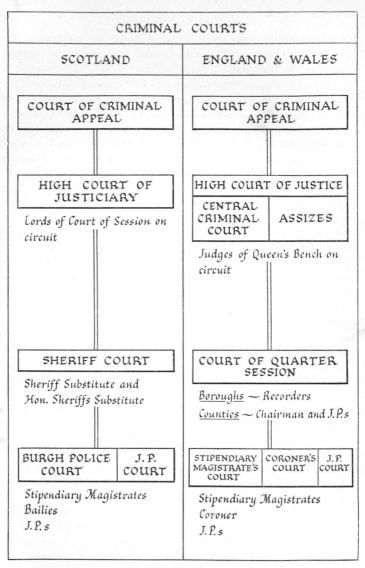

CRIMINAL COURTS	
SCOTLAND	ENGLAND & WALES

SCOTLAND

COURT OF CRIMINAL APPEAL

HIGH COURT OF JUSTICIARY

Lords of Court of Session on circuit

SHERIFF COURT

Sheriff Substitute and Hon. Sheriffs Substitute

BURGH POLICE COURT — J. P. COURT

Stipendiary Magistrates
Bailies
J. P. s

ENGLAND & WALES

COURT OF CRIMINAL APPEAL

HIGH COURT OF JUSTICE

CENTRAL CRIMINAL COURT — ASSIZES

Judges of Queen's Bench on circuit

COURT OF QUARTER SESSION

<u>Boroughs</u> — *Recorders*
<u>Counties</u> — *Chairman and J.P.s*

STIPENDIARY MAGISTRATE'S COURT — CORONER'S COURT — J. P. COURT

Stipendiary Magistrates
Coroner
J. P. s

British Law Courts and Justice: Criminal Courts

English PUBLIC PROSECUTOR are in charge of the prosecution. Procedure in a criminal court is usually familar to the public because of newspaper reports of sensational trials. There are many rules about EVIDENCE. It should be, according to the oath that witnesses have to take (except those like Quakers who refuse to take oaths and are permitted to "affirm") "the truth, the whole truth and nothing but the truth". The evidence of a witness should be what he or she has actually seen or heard; what someone else has told him is only "hearsay evidence" and is not allowed. Witnesses for the prosecution are first of all examined by the Procurator Fiscal or Prosecutor and then cross-examined by the defence counsel, while defence witnesses are first examined by the counsel for the defence and then cross-examined by the prosecution counsel. In addition to the evidence of someone who has witnessed an offence, it usually happens also that circumstantial evidence is considered, that is, certain circumstances that suggest but do not prove guilt. The JURY of "honest men and women" before whom the case is tried is composed of ordinary householders in the district and is guided by the judge on points of law during the case and at the end in his summing-up; their duty is to decide on the facts, which means also on the reliability of the witnesses. The penalty to be imposed on the guilty person is a matter for the judge, but there are certain rules to guide him in deciding whether it should be a fine or imprisonment and whether it should be a short or a long term of imprisonment. CAPITAL PUNISHMENT is reserved now for cases of murder and treason. Many countries have abolished capital punishment without any increase in the number of murders; but attempts to suspend capital punishment were made in Parliament in 1948 and 1956 only to be defeated in the House of Lords. By the HOMICIDE ACT (1957), capital punishment is restricted to (a) murder accompanied by theft, (b) murder committed while resisting arrest or escaping from prison, (c) murder of police officers or prison officers, (d) murder by shooting or causing explosions, (e) murder by a person who has already committed a murder.

Scottish and English Criminal Law. Scotland has a different

legal system from that of England, one of the rights reserved
to Scotland by the Treaty of Union, 1707. The differences in
criminal procedure are considerable. (1) In England, the accused
in a serious case like murder appears in public before a magistrate
for a PRELIMINARY HEARING to see whether the evidence is
sufficient to justify the accused being sent to the Assizes. In
Scotland, such a preliminary hearing takes place in private
before a Sheriff. It has been argued that a preliminary hearing
in public often prejudices the accused's chances of a fair trial
later as people who might have to act as jurors could be influenced
by newspaper reports of the hearing. Changes have been
advocated that might bring English procedure more into line
with Scottish procedure in this respect. (2) In the cases of fatal
accidents, suicides and murders, similar publicity is given in
England to the proceedings in the Coroner's Court, where again
evidence may be given that could prejudice the accused's chances
later. The publicity surrounding a CORONER'S INQUEST on a
suicide in England also causes great distress to relatives and
friends and the Scottish method whereby the local Procurator
Fiscal carries out his inquiries in private seems much more
humane. (3) In the matter of proving guilt, Scots law will not
accept the evidence of one witness if it is not corroborated by
other evidence, however definite the evidence and however reliable
the witness, whereas such evidence can be accepted in an English
law-court. (4) The Scottish courts have three possible verdicts
instead of the two—"Guilty" and "Not Guilty"—in the English
courts. This third verdict, "Not Proven", has often been criticized
as leaving a stigma on a person; but it seems a fair enough
judgement where the person has committed the crime or offence
but where the evidence is not strong enough to justify the verdict
of "Guilty". A person who has committed an offence or crime
in England might be able to leave the court without a stain on
his name; and his chances are increased by the fact that in an
English court the jury must arrive at a unanimous decision,
whereas in Scotland, a majority verdict is accepted. In England,
a jury's failure to agree may mean that they have to be discharged
and a new trial arranged. Another small difference between the

two courts relates to the juries: in England the number of persons on the jury is twelve and in Scotland fifteen.

Scottish and English Civil Law. There is another kind of court to which a man may have recourse—the CIVIL COURT, in which he may bring an action against another person, e.g. a claim for damages or compensation, or divorce, etc. The courts range from the Small Debt Court to the House of Lords and cases can go by appeal from the lower courts to the higher. There are differences also between the civil law of Scotland and that of England, although in the last half century the two countries have tended to draw closer to one another in this sphere. Formerly, an Englishman could dispose of his property as he wished; for example, he could ignore his eldest son or only son and "cut him off with a shilling". In Scotland, the rights of the widow and children have been protected for centuries; and since 1938 similar protection has also been given in England. As everyone knows, it is easier for a young couple to get married in Scotland than in England. In England, a minor (or a person under twenty-one) cannot be married if the parent objects but in Scotland there is no such impediment. Up to the middle of the nineteenth century, it was possible for a man and woman to become husband and wife by a mutual declaration to that effect before two witnesses in Scotland. This led to many a daring or unscrupulous English adventurer eloping with a young heiress across the Border to Scotland. Places near the Border like Gretna Green became so notorious for such runaway marriages that by an Act of 1856 it became necessary for one of the couple to have been resident in Scotland for three weeks before the marriage; and, by another Act of 1939, a marriage had to be celebrated before a clergyman or a registrar. Gretna Green became so linked in the public mind with runaway marriages that even today young couples (including some from Scotland) make for this small Border village, as if it is the only place for runaways to be married. Another difficulty for English couples is the restriction on the time during which marriages are permitted: up to 1886 the ceremony had to take place between 8 a.m. and noon, but from that year the time was extended to 3 p.m.

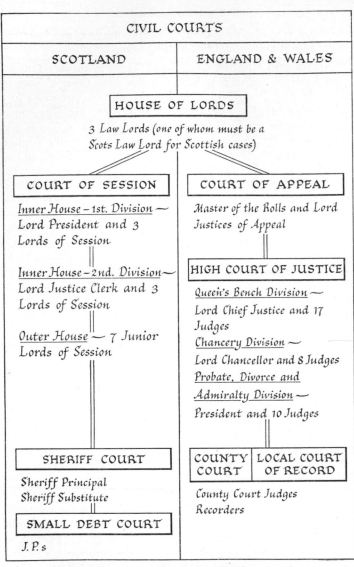

CIVIL COURTS

SCOTLAND	ENGLAND & WALES

HOUSE OF LORDS

3 *Law Lords (one of whom must be a Scots Law Lord for Scottish cases)*

COURT OF SESSION

<u>Inner House – 1st. Division</u> —
Lord President and 3
Lords of Session

<u>Inner House – 2nd. Division</u> —
Lord Justice Clerk and 3
Lords of Session

<u>Outer House</u> — 7 Junior
Lords of Session

SHERIFF COURT

Sheriff Principal
Sheriff Substitute

SMALL DEBT COURT

J. P. s

COURT OF APPEAL

Master of the Rolls and Lord
Justices of Appeal

HIGH COURT OF JUSTICE

<u>Queen's Bench Division</u> —
Lord Chief Justice and 17
Judges
<u>Chancery Division</u> —
Lord Chancellor and 8 Judges
<u>Probate, Divorce and
Admiralty Division</u> —
President and 10 Judges

COUNTY COURT | **LOCAL COURT OF RECORD**

County Court Judges
Recorders

British Law Courts and Justice: Civil Courts

In both countries, the marriage of persons within the prohibited degrees of affinity (according to the Bible) was not regarded as valid; but by the Deceased Wife's Sister Act of 1908 it became legal for certain persons related by marriage. There are other very important differences between the civil law in Scotland and England, particularly in regard to property and land tenure. There is, for example, nothing in England similar to the Scottish system of feuing land, whereby, for the payment of a feu-duty or a fixed annual sum to the superior of the land, a man acquires the rights of ownership with certain restrictions.

The British Constitution. The constitution of Great Britain is often regarded with bemused admiration by foreign visitors and observers. They find it difficult to reconcile with a modern state the age-old pageantry of royal processions at state functions like the opening of Parliament. The paradoxes of a CONSTITUTIONAL MONARCH who "reigns but does not govern", who opens Parliament each session with a "Queen's Speech" written by the Prime Minister and Cabinet, who is head of the national church but leaves the choice of bishops to the Prime Minister—all these and many other seeming anomalies puzzle the foreigner. And yet he knows that there is no great European state which has been so free of revolution in the last three hundred years, and that whereas monarchies have fallen in Europe like ninepins, the British monarchy remains as firmly fixed as ever. As the powers of the monarchy in Britiain have declined, its position in the state has become more secure. There are other constitutional monarchies in Europe, particularly in the Scandinavian countries, which can also be considered successful; and there, it is interesting to note, the constitutions are modelled on that of Britain. Another cause for the bewilderment of foreign vistors is the FLEXIBILITY of the constitution, the ease with which changes are made, in comparison, for example, with the United States, where there is a RIGID CONSTITUTION, a paper document to which amendments can be made only with great difficulty. Part of the British constitution is contained in its laws, some of which like the Bill of Rights, the Petition of Right, Magna Carta and the Habeas Corpus

Act have been described as the corner-stones of the constitution.
But changing the laws of the country is not difficult, provided
public opinion and the Government of the day are willing to
support the change. Even such an important law as the Habeas
Corpus Act has been suspended on more than one occasion,
mainly during wartime, to allow the Government to take action
against suspected persons without the need for a trial. Parliament,
it has been said, can do everything but make a man a woman or a
woman a man. Other important parts of the constitution are
called CONVENTIONS, customs that have been hallowed by the
passage of time and have acquired the sanctity of laws. Such is,
for example, the convention that the Prime Minister must be a
member of the House of Commons. This is only a twentieth-
century convention. The last Prime Minister in the House of
Lords, the Marquess of Salisbury, retired only in 1902, and yet
already this convention has a validity as great as any law. The
history of the office of Prime Minister, for almost two centuries
unrecognized by any Act of Parliament, shows the importance of
conventions in the constitution. There is hardly any more important development in the constitution in modern times than that
of the office of Prime Minister and his relation to the Cabinet;
but it has happened almost entirely without any need for an Act
of Parliament. Circumstances at one time or another have made
it necessary to take a new course of action, which has provided
the basis for still more changes. A century ago, Tennyson
wrote that Britain is a land

> "where freedom slowly broadens down
> From precedent to precedent".

Most observers of the political scene would be inclined to the
view that, although the main tendency in Britain over the
centuries has been towards freedom, there have been at certain
times developments which, unchecked, might have led to the
curtailment of the liberties of the people. Such, for example,
has been the growth in modern times of the powers of the
bureaucracy, the trade unions and the party system. The British
press takes an interest in exposing (sometimes, it must be

confessed, in a most sensational manner) the abuses and scandals of the bureaucracy and other bodies in the country; to a certain extent, the press merits the titles of "the watch-dog of the public" or "the Fourth Estate" that have been given to it. But in the last resort Parliament remains the open forum for discussion of the nation's affairs and redress of grievances.

SOURCE EXTRACT

King George V and his Ministers

House of Commons

A letter is written to the King every day by the Leader of the House of Commons, describing the proceedings of the House. A telegram briefly reporting any outstanding particulars in the proceedings is sent every evening by one of the Whips.

Cabinet

1. No change is made in the constitution of the Ministry until the King's approval has been obtained.

2. No mention should be made publicly or privately of any matters which have transpired in Cabinet, without the approval of His Majesty being first obtained.

3. Before a Minister goes abroad he should acquaint the King of his intention to do so.

Foreign Office

All important Foreign Office Despatches are submitted to His Majesty before being sent abroad.

Ecclesiastical Preferment

A very important responsibility. The Archbishop of Canterbury will be found very fair and liberal-minded with a wide knowledge of the personnel of the Church and always ready to advise. It is important that the letters which convey the offer of important preferment should be written by the Prime Minister himself.

Honours and Appointments

It is hoped that a firm hand will be kept on the distribution of Honours. With the exception of the last Government, the bestowal has been extravagant. Especial care should be taken with regard to appointments to the Privy Council. Mr. Gladstone said that a Privy Councillorship used to be regarded as a greater honour than a Peerage.

Before any person is offered an Appointment under the Crown, or an Honour, the King's approval should be obtained, until which time the individual in question should not be approached on the subject.

All recommendations for Honours are submitted in conjunction with the Prime Minister with the exception of the Order of Merit and the Royal Victorian Order (which are made on the King's initiative). . . .

The King deprecates the bestowal of Honours on Ministers while in Office.

King George V's Memorandum to Ramsay MacDonald, 1924, quoted in Harold Nicolson: King George the Fifth.

EXERCISES

1. Why did George V think it necessary to send the above memorandum to Ramsay MacDonald?
2. Explain: Prerogative of mercy, collective responsibility, surtax, parliamentary burgh, Dean of Guild, Bailie, Alderman, Lord Mayor, Lord Provost, hearsay evidence, solicitor, writer, barrister, advocate, coroner, convention of the constitution, rigid constitution.
3. Write short notes on: Convention of Royal Burghs, Parish Councils, District Councils, Homicide Act of 1957, Jury system in Scotland, National Boards.
4. Outline the main sources of Government revenue, distinguishing between direct and indirect taxation.
5. What are the main services administered by a town council or county council? Describe the work of a major committee of a town or county council.
6. What are the main differences in procedure in English and Scottish criminal courts?
7. What are the main differences between English and Scottish civil law?

GLOSSARY OF POLITICAL AND ECONOMIC TERMS

Abrogation, Unilateral. Renunciation of a treaty by one of the signatories.

Administration. In U.S.A., the Government.

Afrikaans. Language, similar to Dutch, spoken by people of Dutch descent in South Africa.

Afrikaner. White inhabitant of Dutch descent in South Africa (also called "Boer").

Aggression. Attack; generally used to describe attack by armed forces of one country on another.

Amnesty. Act of pardon for political offenders or rebels.

Annexation. Forceful acquisition of territory.

Anti-Semitism. Hostility and prejudice against the Jews, particularly strong in Nazi Germany.

A.N.Z.A.C. Australian and New Zealand Auxiliary Corps.

Apartheid. (Afrikaans word meaning "separateness".) Racial segregation policy practised by white people of South Africa.

Arbitration. Settlement of a dispute by arbiter or independent judge.

A.R.P. Air Raid Precautions, an organization for defence against air raids in Britain in the Second World War.

Aryan. Belonging to Indo-European group of languages or peoples, contrasted with Semitic and other groups.

Attrition. Wearing down. War of attrition—a war depending on which side can last the longer.

Authoritarian. Used of states which are ruled by dictators and which emphasize authority; contrasted with democratic.

Autonomy. Self-government.

Balance of Payments. Balance between the overseas payments (for imports and invisible imports) and receipts (for exports and invisible exports).

Balance of Power. Balance between one group of powers and another. (The traditional foreign policy of Britain was to maintain a balance of power in Europe.)

Balfour Declaration. A promise made in 1917 by A. J. Balfour (later Earl Balfour), Foreign Secretary, that the British Government would found a Jewish national home in Palestine, provided that the civil and political rights of the non-Jewish communities would not be prejudiced.

Benelux. Abbreviation for customs union formed by Belgium, the Netherlands and Luxembourg in 1947.

Bilateral Agreement. Agreement between two parties, as compared with a multilateral agreement, signed by more than two parties.

Blitz. Colloquial word used of a heavy raid or series of raids on Britain in Second World War.

Blitzkrieg. (German word meaning "lightning war".) Used to describe the German type of warfare in which the enemy is overwhelmed by sudden, concentrated attacks on land and from the air.

Blockade. Prevention of supplies reaching an enemy, by sea as in German blockade of Britain in 1914–18 and 1939–45 or by land as in Russian blockade of Berlin, 1947–48.

Boer. (Afrikaans word meaning "farmer".) Settler of Dutch descent in South Africa.

Bolshevism. (From Russian word "Bolsheviki", the majority at the time of the split in the Russian Social Democratic Party in 1903.) An alternative name for Communism, particularly in connection with the Russian Revolution of 1917.

Bourgeoisie. (French word meaning "merchants".) Used by Communists to denote the middle classes.

Buffer State. A state between two large powerful states.

Bureaucracy. Government by officials.

Capitalism. The economic system in which the capital (land, buildings, machinery, etc.) is owned (by capitalists) and used for profit.

Cession. Surrender of territory.

Civil Disobedience. Term applied in India to non-violent refusal to obey the laws.

Closure. Decision to take a vote without further debate in the House of Commons.

Code. A systematic collection of laws or regulations.

Coercion. Controlling by force.

Cold War. A term used to describe tension existing between the Soviet Union and the Western Powers from 1947 onwards.

Collaboration. Used during the Second World War of co-operation with the enemy, particularly in France.

Collective Security. The principle, underlying the United Nations and the League of Nations, of all countries guaranteeing the security of each individual country.

Collectivism. A political system based on state ownership and control, e.g. Socialism, Communism.

Cominform. Abbreviation for the Communist Information Bureau set up in 1947 for co-ordinating propaganda and activities of Communist parties in different states.

Comintern. Abbreviation for Communist International, an association of Communist parties, set up in Moscow in 1920 and dissolved in 1943.

Commando. (*a*) Body of troops in South African War (1899–1902). (*b*) Body of British assault troops in Second World War, or a soldier of such a troop.

Commission. (*a*) A body of persons entrusted with authority. (*b*) Royal Commission, a body of persons authorized by the Government to enquire into and report on certain problems. (*c*) International Commission, a similar body composed of people of different nations.

Common Market. Organization of Belgium, the Netherlands, Luxembourg, France, Italy and West Germany, set up in 1957 in order to have a customs union and a common economic policy.

Communism. A political and economic theory propounded by Karl Marx, aiming at the overthrow of the capitalist system by force, after which a state based on public ownership and control would be set up.

Concentration Camp. (*a*) A camp organized by the British for the maintenance of wives and children of Boer soldiers in the South African War. (*b*) A camp in Nazi Germany for the detention of political opponents.

Condominium. Common rule by two or more nations, e.g. Anglo-French Condominium of the Sudan.

Confederation. A loose union of states, which still retain their independence. (Compare with "Federation".)

Congress. (*a*) A meeting of diplomatic representatives, e.g. Congress of Berlin. (*b*) The legislature of the U.S.A., consisting of the Senate and the House of Representatives.

Congress Party. The Hindu organization, originally the Indian National Congress, set up in 1885.

27

Conscription. Compulsory enlistment for service in the armed forces.

Conservative Party. Name given to British right-wing party since 1832, before which it was called the Tory party. Still called Tories and Unionists (name applied mainly during the period of Irish Home Rule agitation).

Convention. (*a*) Agreement between states, e.g. the Geneva Convention. (*b*) Custom of the British constitution based on tacit agreement. (*c*) Meeting of delegates, e.g. party convention.

Convertible Currency. Currency exchangeable with other currencies.

Corporative State. A state based on organization of trade, industry and professions in corporations, each corporation including representatives of employers and employees.

Coup d'état. (French.) A sudden change of government by a group seizing power.

Covenant. A solemn compact or agreement.

Deflation. The opposite of inflation; a restriction of the circulation of money.

Democratic Party. One of the two main political parties in the U.S.A., the most recent Democratic Presidents being Woodrow Wilson (1912–20), F. D. Roosevelt (1932–45) H. S. Truman (1945–52), and John Kennedy (1960–).

Depressed Area. An area scheduled in the 1930's as requiring special Government assistance because of serious, long-continued unemployment.

Depressed Classes. Non-caste Hindus, also called "Untouchables".

Depression. A period of greatly reduced activity in trade and industry, resulting in unemployment.

Devaluation. A lowering of the value of a currency.

Devolution. Delegation of powers of the central government, a limited form of Home Rule without a separate Parliament.

Disarmament. Reduction or abolition of armaments; restriction of size of armed forces, types of weapons, etc.

Disestablishment. Ending of the connection (of a church) with the state.

Displaced Person. A refugee who has been expelled or has fled from his country and does not want to return to it.

Dominion. (*a*) Name given to the union or federation of Canadian provinces, set up in 1867. (*b*) Name given since 1907 to independent states in the British Empire and Commonwealth.

Dominion Status. The rank of the self-governing and independent states of the British Commonwealth, as defined in the Statute of Westminster (1931).

Dual Mandate. The duty of a colonial power, according to Lord Lugard, British colonial administrator in Africa, (1) to develop the natural resources of a colony so that the native population benefited most; and (2) to allow the world at large to share in the resulting benefit.

Dyarchy. System of dual government.

Eastern Question. The problems connected with the break-up of the Ottoman Empire in the nineteenth and twentieth centuries.

Encirclement. Formation of alliance or alliances between neighbours of a state and against that state.

Enosis. (Greek word, meaning "incorporation".) Used by movement in Cyprus for union with Greece.

Entente. (French.) Friendly understanding between states, e.g. *Entente Cordiale* between Britain and France after 1904.

Executive. Body responsible for the government of a country or management of a business.

F.A.O. Food and Agricultural Organization of the United Nations.

Fascism. (*a*) The political movement founded by Mussolini in Italy after the First World War. (*b*) Ultra-nationalist and authoritarian movements in other states.

Federal. Used of the constitution of the united government of several states, e.g. the U.S.A., which retain their independence in certain internal affairs. (Compare "Confederation".)

Federation. A federal group of states.

Fellah. (Plural "fellaheen".) Egyptian peasant.

Fellow-Traveller. Usually one who sympathizes with Communism but is not a member of the Communist Party.

Fifth Column. A term originally used in the Spanish Civil War to denote those working inside a country on behalf of the enemy.

Franchise. Right to vote.

Free City. An autonomous city, independent of the surrounding country, e.g. Danzig, 1920–39.

Free Port. A port with no tariffs or restrictions on trade, e.g. Trieste since 1954.

Free Trade. Trade without tariffs.

French Union. (*Union Française* in French.) An association of France and her overseas territories, set up in 1946.

Friendly Society. Society for mutual insurance against sickness, death, accident or unemployment, often connected with trade union in the nineteenth century.

Fuehrer. (German for "Leader".) Used of Adolf Hitler, Chancellor of Germany.

Gallup Poll. A test of public opinion by questioning a representative cross-section of the people, as used by Dr. Gallup of the U.S.A.

General Assembly. (*a*) Annual or special meeting of all the member states of the United Nations Organization. (*b*) Annual meeting of ministers and elders of the Scottish Presbyterian churches.

General Strike. Sympathetic strike undertaken by all or most of the trade unions in support of one or more unions in a dispute with their employers.

Geneva Convention. One of various agreements adopted at international conferences at Geneva regarding methods of warfare, treatment of wounded and prisoners of war.

Gestapo. (German abbreviation for *Geheime Staatspolizei*.) Secret political police of Nazi Germany, noted for brutality.

Gold Standards. The systems under which a currency is exchangeable for gold:—(*a*) Full gold standard, as in Britain before 1914; (*b*) Gold bullion standard, as in Britian, 1925–31; (*c*) Gold exchange standard, as in Britain since 1931.

Guerrillas or **Guerillas.** (Spanish.) Bands of armed men conducting irregular warfare.

Guillotine. Cutting short of a debate on a Bill by limiting the amount of time to be spent on different sections of the Bill.

Hague Conferences. Peace conferences at the Hague, 1899 and 1907, which formed agreements about methods of warfare.

High Commissioner. High administrative official in a British dominion or colony or a territory under the League of Nations or United Nations.

Home Guard. Local defence volunteer force in Second World War.

Home Rule. Self-government by a national minority, e.g. Irish, Scottish or Welsh.

House of Commons. Lower house of British Parliament, consisting of 630 elected members.

House of Lords. Upper house of British Parliament, consisting of 2 archbishops, 24 bishops, hereditary peers (of whom 16 are Scottish peers, elected by their fellow-peers at a general election), 9 life peers or peeresses (1959). Over 900 peers entitled to attend but attendances seldom over 100.

House of Representatives. Lower house of the Congress of the U.S.A.; 435 members elected on a population basis every two years.

I.L.O. International Labour Organization.

I.L.P. Independent Labour Party.

Imperial Preference. Reduction of tariffs on imports from other parts of the Empire or Commonwealth.

Imperialism. (1) System of government of an empire with colonial territories. (2) Policy of territorial and economic expansion of modern states.

Indemnity. (1) Exemption from penalties incurred, e.g. granted to those engaged in rebellions. (2) Compensation for loss or damages. (3) Sum paid by defeated country as part of a peace settlement.

Independent Labour Party. Left-wing party founded in 1893, advocates of socialism earlier than Labour party; latterly section of Labour party.

Inflation. A rise in the general price level due to an increase in the supply of money and involving a fall in the value of money.

International Court of Justice. Principal court of arbitration of the United Nations, meeting at the Hague like its predecessors, the Permanent Court of International Justice of the League of Nations, set up in 1921, and the Court of Arbitration set up by the Hague Peace Conference of 1899.

International Labour Organization. Founded in 1919 as part of the League of Nations organization and linked since 1946 with the United Nations.

International Monetary Fund. Set up in 1944 at Bretton Woods, New Hampshire, U.S.A., as part of the United Nations Organization, in order to maintain stable currencies.

Intervention. Interference, usually by armed force, in the affairs of another country.

Invisible Exports. The services such as banking, insurance, shipping, interest on overseas investments, tourist traffic, which bring in money from overseas like exports.

Invisible Imports. The services (as listed above) which involve payments of money overseas.

I.R.A. Irish Republican Army.

Irish Republican Army. An association of Irish Nationalists, who first opposed the British Government and then quarrelled with the Irish Free State Government over the Peace Treaty of 1921, continuing by terrorism to agitate for a united Ireland.

Iron Curtain. The frontiers between the satellite states of the Soviet Union and the rest of Europe.

Isolationism. Policy of avoiding alliances or intervention in foreign affairs.

Jingoism. Aggressive, nationalist policy (first used in 1878).

Judicature. (1) Administration of justice. (2) Body of judges.

Judiciary. The judges of a state.

Khaki Election. An election held during or at the end of a war, as in 1900, 1918 and 1945.

Khedive. (Turkish.) Title given to viceroy of Egypt.

Kremlin. Citadel in Moscow, formerly Imperial Palace and after 1917 the headquarters of the Government of the Soviet Union.

Kulak. (Russian word, meaning "close-fisted person".) Well-to-do Russian peasant.

Labour Party. British left-wing party, representing trade unions and workers' interests generally, founded in 1900 as Labour Representation Committee and named Labour party in 1906; adopted Socialist policy in 1918.

Laissez-faire. (French.) Policy of non-interference by Government, particularly with reference to trade and industry.

Lebensraum. (German word, meaning "living-space".) Used by German Nazis to denote all the lands that were considered vital to maintenance of all Germans' standard of living, i.e. not only Germany but also neighbouring countries.

League of Nations. International organization set up in 1920, with headquarters at Geneva and disbanded in 1946, when the United Nations Organization was established.

Left-wing. Originally used of continental legislative assemblies which are seated in a semi-circle and describing political views that tend towards Socialism or Communism.

Legislation. Process of making laws.

Legislature. A law-making body, e.g. British Parliament, U.S. Congress or Legislative Assemblies of Dominions.

Lend-Lease. A scheme approved by Congress of U.S.A. in 1941 for lending supplies to any country "whose defence the President deemed vital to the defence of the U.S.A."

Liberal Party. Centre party in British Parliament. Originally Whig party in eighteenth century, then after 1868 named Liberal party, the Whigs leaving in 1886 because of Gladstone's Irish Home Rule policy. Gradual decline following split between Asquith and Lloyd George and rise of Labour party.

Liquidation. (1) Winding-up of affairs of a company. (2) Removal of people for political reasons, either by execution or imprisonment, in dictator states.

Little Englander. Name given in mid-nineteenth century to an opponent of Imperialism.

Mandate. (1) Commission to act for another, e.g. from the League of Nations to a member state to govern a colonial territory, which thus became a "mandated territory". (2) Political instructions supposed to be given by electors to the majority party in Parliament by their approval of the election programme.

Mandated Territory. See "Mandate".

Mandatory. Conveying a command, e.g. a mandatory Act of Parliament, one which obliges authorities or individuals to carry out certain duties.

Marshall Plan. Proposal by General George Marshall, U.S. Secretary of State, in 1947 to give financial and economic aid to Europe.

Marxism. Doctrines of Karl Marx; see "Communism".

Middle East. The countries belonging at one time to the Ottoman Empire (the Balkans, Asia Minor, Syria, Lebanon, Palestine, Arabia, Egypt) together with Persia.

Military Occupation. Control of a country by the military forces of another, usually after a war.

Monroe Doctrine. Insistence on non-intervention by European powers in the affairs of the American continent, first enunciated by President Monroe in 1823.

Multilateral Agreement. Agreement signed by more than two parties.

Muslim League (also **Moslem League**). Political organization formed in India in 1906 to seek protection and, later, autonomy for the Muslim or Moslem community.

Nationalization. Bringing industry, transport, services, etc. under public ownership and control; advocated by Labour and Communist parties in Britain.

N.A.T.O. North Atlantic Treaty Organization.

Nazi. Abbreviation for German *Nazional,* first word in the name of the National Socialist Workers' Party of Germany.

Near East. The European countries which were at one time part of the Ottoman Empire (a term used more often in the nineteenth than in the twentieth century).

New Deal. Name given in 1933 by President F. D. Roosevelt to his policy for settling the economic crisis.

Non-Aggression Pact. Agreement between two countries to refrain from attacking one another, e.g. the Russo–German Pact of 1939.

Non-Co-operation. Non-violent resistance to a government's policy by refusing to co-operate; advocated by Gandhi in India on several occasions.

Non-Intervention. Abstaining from or preventing intervention in the affairs of another country.

Non-Aryan. Belonging to a racial group other than the Aryan group, e.g. Semitic; epithet usually applied in Nazi Germany to Jews.

North Atlantic Treaty Organization. Formed in 1949 by Belgium, the Netherlands, Luxembourg, France, Denmark, Iceland, Norway, Italy, Portugal, Britain, Canada and the U.S.A. (Greece, Turkey and West Germany joined after 1949) for mutual defence against the Soviet Union and her satellites.

O.E.E.C., Organization for European Economic Co-operation.

Order-in-Council. An order issued by the Sovereign by and with the consent of the British Privy Council; often preferred by government to Act of Parliament for emergency legislation because of simplified procedure.

Organization for European Economic Co-operation. Set up in 1947 to carry on the Marshall Plan. At first consisted of 16 member-states and later joined by Spain, Yugoslavia and West Germany, in effect, all countries in Europe except the Soviet Union and her satellites.

Orthodox Church. Main Christian church in Eastern Europe; sometimes called the Greek Orthodox Church and also the Russian Orthodox Church.

Ottoman Empire. Empire of the Ottoman Turks in Europe and Asia, with the capital at Constantinople, dissolved in 1922 when the Republic of Turkey was set up with its capital at Ankara.

Pact. An agreement, e.g. Locarno Pact.

Pan-Arabic Movement. A movement for a union or federation of all Arab states.

Pan-Islamism. A movement for federation of all Islamic or Muslim states.

Partition. Division of a country into two are more parts.

Passive Resistance. Abstention from violence in opposing the government or an enemy.

Permissive Measure. An Act of Parliament which gives powers to a body, such as a local council, to carry out some function but does not compel it to do so.

Plebiscite. Direct vote of all electors on a special issue.

Plural Voting. Exercise of two or more franchises at the same election, because of having residence in more than one constituency or because of being a university graduate. (No longer valid.)

Primary Commodities. Food, raw materials, fuels.

Proletariat. Name used by Communists to denote the working classes.

Proportional Representation. Electoral system where the number of seats gained by each party is in proportion to the number of votes cast.

Protection. Policy of protecting home industries and agriculture by tariffs.

Protectorate. Name given to a colony which has asked for or has been given protection by an Imperial Power.

Putsch. (German.) A *coup d'état,* an attempt to seize control of the government of a country.

Quisling. (Name of pro-German traitor in Norway.) A traitor or fifth columnist working inside a country for its overthrow by a foreign power.

Radical. Formerly member of left-wing section of Liberal party; generally one in favour of thorough-going reforms.

Rapprochement. (French.) Re-establishment of friendly relations between states.

28

Ratification. Confirmation of an agreement by signature of each state.

Reactionary. Repressive in internal policy.

Referendum. Name given in certain countries for a plebiscite or direct vote of all electors on a special issue.

Reichstag. (German.) Imperial Parliament.

Reich, Third. (German.) Third Empire; used of the Nazi régime in Germany. (The First Reich was the medieval Holy Roman Empire and the Second Reich was the German Empire of 1871–1918.)

Reparations. Payments by a defeated country to compensate for damages or losses caused by war.

Republican Party. One of the two main political parties in the U.S.A., the most recent Presidents being Calvin Coolidge (1923–28), Herbert Hoover (1928–32) and Dwight D. Eisenhower (1952–60).

Right-wing. (See "Left-wing".) Conservative.

Royal Commission. See "Commission".

Sanctions. (1) Penalities imposed for infringing a treaty or covenant. (2) Measures taken by League of Nations against an aggressor.

Satellite States. States dependent on a Great Power.

Secretary of State. (1) In Britain, a senior cabinet minister, e.g. Secretary of State for Home Affairs. (2) In U.S.A., the minister for foreign affairs.

Security Council. A council of 11 members of U.N.O. set up to consider and act upon any threat to peace. (5 permanent members, representing U.S.A., Britain, France, U.S.S.R., and China, and 6 other members elected for two-year terms.)

Senate. Upper house of U.S. Congress and of other legislatures (Canada, Australia, France, Eire, etc.).

Sinn Fein. (Gaelic for "We Ourselves".) A nationalist movement in Ireland, dating from 1905; responsible for Easter Rising of 1916, successful in 1918 elections but later opposed 1921 settlement and lost influence; now a small but active extremist party.

Slavonic. Belonging to a racial group of Slavs in Central and Eastern Europe. (Russians, Poles, Bulgarians, Croats. Serbs, Czechs, Slovaks, etc.)

Socialism. Political and economic doctrine of Labour party, advocating establishment of society on the basis of public ownership and control of industry, transport, agriculture and trade. Differs from Communism in preference for evolution to revolution.

Sovereignty. Supreme power or authority.

Soviet. (Russian.) Council of elected representatives, e.g. soldiers' soviet, workers' soviet, Supreme Soviet.

Sphere of Influence. Territories not actually annexed but under the influence of an Imperialist Power, e.g. North-west Africa in French sphere of influence in 1900.

Statutory. Laid down by statute or Act of Parliament.

Suffrage. Right to vote; franchise.

Suzerainty. Sovereignty over semi-independent states.

Tariff. List of customs or import duties.

Terms of Trade. Relation between prices of a country's imports and exports.

Tory. Old name, still used, for Conservative.

Tory Democrat. Name given in 1870's and 1880's to section of Conservative party favouring social reform.

Truman Doctrine. Principle of American foreign policy enunciated by President Truman of the U.S.A. in 1947, supporting intervention in Europe in peace-time to counter the influence of the Soviet Union.

Trusteeship Territory. (Formerly "Mandated Territory" under the League of Nations.) Territories, mostly former German or Italian colonies, under the supervision of the United Nations but entrusted to the administration of other powers, e.g. Tanganyika (formerly German East Africa) administered by Britain.

Uitlander. (Afrikaans.) Foreigner.

Ultimatum. Final warning.

Underground Movement. Name given to secret resistance movement in certain countries occupied by Germans, Italians, etc. in Second World War.

U.N.E.S.C.O. United Nations Educational, Scientific and Cultural Organization, set up in 1946.

U.N.I.C.E.F. United Nations International Children's Emergency Fund, set up in 1946.

Unilateral Abrogation. Renunciation of a treaty by one of the signatories.

Union Française. French Union; an association of France and her overseas territories set up in 1946.

United Arab Republic. A union of Egypt and Syria, under Egyptian President. Federated with Yemen in United Arab States.

U.N.R.R.A. United Nations Relief and Rehabilitation Administration, set up in 1943 and disbanded in 1949.

Untouchable. A non-caste Hindu (whom a caste Hindu may not touch).

U.S.S.R. Union of Soviet Socialist Republics.

Vatican City. Independent state governed by the Pope (an area of one square mile, adjacent to St. Peter's, Rome).

Veto. (Latin, "I forbid".) The right to prohibit or to withhold assent; used by British House of Lords, the American President and permanent members of Security Council.

Whigs. One of the two main British political parties in Britain in the eighteenth and early nineteenth centuries. Right-wing section of the Liberal party in the second half of the nineteenth century. Seceded from Liberal party over Home Rule Issue in 1886 and joined Conservatives to form Unionist Party.

W.H.O. World Health Organization (U.N.O.).

Zionism. Movement to make Palestine a Jewish state.

INDEX

	INDUSTRY, AGRICULTURE, TRANSPORT, TRADE	SCIENCE AND MEDICINE
1880	1880 Frozen mutton from Australia	
		1881 Pasteur's inoculation experiment (anthrax)
	1883 Electric railway in Brighton	1882 Tubercle bacillus isolated (Koch)
	{ Benz motor-car	
	1885 { 'Rover' safety-bicycle	
	1889 { Dunlop's pneumatic tyre	
	{ Ferranti's power-station	
1890	1890 Electric trams in Manchester	
		1893 Röntgen's X-rays
	1894 Manchester Ship Canal	
	1895 Diesel engine	
	1896 Hydro-electric scheme for aluminium manufacture (Foyers)	1896 Immunization against typhoid
	1897 Parsons's Turbinia	1897 Thomson's discovery of electron
		1898 Curies' discovery of radium
1900		
	1901 Marconi's transatlantic wireless	1901 Psychoanalysis (Freud)
	1903 Wrights' biplane	
		1904 Fleming's thermionic valve
		1905 Einstein's theory of relativity
		1906 School medical inspection
	1909 { Blériot's Channel flight	
	{ Mass-production of cars (Ford)	1909 Peary at North Pole
1910	1911 First Morris car	1911 Amundsen at South Pole
	1913 Trade Union Act	
	F I R S T	W
1920	1919 Forestry Commission	1919 Atom split by Rutherford
	1921 Railway amalgamation	1921 Insulin used for diabetes
	1926 { Central Electricity Board	
	{ General Strike	
	1928 Lindbergh's transatlantic flight	
1930		1929 Fleming's discovery of penicillin
	1933 Milk Marketing Board	
	1936 Keynes's Theory of Employment	1936 Sulphanilamide discovered
	1937 First helicopter	
		1938 Hahn's nuclear fission experiment
1940		1939 Radar (Watt)
	1941 Whittle's jet-plane S E C O N D	V
		1943 Streptomycin discovered
		1945 Atom Bomb
	1946-8 { Nationalization of main public services, transport, coal	
	{ Guaranteed farm prices	
1950		
	1953 First large electronic computers	1953 { Hydrogen Bomb
		{ Mt. Everest climbed
1955	c. 1955 Tractors in general use	